The Kierkegaard Reader

W9-AYP-822

BLACKWELL READERS

In a number of disciplines, across a number of decades, and in a number of languages, writers and texts have emerged which require the attention of students and scholars around the world. United only by a concern with radical ideas, Blackwell Readers collect and introduce the works of pre-eminent theorists. Often translating works for the first time (Levinas, Irigaray, Lyotard, Blanchot, Kristeva), or presenting material previously inaccessible (C. L. R. James, Fanon, Elias), each volume in the series introduces and represents work which is now fundamental to study in the humanities and social sciences.

The Kierkegaard Reader

Edited by
Jane Chamberlain and Jonathan Rée

BLACKWELL
Publishers

Copyright © Blackwell Publishers Ltd 2001 except selection, organization and appendices copyright © Jane Chamberlain and Jonathan Rée 2001 and general introduction, section introductions and notes copyright © Jonathan Rée 2001

First published 2001

2 4 6 8 10 9 7 5 3 1

Blackwell Publishers Ltd
108 Cowley Road
Oxford OX4 1JF
UK

Blackwell Publishers Inc.
350 Main Street
Malden, Massachusetts 02148
USA

British Library Cataloguing in Publication Data
A CIP catalogue record for this book is available from the British Library.

Library of Congress Cataloging-in-Publication Data

Kierkegaard, Søren, 1813–1855.
[Selections. English. 2001]
The Kierkegaard reader / edited by Jane Chamberlain and Jonathan Rée.
p.   cm. – (Blackwell readers)
Includes bibliographical references and index.
ISBN 0-631-20467-9 (hardcover : alk. paper) – ISBN 0-631-20468-7 (pbk. : alk. paper)
1. Philosophy.   I. Chamberlain, Jane.   II. Rée, Jonathan, 1948– .
III. Title.   IV. Series.
B4372.E5 K53 2001
198′.9–dc21

00-051917

Typeset in 10½ on 12½ pt Bembo
by Best-set Typesetter Ltd., Hong Kong

This book is printed on acid-free paper.

Contents

Acknowledgements

The editors thank Stacey Ake, Tina Bolden, Simon Bott, Danny Chisham, Kirstin Drotner, Christiane Gehron, Jane Hyldgaard, Sophie Leatherbarrow, Kirsten Malmkjaer, Marianne Olsen, Lars Bøgeholt Pedersen, Claude Pehrson, Karin Klitgaard Poulsen, Belinda Ioni Rasmussen, Janet Rée, Beth Remmes, Henri Stuart, Steffi Vogel and Julia Watkin.

The editors and publishers also wish to thank the following for permission to use material:

Extracts from *Papers and Journals: A Selection* by Søren Kierkegaard, translated by Alastair Hannay (Penguin Classics, 1996), reproduced here with permission. Translation Copyright © Alastair Hannay, 1996.

Extract from *Either/Or: A Fragment of Life* by Søren Kierkegaard, translated by Alastair Hannay (Penguin Classics, 1992), reproduced here with permission. Translation Copyright © Alastair Hannay, 1992.

Extracts from *Fear and Trembling* by Søren Kierkegaard, translated by Alastair Hannay (Penguin Classics, 1985), reproduced here with permission. Translation Copyright © Alastair Hannay, 1985.

Extracts from *The Concept of Anxiety* by Søren Kierkegaard, edited and translated by Reidar Thomte and Albert B. Anderson (New Jersey: Princeton University Press, 1980), reproduced here with permission, © Princeton University Press, 1980.

Extracts from *The Point of View for My Work as an Author: A Report to History* by Søren Kierkegaard, translated by Walter Lowrie (Oxford: Oxford University Press, 1939; New York: Harper and Row, 1962), reproduced here with permission, © Harper and Row Publishers, Inc., 1962.

Translated extracts from Kierkegaard's *Journals and Papers* have also been included from the following works: *The Journals of Søren Kierkegaard*, translated by Alexander Dru (London: Oxford University Press, 1938); *The Diary of Søren Kierkegaard*, edited by Peter Rohde, translated by Gerda M. Andersen (New York: Citadel Press, 1960); *The Last Years: Journals 1853–55*, edited and translated by Ronald Gregor Smith (London: Collins, 1965); and a few entries from the notes to Lee Capel's translation of *The Concept of Irony* (London: Collins, 1966). All reasonable efforts have been made to contact the holders of these copyrights. The publishers apologize for any errors or omissions in the above list and would be grateful to be notified of any corrections that should be incorporated in the next edition or reprint of this book.

Introduction: Becoming a Philosopher

Søren Kierkegaard struck many of his Danish contemporaries as an idle dilettante. From his father, a peasant who made a fortune as a wool merchant, he inherited enough to live a comfortable life in the fashionable Copenhagen of the 1840s, conspicuously squandering his time in the streets, theatres and drawing rooms. He had a reputation as an eccentric too: a lonely bachelor who tried to be suave and elegant but did not always succeed, particularly when overtaken by fits of puritanical rage against the practitioners of 'Official Christianity'.

But in truth the main preoccupation of Kierkegaard's days and nights was the laborious cultivation of the arts of philosophical prose. In seclusion, he worked fanatically, composing draft after draft, reading his output aloud to himself to check it for rhythm and tone, and then recomposing over and over again. When he died in 1855 at the age of 42 he left behind thousands of intricately revised manuscript pages – the so-called Journals and Papers – which, apart from being astonishingly original, were eloquent testimony to his sheer capacity for taking pains.

Despite a certain diffidence about placing himself before the public, Kierkegaard made himself into one of the most prolific authors in the Danish language, publishing no fewer than thirty-four meticulously prepared volumes, though in non-commercial editions of little more than 500 copies. Even the more conventional of Kierkegaard's books cover a vast range, from his debut – an attack on his celebrated contemporary Hans Christian Andersen, called *From the Papers of One Still Living* – through an academic treatise (a thesis for Copenhagen University on *The Concept of Irony*) to occasional articles on acting, opera and theatre, and numerous collections of religious meditations, mostly in the form of sermons.

But these relatively straightforward works account for less than half of what Kierkegaard published in his lifetime, and the books for which he is now most remembered were issued without any open declaration of his authorship. They made a point of their indirectness, and their very title pages proclaimed an intention to frustrate conventional expectations. The first of these literary enigmas was *Either/Or*, published in 1843 and billed as 'A fragment of a life, edited by Victor Eremita', comprising 'Part I, containing the papers of A' and 'Part II, containing the papers of B'. Later the same year, Danish readers could also buy *Fear and Trembling* – 'A Dialectical Lyric' (whatever that might be) 'by Johannes de Silentio', and *Repetition*, 'a venture in investigative psychology by Constantin Constantius'. In 1844, these were followed by *Philosophical Fragments, or a Fragment of Philosophy*, 'by Johannes Climacus, S. Kierkegaard responsible for publication', together with *The Concept of Anxiety*, 'a simple and psychologically-orienting deliberation . . . by Vigilius Haufniensis' and *Prefaces*, 'light reading for certain classes according to time and occasion, by Nicolaus Notabene'. *Stages on Life's Way*, published in 1845, sounds imposing until one notices that it is 'by Hilarius Bookbinder', and even *The Sickness Unto Death* (1849) makes a jokey allusion in its subtitle: 'a Christian psychological exposition by Anti-Climacus, edited by S. Kierkegaard'.

The book-buyers of Copenhagen must have been unsettled by all these volumes with blatantly improbable title-pages, and they must have welcomed the fact that *Concluding Unscientific Postscript*, published in the name of 'Johannes Climacus' in 1846, included a brief appendix in which Kierkegaard owned up to being the author of the pseudonymous books – though he complicated the issue by adding that he was 'not an author in the ordinary sense of the word', but rather 'a collaborator who has helped the pseudonyms to become authors'. Indeed he claimed to have no real connection with their writings – 'no opinion of them except as a third party . . . , and not even the most tenuous private connection to them'.[1] The plot thickened in 1851 with the publication of a brief pamphlet entitled *On my Work as an Author* and signed 'S. Kierkegaard'. Kierkegaard again admitted that he was responsible for various pseudonymous works of the previous decade, but announced that he had now abandoned them, with all their 'poetry' and 'aesthetics', in order to concentrate on the 'one thing' that mattered, namely the task of 'becoming a Christian' which he would pursue from now on in plain religious simplicity without any further artifice.[2] Wary readers, however, may have wondered if their author had quite finished teasing them. 'The discerning mind will at the same time recognise', Kierkegaard said, 'that this one thing is the religious, but the religious altogether and utterly transposed into reflection.' The discerning mind, one might add, would also notice that if Kierkegaard was trying to dispel the mystery of his authorship he was going about it in a mysterious way: for how could this 'one thing' survive the process of being 'transposed into reflection'? The religious, he continued paradoxically, has been 'utterly transposed . . . yet in such a way that it is altogether and utterly withdrawn from reflection and restored to simplicity'.[3] It might seem that instead of trying to remove the discord, Kierkegaard was only making it resound more loudly. A later explanation entitled *The Point of View for My Work as an Author*, found amongst Kierkegaard's papers and published four years after his death, is subtitled 'A Report to History', but for better or worse it kept the doubts open – doubts as to whether 'the author is an aesthetic or a religious author',[4] as well as doubts about what 'religiousness' can really mean.[5] Another posthumously published work – the unfinished early novella *Johannes Climacus* – suggests a rather different and perhaps more revealing point of view on Kierkegaard's authorship as a whole: his sense of the awesome difficulty of 'becoming a philosopher'.[6]

From Romantic Sentiment to Socratic Comedy

The main effect of Kierkegaard's writings on his first readers was puzzlement shading into exasperation, and his explanations did little to dispel it. Since his death, however, this puzzlement has been wrapped up in several layers of reinterpretation.

In a first phase, Kierkegaard was regarded mainly as a romantic memoirist, whose masterpieces were not so much the works he published in his lifetime as the confessions contained in the posthumous *Point of View* and the anguished self-analyses he confided to his journals. A nine-volume selection from these private papers was published between 1869 and 1881, and it evoked a figure rather like Goethe's Werther, or perhaps a second 'melancholy Dane' – a nineteenth-century Hamlet who brought ruin on himself and others through a sickly excess of thought, sensitivity and perceptiveness.[7] The essence of Kierkegaard's existence, according to this romantic interpretation, lay in his unconsummated passion for Regine Olsen, whom he met in 1837 when she was 15 and he 24. They announced their engagement in 1840, but he revoked it a year later. The reasons for his change of mind are quite unclear, but it has always been tempting to speculate that he felt unworthy of any happiness she might bring him, and that his subsequent regrets, energetically repressed, led to a pathologically intense Christian piety which was to drive him, maddened by grief, to an early grave.[8]

The second Kierkegaard, in contrast, is a participant in twentieth-century theological debates. He is usually taken as representing a philosophical position called 'Christian existentialism', grounded in corrosive doubt about the possibility of knowledge (as opposed to faith or belief) concerning the fundamental questions of religion. Of course Kierkegaard himself knew nothing of the concept of existentialism, which came into being as the German term *Existentialismus* in 1919, and entered the English language for the first time in 1941.[9] But he was the first writer to use the terms 'exist' and 'existence' (*at existere*, *existents* and *tilværelse* in Danish) to refer specifically to the finitude of individual human lives, and by implication their contingency, arbitrariness and absurdity. During World War I the German philosopher Karl Jaspers found 'illumination' through reading Kierkegaard in German translation, and his *Psychology of Worldviews* (1919) portrayed Kierkegaard as the first and greatest philosopher of *Existenz* – a thinker, that is, of 'present individuality' and 'the moment', who focused on the agonies of 'choosing one's self' and striving for 'authenticity [*Echtheit*] of mental life'.[10] Many of these 'existentialist' themes were taken up by Jaspers's young colleague Martin Heidegger in *Being and Time* (1927),[11] and then by Jean-Paul Sartre in *Being and Nothingness* (1943).[12]

But if the existentialist Kierkegaard was popular for a while, he was also widely criticized – for example in Martin Buber's *I and Thou* (1922), Theodor Adorno's *Kierkegaard* (1933) and Georg Lukács's *The Young Hegel* (1948) – as a stubborn individualist and irrationalist. But then a third Kierkegaard slowly made his way onto the scene. He could be called the 'literary-deconstructionist' Kierkegaard as opposed to the romantic-sentimental or religious-existentialist Kierkegaard, and he started to come into his own in the 1990s.[13] His special claim to attention was the theme of 'indirect communication', through which he fused his philosophical ambitions with literary experimentation. Kierkegaard discussed indirect communication in *On my Work as an Author* and *The Point of View*, but he gave a far subtler account of it in *Concluding Unscientific Postscript*, where he explained that the most important philosophical truths are so personal and passionate that any attempt to express them directly will convey nothing except the fact that they have not been understood.[14] On this basis, the exuberant variousness of Kierkegaard's published works – which puts him in the company not only of great philosophical stylists such as Seneca, Montaigne and Nietzsche, but also of literary writers from Sterne and Dostoevsky to Kafka and Beckett – can be interpreted not merely as the fancy embellishment of a philosophical point of view, but also as a serious attempt to put the theory of indirect communication into practice.[15]

One thing that never fluctuated in Kierkegaard's philosophical writings was what he himself called, in the subtitle of his doctoral thesis, a 'constant reference to Socrates'. Socrates is traditionally regarded as the progenitor of the entire Western tradition of philosophy, but he is unusual amongst intellectual father-figures in that he left no written legacy: not a single lecture, treatise, dialogue or poem, nor even an enigmatic fragment. And this was entirely apt, since Socrates had no ambition to impart knowledge: he believed he was an ignorant fool whose only advantage over other ignorant fools was that he knew what he was.[16] His teaching therefore consisted entirely in listening and responding, silence and laughter. His was an art not of the permanent and monological written word but of the ebbs and flows of intimate conversation, punctuated by occasional bursts of hilarity. Socratic wisdom was a matter not of knowledge but of irony.

According to conventional accounts of the history of philosophy, the thinkers who came after Socrates made steady improvements to his legacy and eventually built it up into the imposing edifice of modern knowledge, both philosophical and scientific. As a student at Copenhagen University, the young Kierkegaard would have been told that the seed planted by Socrates had been nurtured by Plato and Aristotle; that the plant had been pruned by the rigorous Descartes, father of 'modern philosophy'; and that it had recently blossomed into 'speculation', or the philosophy of German idealism as expressed in the works of Georg Wilhelm Friedrich Hegel. Hegel thought of himself as having renovated Socrates's ramshackle dialectic, adapting it to the purposes of positive logic rather than negative irony. In Hegel's hands, the dialectic was supposed to model the laborious movements of the human Spirit itself as it made its steady historical progress towards an absolute comprehension of everything. The dialectic was the means by which Spirit would arrive at a complete understanding not only of God and Nature but also of its own evolving consciousness of itself and the world. Hegelian logic, in short, was to be the ultimate solution to all philosophical riddles.

But Hegel died in Berlin in 1831 – the year Kierkegaard entered Copenhagen University – without entirely completing the final synthesis of all possible forms of knowledge. And Kierkegaard soon came to the conclusion that the Hegelian dream was fundamentally flawed, and indeed that the complacent optimism of his Hegelian teachers was the very antithesis of authentic philosophy: Hegel's positive dialectic, far from being the ultimate fulfilment of Socratic promise, was the kind of pompous folly that would have made Socrates laugh like a drain. So Kierkegaard set himself the task of becoming an ironist – of writing philosophy in a way which would revive the negative spirit of Socrates and relaunch the Socratic campaign against inflated pomposity – only this time not by writing nothing, but by writing everything, and writing endlessly, in dozens of varieties of style and genre.

Kierkegaard crammed his writings with allusions not only to the famous classical philosophers, but also to the dozens of unillustrious extras who populate the pages of ancient histories of philosophy – especially Diogenes Laertius's third-century *Lives of the Philosophers*, pregnant as it was with insignificance, gossip and human inconsequentiality. He also paid elaborate tribute to writing for the stage, from the tragedies of Sophocles and Shakespeare to the comedies of Ludvig Holberg, Johan Ludvig Heiberg and Eugène Scribe, the operas of Mozart, and popular farces and pantomimes. But above all he took up the narrative traditions of the Bible, and of Virgil, Aesop, Rabelais, Cervantes, Diderot and Goethe, telling stories and stories within stories, and orchestrating a profuse plurality of different voices – didactic, fatuous, anecdotal or sarcastic, reassuring or confessional, trustworthy, pedantic or unreliable – in any succession or combination that might serve the ironic turn.

As a devotee of Socrates, Kierkegaard was concerned above all to remind his readers of what he called 'possibility' – in other words, the non-necessity or surprisingness of the ways of the world. According to Kierkegaard, it was the characteristic vice of philosophical thinking to try to cover possibility up, and thus block our access to our freedom – a freedom which, for Kierkegaard, meant not the arbitrariness of a subjective will, but the openness, inexplicability and indeterminacy of the future, the present and the past, and indeed of the world as a whole.[17]

Kierkegaard's conception of freedom as possibility can also be described as a cheerful incredulousness about all attempts at complete and absolute explanations. He knew that one insight does not exclude another, and no doubt that is why he practised stylistic diversity on a scale unequalled by any other philosophical writer. The titles of some of his most famous books sound preachy and grim – *Fear and Trembling, Sickness unto Death* and *Concept of Anxiety* for instance – and they must have deterred many potential readers. He has acquired a reputation as a specialist in intellectual gloom whose works, for those who are sad enough to like them, will always be enveloped in a haze of golden tears. Yet Kierkegaard was one of philosophy's greatest comedians, and readers approaching him for the first time should brace themselves for some serious bouts of Socratic laughter.

Kierkegaard in Translation

As a young man, Kierkegaard found it easier to write Latin than his native Danish, and he could also write German if he chose. But all his literary works – published, unpublished or private – were composed in Danish. And Danish, though a rich and supple medium for both poetry and philosophy, is the first language of a comparatively small national community. Translators from Danish have never been numerous, but it is largely through their labours that Kierkegaard's work has been transmitted to posterity – for Kierkegaard has the unusual distinction (he shares it with the authors of the Bible) of being read far more in translation than in his own words.

No translations are perfect. In some cases they may be improvements on their originals, for there is nothing to stop translators from rearranging clauses to straighten the flow of an argument, eliminating obstacles, removing distractions, correcting errors or refocusing images. But every improvement is an infidelity, if not a distortion. Even when translations are so good that no conceivable revision could improve them, they cannot fail to spoil the tonal balances and contrasts of their originals: they are like colour filters or perspective drawings, enhancing certain features of a landscape while obscuring others, closing down ambiguities that might have been fruitful or altering patterns of resonance in both sound and sense.

In addition, translations always stand in awkward reciprocal relations to literary and linguistic history, and indeed to previous translations. For one thing, translators are expected to write more or less in the language of their time, even when working on ancient authors; and changes in linguistic environments will ensure that translations become obsolete even when their originals do not. Secondly, translators often have to be innovators in their own languages, creating new terms, new turns of phrase, new senses for old words, even new sentence-patterns, and thus contributing to the process of linguistic change to which their own work will eventually succumb. And thirdly, they have to be alert to layers of previous translations in the languages with which they are working: works in modern European languages, for example, will often contain a more or less concealed sediment of debts and allusions to established translations (and established mistranslations) from Greek and Latin classics, or from Shakespeare, Goethe or Molière or – most pervasively, particularly in a writer like Kierkegaard – from the Bible, whose words, in various translations, have been incorporated wholesale into ordinary Greek, Latin, German, English and Danish, but not always in the same way. (It may make a difference, for instance, whether we think of the binding of Isaac in terms of an English 'burnt offering' or a Latin *holocaustum*; and it is signifi-

cant that the phrase from St Paul which comes out in English as the strik-
ingly poetic 'twinkling of an eye' is translated into Danish as *øieblik* and into
German as *Augenblick* – terms which have been taken up into everyday language as ordinary secular expressions meaning a moment or instant of time.)[18]
The main rule for readers who rely on translations must be to obtain as many
of them as possible, read them promiscuously, and avoid becoming wholly
dependent on any one translator.

The translation of philosophy also poses some uncomfortable problems of
its own – grievous dilemmas with which no competent translator can ever
feel at ease. The first problem is that, while translation in general can be
roughly defined as the attempt to render identical meanings in a different
language, philosophy is the discipline that specializes in meanings that are
hard – if not impossible – to pin down. The arts of philosophical reading
and writing involve struggles to extract clear sense from difficult expressions,
and if the difficulty is removed or neglected, then the philosophy will disappear as well. Like other philosophers, Kierkegaard was capable of coming
out with carefully crafted sentences which even the most learned and experienced native speakers may find hard to fathom, even after days, weeks or
years of hard hermeneutic labour. Translators who are lucky enough to clarify
a dark meaning – perhaps penetrating it better than its author ever did – will
then face an awkward choice between expressing their hard-won clear interpretation or translating the convoluted phrases on which they have based it.
And translators who come to the conclusion that an obscurity is inherent
and ineradicable will face an equally intractable problem, for how can one
construct a sentence in another language that will have the same meaning as
a sentence that cannot be understood?

Another problem for philosophical translators is posed by the use of
foreign phrases. Kierkegaard's Danish is strewn with fragments of raw Greek,
Latin or German, and presumably he thought they could not pass without
loss into Danish. But if translators seek to reproduce the experience of the
original by leaving these foreign phrases untranslated, they will not be
thanked by modern readers, who mostly lack the linguistic equipment that
Kierkegaard took for granted, and who may in any case interpret them differently. And in the third place, the vocabulary of Danish, like that of every
other modern European language, contains numerous philosophical words
which carry a strong interlinguistic charge and a bulky freight of previous
translations, even though they may strike ordinary native speakers as having
entirely obvious home-grown meanings. When Kierkegaard uses ordinary
Danish terms like *begreb* or *forestilling*, for instance, it is not enough to translate them by equally ordinary English words like *idea* or *impression*. For one
thing these English words are themselves Greek-Latin imports trailing their

own clouds of philosophical glory; and for another Kierkegaard's words picked up on the differentiation which Kant and Hegel made in German between *Begriff* and *Vorstellung* (which were once translated into English as *notion* and *idea* respectively, though *concept* and *representation* are nowadays usually preferred). Conversely, the fact that all modern European languages contain words which stem from philosophical Greek and Latin can lure translators into a false sense of security, and there is no guarantee that Danish terms like *kategorisk* or *æsthetisk* or *erotisk* have exactly the same meaning as their clones in other vernaculars (*categorical*, *aesthetic* and *erotic* in English for example).

But Kierkegaard presents the philosophical translator with further difficulties of a quite special kind. Like Nietzsche, he took great care with the rhythms, tunes, manners and tones of his language, so a translator who wants to be true to his poetic achievement may have to settle for doing less than justice to the literal meanings of his words. Kierkegaard also played extensively on his reader's imagination: like the comic actor he described in *Repetition*,[19] he was able to conjure up whole scenes with a tiny gesture, and attentive translators need to visualize Kierkegaard's image for themselves and find ways of evoking it in their own language, rather than contenting themselves with dictionary equivalents of his words.

The history of English translations of Kierkegaard falls into three phases, corresponding very roughly to the three phases in the reception of his doctrines. The first was inaugurated in 1935 with a version by Knud Fick of a chapter torn from its context in *Either/Or*, presumably because of its commercial-sounding title, and 'The Diary of a Seducer' must have provided many furtive readers with their first experience of philosophical disappointment. It was followed in 1936 by a meticulous version of *Philosophical Fragments* by David Swenson, a member of the Swedish-speaking community in Minnesota who had happened upon the Danish text in a local library in 1898. Swenson devoted all the labours of his adult life to rendering Kierkegaard into English, but he was handicapped by perfectionism, and after his death in 1940 his manuscripts were taken over by the fluent Walter Lowrie, who finished Swenson's *Concluding Unscientific Postscript* in 1941 and his *Either/Or* in 1941 and 1944. Meanwhile Alexander Dru provided a generous and well-translated selection from the Journals and Papers in 1938, and Walter Lowrie produced a very influential version of *The Point of View* in 1939.

Dru, Swenson and Lowrie, followed by Lee Capel in 1966 with an excellent translation of *The Concept of Irony*, created an English Kierkegaard who was fluent, relaxed and companionable. From the 1960s onwards their approach has been corrected and regimented by the monumental work of

Howard Hong and Edna Hong, who, with the help of various assistants, have presented readers with a Kierkegaard who is admirably systematic, though sometimes rather short on charm and style. They started in 1967 with what became a seven-volume translation of the Journals and Papers, and in 1970 they undertook an English edition of all the works that Kierkegaard ever published or prepared for publication, with historical introductions, notes, indexes and lavish supplements drawn from Journals and Papers.

The twenty-five-volume set of *Kierkegaard's Writings* was completed in 1998, and it will inevitably have a decisive effect on English-language responses to Kierkegaard. But the scale and uniformity of the edition must also give rise to some misgivings. As is natural in a project which aims to be definitive, the claims of poetic imitation have been subordinated to those of consistent word-by-word equivalence: Hong and Hong always use 'upbuild-ing' instead of 'edifying' for *opbyggelige*, for instance, and they insist on trans-lating *elskov* as 'erotic love' in order to distinguish it from *kærlighed*, though at the risk of distracting all but the most innocent of readers. Moreover they make little attempt – unlike some of their predecessors – to capture the colourings and tones of Kierkegaard's many voices and those of his assorted pseudonyms, or to emulate his humour and comic timing.

The third phase in the history of English Kierkegaard-translation is as yet more a hope than an established fact, but the versions of *Fear and Trembling*, *The Sickness Unto Death*, *Either/Or* and *Papers and Journals: A Selection* which have been produced by Alastair Hannay since 1985 have done a lot to restore the idea that reading Kierkegaard might be a life-changing pleasure rather than a wearisome academic duty.

This anthology aims to demonstrate the diversity of Kierkegaard's transla-tors as well as that of his philosophical writings. It displays classic work by Lowrie, and by Hannay and Capel, as well as a sample from the workshop of Hong and Hong. (Where they have special significance, the words of the Danish original have been supplied in parenthesis.) The anthology also includes several new translations by the editors, undertaken on the principle that the only way to criticize one translation is by writing another. It con-cludes, however, with a glossary of largely untranslatable terms.

Editors' Note

Editorial interpolations are enclosed in square brackets. Quotations from the Bible are from the Authorized Version. References to Kierkegaard's Journals and Papers use the established three-part notation (e.g. XI A 136). Ref-erences to published works are keyed to *Kierkegaard's Writings* (see Bibliography below, p. 385), with volume number and page (e.g. KW VIII, p. 32). Uncredited translations are our own.

Notes

1   See below, p. 281.
2   See below, pp. 290–6.
3   See below, p. 292.
4   See below, p. 300.
5   See Joakim Garff, 'The Eyes of Argus: *The Point of View* and Points of View on Kierkegaard's Work as an Author', in Jonathan Rée and Jane Chamberlain (eds), *Kierkegaard: A Critical Reader* (Oxford: Blackwell, 1998), pp. 75–102.
6   See below, pp. 354, 371–2.
7   See for example Harold V. Martin, *Kierkegaard the Melancholy Dane* (London: Epworth Press, 1950).
8   Cf. Georg Lukács, 'The Foundering of Form against Life', Sören Kierkegaard and Regine Olsen' (1909), translated by Anna Bostock in *Soul and Form* (London: Merlin, 1974), pp. 28–41.
9   See *Oxford English Dictionary*, s.v. 'existentialism'.
10 See Karl Jaspers, *Psychologie der Weltanschauungen* (Berlin: Springer, 1919), pp. 12, 31, 95 etc. See also Karl Jaspers, 'Intellectual Autobiography', in Paul Arthur Schilpp (ed.), *The Philosophy of Karl Jaspers* (La Salle: Open Court, 1957), pp. 26, 86. German versions of Kierkegaard had begun to appear as early as the 1870s, but Jaspers relied on the translations by Hermann Gottsched and the violently anti-Kierkegaardian Christoph Schrempf in the influential twelve-volume *Gesammelte Werke* (Jena: Diedrichs, 1909–15; second edition 1922–5).
11 *Being and Time* contains many echoes of Kierkegaardian themes (e.g. existence, anxiety, repetition, idle talk, the moment and guilt), perhaps transmitted through Jaspers. Heidegger is open to the suspicion that he covered up the extent of his debt, and he acknowledged Kierkegaard only in three dismissive footnotes (e.g. 'he remained completely dominated by Hegel and by ancient philosophy as Hegel saw it'). See Martin Heidegger, *Being and Time* (1927), translated by John Macquarrie and Edward Robinson (Oxford: Blackwell, 1962), p. 494; see also pp. 492, 497.
12 *Being and Nothingness* paid tribute to Kierkegaard as a thinker who understood 'ambiguity', 'irony' and 'anxiety' and thus provided a relief from the universalism of Hegel and the 'seriousness' of Marx; see Jean-Paul Sartre, *Being and Nothingness* (translated by Hazel E. Barnes, 1956; London: Methuen, 1958), pp. 29, 94 n. 12, 239, 580. See also Sartre's 'Kierkegaard: the Singular Universal' (1956), in *Between Existentialism and Marxism*, translated by John Matthews (London: New Left Books, 1974), pp. 141–69.
13 See for example Paul Ricoeur, 'Philosophy after Kierkegaard' (1963), Jacques Derrida, 'Whom to Give to (Knowing Not to Know)' (1992), and Sylviane

Agacinski, 'We Are Not sublime: Love and Sacrifice, Abraham and Ourselves' (1996), in Rée and Chamberlain, *Kierkegaard*, pp. 9–25, 129–50, 151–74.

14   See below, pp. 232–8.

15   See George Steiner, 'The Wound of Negativity', and Gabriel Josipovici, 'Kierkegaard and the Novel', in Rée and Chamberlain, *Kierkegaard*, pp. 103–13, 114–28.

16   See Plato, *Apology of Socrates*, 20d–22a.

17   See below, pp. 158–72, 231–85.

18   Cf. Genesis 22, 8; I Corinthians 15, 51–2.

19   See below, pp. 139–41.

1

Journals and Notebooks

When Kierkegaard died in 1855, his desk and workroom were found to contain tens of thousands of manuscript pages, together with thirty-six bound volumes of journals. Under the terms of Kierkegaard's will they were inherited by his brother-in-law, J. C. Lund, who found them too much to handle and passed them on to Kierkegaard's older brother Peter. Peter too was a reluctant beneficiary. He had already spoken out in public to defend the Danish State Church from his unruly sibling's attacks, and after his appointment as bishop of Aalborg in 1856 he had to consider the dignity of his office as well. He found one manuscript which he deemed suitable for immediate publication as a book – *The Point of View for My Work as an Author*, which appeared in 1859[1] – and entrusted the rest to the care of an assistant, H. P. Barfod. The first volumes of Barfod's *Efterladte Papirer* appeared in 1869, kindling a new public interest in Kierkegaard, and the edition was brought to completion in nine volumes by the German theologian Hermann Gottsched in 1881. It has since been replaced by a far fuller one (1909–48, 1968–70), and a definitive and comprehensive new edition is now in preparation.

Back in 1843, however, Kierkegaard had written of the 'consolation' he found in the thought that 'after my death no one will find among my papers a single explanation as to what really filled my life'.[2] And in 1854 he contemplated his posthumous fate with rueful glee: 'When I die,' he wrote, 'there will be something for professors!' They will 'lecture away', he thought, explaining the truth about Kierkegaard, though 'perhaps with the additional remark that the peculiarity of this man is that he cannot be lectured about'.[3]

But the notebooks contain some of Kierkegaard's finest writing on his greatest themes: about wisdom as entailing paradox or absurdity, about Hegel and 'the System' as the antithesis of Socratic wisdom and irony, about the comical absurdity of professordom, and above all about the incomprehensibility of what it is most important for us to understand: the meaning of our finite individual lives.

Notes

1 See below, pp. 297–342.
2 See below, p. 18.
3 See below, p. 24.

Journals and Notebooks

What I really lack is to be clear in my mind *what I am to do*, not what I am to know, except in so far as a certain understanding must precede every action. The thing is to understand myself, to see what God really wishes *me* to do; the thing is to find a truth which is true *for me*, to find *the idea for which I can live or die*. What would be the use of discovering so-called objective truth, of working through all the systems of philosophy and of being able, if required, to review them all and show up the inconsistencies within each system; – what good would it do me to be able to develop a theory of the state and combine all the details into a simple whole, and so construct a world in which I did not live, but only held up to the view of others; – what good would it do me to

Alexander Dru's translation of a generous selection of *The Journals of Søren Kierkegaard*, published in 1938, did more than anything else to establish Kierkegaard's reputation in English (not least with W. H. Auden, who produced an abridgement in 1956). It has been followed by several versions: not only the unwieldy *Søren Kierkegaard's Journals and Papers* by Howard V. Hong and Edna H. Hong (7 vols, 1967–78) but also *The Diary of Søren Kierkegaard*, edited by Peter Rohde, translated by Gerda M. Andersen (1960), *The Last Years: Journals 1853–55*, edited and translated by Ronald Gregor Smith (1965) and *Papers and Journals: A Selection*, edited and translated by Alastair Hannay (1996). The selections given here also include a few entries from the notes to Lee Capel's *The Concept of Irony* (1966), and are designed to display some of the variety not only of Kierkegaard's manuscripts, but also of his translators. All extracts are referenced by the conventional three-part notation giving notebook number (roman numeral), category (A = autobiographical, B = drafts for published works, C = reading notes) and identifying number (arabic numeral). This notation is followed by the date of composition (sometimes uncertain) and the initial of the translator – Andersen, Capel, Dru, Hannay or Smith.

be able to explain the meaning of Christianity if it had *no* deeper significance *for me and for my life*; – what good would it do me if truth stood before me, cold and naked, not caring whether I recognised her or not, and producing in me a shudder of fear rather than a trusting devotion?

I A 75; August 1835 (D)

Philosophy and Christianity can never be united. . . .

I A 94; October 1835 (H)

People understand me so little that they fail even to understand my complaints that they do not understand me.

I A 123; February 1836 (H)

There are many people who reach their conclusions about life like schoolboys; they cheat their master by copying the answer out of a book without having worked out the sum for themselves.

I A 322; January 1837 (D)

At every step philosophy sloughs a skin into which creep its worthless hangers-on.

II A 11; January 1837 (D)

[The humorist can never] really become a systematizer, for he looks on every system as a renewed attempt . . . to blow the world apart with a single syllogism; whereas he himself has caught sight of the incommensurable which the philosopher can never compute and must therefore despise. He lives in life's fullness and so feels how much is always left over, even if he has expressed himself in the most felicitous manner possible. . . . The systematizer believes he can say everything, and that whatever cannot be said is wrong and unimportant.

II A 140; 1837 (H)

I stand like a lonely pine-tree egoistically shut off, pointing to the skies and casting no shadow, and only the turtle-dove builds its nest in my branches.

II A 617; July 1837 (D)

Irony, to be sure, can bring about a certain repose (one which must correspond to the peace following the humorous development). . . . The repose induced through irony can bring about a certain love, the love whereby Socrates comprehended his disciples (Hamann [J. G. Hamann, 1730–88] calls it spiritual pederasty); but it is nevertheless egoistic because he stood for them as their deliverer expanding their anxious expressions and perspectives in his higher consciousness and comprehension [*overblik*]. But the diameter of the ironist's movement is not as great as that of the humorist. . . . The highest polemical movement of the ironist is *nil admirari* [wonder at nothing]. Irony is egoistical, it combats Philistinism and yet it remains. It rises in the individual like a song bird, ascends into the air gradually casting off ballast until it runs the risk of ending in an 'egoistical devil may care' – for irony has not yet killed itself by seeing itself, and this happens when the individual comes to see himself in the illumination of irony. Humour is lyrical (the deepest seriousness towards life), deep poesy which cannot fashion itself as such and therefore crystallises itself under the most baroque forms.

II A 102; July 1837 (C)

Paradox is the intellectual life's authentic pathos, and just as only great souls are prone to passions, so only great thinkers are prone to what I call paradoxes, which are nothing but grand thoughts still wanting completion.

II A 755; 1838 (H)

Idées fixes are like cramp in the foot – the best cure is to stamp on it.

II A 230; July 1838 (D)

Hegel is a Johannes *Climacus* who does not storm the heavens, like the giants, by putting mountain upon mountain, but climbs aboard them by way of his syllogisms.

II A 335; January 1839 (H)

Whether this preface will be long or short I do not at this moment know. Only one thought fills my soul: a longing and a thirst to lose myself in the lyrical undergrowth of the foreword, to cast myself into it. Just as the poet feels now moved lyrically, now drawn to the epic, so as a prose writer I feel at this moment an indescribable satisfaction in abandoning all objective thought in order to vent myself in hopes and desires, in a secretive whispering with the reader, in an Horatian *susurratio* [murmur] at eventide.[1] A preface should always be conceived in the illumination of twilight as this is undeniably the most beautiful. It fills one therefore with wonder to read that our Lord used to walk in the cool of the day (*Genesis*) at eventide, when the bustle of objective thought resounds solemnly in the distance like the scythe of the reaper.[2]

II A 432; May 1839 (C)

At the present time my existence is like that of a piece on the chessboard, of which the opponent says: that piece cannot move – like a deserted spectator, for my time is not yet come.

II A 435; May 1839 (D)

Next to taking off all my clothes, owning nothing in the world, not the least thing, and then throwing myself into the water, I find most pleasure in speaking a foreign language, preferably a living one, in order to become *entfremdet* [estranged] from myself.

III A 97; 1841 (H)

My doubt is terrifying – nothing can stop me – it has the hunger of a curse. I consume every *Raisonnement* [argument], every comfort and assurance. I overtake every resistance with the speed of 10,000 miles per second.

III A 103; 1841 (C)

A friend is not what we philosophers call the necessary other, but the superfluous other.

III A 119; 1841 (H)

Strangely enough, philosophy steadily advances, and in spite of there being in the whole crowd of philosophers not one single player but simply people keeping score.

III B 192; 1842 (H)

The nature of original sin has often been considered, and yet the principal category has been missing – it is dread [*angst*], that is what really determines it; for dread is a desire for what one fears, a sympathetic antipathy; dread is an alien power which takes hold of an individual, and yet one cannot extricate oneself from it, does not wish to, because one is afraid, but what one fears attracts one. Dread renders the individual powerless, and the first sin always happens in a moment of weakness; it therefore lacks any apparent accountableness, but that want is the real snare.

III A 233; May 1842 (D)

After my death no one will find among my papers a single explanation as to what really filled my life (that is my consolation); no one will find the words which explain everything and which often made what the world would call a bagatelle into an event of tremendous importance to me, and which I also look upon as something insignificant when I take away the secret gloss which explains all.

IV A 85; 1843 (D)

It is perfectly true, as philosophers say, that life must be understood backwards. But they forget the other proposition, that it must be lived forwards. And if one thinks over that proposition it becomes more and more evident that life can never really be understood in time because at no particular moment can I find the necessary resting-place from which to understand it – backwards.

IV A 164; 1843 (D)

If Hegel had written the whole of his *Logic* and then said, in the Preface, that it was merely an experiment in thought in which he had even begged the question in many places, then he would certainly have been the greatest thinker who had ever lived. As it is he is merely comic.

V A 73; 1844 (D)

In the realm of thought there is a haggling, an up-to-a-certain-point under-standing, which just as surely leads to nonsense as good intentions lead to hell.

V A 9; 1844 (H)

Danish philosophy – if there ever comes to be such a thing – will differ from German philosophy in definitely not beginning with nothing or with no presuppositions whatever, or explaining everything by mediating. It will begin, on the contrary, with the proposition that there are many things between heaven and earth which no philosophy has explained.

Incorporating this proposition in philosophy will provide the necessary corrective and will also cast a humorously edifying warmth over the whole.

V A 46; 1844 (H)

The accursed mendacity which entered philosophy with Hegel . . .

V A 98; 1844 (H)

Even if the system politely assigned me a guest-room in the attic so I could come along all the same, I'd still prefer to be a thinker who is like a bird on a twig.

VI A 66; 1845 (H)

Why did Socrates compare himself to a gadfly? Because he only wished to have ethical significance. He did not wish to be admired as a genius standing apart from others, and fundamentally, therefore, make the lives of others easy, because they could then say, 'it is all very fine for him, he is a genius.' No, he only did what every man can do, he only understood what every man can understand. Therein lies the epigram. He bit hard into the individual man, continually forcing him and irritating him with this 'universal'. He was a gadfly who provoked people by means of the individual's passion, not allow-ing him to admire indolently and effeminately, but demanding his self of him. If a man has ethical power people like to make him into a genius, simply to be rid of him; because his life expresses a demand.

VII¹ A 69; 1846 (D)

That several of Plato's dialogues end without any concrete result has a far deeper reason than I have hitherto thought. Indeed Plato emulated Socrates's maieutic method which incites the listener to independent thinking and therefore does not draw any conclusion, but leaves a sting. This is an excel-lent parody of the modern method of learning by rote, which brings out everything at once, the sooner the better, a method that does not arouse any independent mental activity, but only causes the student to repeat by rote.

VII¹ A 74; 1846 (A)

In relation to their systems most systematisers are like a man who builds an enormous castle and lives in a shack close by; they do not live in their own enormous systematic buildings. But spiritually that is a decisive objection. Spiritually speaking a man must be the building in which he lives – otherwise everything is topsy-turvy.

VII[1] A 82; 1846 (D)

There has probably existed many an author more acute and with greater genius than I, but I would like to see one who with keener acumen has reduplicated his very thinking to the second power of dialectics. It is one thing to be a keen thinker in books, another to reduplicate dialectically one's thinking in one's own existence. The former is like a game with no stakes, played merely for the sake of the game, whereas reduplication is like a game the enjoyment of which is intensified by playing for big stakes. Dialectics in books represents only thinking, but reduplication of the thinking means action in life. But a thinker who fails to reduplicate the dialectics of his thinking will constantly develop new illusions. His thinking never receives the final test of action. Only the ethical thinker, by acting, can safeguard himself against communicating illusions.

VIII[1] A 91; 1847 (A)

Something about my punctuation. In regard to spelling I bow unconditionally to authority (Molbech):[3] it never occurs to me to investigate further, for I know that on this point I lack knowledge, wherefore I willingly admit that I believe every fair-to-middling Danish author is perhaps more diligent in this respect than I.

Punctuation is something else again; in that I do not bow unconditionally to anyone, and I greatly doubt whether there is any Danish author who can match me in that respect. My whole structure as a dialectician with an unusual sense of the rhetorical, my constant intercourse with my thoughts by silent conversations, my experience in reading aloud: all these must needs make me excel in this respect.

That is why I make distinctions in my punctuation. In a scientific paper I use my punctuation differently from the way I use it in rhetorical writing. This probably already will be quite enough for most people, who only acknowledge one grammar. It goes without saying that in regard to punctuation I certainly would not dare to proffer my writings as direct examples for schoolboys or quite young people. Similarly, a good Latin teacher usually does not teach his students the finer shades of that language, such as the delightful little mysteries of the conjunctive mood, but he himself will use them. Unfortunately I do not really know any Danish author who, in an ideal sense, pays proper attention to punctuation; they merely follow the grammatical norm. My punctuation deviates especially in rhetorical matters, because there it becomes more evolved. What particularly occupies me is the architectonic-dialectical phenomenon that the eye sees the structure of the sentences which at the same time, when one reads them aloud, becomes their rhythm – and in my mind's eye I always visualize a reader reading aloud. – That again is the reason why I sometimes use commas very sparingly. For instance, where I want a subdivision under a semicolon, I do not place a comma between such sentences. I write, for example, 'what one owes to another or what one owes to oneself.' In this respect I keep up a constant feud with compositors who, with their best intentions, put commas everywhere and by doing so disturb my rhythm.

In my opinion most Danish stylists use their full stops quite erroneously. They cut up their discourse in nothing but short sentences with the result that logic is deprived of the respect it should command, that propositions which logically are dependent instead become co-ordinated by each forming a separate sentence.

Above all I must repeat that I imagine to myself readers reading aloud and therefore well versed in following the vibration of every thought into its last recess, and also able to recreate this with the voice. I am willing to submit, with complete confidence, to the test that an actor or orator used to modulating should read, as an experiment, a small fragment of my discourses: and I am convinced that he will admit that *much* of what ordinarily he must determine for himself, *much* that otherwise is elucidated by instructive hints on the part of the author, in my text he will find to be indicated by punctuation. Abstract, grammatical punctuation in no wise suffices when it comes to the rhetorical, particularly if this is spiced up with a dash of the ironical, the epigrammatic, the subtle, and what, in the sense of the idea, would be the malicious, etc.

VIII[1] A 33; 1847 (A)

To reduplicate is to be what one says.

IX A 208; 1848 (H)

That's actually how I'm treated here in Copenhagen. I'm looked upon as a kind of Englishman, a half-crazy eccentric, with whom let's all of us, notables and street-urchins alike, imagine we can make sport.

IX A 288; 1848 (H)

The Difference between a Real Thinker and a Professor. The real thinker always presents the crux of a matter; that is exactly where his eminence lies – only a few can follow him. Then along comes the professor; he takes away the 'paradox' – and a sizeable crowd . . . can understand him; and then the truth is now thought to have become truer!

Even if an eminent thinker came up with the thought of a 'system' he would never get it finished – he would be too honest for that. But just one little hint to the professor of what he is engaged in – and the professor has the system finished in a trice. [. . .]

A real thinker can only think comically of the professor. The professor is what Leporello [the servant] is to Don Giovanni, only more so for falsely accrediting to himself a great esteem in the eyes of pseudo-intellectuals.

X^1 A 573; 1849 (H)

Take away the paradox from a thinker and you have a professor.

X^1 A 609; 1849 (H)

No one says 'I'. One person talks in the name of the century, one in the name of the public, one in the name of science, one on behalf of his official position, and everywhere their lives are guaranteed by the tradition that 'others', 'the others', are doing the same thing.

X^1 A 628; 1849 (H)

People have an infantile and conceited idea of human reason, especially in our age, since they never speak of a thinker, a reasoning man, but of pure reason and such like, which do not even exist, inasmuch as probably no one, be he Professor or what have you, is pure reason. Pure reason is a fantasy and a phantastical lack of boundaries that finds itself at home where, in the absence of negative concepts, one conceives of everything, like the witch who ended by devouring her own stomach.

X^2 A 354; 1850 (C)

The absurd is a category. . . .

X^6 B 79; 1850 (H)

What makes the difference in life is not what is said, but how it is said. As for the 'what,' the same thing has already been said perhaps many times before – and so the old saying is true: there is nothing new under the sun, the old saying which is always new. . . .

X^2 A 466; 1850 (D)

Socrates always talked exclusively of food and drink – but really he was talking and thinking all the time of the infinite.

The others are always talking, and in the loudest voices, about the infinite, but really they are talking and thinking all the time about food and drink.

X^4 A 497; 1852 (H)

They say: In Socrates philosophy was *still just* (N.B. this 'still just') – *still just* a life. In Plato, however (in other words we have progress, we are moving upwards), it becomes (up we go) doctrine. Then it becomes science. And so it goes with philosophy, on up to our own time when we stand on the pinnacle of science and look back on Socrates as on a lower plane because philosophy was still only a life.

X^5 A 113; 1853 (H)

Is this the road to London? Indeed, but only if you turn round.

X^5 A 113; 1853 (H)

Something on style. How childish it is to be deceived by such things – alas, how true were Socrates's words: 'It seems to me that now that I am 70 years old I should no longer polish up my style like a boy' – and though it very rarely occurs to me now to do so, still, suddenly my old urge may be aroused, a little sadly, to take delight in the linguistic form. You see, I believe that as a prose-writer I am able to achieve, merely through linguistic form, beautiful and true effects not to be surpassed by a poet.

As an example let me take an idea (and it is precisely this example that forced itself upon my attention today and pleaded its cause so eloquently that it actually made me seize my pen for the sake of such childishness); an idea, I say, inherently rather succinct: Everything disappoints – hope or the hoped for. (*Marginal note*: The phrase: 'Hope disappoints or the hoped for' is by Schopenhauer.)[4] Already there is form, as the dash represents form. But perhaps the idea is too summarily expressed. The idea may also be expressed by a somewhat longer phrase and then a linguistic twining: Everything disappoints: Hope, the hoped for does not come, or the hoped for comes – and disappoints. (*Marginal note*: That hope disappoints is quite an ordinary remark; what must be stressed is the second clause. Therefore, if I imagined a person who passionately had experienced that 'the hoped for disappoints' this special linguistic form will attract him or satisfy him. On hearing the first part he will become impatient and think: must we hear this nonsense again now, but then the formulation of the next sentence will satisfy him completely.)

XI^1 A 214; 1854 (A)

Style. So I have sometimes sat for hours, in love with the sound of words. That is to say, when the pregnancy of the thought is echoed I have been able to sit for hours on end, like a flute-player entertaining himself with his flute. Most of what I have written has been said over many many times, often perhaps a dozen, before it was written down. The structure of my sentences could be called a world of memories, so much have I lived in and enjoyed and experienced the life of these thoughts and their search for form – even if in a certain sense they most often had found their form straightaway – until every point, down to the least significant (this was the later work, the stylistic business – everyone who really has thoughts has also immediate form) had its proper place, so that the thought could feel, as one says, that it was well organized in the form. . . .

XI¹ A 214; 1854 (S)

When I die, there will be something for professors! These wretched rascals! And it does not help, it does not help in the least, even if it is printed and read over and over again. The professors will still make a living from me, and they will lecture away, perhaps with the additional remark that the peculiarity of this man is that he cannot be lectured about.

XI¹ A 136; 1854 (S)

Even before Hegel there lived philosophers who undertook to explain existence and history. And it is doubtless true of all such attempts that Providence must really smile at them. He has not perhaps exactly laughed at them, for they had a certain human and honest seriousness about them.

But Hegel – oh, let me think in a Greek manner! – how the Gods must have guffawed! Such a miserable professor, who penetrated the necessity of all things, and then got it all off by heart: ye gods!

XI¹ A 180; 1854 (S)

The temporal – the eternal. The temporal is a snail's pace, spreading out in time and space; the eternal is the intensive which hurries to meet death.

XI¹ A 468; 1954 (S)

The deceptive with Socrates. The deceptive with Socrates is that his irony is so witty, his intellectuality so eminent, that one is tempted to forget completely that at the same time his actions are a matter of life and death.

You read Plato's *Apology* and are enchanted: how infinitely witty he is, how pointed every word, how absolutely right – alas! And we who are corrupted by the accursed nonsense that the great thing is to be an author, we are tempted to read him as though he were an author, a witty author who might carry off the palm in the newspapers – but he is playing for life and death.

My life shows something similar, in a smaller measure. For my personal existence is worth much more, it is much more exhausting than my writings . . .

How true and how Socratic is this view of Socrates, that to understand, truly to understand, is to be! For us more ordinary men these things are distinct, and remain so: it is one thing to understand, and another to be. Socrates is on such a high level that he abolishes this difference – and that is why we cannot understand him, in the deepest, Socratic sense. I can point to him from a distance, but I doubt whether if I had been his contemporary I could have borne with him. . . .

XI¹ A 430; 1854 (S)

Immortality. One of our poets (Ingemann)[5] is of the sentimental view that even insects are immortal.

The man is right, and one could almost be tempted to say that if such men as are born nowadays *en masse* are immortal, then it does not seem unreasonable that insects too should be immortal.

This is right tea-table gossip, so cheery and so touching, real priests' chatter, for they always excel in cheerily watering down every idea till it is nothing at all, or even something disgusting! Immortality was once the lofty goal which the heroes of mankind looked up to, humbly confessing that this reward was so excessive that it was quite incommensurate with their greatest efforts – and now every louse is immortal!

XI[1] A 463; 1854 (S)

Once man understood little, but that little moved him profoundly. Now he understands much, but it does not move him, or it moves him only superficially, like a grimace.

XI[1] A 480; 1854 (S)

In order to swim one strips oneself naked – in order to aim at the truth one must undress in a much more inward sense, one must take off the inward clothing of thoughts, ideas, selfishness, and the like, before one is naked enough.

XI[1] A 227; 1854 (S)

Suppose – and let us not skimp the number – that there were 100,000 words in Latin declined like *mensa*; suppose that they were written, one below the other, on an enormous sheet of paper – and all in order to impress a grammarian. Would it impress him in the least? No, not in the least. *Mensa*, he would say, is the declension, the rest, the combined number of them, is a matter of indifference, it would even be a waste of time for me to get to know the whole list. Only with *dominus* do we reach the second declension, but *dominus* does not follow *mensa*. In a dictionary, I would say, these 100,000 words have their significance, as vocabulary; but they have no grammatical significance. Or (to change the picture somewhat) if *mensa* thought of putting itself at the top of this list of 100,000 words in order to impress a grammarian, would he be impressed? Not in the least. My dear *mensa*, he would say, what concerns me is the declension, and you misunderstand yourself and your significance if you suppose that you are more significant because you are at the head of a list of 100,000 words that are declined like yourself. In fact you are mad, dear *mensa*, if you suppose you can put yourself at the head of what is nothing. For the 100,000 words are grammatically equal to zero. You are not therefore at the head of anything, it is just something you make yourself and the 100,000 imagine, or they do it to you.

And thus with numbers. Only the illustration does not express (and to this extent is unsuitable) that in the realm of words it is accidental which word is the paradigm among the 100,001 words. In the realm of spirit it is not accidental who will provide the declension; but the words which are declined on this model, the imitations, have no significance at all.

XI¹ A 92; 1854 (S)

On being related objectively to one's own subjectivity. Most men are blunted I's. What was given us by nature as a possibility of being sharpened to an I is quickly blunted to a third person (like Baron Münchhausen's dog, a greyhound which wore down its legs and became a dachshund).⁶

It is quite a different matter to be related objectively to one's own subjectivity.

Take Socrates: he is not third-personal in the sense that he avoids danger or exposing himself and risking his life, as one would do if one were third-personal and not an I. Not at all. But in the midst of danger he is related objectively to his own personality, and at the moment when he is condemned to death he speaks of the condemnation as though he were a third person. He is subjectively raised to the second power, he is related to objectivity as a true poet wishes to be related to his poetic production: this is the objectivity with which he is related to his own subjectivity. This is a work of art. Otherwise one gets either an objective something, an objective stick of furniture which is supposed to be a man, or a hotch-potch of casual and arbitrary happenings. But to be related objectively to one's own subjectivity is the real task.

XI¹ A 97; 1854 (S)

Notes

1   Presumably an allusion to Horace (Quintus Horatius Flaccus, 65–8 BCE), *Odes*, I, ix, ll. 19–20: 'Lenesque sub noctem sussurri composita repentatur hora' ('And low whispers at the hour of tryst, as night draws on').
2   Cf. Genesis 3, 8: 'And they heard the voice of the Lord God walking in the garden in the cool of the day.'
3   Christian Molbech (1783–1857), Danish philologist.
4   'So täuscht uns also bald die Hoffnung, bald das Gehoffte'; see Arthur Schopenhauer (1788–1860), *Die Welt als Wille und Vorstellung*, Vol. II (1844), supplement to Book IV, Ch. 46: 'On the Vanity and Suffering of Life'.
5   Bernhard Severin Ingemann (1789–1862).
6   Jerom Karl Friedrich, Baron von Münchhausen (1720–97), German officer whose fantasies and delusions were embroidered by the poet Rudolf Erich Raspe and published in 1787.

2

The Concept of Irony

Kierkegaard completed his eleven years as a student at Copenhagen University in September 1841, with a seven-and-a-half-hour public defence of a dissertation on *The Concept of Irony with Continual Reference to Socrates*. He had obtained special permission from the king to submit his dissertation in Danish instead of Latin, on the ground that the modernity of the topic made Latin inappropriate, as did the need to make extensive use of German sources. But he produced a summary in Latin, which was also the language of the oral examination. Despite reservations about the wildness of his style, the examiners admitted him to the degree of Master in the Faculty of Philosophy, which would eventually entitle him (not that he ever cared) to be called Dr Søren Kierkegaard.

Kierkegaard approached the concept of irony in the light of what was by then a commonplace account of recent developments in philosophy. It was taken for granted that a completely new philosophical epoch had been inaugurated at the end of the last century by Immanuel Kant. Kant's three *Critiques* (*Pure Reason*, 1781, *Practical Reason*, 1788, and *Judgement*, 1790) had succeeded – so it was thought – in reviving something called 'idealism', but in a form quite distinct both from Plato's theory of heavenly 'forms' and from Berkeley's 'immaterialism'. According to Kantian idealism (also known as 'the critical philosophy'), our own mental activity plays an indispensable role in the constitution of the world. It followed that objective reality is to some degree invented by us, rather than existing independently and waiting to be experienced or observed.

The first generation of post-Kantians, however, had sought to take Kant's idealism further. Kant, they noted, treated the world as if it were a resultant of two forces: the human mind on the one hand and a mysterious 'thing in itself' (*ding an sich*) on the other. But since by definition we could never know 'things in themselves' as such, it seemed reasonable to dismiss them as cumbersome and unwanted residues of pre-critical dogmatism, quite super-fluous to the needs of the new idealism. According to Johann Gottlieb Fichte, author of *The Science of Knowledge* (*Wissenschaftslehre*, 1794–5), the entire objective world of the 'not-self' is a creation of the free activity of the 'absolute self', and this implied that self-consciousness was to be attained not through introspection but through a process of mirroring or 'reflection' in the world.

Fichte's notion of the self-creating self had an immediate appeal for a group of German writers who rejected the long tradition of reverence for the ancient classics in favour of a revival of medieval romances and the works of Shakespeare, conceived as spontaneous if fragmentary expressions of living genius as opposed to slavishly perfect applications of deadly classical rules. In particular Friedrich Schlegel applied Fichte's notion of the self to poets and artists as opposed to the rest of humanity. This required that authentic creators be 'ironists' in the tradition of Socrates, always able to make light of what everyone else takes seriously. Hegel, however, had then begun to sneer at 'romantic irony' (notably in the lecture courses on fine art delivered in Berlin in the 1820s and published posthumously in 1835), arguing that romanticism was finished as an artistic movement and that its notion of 'divine creative genius' was mere *Nachschwatzen* or vain babble.

The basic aim of Kierkegaard's dissertation was to establish a clear dis-tinction between the romantic irony which Hegel had criticized and genuine Socratic irony, and then to defend the following theses, as spelt out in his Latin synopsis:

– Hegel's account of irony applies not to its ancient form but only to its modern one.
– Socrates was not only an employer of irony, but a devotee, so that in the end he succumbed to it himself.
– Just as philosophy begins with doubt, so a truly human life begins with irony.[1]

The dissertation was quite long (350 pages) and fell into two parts. The first was an attempt to establish historically that Socrates was essentially an ironist, while the second expounded the concept of irony in general. The first extract given below ('For Orientation', pp. 30–40) comes from the opening of the second part, where Kierkegaard explains how romantic irony has become unfashionable, and manifestly ridiculous in its attempt to gain public adulation for its stance of lofty indifference to the public. But he also points out that it is entirely fitting for an ironist to be caught in such contradictions, since the disparity between inner truth and outward appearance is what irony is all about. The second extract ('Irony after Fichte', pp. 40–50) comes from near the end of the dissertation, and criticizes the romantic appropriation of Fichtean idealism in terms which are very close to Hegel's own.

Ten years after writing it, Kierkegaard was to look back on his dissertation with distaste. He had tried to be 'super-clever and objective and positive', he said: 'I could not resist pointing out that it was a defect on the part of Socrates to disregard the whole. . . . What a Hegelian fool I was!'[2] But despite its occasional pomposities and conventional academic form, *The Concept of Irony* anticipated many of Kierkegaard's later literary and philosophical experiments. It gave elaborate formulation to the issue which, for Kierkegaard, would always be central to the interpretation of Western philosophy: the relation between Socrates and Hegel. Moreover irony would never cease to remain the key category in terms of which Kierkegaard conceived his work – irony considered not only as a figure of speech but also as a method of communicating or teaching and indeed as a style of life. Kierkegaard summarized the position very near the end of the dissertation: 'If we must warn against irony as a seducer,' he wrote, 'we must also praise it as a guide.'[3]

Notes

1   *The Concept of Irony*, 'Theses'; cf. KW II, pp. 5–6.
2   *Journals and Notebooks*, XI^2 A 108 and X^3 A 477; cf. KW II, pp. xiv, xv.
3   *The Concept of Irony*, part two: 'Irony as a Mastered Moment: The Truth of Irony'; cf. KW II, pp. 5–6; see also p. 327.

The Concept of Irony, with Continual Reference to Socrates
by S. A. Kierkegaard

For Orientation

There was a time not so long ago when a man could make his fortune here with a morsel of irony, one which compensated for all defects in other respects and helped a man to make his way honourably through the world, which gave one the appearance of being cultivated and having had a look at life and some understanding of the world, which signified to the initiated that one was a member of a widespread intellectual Freemasonry. One still encounters an occasional representative of this bygone age who has pre-served that delicate and meaningful smile ambiguously revealing so much, that intellectual air of nobility with which he was so successful in his youth and upon which he built his future in the belief that he had overcome the world.[1] But alas, this was a disappointment! His searching eye looks in vain for a kindred spirit, and were not his golden age still a fresh memory for some, the play of his countenance would remain a mysterious hieroglyph for his contemporaries, among whom he lives as a stranger and alien.[2] Our age demands something more: it demands, if not lofty, then at least loud-voiced pathos, if not speculation then surely results, if not truth then conviction, if not honesty then certainly affidavits to that effect, if not emotion then inces-sant talk about it. It therefore mints quite a different species of privileged

The Concept of Irony has been translated by Howard V. Hong and Edna H. Hong (*Kierkegaard's Writings*, vol. II, 1989); but this version was preceded by an outstanding translation by Lee M. Capel (1966), from which these (very lightly amended) extracts have been drawn.

faces. It will not tolerate the mouth to be closed defiantly nor the upper lip to quiver prankishly. No, it demands that the mouth drop open, for how else is one to visualize a true and genuine patriot except he be making speeches, how else should one visualize the dogmatic face of a profound thinker except with a mouth able to swallow the whole world, how else could one imagine a virtuoso on the cornucopia of the living word except with a mouth wide open? It will not tolerate a man to stand still and become immersed in himself, to walk slowly is already suspect, and how could one even think of such a thing in the animated moment in which we live, this fateful hour which everyone agrees is pregnant with the extraordinary? It despises isolation, and how could it possibly tolerate a human being getting the preposterous idea of going through life alone, an age which, hand in hand and arm in arm (like itinerant journeymen and mercenaries), lives for the Idea of community?★

While irony is far from being especially familiar to our age, it does not follow that it has completely vanished. Neither is our age an age of doubt, yet there are still many expressions of doubt remaining from which one can study doubt, as it were, although there remains a qualitative difference between a speculative doubt and a vulgar doubt about this or that. In oratorical discourse there frequently occurs a figure of speech which bears the name of irony and whose characteristic is this: to say the opposite of what is meant. With this we already have a determination present in all forms of irony, namely, the phenomenon is not the essence but the opposite of the essence. When I speak the thought or meaning is the essence, the word the phenomenon. These two moments [*Momenter*] are absolutely necessary, and it is in this sense that Plato has remarked that all thinking is a dialogue. Now truth demands identity, for if I have the thought without the word, I do not have the thought; and if I have the word without the thought, I do not have the word, since it may not be said that infants and the demented speak. When next I consider the speaking subject, I again have a determination present in all forms of irony, namely, the subject is negatively free. If I am conscious when I speak that what I say is my meaning, and that what is said is an adequate expression for my meaning, and I assume that the person with whom I am speaking comprehends perfectly the meaning in what is said, then I am bound by what is said, that is, I am here positively free. Here applies the ancient line: *semel emissum volat irrevocabile verbum* ['our words, once uttered, fly off beyond recall']. Furthermore, I am bound in relation to myself and cannot detach myself whenever I choose. If, on the other hand, what is said

★   This is not intended to disparage or belittle the serious pursuits of the age, yet it is certainly to be wished that the age were more serious about its seriousness.

is not my meaning, or the opposite of my meaning, then I am free both in relation to others and in relation to myself.

The ironic figure of speech cancels [*hæver*] itself, however, for the speaker presupposes his listeners understand him, hence through a negation of the immediate phenomenon the essence remains identical with the phenomenon. When it sometimes happens that such an ironic figure of speech is misunderstood, this is not the fault of the speaker, except insofar as he has taken up with such an underhanded patron as irony which is as fond of playing pranks on its friends as its enemies. We say of such an ironic turn of speech: it is not serious about its seriousness. The expression may be serious enough to strike terror, yet the knowing listener is initiated into the secret concealed behind it, and precisely through this the irony is again cancelled. The most common form of irony is when one says something seriously which is not seriously intended. The other form of irony is when one says something facetiously, as a jest, which is intended seriously, although this occurs more seldom.* As previously remarked, however, the ironic figure of speech cancels itself. It is like a riddle and its solution possessed simultaneously. The ironic figure of speech also contains an attribute characteristic of all forms of irony, namely, a certain exclusiveness deriving from the fact that although it is understood, it is not directly understood. Hence this figure of speech looks down, as it were, on plain and ordinary discourse immediately [*øieblikkelig*] understood by everyone; it travels in an exclusive incognito, as it were, and looks down from its exalted station with compassion on ordinary pedestrian speech. In everyday affairs this ironic figure of speech occurs chiefly in the higher circles as a prerogative belonging to the same category as that *bon ton* [good breeding] requiring one to smile at innocence and regard virtue as a kind of prudishness, although one still believes in it to a certain extent.

Insofar as the higher circles (naturally this must be understood according to an intellectual protocol) speak ironically – just as kings and rulers speak French so as not to be understood by commoners – to this extent irony is in the process of isolating itself, for it does not generally wish to be understood. Here the irony does not cancel itself. It is, furthermore, merely an inferior form of the ironic conceit which desires witnesses in order to convince and reassure itself, for it is merely an inconsistency which irony has in common with every negative standpoint that while according to its concept it is isolation, it nevertheless seeks to constitute a society, and, when it cannot

---

*   This most often occurs in connection with a certain despair, and is therefore usually found in humorists; for example, when Heine [the poet Heinrich Heine] in the most facetious tone deliberates upon which is worse: a toothache or a bad conscience, and decides in favour of the first.

elevate itself to the Idea of community, seeks to realize itself in conventicles. But there is as little social unity in a coterie of ironists as there is truly honesty among a band of thieves. If we now disregard that aspect of irony which it opens to the conspirators and consider it in relation to the uninitiated, in relation to those against whom its polemic is directed, in relation to the existence [tilværelse] it conceives ironically, then it usually expresses itself in two ways. Either the ironist identifies himself with the nuisance he wishes to attack, or he enters into a relation of opposition to it, but in such a way, of course, that he is always conscious that his appearance is the opposite of what he himself subscribes to, and that he experiences a satisfaction in this disparity.

In relation to a foolishly inflated wisdom which knows about everything it is ironically correct to go along with it, to be transported by all this knowledge, to goad it on with jubilant applause into rising ever higher and higher in an always greater and greater lunacy, although through all this the ironist is himself aware that the whole thing is empty and void of content. In relation to an insipid and inane enthusiasm it is ironically correct to outbid this with ever more and more elated exultation and praise, although the ironist is himself aware that this enthusiasm is the greatest foolishness in the world. Now the more the ironist succeeds in deceiving and the better his falsification progresses, so much the greater is his satisfaction. But he experiences this satisfaction in solitude, and his concern is precisely that no one notices his deception. – This is the form of irony which occurs more seldom, though it is equally profound and easier to effect than the irony appearing in the form of an opposition. In particular, one sometimes sees it employed against a man who is on his way toward suffering from some fixed idea, against a man who deludes himself into thinking he is handsome or has especially handsome side-whiskers, or imagines he is witty or that he once said something so funny that it cannot be repeated often enough, or against a man whose whole life is contained in a single event, as it were, which he constantly reverts to and which anyone can induce him to relate at any moment if one but knows the right spring to press, etc. In all these instances it is the ironist's pleasure to seem ensnared by the same prejudice imprisoning the other person. It is one of the ironist's chief satisfactions to discover such weaknesses everywhere, and the more distinguished the person in whom they are found, so much the more does it please the ironist to have him in his power and make a fool of him unawares. Hence even a distinguished individual becomes for the ironist at times like a puppet, a marionette, to which he has attached strings and which he can cause to perform whatever movements he wishes according to the way he manipulates the strings. And curiously enough, it is the weaker aspects in man that come much closer to being Chladni figures[3] and which constantly become visible when one bows correctly, rather than his better aspects; for the former seem to bear in them-selves a natural necessity, whereas one so often has cause to lament the fact that the better aspects are subject to inconsistencies.

It is equally characteristic of irony, however, to make its appearance through a relation of opposition. In relation to a superabundance of wisdom, to be so ignorant, so stupid, to be as much of a bumpkin as possible, yet always so amiable and eager to learn that the landlords of wisdom take plea-sure in letting one poach on their well-stocked preserves. In relation to a sentimental and inane enthusiasm, to be too dense to grasp the sublime which inspires others, yet all the while to evince the good will which so earnestly desires to grasp and comprehend what has heretofore remained a mystery – these, I say, are perfectly normal expressions of irony. And the more guileless the stupidity of the ironist seems, and the more honest and unfeigned his efforts appear, so much the greater is his joy. It will be seen from this that it is as ironic to appear wise though one is ignorant as to appear ignorant though one is wise. – Irony may exhibit itself through a relation of opposi-tion in a still more indirect fashion when it chooses the simplest and most limited human beings, not in order to mock them, but in order to mock the wise.

In all these instances irony exhibits itself most nearly as conceiving [opfatter] the world, as attempting to mystify the surrounding world not so much in order to conceal itself as to induce others to reveal themselves. But irony may also manifest itself when the ironist seeks to lead the outside world astray respecting himself. In our time when the social situation makes a secret love affair almost impossible, when the city or commune most often has already had the banns of the happy couple read several times from the pulpit before the parson has done it once; in our time when society would con-sider itself robbed of one of its dearest prerogatives did it not have the power to fasten the knot of love, and, at its own invitation (not the parson's) to have much to say about it, so that a love affair only acquires its validity by being publicly discussed, while an understanding entered into without the knowl-edge of the community is almost regarded as invalid, or at least as a shame-ful invasion of its prerogatives – just as a sexton regards suicide as a disgraceful stratagem designed to sneak oneself out of the world – in our time, I say, it may occasionally seem necessary for a person to play false if he does not wish the city to take upon itself the honourable task of proposing for him, so that he need only present himself with the customary facial expression of one about to propose in the manner of Peder Erik Madsen with white gloves and a written sketch of his future prospects in his hand, together with other magical charms (not to mention a trustworthy aide-memoire) to be used in the final assault.[4] If there be still other external circumstances that make a certain secrecy necessary, such mystification becomes increasingly pure and simple dissemblance. But the more the individual conceives these mystifications as episodes in his own love affair, and the more abandoned his joy at having directed everyone's attention to a wholly different object, so much the more does irony manifest itself. The ironist enjoys the whole infinity of love, and the amplification which others seek by having confidants, this he induces by having trusted intimates who yet know nothing. Similar mystifications are sometimes also necessary in literature when one is everywhere surrounded by a multitude of vigilant literati who discover authors about the same way that Polly Panderer [the marriage-broker] arranges matches. Indeed, the less it is an external reason determining one to play hide and seek (family considerations, concern for promotion, timidity, etc.), and the more it is a certain inward infinity which seeks to emancipate one's work from every finite relation to oneself, desires to be absolved from all the condolences of fellow sufferers and all the congratulations of that endearing brotherhood of authors – so much the more does irony manifest itself. And should it progress so far that it is possible to induce some crowing rooster, who would so dearly love to lay an egg, to allow the paternity to be imputed to him, half averting and half reinforcing people in their delusion, then the ironist has won the day. If one wishes on occasion to divest oneself of the habit which everyone must dutifully put on and wear according to his social position – and in our time one might very easily be tempted, if now and then one wishes to know he is at least better off than a convicted criminal and dares to show himself attired in other than the clothes of the work-house – then here too a certain mystification will be necessary. But the more it is a finite consideration that determines one to engage in such mystifications, as when a merchant travels incognito in order to expedite the successful outcome of a speculative investment, a king in order to surprise his custom house functionaries, a police inspector to come for once as a thief – in the night,[5] a person in the most subordinate position in the state with fear for high-ranking superiors, etc., then the more it approximates plain and simple dissemblance. On the other hand, the more it springs from the need once in a while to be a human being and not always and forever chancellor, and the more poetic infinity inheres in it and the more artfully the mystification is accomplished, so much the more does irony manifest itself. And should he wholly succeed in leading people astray, perhaps to be arrested as a suspicious character or involved in interesting domestic situations, then the ironist has attained his wish.

But the outstanding feature of irony in these and similar instances is the subjective freedom which at every moment has within its power the possibility of a beginning and is not generated from previous conditions. There is something seductive about every beginning because the subject is still free, and this is the satisfaction the ironist longs for. At such moments actuality loses its validity for him; he is free and above it. This is something which the Roman Catholic Church understood in certain points, and on various occasions during the Middle Ages it used to elevate itself above its absolute reality and conceive itself ironically, e.g., in The Feast of the Ass, The Feast of Fools, Easter Humour, etc. A similar sentiment was the basis for allowing Roman soldiers the liberty of reciting satirical verses over the triumphator. Here one was conscious both of the majesty of life and the reality of glory, yet at the same time ironically above it. Similarly, there was much irony concealed in the life of the gods of Greece without ever needing the railleries of a Lucian, for not even the heavenly actuality of the gods was spared the piercing blasts of irony.[6] As certain as it is that there is much existence [tilværelse] which is not actuality, and that there is something in personality which is at least momentarily incommensurable with actuality, so also it is certain that there resides a truth in irony. Add to this that thus far we have merely conceived irony as a momentary expression, so that in all these instances we may still not speak of pure irony, or irony as a standpoint. On the other hand, the more the consideration of the relation between actuality and subject, as occasionally asserted here, draws into its orbit, the more we approach the point where irony exhibits itself in its usurped totality.

A diplomat's conception of the world is in many respects ironical, and the famous statement of Talleyrand[7] that man was given speech not in order to reveal his thoughts but to conceal them expresses a deep irony against the world, and from the perspective of statecraft corresponds perfectly to another authentic diplomatic thesis: *mundus vult decipi, decipiatur ergo* ['the world wants to be deceived, so let it be deceived']. But it does not at all follow that the diplomatic world regards existence ironically; on the contrary, there are many things it would seriously maintain. – The difference between all the expressions of irony suggested here is therefore merely a quantitative one, a more or a less. On the other hand, irony in the eminent sense differs qualitatively from the kind of irony described here, just as a speculative doubt differs qualitatively from a vulgar and empirical doubt. Irony in the eminent sense directs itself not against this or that particular existence [enkelte tilværende] but against the whole given actuality of a certain time and situation. It has, therefore, an apriority in itself, and it is not by successively destroying one segment of actuality after the other that it arrives at its total view, but by virtue of this that it destroys in the particular. It is not this or that phenomenon but the totality of existence [tilværelse] which it considers *sub specie ironiæ* [from the point of view of irony]. To this extent one sees the propriety of the Hegelian characterisation of irony as infinite absolute negativity.

Before we proceed to a closer discussion of this, however, it seems appropriate to orient ourselves in the conceptual landscape [*begrebs-omgivelse*] wherein irony has its abode. In this regard one must distinguish between what we shall call an executive irony★ and a contemplative irony.

We shall begin with what I have ventured to call executive irony. Insofar as irony asserts a relation of opposition in all its various nuances, it might seem as if irony were identical with dissembling,† and for the sake of brevity one usually translates the word 'irony' as dissemblance. But whereas dissemblance describes more the objective act by which the disparity between

---

★ Belonging to executive irony, or dramatic irony as it might be called, is also the irony of nature, since this is not conscious in nature except for one who has an eye for it, for whom it is then as if nature were like a person playing tricks on him, or confiding to him its pain and sorrow. This disparity is not present in nature for one who is too natural and too naïve, but only exhibits itself for one who is himself ironically developed. In his *Symbolik des Traumes* (1821), Schubert [Gotthilf Heinrich von Schubert (1780–1860)] has a judicious selection of a multitude of such ironic features in nature. He remarks that nature has with deep mockery 'strangely conjoined mirth with lament, joy with sorrow, like the voice of nature in the music of the wind on Ceylon, which sings frightfully merry minuets in tones of a deep, wailing, heart-rending voice'. He calls attention to the fact that nature has ironically juxtaposed the most remote extremes: 'Following immediately after the rational and moderate human being – in the free association of ideas of natural species – comes the absurd ape, after the intelligent and immaculate elephant the unclean swine, after the horse the ass, after the repulsive camel the slender deer, and after the bat, which, being dissatisfied with the usual lot of the mammal, imitates the bird, comes the mouse, which, being dissatisfied in the opposite sense, scarcely ventures forth from the deep.' Now all such features are not in nature, but the ironic subject perceives them in nature. Similarly, one may also regard every deception of the senses as an irony of nature. But to become conscious of this requires a consciousness which is itself ironical. Indeed, the more polemically developed an individual is, the more irony he will find in nature. Such a view of nature belongs, therefore, more to the romantic than to the classical development. Greek harmoniousness found it hard to attribute such sarcasm to nature. Allow me to illustrate this point by means of an example. In happy Greece nature was seldom witness to anything but the gentle and mild harmonies of an evenly tempered soul, for even the Greek sorrow was beautiful, hence Echo was a friendly nymph. In Nordic mythology, however, where nature resounded with wild shrieks, where the night was not luminous and clear but dark and overcast, full of dread and terror, where grief was not assuaged by quiet recollection but by a deep sigh and an eternal forgetting, there Echo became a troll. Thus in Nordic mythology Echo is called *Dvergmaal* [dwarf-language] or *Bergmaal* [mountain-language]. (Cf. Jakob and Wilhelm Grimm, *Irische Elfenmärchen* [their translation of Thomas Croker, *Fairy Legends and Traditions of the South of Ireland*, 1825], see also *Færoiske Quæder* [*Folk-songs of the Faeroe Isles*] 1822.) This irony in nature has here been accorded a place in a footnote because it is essentially only apparent for an individual oriented in humour, since it is essentially only through a consideration of sin in the world that the ironic conception of nature makes its appearance.

† Irony is conceived in this way by Theophrastus [Greek philosopher, pupil of Plato] in his *Characters*, 1: '*Peri eironeias*' ('*On Irony*'). Here irony is defined as follows: *prosōpoiésis epi kheirōn praxeōn kai logōn* [the feigning of action and thought for the worse], (*simulatio dissimulatioque fallax et fraudulenta*) [false and fraudulent dissembling and concealment].

essence and phenomenon is effected, irony is also descriptive of a subjective satisfaction, for it is by means of irony that the subject emancipates himself from the constraint imposed upon him by the continuity of life, whence it may be said of the ironist that he 'cuts loose'. To this must be added that dissemblance, insofar as one wishes to relate it to the subject, has a purpose, a purpose foreign to dissemblance itself. Irony, on the other hand, has no purpose, its purpose is immanent in itself, a metaphysical purpose. The purpose is none other than irony itself. When an ironist exhibits himself as other than he actually is, it might seem as if his purpose were to induce others to believe this. His actual purpose, however, is merely to feel free, and this he is through irony. Irony has, therefore, no external purpose but is self-purposive. It follows that irony is quite different from Jesuitism, for in Jesuitism the subject is free regarding the choice of means with which to accomplish his purpose, but not at all free in the ironic sense where the subject has no purpose.

Insofar as it is essential for irony to have an external which is the opposite of the internal, it might seem as if irony were identical with hypocrisy. In Danish one occasionally finds irony translated as *Skalkagtighed* [mischievousness], and a hypocrite is usually called an *Øienskalk* [fraud]. But hypocrisy properly belongs to the moral sphere, for the hypocrite constantly strives to seem good though he is evil. Irony, on the other hand, belongs to the metaphysical sphere, for the concern of the ironist is merely to seem other than he actually is. As he therefore conceals his jest in seriousness and his seriousness in jest (like the music of the wind on Ceylon), so it may also occur to him to seem evil though he is good. It must be borne in mind, however, that moral determinations are essentially too concrete for irony.

But irony has a theoretical or contemplative aspect. Were we to consider irony an inferior moment [*moment*], we might allow it to be a sharp eye for what is crooked, wry, distorted, for what is erroneous, the vain in existence [*tilværelse*]. In conceiving this it might seem as if irony were identical with ridicule, satire, persiflage, etc. Naturally, it has an affinity with this insofar as it, too, perceives what is vain, but it differs in setting forth its observation. It does not destroy vanity, it is not what punitive justice is in relation to vice, nor does it have the power of reconciliation within itself as does the comic. On the contrary, it reinforces vanity in its vanity and renders madness more mad. This is what might be called irony's attempt to mediate the discrete moments, not in a higher unity but in a higher madness.

If we consider irony as it directs itself against the whole of existence [*tilværelse*], it here again sustains the opposition between essence and phenomenon, between the internal and the external. It might seem that as absolute negativity it is identical with doubt. It must be borne in mind, however, that doubt is a conceptual determination while irony is the being-for-itself of subjectivity. Again, it must be remembered that irony is essentially practical, that it is only theoretical in order to become practical again, in other words, it is not concerned with the irony of the situation but only with that of itself. Hence when irony gets wind of the fact that there must be something concealed behind the phenomenon other than what is contained in the phenomenon, this is merely what irony has always been so keen about telling everybody, namely, that the subject feels free, and so the phenomenon never acquires any reality for the subject. The movement is the direct opposite. With doubt the subject constantly seeks to penetrate the object, and his misfortune consists in the fact that the object constantly eludes him. With irony, on the other hand, the subject is always seeking to get outside the object, and this he attains by becoming conscious at every moment [øieblik] that the object has no reality. With doubt the subject is witness to a war of conquest in which every phenomenon is destroyed, because the essence always resides behind the phenomenon. But with irony the subject constantly retires from the field and proceeds to talk every phenomenon out of its reality in order to save himself, that is, in order to preserve himself in his negative independence of everything.

Finally, insofar as irony becomes conscious of the fact that existence [tilværelse] has no reality, thereby expressing the same thesis as the pious disposition, it might seem as if irony were a species of religious devotion. In religious devotion, if I may be permitted to put it this way, the lesser actuality, that is to say, the relationship to the world, also loses its validity; but this only occurs insofar as the relationship to God at the same moment asserts its absolute reality. The devout mind also affirms that all is vanity, but this is only insofar as this negation thrusts aside all interference and allows the eternally existent [bestaaende] to become manifest. Add to this that when the devout mind perceives all is vanity, it makes no exception regarding its own person, makes no fuss [ophævelser] respecting itself; on the contrary, this, too, must be thrust aside so the divine will not be impeded by its resistance, but pour itself out in the mind made receptive by religious devotion. Indeed, we see from the more penetrating writings for edification that the pious mind regards its own finite personality as the most wretched of all. With irony, on the other hand, when everything else becomes vain, subjectivity becomes free. And the more vain everything becomes, so much the lighter, more vacuous, more evanescent becomes subjectivity. Whereas everything else becomes vain, the ironic subject does not himself become vain but saves his own vanity. For irony everything becomes nothingness, but nothingness may be taken in several ways. The speculative nothingness is that which at every moment is vanishing for concretion, since it is itself the demand for the concrete, its *nisus formativus* [formative impulse]. The mystical nothingness is a nothingness for representation, a nothingness which yet is as full of content as the silence of the night is eloquent for one who has ears to hear. Finally, the ironic nothingness is that deathly stillness in which irony returns to 'haunt and jest' [*spøger*] (this last word taken wholly ambiguously).

Irony after Fichte

It was in Kant, to recall a rather well-known fact, that modern speculation, now feeling itself full grown and of age, became tired of the tutelage in which it heretofore had lived under Dogmatism and went like the Prodigal Son to his father to demand that he divide and apportion to him his inheritance.[8] The outcome of this settlement is well known, as is also the fact that speculation did not need to go abroad in order to squander its fortune, for prosperity was nowhere to be found. Indeed, the more the ego became involved in scrutinising the ego in the Critical [Kantian] philosophy, the more emaciated the ego became, until it ended by becoming a *Gespenst* [spectre, ghost] as immortal as the husband of Aurora.[9] The ego was like the crow, which, deceived by the fox's praise of its person, lost the cheese.[10] Thought had gone astray in that reflection continually reflected upon reflection, and every step forward naturally led further and further away from all content. Here it became apparent, and it will ever be so, that when one begins to speculate it is essential to be pointed in the right direction. It failed to notice that what it sought for was in the search itself, and since it refused to look for it there, it was not in all eternity to be found. Philosophy was like a man who has his spectacles on but goes on searching for them; he searches for what is right in front of his nose, but he never looks there and so never finds them.

Now that which is external to experience, that which collided with the experiencing subject like a solid body, after which each recoiled from the force of the impact in its own direction; *das Ding an sich* [thing in itself], which constantly persisted in tempting the experiencing subject (as a certain school in the Middle Ages believed the visible emblems in the Eucharist were present in order to tempt the believer); this externality, this *Ding an sich* was what constituted the weakness in Kant's system. It even became a problem whether the ego itself was not a *Ding an sich*. This problem was raised and then resolved by Fichte.[11] He removed the difficulty connected with this *an sich* by placing it within thought, that is, he rendered the ego infinite as I = I. The producing ego is the same as the produced ego; I = I is the abstract identity. With this he emancipated infinite thought. But this infinite thought

in Fichte is like every other Fichtean infinity (his ethical infinity is incessantly striving for striving's own sake, his aesthetic infinity is perpetual production for production's own sake, God's infinity is continual development
for development's own sake), that is, a negative infinity, an infinity without
finitude, an infinity void of all content. Hence when Fichte rendered the ego
infinite he asserted an idealism in relation to which all actuality became pale,
an acosmism in relation to which his idealism became actuality, notwithstanding the fact that it was docetism.[12] With Fichte thought was rendered
infinite, and subjectivity became infinite absolute negativity, infinite tension
and longing. Fichte hereby acquired a significance for knowing [*videnskab*].
His *Science of Knowledge* rendered knowledge infinite. But that which he
rendered infinite was the negative, hence in place of truth he acquired certainty, not positive but negative infinity in the infinite identity of the ego
with itself. Instead of positive endeavour, i.e. happiness, he obtained negative
endeavour, i.e. an ought. Inasmuch as Fichte had the negative his standpoint
acquired an infinite enthusiasm, an infinite elasticity. Kant lacks the negative
infinity, Fichte the positive. In this way Fichte receives an absolute return on
his method, for knowing here becomes a whole out of a part. But because
Fichte maintained the abstract identity as I = I, and in his idealistic realm
would have nothing to do with actuality, he thus acquired the absolute beginning from which, as has so often been discussed, he sought to construct the
world. The ego became the constitutive principle. But as the ego is merely
formally hence negatively conceived, Fichte essentially got no further than
the infinite, elastic *molimina* [efforts] towards a beginning. He has the infinite
longing of the negative, its *nisus formativus* [formative impulse], but has it as
an urgency which cannot get under way, has it as a divine and absolute impatience, as an infinite power which yet accomplishes nothing because there
is nothing to which it can be applied. It is a potentiation and an exaltation
mighty like a god, which is able to lift the whole world but has nothing to
lift. With this the starting point of philosophy is brought to consciousness –
the presuppositionlessness with which it begins – and yet the enormous
energy of this beginning brings it no further. In order for thought, subjectivity, to acquire truth and content it must allow itself to be born: it must
sink down into the depths of the substantial life and allow itself to be concealed in this as the Church is concealed in Christ. It must – half anxiously,
half sympathetically, half shrinking backwards, half surrendering itself – allow
the waves of the substantial ocean to close over itself, just as in the moments
of enthusiasm the subject almost becomes absent to himself and sinks down
into that which inspires, yet all the while experiencing a quiet shudder
because it concerns his very life. But this requires courage, and yet it is necessary; for everyone who shall save his soul shall lose it.[13] Nor is this the

courage of desperation, for as Tauler has so beautifully expressed it in a more concrete context:

> *Doch dieses Verlieren, dies Entschwinden*
> *Ist eben das echte und rechte Finden.*
> [Yet loss and vanishing of this kind
> Are nothing else but truly to find.][14]

It is well known that Fichte later abandoned this position, which found many admirers and few disciples, and in various writings sought in a more edifying fashion to pacify and diminish this earlier *pléropsoria* [full assurance].[15] On the other hand, it would appear from the posthumous works published by his son that he also sought to become lord and master over this negative infinity by immersing himself in the very essence of consciousness. As this does not concern this investigation, however, I shall confine myself to one of the standpoints attaching itself to the earlier Fichte, namely, with the irony of Schlegel and Tieck.[16]

In Fichte subjectivity had become free, infinite, and negative. But in order for it to emerge from this movement of emptiness, wherein it moved in infinite abstraction, it had to be negated; in order for thought to become actual it had to become concrete. With this there emerges the question of metaphysical actuality. The Fichtean principle that subjectivity, the ego, has constitutive validity, that it alone is the almighty, was seized upon by Schlegel and Tieck and with this they proceeded to operate in the world. But this involved a double predicament: first, the empirical and finite ego was confounded with the eternal ego; and secondly, metaphysical actuality was confused with historical actuality. An abortive metaphysical standpoint was thus applied directly to actuality. Fichte wanted to construct the world, by means of a systematic construction; Schlegel and Tieck, on the other hand, wanted to inherit a world.★

Here it is evident that this irony was not in the service of the world spirit. It was not a moment [*moment*] of the given actuality that was to be negated and displaced by a new moment; no, all historical actuality was negated to make room for a self-created actuality. It was not subjectivity that was here to appear, for subjectivity was already given by the conditions of the world; no, it was an exaggerated subjectivity, a subjectivity raised to the second

★ This ironic endeavour did not end with Schlegel and Tieck, but has found an extensive following in Young Germany [a radical literary movement of the 1830s, dedicated to Schlegel's romanticism and Saint-Simon's socialism]. In the general discussion of this standpoint, therefore, many a consideration is directed at Young Germany.

power. It will be seen from this that such an irony was wholly unwarranted, and that Hegel's efforts to oppose it were quite in order.

Irony* now appeared as that for which nothingness was an existent [bestaaende], as that which was through with everything, yet at the same time as that which had absolute power to do everything. If it allowed something to stand [bestaae], it knew it had the power to destroy it, and it knew this at the same moment [øieblik] it allowed it to endure [bestaae]. If it posited something, it knew it had the authority to abrogate [ophæve] it, and it knew this at the same moment it posited it. It knew itself to be in complete possession of the absolute power to bind and to loose. It was as much lord over the Idea as over the phenomenon, and it destroyed the one by the other. It destroyed the phenomenon by showing that it did not correspond to the Idea, and it destroyed the Idea by showing that it did not correspond to the phenomenon. Moreover, it was quite correct in both cases, since the Idea and the phenomenon are only in and with each other. But through all this irony rescued its sorrowless life. To do all this was given to the subject man: Behold, who is great like unto Allah, and who can stand [bestaae] before him?

But actuality (the historical actuality) relates in a twofold way to the subject: partly as a gift which will not admit of being rejected, and partly as a task to be realized. The disparate way in which irony related to actuality is sufficiently indicated by the fact that the ironic orientation is essentially critical. Both its philosopher (Schlegel) as well as its poet (Tieck) are critical. Hence the Sabbath – which our age believes in so many ways has already arrived – was not used in order to rest from historical labours but to criticize. But criticism usually excludes sympathy, and there is a criticism for which there is no more anything abiding [bestaaende] than there is anything innocent to a suspicious policeman. But one did not criticize the old classics, nor did one criticize consciousness as did Kant – one criticized actuality itself. Now there might well have been much in actuality in need of a critique, and evil in the Fichtean sense of indolence and laziness might well have become rampant and its *vis inertiæ* [force of inertia] in need of a rebuke, in other words, there might well have been much in existence [tilværende] which, precisely because it was not actuality, must be sheared away. But it was in no way defensible to direct its critical onslaught against the whole of actuality. I need scarcely remind the reader that Schlegel was critical, but that

---

* Throughout this discussion I use the expressions: *irony* and the *ironist*, but I could as easily say: *romanticism* and the *romanticist*. Both expressions designate the same thing. The one suggests more the name with which the movement christened itself, the other the name with which Hegel christened it.

Tieck was no less critical will surely be admitted if one will consider that his polemic against the world is deposited in his dramas, and that these pre-suppose a polemically developed individual in order to be understood – a fact which has caused them to become proportionately less popular than they deserve to be in light of their genius.

When in the foregoing I said that actuality offers itself partly as a gift, this was intended to express the relation of the individual to the past. This past will have validity for the individual, will not be overlooked or ignored. Irony, however, acknowledges no past. This is due to the fact that it sprang from metaphysical investigations. It confounded the temporal ego with the eternal ego, and as the eternal ego has no past, so neither does the temporal. Insofar as irony should be so conventional as to accept a past, this past must then be of such a nature that irony can retain its freedom over it, continue to play its pranks on it. It was therefore the mythical aspect of history, saga and fairy-tale, which especially found grace in its eyes. Authentic history, on the other hand, wherein the true individual has his positive freedom because in this he has his premises, must be dispensed with. To this end irony behaved like Her-cules wrestling with Antæus, for the latter could not be overcome so long as he stood firmly on the ground; but Hercules lifted Antæus off his feet and in this way overpowered him. Irony did the same to all historical actuality. With a twist of the wrist all history became myth, poetry, saga, fairy-tale – irony was free once more. Now it took its choice, had its own way, and did exactly as it pleased. It was particularly fond of Greece and the Middle Ages, but without becoming lost in historical conceptions which it knew were *Dichtung und Wahrheit* [poetry and truth].[17] At one moment it dwelt in Greece beneath the beautiful Hellenic sky, lost in the presentational [*præsentiske*] enjoyment of the harmonious Hellenic life, dwelt there in such a way that it had its actuality in this. But when it grew tired of this arbitrarily posited actuality it thrust it away so far that it wholly disappeared. Hellenism had no validity for it as a world historical moment, but it had validity, even absolute validity, because irony was pleased to have it so. Next, it concealed itself in the virgin forests of the Middle Ages, listened to the mysterious whisperings of the trees and built nests in their leafy tops, or hid itself in dark hollows, in short, sought its actuality in the Middle Ages in the company of knights and troubadours, became enamoured of a noble maiden on a snorting horse with a falcon trained for hunting perched on her outstretched right forearm. But no sooner had this love-affair lost its validity than the Middle Ages were spirited away back into infinity, dying away in ever weakening contours on the backdrop of consciousness. The Middle Ages had no validity for it as a world historical moment, but it had validity, even absolute validity, because irony was pleased to have it so.

The same thing repeats itself in every theoretical domain. A particular religion was momentarily absolute for it, yet it knew full well that the reason it was absolute was merely because irony was pleased to have it so. At the next moment it wanted something else. It therefore taught with *Nathan der Weise* that all religions were equally good, Christianity perhaps the worst, and for a change it even fancied being a Christian.[18] It behaved in identical fashion with philosophical [*videnskabelig*] matters. It condemned and denounced every philosophical standpoint, was for ever passing sentence, always in the judgement seat, yet never investigated any of them. It always placed itself above the object, which was also quite natural, for only now should actuality really begin. Irony had sprung from the metaphysical problem concerning the relation of the Idea to actuality, but metaphysical actuality is beyond time, hence it was impossible for the actuality desired by irony to be given in time.

It is this condemning and denouncing behaviour of irony that Hegel particularly censures in Friedrich Schlegel.[19] In this respect one cannot overrate Hegel's great contribution to the conception of the historical past. He does not reject the past but conceives [*begriber*] it; he does not dismiss other philosophical standpoints but overcomes them. Hegel has therefore put a stop to all that incessant chatter to the effect that only now shall world history begin, as if it should begin precisely at four o'clock or in any event certainly before five. And if one or another Hegelian has got up such enormous world historical momentum that he cannot stop, but strikes out devil-may-care with awesome speed, then Hegel is not to blame for this. While more can be accomplished with respect to contemplation than Hegel has done, still no one who has any concept of the significance of actuality will be so ungrateful as to go beyond Hegel so hastily as to forget what he owes him, that is, if he has ever really understood Hegel. But if it be asked what gives irony the right to behave in this way, it must be answered that this is because irony knows the phenomenon is not the essence. The Idea is [*er*] concrete and must therefore become [*blive*] concrete, but this becoming [*bliven*] concrete of the Idea is the historical actuality. Within this historical actuality every particular segment has its validity as a moment [*moment*]. This relative validity, however, is not acknowledged by irony. First historical actuality has absolute validity for irony, then none at all, for irony has itself assumed the momentous task of establishing actuality.

But actuality for the individual is also a task to be realized. In this connection one would think that irony would show itself to advantage, for since it had gone beyond every given actuality, surely it must have something good to set in its place. But this is not the case. As irony contrives to overcome historical actuality by making it hover, so irony itself has in turn become hovering. Its actuality is sheer possibility. In order for the acting individual to be able to fulfil his task in realizing actuality, he must feel himself assimilated into a larger context, must feel the seriousness of responsibility, must feel and respect every rational consequence. But irony is free from all this. It knows itself to be in possession of the power to begin from the beginning whenever it pleases, for nothing in the past is binding upon it. Moreover, as irony in infinite freedom enjoys a critical satisfaction in theoretical concerns, so in practical affairs it relishes a similar divine freedom acknowledging no bonds, no chains, but, abandoning itself heedlessly to reckless play, romps like a leviathan in the deep.[20] Irony is free, to be sure, free from all the cares of actuality, but free from its joys as well, free from its blessings. For if it has nothing higher than itself, it may receive no blessing, for it is ever the lesser that is blessed of a greater. This is the freedom for which irony longs. It therefore keeps watch over itself, and fears nothing so much as that one or another impression may overwhelm it. For when the individual is free in this way, only then does he live poetically, and it is well known that irony's great demand was that one should live poetically.

But by 'living poetically' irony understood something other, something more, than what this signifies to every rational person with some regard for the worth of a human being, some sense for what is original in man. It did not understand by this the artistic seriousness which lends assistance to the divine in man, which listens hushed and silently to the voice of what is unique in individuality, disclosing to it its movements so as to predominate in the individual, and so cause the whole of individuality to develop harmoniously into a form which culminates in itself. It did not understand by this what the pious Christian understands when he becomes conscious of the fact that life is an upbringing, an education, which, to be sure, is not going to make him other than he is (for the Christian God is not in possession of the infinite negative omnipotence of the Mohammedan God, for whom a man as huge as a mountain and a flea as large as an elephant are as possible as a mountain as small as a man and an elephant as minute as a flea, because all things might easily be quite other than they are), but which shall develop the very seeds God has planted in man, since the Christian knows himself as that which has reality for God. Here the Christian lends assistance to God and becomes his accomplice as it were in perfecting the good work God has begun.

But irony did not merely intend to lodge a protest against all that baseness which is no more than a wretched product of its environment, a protest against all the mediocre types with which the world is unfortunately rich enough. No, irony desired something more. It is one thing poetically to produce oneself [*at digte sig selv*], quite another to allow oneself to be poetically produced. The Christian allows himself to be poetically produced, and in this respect a simple Christian lives far more poetically than many a gifted head. But even one who poetically produces himself in the Greek sense acknowledges that he has been assigned a task. It is also of the utmost importance for him to become conscious of what is original in him, and this originality is the limit within which he poetically produces, within which he is poetically free. Individuality has a purpose which is absolute, therefore, and its activity consists in realizing this purpose, and in and through this realization to enjoy itself, that is to say, its activity is to become *für sich* [for itself] what it is *an sich* [in itself].[21] But as the average person has no *an sich* but becomes whatever he becomes, so neither does the ironist. This is not because he is merely the product of his environment; on the contrary, he stands completely above his environment. No, to be able to live poetically, to be able poetically to create himself to advantage, the ironist must have no *an sich*. Hence irony lapses into the very thing it most opposes, for the ironist acquires a certain similarity to a thoroughly prosaic person, except that he retains the negative freedom whereby he stands poetically creating above himself. Accordingly, the ironist most often comes to [*bliver til*] nothing, for it is the case with man, unlike God, that nothing can come [*bliver*] of nothing. But the ironist constantly preserves his poetic freedom, and when he notices that he is becoming [*bliver til*] nothing, he includes even this in his poetizing. For it is well known that to become nothing at all was one of those poetic attitudes and vocations in life made valid by irony, indeed it was the most distinguished of them all.

In the poetry of the romantic school, therefore, a *Taugenichts* [good-for-nothing] is always the most poetic character; and what the Christian talks so much about during agitated seasons, namely, to become a fool in the world,[22] this the ironist realizes in his own fashion – except that he feels no martyrdom but the highest poetic enjoyment. But this infinite poetic freedom, already suggested by the fact that to become nothing at all is itself included, is expressed in a still more positive way, for the ironic individual has most often traversed a multitude of determinations in the form of possibility, poetically lived through them, before he ends in nothingness. For irony, as for the Pythagorean doctrine [of the transmigration of souls], the soul is constantly on a pilgrimage, except irony does not require such a long time to complete it. But if irony is a little skimpy with time, it doubtless excels in the multiplicity of determinations. And there is many an ironist who, before finding repose in nothingness, has traversed a far more extraordinary fate than the cock in Lucian, which had first been Pythagoras himself, then Aspasia the ambiguous beauty from Miletus, Crates the Cynic, a king, a beggar, a satrap, a horse, a jackdaw, a frog, and a thousand other things too long to tell, and finally a cock, and this more than once because it found most satisfaction in this.[23] All things are possible for the ironist. Our God is in the heavens: he hath done whatsoever he hath pleased;[24] the ironist is on earth, and does just as he likes. Still, one cannot blame the ironist because he finds it so difficult to become something, for it is not easy to choose when one has such an enormous range of possibilities. For a change he even deems it appropriate to let fate and accident decide for him. He therefore counts on his fingers like a child: rich man, poor man, beggar man, etc. As all these determinations merely have the validity of possibility, he can even run through the whole lot almost as quickly as a child. What costs the ironist time, however, is the care he lavishes on selecting the proper costume for the poetic personage he has poetized himself to be. In this matter the ironist has great skill, not to mention a considerable assortment of masquerade costumes from which to make a judicious selection. Now he strolls about with the proud mien of a Roman patrician in trimmed toga, now he is sitting in the *sella curulis* [official throne] with weighty Roman seriousness, now he disguises himself in the humble cloth of a penitent pilgrim, now he crosses his legs like a Turkish pasha in his harem, flits airily about like a bird, a lovesick cyther player. This is what the ironist means when he maintains that one should live poetically, and this is what he attains by poetically producing himself.

But let us return to our previous remark that it is one thing poetically to produce oneself, quite another to let oneself be poetically produced. The man who allows himself to be poetically produced also has a specific given context to which he must accommodate himself, and hence is not a word without meaning for having been divested of connection and context. But for the ironist this context (this pretext he would say) has no validity, and as he is not inclined to fashion himself to suit his environment, so his environment must be fashioned to suit him, that is, he not only poetically produces himself but his environment as well. The ironist is reserved [*indesluttet*] and stands aloof; he lets mankind pass before him, as did Adam the animals, and finds no companionship for himself. By this he constantly comes into collision with the actuality to which he belongs. It is therefore essential for him to suspend what is constitutive of actuality, that which orders and sustains it: ethics [*sædelighed*] and morals [*moral*]. Here we have arrived at the point which has been the special object of Hegel's attack. Whatever is substantial [*bestaaende*] in the given actuality has only poetic validity for the ironist, indeed he even lives poetically. When the given actuality loses its validity for the ironist, therefore, this is not because it is an outlived actuality which shall be displaced by a truer, but because the ironist is the eternal ego for whom no actuality is adequate. Here it is evident how this relates to the fact that the ironist sets himself above ethics and morals, a thing even Solger declaims against when he asserts that this is not what he means by irony.[25] Still, it cannot properly be said that the ironist sets himself above ethics and morals, for he lives much too abstractly, much too metaphysically and aesthetically ever to arrive at the concretion formed by ethics and morals. Life is for him a drama, and what engrosses him is the ingenious unfolding of this drama. He is himself a spectator even when performing some act. He renders his ego infinite, volatizes it metaphysically and aesthetically, and should it sometimes contract as egoistically and shallowly as possible, at other times it unfurls so loosely and dissolutely that the whole world may be accommodated within it. He is inspired by the virtues of self-sacrifice as a spectator is inspired by them in a theatre, and he is a severe critic who well knows when such virtues become insipid and false. He even feels remorse, but aesthetically not morally. At the moment of remorse he is aesthetically above his remorse examining whether it be poetically correct, whether it might be a suitable reply in the mouth of some poetic character.

Because the ironist poetically produces himself as well as his environment with the greatest possible poetic licence, because he lives completely hypothetically and subjunctively, his life finally loses all continuity. With this he falls completely under the sway of mood [stemning]. His life is sheer mood. Now it is certain that a mood may be very true, and surely no earthly life is so absolute as to be unacquainted with the oppositions inherent in this. But mood, in a healthy life, is merely an intensification [potensation] of what otherwise animates and moves a human being. A serious Christian well knows that there are moments when he is more deeply and forcefully affected by the Christian life than others, but he does not become a heathen when this mood has passed. Indeed, the more healthy and seriously he lives, the more will he become a master of moods, that is to say, so much the more will he humble himself through this and thereby save his soul. But as the ironist has no continuity, so the most contrary moods are allowed to displace each other. Now he is a god, now a grain of sand. His moods are as accidental as the incarnations of the Brahma. Although believing himself to be free, the ironist succumbs to the most terrible law of the irony of the world and toils in the most awful bondage. But the ironist is a poet, and so it does not always appear that he is a ball for the irony of the world to sport with. He poetizes everything, including his moods. To be truly free he must have control over moods, one must instantly displace another. When it sometimes happens that his moods displace one another so preposterously that even he notices all is not right, he poetizes further. He poetizes that it is he who evokes the mood, and he keeps on poetizing until he becomes so spiritually palsied that he must cease. The mood itself has therefore no reality for the ironist, and he seldom airs his moods except in the form of an opposition. His grief conceals itself in the exclusive incognito of jesting, his joy is enveloped in lament. Now he is on his way to the cloister, but on the way he visits the mount of Venus; now he is journeying to the mount of Venus, but stops at a cloister long enough to pray.[26] The philosophical pursuits of irony are likewise dissolved in mood. It is this which Hegel censures in Tieck, and which is particularly apparent in the latter's correspondence with Solger: at one moment he is absolutely certain, at the next he conducts further inquiries, now he is a dogmatist, now a doubter, now it is Jacob Böhme who moves him, now the Greeks, etc. – sheer mood.[27] As there must always be a bond uniting these oppositions, a unity into which these intense dissonances of mood resolve themselves, so upon closer examination one will even find such a unity in the ironist. Boredom is the only continuity the ironist has. Yes, boredom: this eternity void of content, this bliss without enjoyment, this superficial profundity, this hungry satiety. But boredom is the negative unity assimilated into personal consciousness, the negative unity into which opposites disappear. That both Germany and France at this moment have only too great a number of such ironists, and no longer need to be initiated into the secrets of boredom by some English lord, the travelling member of a spleen club; and furthermore, that one or another youthful ward of Young Germany and Young France would long ago have died of boredom had not their respective governments been so fatherly as to arrest them in order to give them something to think about – all this will scarcely be denied by anyone. If anyone wishes to have a splendid image of such an ironist, who, by his very doubleness in existence [*existents*], lacked existence, then let me remind him of Asa-Loke.[28]

It is evident from this how irony remains thoroughly negative: in a theoretical dimension it establishes a disparity between Idea and actuality, actuality and Idea; and in the practical dimension between possibility and actuality, actuality and possibility.

Notes

1   Cf. John 16, 33: 'Be of good cheer; I have overcome the world.'
2   Cf. Ephesians 2, 19: 'Now therefore ye are no more strangers and foreigners, but fellow-citizens with the saints.'
3   *Klangfigurer:* patterns produced when a glass plate sprinkled with sand is made to resound by a violin bow, named after the acoustician E. F. F. Chladni (1757–1827).
4   Kierkegaard refers to a character in the play *Den Stundesløse* ('The Fidget', 1731) by Ludvig Holberg (1684–1754).

5   Cf. I Thessalonians 5, 2: 'the day of the Lord so cometh as a thief in the night'.

6   Kierkegaard refers to the Greek satirist Lucian (c.125–90).

7   The French statesman Charles de Talleyrand (1754–1838).

8   Kierkegaard alludes to Kant's essay 'Was ist Aufklärung?' ('What is Enlighten-ment?', 1784), which begins by stating that 'enlightenment is man's release from his self-incurred tutelage'. The parable of the Prodigal Son is told in Luke 15, 12–32.

9   Kierkegaard alludes to Tithonos, a figure in Greek myth who was exempted from mortality but not from old age; he dwindled to a disembodied voice and was transformed into a grasshopper. Cf. Journals and Papers, I A 302: 'The whole idealistic development in Fichte, for example, discovered an Ego, an immortal-ity, to be sure, but without content, like the husband of Aurora who, although immortal, was without eternal youth and so ended by becoming a grasshopper. Similarly, Fichte dumped the empirical ballast overboard in despair and so cap-sized.'

10 An allusion to Aesop's fable, 'The Fox and the Crow'.

11 Johann Gottlieb Fichte (1762–1814), disciple of Kant, persecuted for alleged atheism, who put forward a version of 'Idealism' (as opposed to 'Dogmatism') which made phenomena depend not on the objective thing in itself but on the subjective ego.

12 Acosmism is the doctrine that the physical world does not exist as such, but is only a manifestation of divine power; docetism states that Christ was human only in appearance and not in reality.

13 Cf. Matthew 10, 39: 'He that loseth his life for my sake shall find it.' See also Mark 8, 35, Luke 9, 24, and John 12, 25.

14 Kierkegaard refers to Johannes Tauler (c.1300–61), Nachfolgung des armen Lebens Christi (1821), but it is now thought that this work has nothing to do with Tauler.

15 Cf. Colossians 2, 2: 'the full assurance of understanding'.

16 Friedrich Schlegel (1772–1829), advocate of orientalism and medievalist roman-ticism, and translator of Shakespeare, and Ludwig Tieck (1773–1853), romantic poet, novelist and dramatist, translator of Shakespeare and other English poets.

17 Kierkegaard alludes to Aus meinem Leben: Dichtung und Wahrheit (1833), the auto-biography of Johann Wolfgang von Goethe (1749–1832).

18 An allusion to the opinion of the hero of the play Nathan der Weise (1779) by Gotthold Ephraim Lessing (1729–81).

19 Kierkegaard refers to Hegel's discussion of Tieck in a review of posthumous works by K. W. F. Solger (1780–1819), which appeared in 1828. Solger had crit-icized romanticism, but not as severely as Hegel would have liked. Kierkegaard discusses Solger's view of irony at length elsewhere in 'Irony after Fichte' in The Concept of Irony, cf. KW II, pp. 308–23.

20 Cf. Psalms 104, 26: 'There go the ships; there is that leviathan, whom thou hast made to play therein.'

21 According to Hegel, progress consists in spirit becoming 'for itself' what it has always been 'in itself'.

22 Cf. I Corinthians 3, 18: 'If any man among you seemeth to be wise in this world, let him become a fool, that he may be wise.'

23 Kierkegaard alludes to Lucian's satire 'The Dream, or the Cock'.

24 Psalms 115, 3: 'But our God is in the heavens: he hath done whatsoever he hath pleased.'

25 See above, n. 19.

26 In the Middle Ages, various mountains in southern Germany were associated with Venus, who presided over a world of dissipated sensuality and lured young knights such as Tannhäuser.

27 Jacob Böhme (1575–1624), puritan mystic and enthusiast, much admired by the German romantics, and founder of the Behmenist movement.

28 The cunning devil-god (also known as Loge) of Norse myth.

3

Either/Or

In October 1841, about a month after the examination of his dissertation on irony, Kierkegaard left Copenhagen to spend the winter in Berlin. The main purpose of the visit was to attend the lectures of F. W. J. Schelling, whose early work had been an inspiration to Hegel many years before, and who was now by far the most eminent and revered philosopher in Germany. Schelling's lectures were on the theme of 'Philosophy and Revelation', and they attracted an audience of enthusiasts from all over Europe, including the young revolutionaries Michael Bakunin and Friedrich Engels.

Schelling seems to have disappointed everybody. The incandescent intellectual adventurer of the turn of the century had evidently turned into a mediocre and complacent compromiser. Karl Marx captured the mood of the moment when he accused him of having no topic except 'I . . . Schelling', and derided his claim to have transcended and reconciled flesh and idea, body and mind, philosophy and theology, and every other dualism. Schelling's only merit, according to Marx, was his remarkable knack for 'uniting philosophy with diplomacy'.[1]

Kierkegaard too was deeply unimpressed. Everything Schelling said was 'unbearable nonsense', he thought – a combination of harebrained philosophy and incompetent scholarship, bound together by 'an insolence which no other philosopher can match'. 'I am too old to listen to lectures,' he concluded, 'and Schelling too old to give them.'[2] And in any case, 'Schelling is a most insignificant man to look at – he looks like a tax collector.'[3]

Kierkegaard kept himself busy in Berlin nevertheless. He attended many other boring lectures, took daily lessons to perfect his German, and went as often as he could to the opera (particularly Mozart's *Don Giovanni*). For a while he made no progress with his own work, complaining of a 'monstrous productivity block'; but after a month or two he was 'writing furiously'. He told his good friend Emil Boesen that he had given up his former manner, and was adopting a 'purely literary' style instead of an academic and 'expository' one; indeed he was struggling to put together a work of fiction or 'pure invention', which he planned to call *Either/Or*.[4]

Kierkegaard brought the manuscripts of *Either/Or* back to Copenhagen in March 1842, and the whole work was published in February 1843. There was no mention of Kierkegaard's name, however, the book being described as 'edited by Victor Eremita' ('Victor the Hermit'). And Victor's preface provides some strong if baffling clues as to the games Kierkegaard might be playing with his readers.

In his first sentence Victor reveals himself as something of a philosophical ironist, in the sense that he entertains doubts about 'the familiar philosophical proposition that the outer is the inner, the inner the outer'. He has devoted himself to reading about such discrepancies and investigating them on his own account, in the hope of being able eventually 'to fill a gap in the philosophical literature'. On occasion he has despaired, but now, by a remarkable stroke of good fortune, he has come into possession of a collection of papers which provide the perfect illustration of his themes, and 'corroborate my suspicion that the outer is not, after all, the inner'. He was now putting these documents before the public under the title *Either/Or*.

Victor explains that he originally found the papers as a result of a turbulent but totally one-sided affair of the heart. It had started some years before, probably in 1835, and as far as he was concerned it had been love at first sight. Oddly enough, its object was not a girl, nor yet a woman or a boy or a man, but . . . a writing desk. ('Desire, as is well known, is very sophistical', Victor says.) He glimpsed the fatal beauty in a second-hand dealer's window, and fell immediately under its spell. Before long he was creating pretexts for passing the shop every day to steal some furtive but lascivious glances. He did not need a desk, and he had no money to spare, but by then it was too late: the creature had 'acquired a history' for him and after much prevarication he entered the shop and paid the price with trembling hands. The trophy was carried up to his rooms, and for many months he enjoyed deep happiness in its company – getting to know its contours, its intricate runners and compartments, and stowing his most precious treasures inside. 'Desire', as Victor remarks, 'is very eloquent.'

But the affair could not last. Early one morning the following summer, Victor was preparing to visit a friend for a rural vacation, which of course would mean leaving his beloved on its own in Copenhagen. There was a drawer in the desk where he kept his money, but he found that it had somehow jammed itself shut. As he was wrestling with the drawer Victor could hear the coachman blowing his horn outside. 'The blood rushed to my head; I was furious and . . . so I decided to take a dreadful revenge.' In a fit of jealous fury, he bludgeoned his sweet and uncomplaining companion with an axe. The money drawer stayed stubbornly closed, but all of a sudden an unsuspected cubby hole sprang open on the other side, revealing a large cache of old manuscripts. Victor blessed his dear desk and begged it to excuse him, for the discovery was not only delightful in itself, but also a confirmation of what, as an ironist, he had suspected all along: that everyone has their secrets, so that 'the outer is not the inner after all'.

Forgetting all about the money, Victor placed the papers in an old mahogany gun case and rushed out with it to catch the waiting coach. After a few days settling in at his friend's house he began to go out on his own with the case under his arm, seeking romantic forest glades where he could study the papers in peace. His host was impressed by what he took to be Victor's new-found passion for shooting, and Victor was happy to leave the misunderstanding intact.

The manuscripts turned out to fall into two groups, one written in a clear and businesslike script filling uniform columns on legal foolscap, the other in an informal but elegant hand on luxurious quarto letter-vellum with generous margins. The foolscaps contained copies of letters which Victor found to be 'ethical in content', in the sense that they are attempts to persuade their recipient to choose a solid life of marriage and good works. He therefore ascribes them all to a single writer whom he decides to call 'B', though internal evidence makes it fairly certain that B was a retired judge by the name of William.

The quartos are far more problematic. Their theme is certainly not 'ethical', and Victor therefore decides to classify them as 'aesthetic' (in the sense of unreflective sensuality rather artistic refinement). But they are very miscellaneous, and Victor finds it difficult to unravel their authorship, especially as the largest section – entitled 'The Diary of a Seducer' – has ostensibly been copied from some manuscripts stolen from a friend who had left them in an open drawer of his desk.

Victor dismisses this new tale of a desk as a subterfuge: we are all familiar, are we not, with the 'old literary device' by which 'one author is enclosed inside another like the boxes in a Chinese puzzle'? He therefore concludes that, despite appearances, the quarto papers can all be attributed to a single author, an irresponsible sensualist with a literary streak whom he decides to call 'A'.

The perspectives of A and B could hardly be more different, but after reflecting for a further five years, Victor settles on the conclusion − 'unhistorical', 'improbable' and 'unreasonable' though he admits it to be − that A and B were really one and the same person, experimenting with two different styles of thinking and writing. And that, he explains, is why he has decided to publish them all together under the title *Enten-Eller: Et Livs-Fragment*, or *Either/Or: A Fragment of Life*.[5]

Victor's reasoning is strained, of course, if not entirely cracked. The idea of having to choose between alternative ways of life loses its force if the same person − an ironist perhaps, who maintains a distance between the inner and the outer − can combine them both. Moreover B's papers also include the work of someone else, in the form of a transcript of a sermon whose theme happens to be that our life-choices never matter much: they make no real difference, because 'in relation to God we are always in the wrong'.[6] A's papers themselves include an 'ecstatic discourse' on the theme of 'either/or', which makes much the same point: 'Marry, and you will regret it; do not marry, and you will also regret it; . . . whether you laugh at the stupidities of the world or you weep over them, you will regret it either way; . . . trust a girl and you will regret it; do not trust her and you will also regret it; . . . hang yourself or do not hang yourself, you will regret it either way.'[7] And the same might be said, Victor reflects in his Preface, of the papers he is offering us under the title *Either/Or*: 'Read them or do not read them, you will regret it either way.'[8]

The title may therefore be misleading. *Either/Or* does not necessarily imply a choice between *either* the 'aesthetic' quartos of A, *or* B's 'ethical' foolscaps. If there are choices to be made, they arise equally within every part of the book. Indeed, its overall architecture is itself systematically unsettling.

Preface (by Victor Eremita)
  ONE: THE PAPERS OF A
  1   *Diapsalmata* (A collection of epigrams and anecdotes of which the following are typical: 'A fire broke out backstage in a theatre, and a clown came out to inform the audience; they thought it was a joke and applauded.' Or 'What the philosophers say about actuality is often as disappointing as a sign seen in a shop window saying "Pressing done here"; but when you bring your clothes to be ironed, you will have been fooled: the sign itself is for sale.')[9]
  2   *The Immediate Stages of the Erotic, or the Musical Erotic* (An essay based on the idea that music expresses what Christianity denies: the spirit of sensuality which, since it exists 'not in a single moment [*moment*] but in a succession of moments' can be expressed only in music, especially in

Mozart's portraits of the dreamy love-crazed Cherubino in *The Marriage of Figaro*, Papageno the desperate wife-hunter in *Magic Flute*, and above all the insatiable seducer-hero of *Don Giovanni*.)[10]

3 *The Ancient Tragical Motif as Reflected in the Modern* (An essay in fragmentariness, discussing ancient and modern tragedy with special reference to Antigone, and designed to be read to a club called the *Symparanekromenoi* or 'fellowship of the dead'.)

4 *Shadowgraphs: A Psychological Pastime* (Another lecture to the *Symparanekromenoi*, discussing a variety of modern heroines of reflective grief, including Mozart's Elvira and Goethe's Gretchen.)

5 *The Unhappiest One* (Another address to the *Symparanekromenoi* – a lecture on the question of who deserves the distinction of being called unhappier than anyone else.)

6 *The First Love* (An over-the-top essay in praise of a simple comedy by Eugène Scribe.)

7 *Crop Rotation: An Attempt at a Theory of Social Prudence* (A solemn discussion of the uses of boredom.)

8 *The Diary of a Seducer* (An account of a character called Johannes and how he conducted a cynical campaign of courtship, together with an exchange of letters between him and his victim Cordelia, and a preface by a third party who claims to have discovered the diary in a friend's desk.)

TWO: THE PAPERS OF B (LETTERS TO A)

9 *The Aesthetic Validity of Marriage* (A careful but sanctimonious defence of the married state, addressed to 'My Friend'.)

10 *Equilibrium between the Aesthetic and the Ethical in the Development of Personality* (A second letter to 'My Friend', attempting to reassert the idea of absolute and binding life-choices.)

11 *Ultimatum* (A valedictory letter, mostly transcribing a sermon on 'The Edification to be found in the thought that in relation to God we are always in the wrong'.)

Either/Or as a whole is structured a bit like a drawing of an impossible object: you can never be sure that any given element of the picture is really reliable, nor whether it is designed to complement the others or to conflict with them. Or again, it is like a six-part musical canon, with different voices chiming in one after the other: first Victor the editor, then the aesthetician A, followed by Johannes the Seducer, Cordelia his prey, Judge William, and the preacher of the sermon on how we are always in the wrong.

Or again, *Either/Or* can be seen as enacting a kind of rotation, in the sense of the chapter on 'Crop Rotation' printed below. The chapter's subtitle

('Forsøg til en social Klogskabslære') could be translated as 'an essay towards a theory of social prudence' – a kind of exploratory *How to Make Friends and Influence People*, but written in a style calculated to alienate its readers. The author appears to be an ironist of the kind Kierkegaard ridiculed in *The Concept of Irony*, a specialist in the ways of boredom.[11] His message is that if you want to avoid stagnation, the solution is not so much to abandon your native soil as to vary the way you cultivate it. In other words: rotate your crops.

Notes

1 Karl Marx, letter to Ludwig Feuerbach, 3 October 1843; translated by Jack Cohen in Karl Marx and Friedrich Engels, *Collected Works*, Vol. 3 (London: Lawrence and Wishart, 1975), p. 350.

2 Letter to Peter Kierkegaard (1805–88), 6 February 1842, cited by Howard V. Hong and Edna H. Hong in *The Concept of Irony*, KW II, pp. xxii–xxiii.

3 Letter to Peter Johannes Spang (1796–1846), 18 November 1841, cited in ibid., KW II, pp. xx–xxi.

4 Letter to Emil Boesen (1812–81), 6 January 1842, cited by Howard V. Hong and Edna H. Hong in *Either/Or*, KW III, p. vii.

5 See *Either/Or*, Preface by the Editor (Victor Eremita); cf. KW III, pp. 3–15.

6 See 'The Edification to be found in the thought that in relation to God we are always in the wrong', *Either/Or*, Part II, 'Ultimatum'; cf. KW IV, pp. 339–54.

7 See *Either/Or*, Part I, 'Diapsalmata', cf. KW III, pp. 38–40; the passage alludes to Diogenes Laertius's account of Socrates: 'Someone asked him whether he should marry or not, and received the reply, "You will regret it whichever you do." ' See *Lives of the Philosophers* II, 33.

8 *Either/Or*, Preface; cf. KW III, p. 14.

9 Cf. KW III, pp. 30, 32.

10 Cf. KW III, pp. 56–7.

11 See above, p. 50.

Either/Or: A Fragment of Life
edited by Victor Eremita

Crop Rotation: An Attempt at a Theory of Social Prudence

People of experience maintain that it is very sensible to start from a principle. I grant them that and start from the principle that all men are boring. Or will someone be boring enough to contradict me in this? This principle possesses to the highest degree that power of repulsion one always requires of any negative that genuinely provides the principle of motion. Not merely is it repellent, it is infinitely forbidding; and the person with this principle behind him must necessarily have an infinite momentum to make discoveries with. For if my principle is true, to slacken or increase one's impetus one need only consider with more or less moderation how ruinous boredom is for man; and if one wants to risk doing injury to the locomotive itself by pressing the speed to the maximum, one need only say to oneself: 'Boredom is the root of all evil.' Strange that boredom, so still and static, should have such power to set things in motion. The effect that boredom exercises is altogether magical, except that it is not one of attraction but of repulsion.

How ruinous boredom is everyone also recognizes in relation to children. So long as children are enjoying themselves, they are always well-behaved.

The first English translation of *Either/Or* was begun by David Swenson, completed by Walter Lowrie, and published in 1944. It was joined in 1987 by a painstaking and fully annotated version by Howard V. Hong and Edna H. Hong (*Kierkegaard's Writings*, vols III, IV). This extract is taken from the fresh and fluent translation published in 1992 by Alastair Hannay, which has been checked against the original and lightly amended where necessary.

This can be said in the strictest sense, since if they sometimes get out of control even in play, really that is because they are beginning to get bored; boredom has already set in, though in a different way. So in choosing a nursemaid one pays attention not just to her sobriety, faithfulness and decency; one also takes into consideration, aesthetically, her ability to amuse the children. And one would not hesitate to dismiss a nursemaid lacking in this qualification even if she possessed all other desirable virtues. Here, indeed, the principle is clearly acknowledged; but so remarkable are the ways of the world, so much have habit and boredom gained the upper hand, that justice is done to aesthetics only in the case of the nursemaid. Were one to demand divorce on the grounds that one's wife was boring, or a king's abdication because he was boring to look at, or a priest thrown out of the land because he was boring to listen to, or a cabinet minister dismissed, or a life-sentence for a journalist, because they were dreadfully boring, it would be impossible to get one's way. What wonder, then, that the world is regressing, that evil is gaining ground more and more, since boredom is on the increase and boredom is the root of all evil.

We can trace this from the very beginning of the world. The gods were bored so they created man. Adam was bored because he was alone, so Eve was created. From that time boredom entered the world and grew in exact proportion to the growth of population. Adam was bored alone, then Adam and Eve were bored in union, then Adam and Eve and Cain and Abel were bored *en famille*, then the population increased and the peoples were bored *en masse*. To divert themselves they conceived the idea of building a tower so high it reached the sky. The very idea is as boring as the tower was high, and a terrible proof of how boredom had gained the upper hand. Then the nations were scattered over the earth, just as people now travel abroad, but they continued to be bored. And think of the consequences of this boredom! Man stood high and fell low, first with Eve and then the tower of Babel. Yet what was it that stayed the fall of Rome? It was *panis* and *circenses* [bread and circuses].[1] What is it people do nowadays? Do they think of ways of diverting themselves? Quite the contrary, they accelerate the ruin. They think of calling a constitutional assembly. Can anything more boring be imagined, as much for the gentlemen taking part as for those who have to read and hear about them! There is a proposal to improve the State's economy through savings. Can anything more boring be imagined? Instead of increasing the national debt, it is proposed to pay it off. From what I know of politics, it would be an easy matter for Denmark to take out a loan of fifteen millions. Why does no one think of that? That some person is genius enough not to pay his debt, that at least is something one hears of now and then; why shouldn't a state be able to do the same if only all are agreed? So we take out a loan of fifteen millions yet use it not to pay our debts but for public pleasure. Let us celebrate the thousand year reign with joy and merriment. Just as there are boxes everywhere to put money in, so there should be bowls of money everywhere. Everything would be free, people would go to the theatre free, have free access to the streetwalkers, take free drives to the park, be buried free of charge, have someone speak over their coffin free of charge; for when one always has money in hand everything is in a sense gratis. No one need own property. An exception would be made just in my own case. I personally reserve 100 dollars a day permanently in the Bank of London, partly because I cannot do with less, partly because it was I who came up with the idea, and finally because one never knows whether I might come up with a new idea when the fifteen millions are used up. What would this affluence lead to? Everything great would pour into Copenhagen, the greatest artists, actors and dancers. Copenhagen would become another Athens. What would be the result? Men of wealth would all settle in this city, among them very likely the Shah of Persia and the King of England. So here is my second idea. We kidnap the Shah. It may be objected that there would then be rebellion in Persia, a new Shah would be placed on the throne – it has happened so often before – and the price for the old Shah would drop. In that case, my idea is we sell him to the Turks; they will know how to convert him into cash. And then there is something else our politicians seem entirely to overlook. Denmark holds the balance of power in Europe. No more fortunate existence can be imagined. I know it from my own experience. I was once the balance of power in a family and could do as I pleased; it was never I that suffered, always the others. Oh that my words might reach your ears, you who sit in high places to advise and rule, you king's men and men of the people, wise and understanding citizens of all classes! Have a care! Old Denmark is foundering, what a sorry fate, and most fateful of all, it is going under from boredom. In ancient times he who sang the praises of the dead king most beautifully became the new king. In our time he should be king who comes up with the best witticism, he the crown prince who provides the occasion for its utterance.

But how you carry me away, beauteous, sentimental enthusiasm! Is this the way I should be opening my mouth to address my contemporaries, initiating them into my wisdom? Not at all. For my wisdom is really not *zum Gebrauch für Jedermann* [for everyone's use], and it is always more prudent to keep one's rules of prudence to oneself. Disciples, then, I have no wish for, but should someone happen to be present at my deathbed, and if I was sure it was all over with me, I might perhaps in a fit of philanthropic delirium whisper my teaching in his ear, uncertain whether I had done him a service or not. There is so much talk of man's being a social animal; basically he is a beast of prey, as one can ascertain not merely by consideration of his teeth. All this talk of sociability and society is in part, therefore, an inherited hypocrisy, in part a calculated deceit.

So all people are boring. The word itself indicates the possibility of a sub-division. 'Boring' can describe a person who bores others as well as one who bores himself. Those who bore others are the plebeians, the mass, the endless train of humanity in general. Those who bore themselves are the elect, the nobility; and how strange it is that those who don't bore themselves usually bore others, while those who do bore themselves amuse others. The people who do not bore themselves are usually those who are busy in the world in one way or another, but that is just why they are the most boring, the most insufferable, of all. This species of animal life, surely, is not the fruit of man's desire and woman's pleasure. Like all lower forms of life, it is distinguished by a high degree of fertility and multiplies beyond belief. Inconceivable, too, that nature should need nine months to produce creatures like these which one would rather suppose could be produced by the score. The other class of men, the select, are those who bore themselves. As remarked above, gen-erally they amuse others, outwardly occasionally the mob, in a deeper sense their fellow initiates. The more profoundly they bore themselves, the more powerful a means of diversion they offer others, when boredom reaches its zenith, either by dying of boredom (the passive form) or (the active form) by shooting themselves out of curiosity.

Idleness, it is usually said, is the root of all evil. To prevent this evil one recommends work. However, it is easy to see from the remedy as well as the feared cause that this whole view is of very plebeian extraction. Idleness as such is by no means a root of evil; quite the contrary, it is a truly divine way of life so long as one is not bored. Certainly, idleness may lead you to lose your fortune, and so on, but of such things the man of noble nature has no fear; what he fears is boredom. The Olympian gods were not bored, they prospered in happy idleness. A beauty who neither sews nor spins nor irons nor reads nor makes music is happy in her idleness, for she is not bored. So, far from idleness being the root of evil, rather it is the true good. The root of evil is boredom, and that is what must be kept at bay. Idleness is not evil; indeed, one can say that any human who lacks appreciation of it proves he has not raised himself to the level of humanity. There is a kind of restless activity that keeps a person out of the world of spirit and puts him in a class with the animals, which from instinct must always be on the go. There are people with an extraordinary gift for transforming everything into business, whose whole life is business, who fall in love and marry, listen to a joke and admire a work of art with the same zealous sense of affairs with which they work in the office. The Latin proverb, *otium est pulvinar diaboli* [leisure is the pillow of the devil], is perfectly correct, but when one isn't bored the devil gets no time to lay his head on that pillow. Yet in so far as people think it is characteristic of man to work, idleness and industry are properly opposed to each other. My own assumption is that it is characteristic of man to amuse himself; my opposites are therefore no less correct.

Boredom is demonic pantheism. If we remain in it as such it becomes evil; on the other hand, as soon as it is annulled [*ophæves*] it is true. But one annuls it only by amusing oneself – *ergo* one ought to amuse oneself. Saying work annuls it is to betray confusion, for though idleness, certainly, can be annulled by industry, seeing the latter is its opposite, boredom cannot, as one also sees that the busiest workers of all, those who in their officious buzzing about most resemble humming insects, are the most boring of all; and if they don't bore themselves, that's because they have no idea what boredom is; but in that case boredom is not annulled.

Boredom is partly an immediate talent, partly an acquired immediacy. Here the English are, on the whole, the paradigmatic nation. One seldom encounters a born talent for indolence, one never meets it in nature; indolence belongs to the world of spirit. Occasionally you meet an English traveller, however, who is an incarnation of this talent, a heavy immovable groundhog whose linguistic resources are exhausted in a single one-syllable word, an interjection with which he signifies his greatest admiration and most profound indifference, because in the unity of boredom admiration and indifference have become indistinguishable. No other nation but the English produces such natural curiosities; other nationals are always a little more lively, not so absolutely stillborn. The only analogy I know is the apostle of empty enthusiasm, who also journeys through life on an interjection – that is, people who are always making a profession of enthusiasm, everywhere making their presence felt, and whether something significant or insignificant is taking place, cry 'Ah!' or 'Oh!', because for them the difference between significant and insignificant has become undone in enthusiasm's blind and blaring emptiness. The acquired form of boredom is usually a product of a mistaken attempt at diversion. That the remedy for boredom can bring boredom about in this way seems doubtful, but it does so only to the extent that it is incorrectly applied. A misconceived, generally eccentric form of diversion also has boredom within it, and that is the way it finds its way out and proves to be the immediate. As with horses one distinguishes between blind staggers and sleepy staggers, but calls them both staggers, we can also make a distinction between two kinds of boredom which are still united in being specifications of boredom.

Pantheism, in general, contains the quality of fullness; with boredom it is the opposite, it is based on emptiness, but is for that very reason a pantheistic category. Boredom rests upon the nothingness that winds its way through existence; its giddiness, like that which comes from gazing down into an infinite abyss, is infinite. That the eccentric form of diversion mentioned above is based on boredom can also be seen from the fact that the diversion reverberates without making an echo, just because in nothing there isn't even enough to make an echo possible.

Seeing that boredom is the root of all evil, as enlarged on above, what more natural than to try to overcome it? But here, as everywhere, cool deliberation is clearly called for lest in one's demonic obsession with boredom, in trying to avoid it one only works oneself further into it. 'Change' is what all who are bored cry out for. With this I am entirely in agreement, only it is important to act from principle.

My own departure from the general view is adequately expressed in the phrase 'crop rotation'. This phrase might seem to contain an ambiguity, and in wanting to make it commodious enough to cover the general method, I should have to say that the method of rotation consisted in constantly changing the soil. That, however, is not the sense in which the farmer uses it. Still, I will adopt this use for a moment, so as to talk of that 'crop rotation' which depends on the unlimited infinity of change, on its extensive dimension.

This rotation is the vulgar, the inartistic method, and is based on an illusion. One is tired of living in the country, one moves to the city; one is tired of one's native land, one travels abroad; one is *europamüde* [tired of Europe], one goes to America, and so on; finally, one indulges in a dream of endless travel from star to star. Or the movement is different but still in extension. One is tired of dining off porcelain, one dines off silver; one tires of that, one dines off gold; one burns half of Rome to get an idea of the conflagration at Troy. This method defeats itself; it is the bad infinite [*slette uendelighed*].[2] And what did Nero achieve?[3] No, Antonine was wiser; he says, 'It is in your power to review your life, to look at things you saw before, from another point of view.'[4]

The method I propose consists not in changing the soil but, as in the real rotation of crops, in changing the method of cultivation and type of grain. Here, straightaway, we have the principle of limitation, which is the only saving one in the world. The more you limit yourself, the more resourceful you become. A prisoner in solitary confinement for life is most resourceful, a spider can cause him much amusement. One thinks of one's schooldays. When one is at the age when no aesthetic considerations are taken in the choice of one's teachers and the latter are for that very reason often very boring, how inventive one is! How amusing to catch a fly and keep it imprisoned under a nut shell and watch how it rushes about with the shell! What pleasure one can get by cutting a hole in the desk to imprison a fly in it, and spy down on it through a piece of paper! How entertaining it can be to hear the monotonous drip from the roof! How thorough an observer one becomes, the slightest noise or movement does not escape one! Here we have the extreme of the principle that seeks relief, not extensively, but intensively.

The more inventive one can be in changing the mode of cultivation, the better; but every particular change comes under the general rule of the relation between *remembering* and *forgetting*. The whole of life moves in these two currents, so it is essential to have control over them. Only when one has thrown hope overboard is it possible to live artistically; as long as one hopes, one cannot limit oneself. It is really beautiful to see a man put out to sea with the fair wind of hope, one can use the opportunity to be taken in tow, but one should never have it aboard one's own ship, least of all as a pilot; for hope is a faithless steersman. Hope was therefore also one of the dubious gifts of Prometheus; instead of the foreknowledge of the immortals, he gave men hope.[5]

To forget – all men want to do that, and when they come across something unpleasant they always say, 'If only I could forget!' But forgetting is an art that must be practised beforehand. Being able to forget depends always on how one remembers, but how one remembers depends in turn on how one experiences reality. The person who sticks fast in it with the momentum of hope will remember in a way that makes him unable to forget. *Nil admirari* [wonder at nothing] is therefore the real wisdom of life. Every life-situation must possess no more importance than that one can forget it whenever one wants to; each single life-situation should have enough importance, however, for one to be able at any time to remember it. The age that remembers best, but is also the most forgetful, is childhood. The more poetically one remembers, the more easily one forgets, for remembering poetically is really just an expression for forgetfulness. In remembering poetically, what was experienced has already undergone a change in which it has lost all that was painful. To remember in this way, one must be careful how one lives, especially how one enjoys. If one enjoys without reservation to the last, if one always takes with one the most that pleasure can offer, one will be unable either to remember or to forget. For then one has nothing else to remember than a surfeit one wants to forget, but which now plagues you with an involuntary remembrance. So when you begin to notice that you are being carried away by enjoyment or a life-situation too strongly, stop for a moment and remember. No other expedient gives a better distaste for going on too long. One must keep reins on the enjoyment from the beginning, not set all

sail for everything you decide on [*beslutning*]. One indulges in a certain dis-
trust; only then can one give the lie to the proverb which says that no one
can have his cake and eat it too. The carrying of secret weapons is forbidden, indeed, by the police, yet no weapon is as dangerous as the trick of
being able to remember. It is a peculiar feeling when, in the midst of enjoyment, one looks at it in order to remember.

Having perfected the art of forgetting and the art of remembering, one
is then in a position to play battledore and shuttlecock with the whole of
existence.[6]

A person's resilience can really be measured by the power to forget. A
person unable to forget will never amount to much. Whether a Lethe flows
somewhere I do not know, but what I do know is that this art can be developed.[7] Yet it does not at all consist in the total disappearance of particular
impressions; for the art of forgetting is not the same as forgetfulness. It is also
easy to see what very little understanding people in general have of this art,
for usually it is only the unpleasant they want to forget, not the pleasant.
This betrays a complete one-sidedness. For forgetting is the proper expression of the real conversion that reduces experience to a sounding-board. The
reason for nature's greatness is that it has forgotten that it once was chaos,
but this latter thought can recur whenever need be. Since one usually only
conceives of forgetting in relation to what is unpleasant, one usually conceives it as an untamed power that drowns things out. Quite the contrary;
forgetting is a quiet occupation and ought to be exercised as much in relation to what is pleasant as to what is unpleasant. As something past, indeed
precisely as past, what is pleasant contains also an unpleasant side by being
able to arouse a sense of privation. This unpleasantness is overcome by forgetting. The unpleasant has a sting, everyone admits that, and it, too, is
removed by forgetting; but if one pushes the unpleasant aside altogether, as
many of those who dabble in the art of forgetting do, one soon sees what
good that does. In an unguarded moment, it often takes one by surprise with
all the force of the sudden. This is in absolute contradiction to the well-
organized arrangement in a reasonable mind. No misfortune, no hardship, is
so hard to approach, so deaf that it cannot be flattered a little; even Cerberus
accepted honey-cakes, and it is not just young girls one beguiles.[8] One talks
it round and in so doing deprives it of its bite, by no means does one want
to forget it; one forgets it in order to remember it. Yes, even with those memories for which one might think eternal oblivion was the only remedy, one
permits oneself this cunning, and the deft will succeed in the deception. Forgetting is the shears with which one clips away what one cannot use –
though, mind you, under the overall supervision of memory. Forgetting and
memory are thus identical, and the skilfully achieved identity is the

Archimedean point with which one lifts the whole world.[9] In saying that we consign something to oblivion, we suggest that it is simultaneously forgotten yet preserved.

The art of remembering and forgetting will then also prevent one's sticking fast in some particular situation in life and ensure perfect suspension.

So one must be on one's guard against *friendship*. How is a friend defined? A friend is not what philosophy calls 'the necessary other', but the superfluous third. What are the ceremonies of friendship? One thous and thees in a glass, one opens an artery, one mixes one's blood with the friend's. The exact arrival of this moment is hard to determine, but it mysteriously proclaims itself, one feels it, one can no longer use the formal 'You' in addressing each other. Once this feeling has occurred, one can never prove mistaken, as was Gert Westphaler, who discovered that he had been drinking with the public hangman.[10] – What are the infallible marks of friendship? Antiquity answers, *idem velle, idem nolle, ea demum firma amicitia* ['identical desires and identical aversions are the foundation of firm friendship'], and extremely boringly at that. What significance has friendship? Mutual assistance in word and deed. So two friends form a close association in order to be everything to one another, regardless that all the one can be for the other is in the way. Yes, they may help each other with money, on and off with each other's coats, be each other's humble servant, join in a sincere New Year's greeting, likewise in matrimony, birth and burial.

But to abstain from friendship doesn't mean that you are to live without human contact. Quite the contrary, human relationships of this kind may also sometimes take on a deeper surge, except that, although you share the speed of the movement for a time, you always have enough speed in hand to be able to run away from it. One no doubt thinks that such behaviour leaves unpleasant memories, that the unpleasantness consists in the fact that, after having meant something to you, the relation dwindles away into nothing. But this is a misunderstanding. Unpleasantness is a piquant ingredient in the contrariety of life. Besides, the same relationship can acquire significance again in another way. What one must watch out for is never to stick fast, and for that one must have one's forgetting up one's sleeve. The experienced farmer now and then lets his land lie fallow; the theory of social prudence recommends the same. All things, no doubt, will return, but in another way; what has once been taken into rotation remains there but is varied through the mode of cultivation. It is quite consistent, therefore, to hope to meet old friends and acquaintances in a better world; but one does not share the fear of the masses, that they will have changed too much for one to be able to recognize them again. One fears, rather, that they may be unchanged. It is incredible how much significance even an insignificant person can gain through such rational management.

One never enters into *marriage*. Married couples promise each other eternal love. That is all very fine but does not mean very much, for when one is finished with time, one will no doubt be finished with eternity. So if, instead of saying 'forever', the parties said, 'until Easter', or 'until the first May-Day', then at least their words would have meaning for they would have actually said something, something they could perhaps keep to. And how does it go with a marriage? After a little while one party begins to notice that something's wrong; then the other party complains and cries out, 'Faithlessness, faithlessness!' After some time the other party arrives at the same point and a state of neutrality is brought about, in that the mutual faithlessness balances out to the satisfaction and contentment of both. But now it is too late, for there are great difficulties connected with divorce.

Such being the case with marriage, it is not surprising that it has to be stiffened in so many ways with moral supports. When a husband wants to be divorced from his wife, people cry, 'He is contemptible, a scoundrel', etc. How silly, and what an indirect attack upon marriage! Either marriage has reality in it, in which case he is sufficiently punished by forfeiting the latter; or it has no reality in it, in which case it is indeed absurd to abuse him, for he is wiser than others. If a man grew tired of his money and threw it out of the window, no one would say he was a contemptible person; for either the money has reality, and then he is sufficiently punished by depriving himself of it, or it has no reality, and then indeed he is wise.

One must always be careful not to enter into any life-relation in which one can become several. For this reason friendship is already dangerous, even more so marriage. A married couple are indeed said to become one, but this is a very dark and mysterious saying. When you are several you have lost your freedom and cannot order travelling boots when you will, cannot roam aimlessly about. If you have a wife it is difficult; if you have a wife and may have children, it is troublesome; if you have a wife and do have children, it is impossible. We do, indeed, have the example of a gypsy woman carrying her husband on her back through life, but for one thing it is a rare occurrence, and for another, in the long run wearisome – for the husband. Besides, in marriage one falls into extremely fateful line with practice and custom, and, like wind and weather, practice and custom are very hard to pin down. In Japan, I am told, it is practice and custom for the husbands too to lie in childbed. Why shouldn't the time come when Europe introduces the customs of foreign countries?

Friendship is already dangerous, marriage still more so, for the woman is and will remain the husband's ruin as soon as he enters into a permanent relation with her. Take a young man, ardent as an Arabian horse, let him marry, he is lost. First of all the woman is proud, then she is weak, then she faints, then he faints, then the whole family faints. A woman's love is only dissimulation and weakness.

But not entering into marriage need not mean that one's life lacks eroticism. The erotic should also have infinitude, but poetic infinitude, which can just as well be limited to an hour as to a month. When two people fall in love and suspect they are made for each other, the thing is to have the courage to break it off, for by continuing they only have everything to lose and nothing to gain. It seems a paradox and is so, for feeling, not for understanding. In this domain it is especially important to be able to use moods; if one can do that, then one can bring off an inexhaustible variety of combinations.

One never accepts any *vocational responsibility*. If one does so, one simply becomes Mr Anybody, a tiny little pivot in the machinery of the corporate state; you cease to direct your own affairs, and then theories can be of little help. One acquires a title, and in it is contained all the consistency of sin and evil. The law one is then in thrall to is equally boring, whether promotion is rapid or slow. A title is something one can never be rid of again, it would have to be lost through some crime which incurs a public whipping, and even then you are not certain, for you may be pardoned and have your title restored to you by royal decree.

Though one abstains from vocational responsibility, one should not be inactive but stress all occupation that is identical with idleness; one must engage in all kinds of breadless skills. Yet in this connection one should develop oneself not so much extensively but intensively, and in spite of being on in years, prove the truth of the old proverb that it takes little to please a child.

If, then, in accordance with the theory of social prudence, one to some extent varies the soil – for if one were to live only in relation to one person the rotation method would turn out as badly as if a farmer had only one acre of land, the result of which would be to make it impossible for him to let land lie fallow, which is of the utmost importance – then one must also constantly vary oneself, and this is really the secret. To that end one must necessarily have control of moods. Controlling them in the sense of being able to produce them at will is impossible, but prudence teaches how to make use of the instant [*øieblikket*]. As an experienced sailor always looks out searchingly over the water and sees a squall far ahead, so should one always see the mood a little in advance. One must know how the mood affects oneself, and in all probability others, before putting it on. One strokes the strings first to elicit pure tones and see what there is in a person, and the intermediate tones follow later. The more practice you have, the more readily you will be convinced that often there is much in a person which one never considers. When sensitive people, who as such are extremely boring, become angry, they are often very diverting. Teasing in particular is an excellent means of exploration.

The whole secret lies in arbitrariness. People think it requires no skill to be arbitrary, yet it requires deep study to succeed in being arbitrary without losing oneself in it, to derive satisfaction from it oneself. One's enjoyment is not immediate but is something quite different which one arbitrarily injects. You see the middle of a play, read the third part of a book. In this way one derives a quite different enjoyment from the one the author has been so good as to intend for you. One enjoys something entirely accidental, one regards the whole of existence from this standpoint, lets its reality run aground on it. I will give an example. There was someone whose chatter certain circumstances made it necessary for me to listen to. He was ready at every opportunity with a little philosophical lecture which was utterly boring. Driven almost to despair, I discovered suddenly that he perspired unusually profusely when he spoke. I saw how the pearls of sweat gathered on his brow, then joined in a stream, slid down his nose, and ended hanging in a drop at the extreme tip of it. From that moment everything was changed; I could even take pleasure in inciting him to begin his philosophical instruction, just to observe the sweat on his brow and on his nose.

Baggesen says somewhere of a man that he was no doubt a very decent person, but that he had one objection to make to him: nothing rhymed with his name.[11] It is extremely beneficial to let the realities of life neutralize themselves in this way on an arbitrary interest of this kind. You transform something accidental into the absolute and, as such, into an object of absolute admiration. This works particularly excellently when tempers are aroused. For many people this method is an excellent stimulus. One looks at everything in life as a wager, and so on. The more consistently one can sustain the arbitrariness, the more amusing the combinations. The degree of consistency always shows whether one is an artist or a dabbler, for to some extent people all do the same. The eye with which one looks at reality must constantly change. The Neo-Platonists supposed that those human beings who had been less perfect on earth became, after death, more or less perfect animals, depending on their deserts. Those, for example, who had exercised civic virtues on a smaller scale (retail traders) became civic animals, bees for example. Such a view of life, which sees all persons transformed into animals or plants (Plotinus also thought that some were transformed into plants),[12] offers a rich multiplicity of variations. The painter Tischbein has tried to idealize every human being as an animal.[13] His method has the fault of being too serious, and that it seeks a real resemblance.

To the arbitrariness within oneself there corresponds the accidental outside one. One should therefore always keep an eye open for the accidental, always be *expeditus* [prepared] if anything should offer. The so-called social pleasures, for which one prepares eight or fourteen days in advance, have no great interest. Through accident, on the other hand, even the least significant thing can become a rich source of amusement. It is impossible here to go into detail, no theory can stretch that far. Even the most comprehensive theory is still but poverty compared with what, in his ubiquity, the genius easily comes by.

Notes

1　Roman emperors were said to placate their subjects by offering them not freedom and glory but bread and circuses.

2　The phrase *slette uendelighed* alludes to Hegel's notion of *schlechte Unendlichkeit* or 'bad infinity' – an infinity which is imperfect because endlessly incomplete.

3　The Roman emperor Nero (37–68) is said to have set Rome on fire in 64.

4　An allusion to Marcus Aurelius Antoninus (121–80), Roman emperor and Stoic philosopher who wrote in his *Meditations* (VII, 2): 'You can recover your life: Look at things fresh as you used to look at them, for in this consists the new life.' The author of 'Crop Rotation' evidently interpreted this passage quite broadly.

5　In Greek myth, Prometheus gave human beings two dangerous gifts: fire and hope.

6　Battledore and shuttlecock (*Fjæderbold*) is a game similar to badminton, in which the players hit a feathered cork back and forth.

7　In Greek myth, Lethe is the river of forgetting which flows through the underworld, dividing the living from the dead.

8　In Greek myth, Cerberus was the three-headed dog guarding the entrance to the underworld.

9　The Greek mathematician Archimedes (286–212 BCE) is reputed to have said that if he could find a fixed point, and had a long enough lever, he could move the world.

10　A reference to the hero of *Mester Gert Westphaler* (1788), a play by Ludvig Holberg (see above, p. 50, n. 4).

11　A reference to the Danish poet Jens Baggesen (1764–1826).

12　See Plotinus (205–70), *Enneads* III, 4, 2.

13　A reference to Johann Heinrich Wilhelm Tischbein (1751–1829).

4

Fear and Trembling

While seeing *Either/Or* through the press in the winter of 1842–3, Kierkegaard took up work on several other projects, and then, just after his thirtieth birthday on 5 May, he returned to Berlin. He had finally broken with Regine Olsen, but he was euphorically productive: 'the ideas are cascading down on me', he wrote: 'healthy, happy, merry, gay – blessed children born with ease . . .'[1] But after three weeks of elation he went back to Copenhagen because he needed to be near his books.

The problem that preoccupied him was the difference between faith or belief on the one hand and science or knowledge on the other (or, in Danish, between *tro* and *viden*, and in German, *Glauben* and *Wissen*). It was easy to suppose that faith is the prerogative of religion, while knowledge is the speciality of philosophy: hence the long-standing conflict between philosophy and religion, which Schelling was only the latest to fail to resolve. On the other hand the philosophical tradition also harboured a strand of scepticism which offered a quite different approach to the issue. Sceptical philosophers from Socrates on had always maintained that doubt is a far greater intellectual virtue than either knowledge or faith. Scepticism, as advocated for example by Pyrrho of Elis and Carneades, meant cultivating the art of *epokhé* – suspension of judgement – so as to protect oneself against dogmatisms of all kinds, and in the sixteenth century it had been revived by Michel de Montaigne and Pierre Charron. Thereafter, however, the meaning of sceptical doubt began to change, and for Descartes it was a preliminary to the enjoyment of absolute certainties rather than an intrinsically desirable state of mind. Hegel (in his early essay 'Glauben und Wissen', 1802) had sought to improve on Descartes by presenting Christianity as a stage through which we pass on our way to philosophical science: for once everything was thoroughly known and clearly conceptualized, he thought, there would be no more need for faith.

Kierkegaard devoted several works to these issues, including *Repetition* (see below, pp. 115–49), which was completed while he was still in Berlin, *Johannes Climacus* (published posthumously but written probably in 1842; see below, pp. 346–79), and *Fear and Trembling* (*Frygt og Bæven*), which came out on 16 October 1843, the same day as *Repetition*. *Fear and Trembling* has a paradoxical subtitle – *A Dialectical Lyric* – and its authorship was attributed to a manifestly fictional pseudonym called Johannes de Silentio. Its main title comprises an allusion to St Paul, who had enjoined his readers to 'work out your own salvation with fear and trembling';[2] but the text is entirely taken up with the tale of Abraham and Isaac as told in Genesis.

The story starts with the despair of the ageing Abraham. He has faith in God, but he is childless and recoils from the prospect that his property will be inherited by his steward Eleazer. But then, at the age of 86 and with the approval of his 77-year-old wife Sarah, he sires a son called Ishmael with an Egyptian maid called Hagar. Thirteen years later, God presents himself to Abraham, telling him that Sarah herself will now bear him a son, through whom he will become 'father of many nations'. Unfortunately Abraham refuses to take the suggestion seriously. ('Abraham fell upon his face, and laughed, and said in his heart, Shall a child be born unto him that is an hundred years old? and shall Sarah, that is ninety years old, bear?') When Abraham told Sarah, she too 'laughed within herself', which angered God, who expostulated 'Is any thing too hard for the Lord?' A son was indeed born to them in due course, and they named him Isaac. Sarah insisted that Hagar and her wild son be cast out into the desert; but when they were almost dead from thirst, God had mercy on them, revealing a well so that Ishmael and his mother could be saved.[3]

But God was less merciful to Abraham and his son Isaac, subjecting them to a terrible test or 'temptation'.

And it came to pass after these things, that God did tempt Abraham, and said unto him, Abraham: and he said, Behold, here I am.

And he said, Take now thy son, thine only son Isaac, whom thou lovest, and get thee into the land of Moriah; and offer him there for a burnt offering [Latin: *holocaustum*] upon one of the mountains which I will tell thee of.

And Abraham rose up early in the morning, and saddled his ass, and took two of his young men with him, and Isaac his son, and clave the wood for the burnt offering, and rose up, and went unto the place of which God had told him.

Then on the third day Abraham lifted up his eyes, and saw the place afar off.

And Abraham said unto his young men, Abide ye here with the ass; and I and the lad will go yonder and worship, and come again to you.

And Abraham took the wood of the burnt offering, and laid it upon Isaac his son; and he took the fire in his hand, and a knife; and they went both of them together.

And Isaac spake unto Abraham his father, and said, My father: and he said, Here am I, my son. And he said, Behold the fire and the wood: but where is the lamb for a burnt offering?

And Abraham said, My son, God will provide himself a lamb for a burnt offering: so they went both of them together.

And they came to the place which God had told him of; and Abraham built an altar there, and laid the wood in order, and bound Isaac his son, and laid him on the altar upon the wood.

And Abraham stretched forth his hand, and took the knife to slay his son.

And the angel of the Lord called unto him out of heaven, and said, Abraham, Abraham: and he said, Here am I.

And he said, Lay not thine hand upon the lad, neither do thou any thing unto him: for now I know that thou fearest God, seeing thou hast not withheld thy son, thine only son from me.

And Abraham lifted up his eyes, and looked, and behold behind him a ram caught in a thicket by his horns: and Abraham went and took the ram, and offered him up for a burnt offering in the stead of his son.[4]

This haunting story – sometimes known as the *akedah*, from the Hebrew for 'binding' – has attracted a vast amount of commentary, especially amongst Christians, whose practice of reading the Old Testament as a prologue to the New has led them to see the lamb-like Isaac as a prototype of Christ.

For those Christians who have wanted to turn their religion into a variety of philosophical knowledge or an offshoot of ethics (notably Kant and Hegel), the *akedah* has always posed an enormous difficulty. It may be a beautiful story from the point of view of faith, but from an ethical point of view it is obscene: it makes God into a cynical manipulator who was willing to put a child's life at risk in order to demonstrate his total power over his servant Abraham, while Abraham becomes a monster of heartless evil and spineless servility – a man who intended to murder his own child simply because God had apparently asked him to. For Kant, indeed, the fact that it would have been unethical for Abraham to kill his son proved that God could not have asked him to do it.[5]

Fear and Trembling is an exploration of the intersecting issues of ethics, faith, knowledge and doubt raised by the *akedah*; but as its subtitle states, it is a 'dialectical lyric' – a poetical structure as much as a philosophical one.

The first half is distinctly unacademic in style. It begins with a Preface (see below, pp. 78–80) in which Johannes praises Descartes but disclaims all philosophical expertise ('the present author is no philosopher, he has not understood the System'). The section which follows (pp. 80–83) is entitled 'Attunement' ('*Stemning*') and tells the story of a simple man – 'no thinker, he felt no need to go further than faith' – who used to believe that he understood the *akedah*, but is now quite sure he never did. In imagination he repeatedly tries to accompany Abraham on his journey to Mount Moriah with the son he intends to sacrifice there. The man constructs four alternative scenarios between which he cannot choose, but he concludes not with exasperation but with increased admiration for the paradox. The third and last section of the first half is a 'Speech in Praise of Abraham' (not included in this anthology), which reflects on how we all need heroes, together with poets to sing their praises. And what greater hero could we have than Abraham? For Abraham was hero enough to expect the impossible (that God would bless his marriage with a son) and to have faith in the ridiculous (that God wanted him to kill Isaac); and he was also hero enough to keep silent about the matter, both with Isaac and Eliezer, and even with Sarah his wife. Looking back on it we may feel secure in the knowledge that it was 'only a trial', since God would never have allowed Abraham to go through with the deed and kill Isaac; but of course Abraham himself could never have enjoyed any such assurance, and in all his one hundred and thirty years, he 'got no further than faith'.[6]

The second half of *Fear and Trembling* opens with a heading which sounds like an omen of impending academic gloom: 'Problemata'. But it is immediately followed by a subheading which has quite the opposite effect: a 'Preliminary Expectoration', or (to translate it more decorously) 'Preamble from the Heart'. The Preamble (not included in this anthology) takes issue with people who are content with the 'large truths' of 'conventional wisdom' – perhaps including the author of the speech we have just read in praise of Abraham's heroism. They probably know the story of Abraham by heart, but never lose any sleep over it: they are serenely untroubled by the fact that if anyone else behaved like Abraham, it would be 'a sin, a crying sin'. For if religion would have us describe Abraham as willing to make a great sacrifice, ethics compels us to condemn him for contemplating a hideous murder. 'In this contradiction lies the very anguish that can indeed make one sleepless; and yet without that anguish Abraham would not be who he is.' It follows that Abraham cannot really be a hero after all, for 'I can *think* myself into a hero, but not into Abraham; when I reach that height I fall over because what I am offered is a paradox.' Hegel is reputed to be hard to understand, but he is infinitely easier than Abraham. And those who pretend to 'go further' than Abraham are like people who imagine improving Christ's miracles: instead of turning water into wine, they will go further and turn wine back into water. Might we not do better to stop with faith and give up trying to 'suck the life-wisdom out of the paradox'?[7]

We must distinguish clearly between those who genuinely possess the jewel of faith and the 'knights of infinite resignation' who merely think they do. True 'knights of faith' do not appear particularly holy. They have been touched by infinity, but they have never ceased to 'make the movements of finitude' in their ordinary existence, and to do so with complete conviction: they inhabit their finitude knowingly, 'on the strength of the absurd'. They are infinitely more blessed than the 'knights of infinite resignation', who make their holiness visible in their 'bold and gliding gait'. Knights of faith belong entirely 'to the world', they walk like postmen and have 'nothing of the strangeness and superiority that mark the knight of the infinite'. They are outwardly at ease with themselves, like a confident 16-year-old girl or a cheesemonger dozing at dusk; they do not have the 'incommensurability of genius', but they purchase every moment of their lives at the dearest price, doing nothing 'except on the strength of the absurd'. The knights of faith have savoured infinity, but unlike the knights of infinite resignation they have not lost their capacity for finitude; and having relinquished the world infinitely, they have 'taken everything back again, on the strength of the absurd'.[8]

Following this Preamble, and just under halfway through *Fear and Trembling*, the atmosphere changes. Our author, who began by confessing that he was 'no philosopher', now claims that in truth he is 'not a poet', but only a practitioner of 'dialectics'.[9] We are promised that the 'dialectical element' in the story of Abraham will now be extracted for our benefit, and the 'monstrous paradox' of faith expounded systematically in a sequence of three *problemata*.[10] The first *problema* (see below, pp. 84–93) asks whether there can be '*a teleological suspension of the ethical*', in other words, whether there can be ends higher than ethical ends, for whose sake one might be justified in acting unethically. The second *problema* (not included here) asks whether there is '*an absolute duty to God*', and contrasts the lonely figure of Abraham – the 'knight of faith' who has to violate ethical norms out of his individual duty to God – with that of the 'tragic hero' whose beautiful soul is comfortably at home with the rest of the ethical community. For if the tragic hero 'finds his point of rest in the universal, the knight of faith is kept in constant tension'.[11] The third *problema* (see below, pp. 93–104) concerns Abraham's silence – the silence for which, presumably, Johannes de Silentio is named: '*Was it ethically defensible of Abraham to conceal his purpose from Sarah, from Eliezer, from Isaac?*'

For the problem is not just that Abraham's secretiveness might have been hurtful or insulting or rude from the point of view of his wife, his steward and his son, but that ethics itself – or at least ethics as understood by philosophy – is a matter of disclosure, of giving outer expression to inner ethical principles and bearing open witness to them. And it is not just Hegelian philosophy which 'assumes there is no justified concealment', but classical tragedy too: for tragedy depends, as Aristotle knew, on the moment of 'recognition', the explicit revelation of some hidden truth. The point about Abraham, however, is that having made the 'double movement' to infinitude and back he is bound to baffle us: he is not the hero whose tragic destiny is eventually made clear, any more than he is a knight of infinite resignation. He is a paradox, and can be understood only in the way that paradoxes are understood: not by being resolved, but by having their unintelligibility properly acknowledged. The book ends with an Epilogue (see below, pp. 104–6) which pokes fun at the idea of going further than faith.

Notes

1 Letter to Emil Boesen, 25 May 1843, cited in by Howard V. Hong and Edna H. Hong in KW VI, p. xvi.
2 Philippians 2, 12.
3 Genesis 15, 13–18; 16, 3–4; 17, 4, 17; 18, 12–14; 21, 2, 10–20.
4 Genesis 22, 1–13.
5 'We can use, as an example, the myth of the sacrifice that Abraham was going to make by butchering and burning his own son at God's command (the poor child, without even knowing it, even brought the wood for the fire). Abraham should have replied to this supposedly divine voice: "That I ought not to kill my good son is quite certain. But that you, this apparition, are God – of that I am not certain, and never can be, even if this voice rings down to me from visible heaven".' See Immanuel Kant, *The Conflict of the Faculties* (1798), translated by Mary J. Gregor and Robert Anchor in Immanuel Kant, *Religion and Rational Theology*, edited by Allen Wood and George di Giovanni (Cambridge: Cambridge University Press, 1996), pp. 282–5, esp. p. 283 n. See also *Religion within the Boundaries of Mere Reason* (1793), translated in ibid., pp. 124, 204.
6 *Fear and Trembling*, 'Speech in Praise of Abraham', cf. KW VI, p. 23.
7 *Fear and Trembling*, 'Preliminary Expectoration', cf. KW VI, pp. 27, 30, 33, 37.
8 *Fear and Trembling*, 'Preliminary Expectoration', cf. KW VI, pp. 38–40.
9 *Fear and Trembling*, Problema III (a passage not included in this anthology); cf. KW VI, p. 90.
10 *Fear and Trembling*, 'Preliminary Expectoration', cf. KW VI, p. 53.
11 *Fear and Trembling*, Problema II; cf. KW VI, p. 79 n.

Fear and Trembling
by Johannes de Silentio

Preface

Not just in commerce but in the world of ideas too our age is putting on a veritable clearance sale. Everything can be had so dirt cheap that one begins to wonder whether in the end anyone will want to make a bid. Every speculative score-keeper who conscientiously marks up the momentous march of modern philosophy, every lecturer, crammer, student, everyone on the outskirts of philosophy or at its centre is unwilling to stop with doubting everything. They all go further. It would perhaps be malapropos to inquire where they think they are going, though surely we may in all politeness and respect take it for granted that they have indeed doubted everything, otherwise it would be odd to talk of going further. This preliminary step is one they have all of them taken, and presumably with so little effort as to feel no need to drop some word about how: for not even someone genuinely anxious for a little enlightenment on this will find such. Not a gesture that might point him in the right direction, no small dietary prescription for how to go about such a huge task. 'But Descartes did it, didn't he?' A venerable, humble, honest thinker whose writings surely no one can read without being most deeply stirred – Descartes must have done what he has said and said what he has

The first English translation of *Fear and Trembling*, by Walter Lowrie, came out in 1954; it was followed in 1983 by a more rigorous version by Howard V. Hong and Edna H. Hong (*Kierkegaard's Writings*, vol. VI). The extracts used here, comprising about one third of the complete text, are taken from the version published in 1985 by Alastair Hannay. The translation has been checked against the original and lightly amended where necessary.

done. A rare enough occurrence in our own time! Descartes, as he himself repeatedly insists, was no doubter in matters of faith. 'But we must keep in mind what has been said, that we must trust to this natural light only so long as nothing contrary to it is revealed by God himself . . . Above all we should impress on our memory as an infallible rule that what God has revealed to us is incomparably more certain than anything else; and that we ought to submit to the Divine authority rather than to our own judgement even though the light of reason may seem to us to suggest, with the utmost clearness and evidence, something opposite.'[1] Descartes has not cried 'Fire!' and made it everyone's duty to doubt, for Descartes was a quiet and lonely thinker, not a bellowing street-watch; he was modest enough to allow that his method was important only for himself and sprang partly from his own earlier bungling with knowledge. ('Thus my design here is not to teach the Method which everyone should follow in order to promote the good conduct of Reason, but only to show in what manner I have endeavoured to conduct my own . . . But so soon as I had achieved the entire course of study (of my youth) at the close of which one is usually received into the ranks of the learned, I entirely changed my opinion. For I found myself embarrassed with so many doubts and errors that it seemed to me that the effort to instruct myself had no effect other than the increasing discovery of my own ignorance.')[2] – What those old Greeks, whom one must also credit with a knowledge of philosophy, took to be the task of a whole lifetime, doubt not being a skill one acquires in days and weeks; what the old veteran warrior achieved after keeping the balance of doubt in the face of all inveiglements, fearlessly rejecting the certainties of sense and thought, incorruptibly denying selfish anxieties and the wheedling of sympathies – that is where nowadays everyone begins.

Today nobody will stop with faith: they all go further. It would perhaps be rash to inquire where to, but surely a mark of urbanity and good breeding on my part to assume that everyone does indeed have faith, otherwise it would be odd to talk of going further. In those old days it was different. For then faith was a task for a whole lifetime, not a skill thought to be acquired in either days or weeks. When the old campaigner approached the end, had fought the good fight, and kept his faith,[3] his heart was still young enough not to have forgotten the fear and trembling that disciplined his youth and which, although the grown man mastered it, no man altogether outgrows – unless he somehow manages at the earliest possible opportunity to go further. Where these venerable figures arrived our own age begins, in order to go further.

The present author is no philosopher, he has not understood the System, nor does he know if there really is one, or if it has been completed. As

far as his own weak head is concerned, the thought of what huge heads everyone must have in order to have such huge thoughts is already enough. Even if
one were able to render the whole of the content of faith into conceptual
form, it would not follow that one had grasped faith, grasped how one came
to it, or how it came to one. The present author is no philosopher, he is *poetice
et eleganter* [to put it with poetic grace] a freelancer who neither writes the
System nor makes any *promises* about it, who pledges neither anything about
the System nor himself *to* it. He writes because for him doing so is a luxury,
the more agreeable and conspicuous the fewer who buy and read what he
writes. In an age where passion has been done away with for the sake of
science he easily foresees his fate – in an age when an author who wants
readers must be careful to write in such a way that he can be comfortably
leafed though during the after-dinner nap, and be sure to present himself to
the world like the polite gardener's boy in the *Advertiser* who, hat in hand and
with good references from his previous place of employment, recommends
himself to a much-esteemed public.[4] He foresees his fate will be to be completely ignored: has a dreadful foreboding that the scourge of zealous criticism
will more than once make itself felt; and shudders at what terrifies him even
more, that some enterprising recorder, a paragraph swallower who to rescue
learning is always willing to do to other's writings what, to 'preserve good
taste', Trop nobly did to *The Destruction of the Human Race*,[5] will slice him into
sections as ruthlessly as the man who, in the service of the science of punctuation, divided up his speech by counting the words and putting a full-stop after
every fifty and a semi-colon after every thirty-five. No, I prostrate myself
before any systematic bag-searcher: this is not the System, it hasn't the slightest thing to do with the System. I wish all good on the System and on the
Danish shareholders in that omnibus; for it will hardly become a tower.[6] I wish
them good luck and prosperity one and all.

Respectfully
Johannes de Silentio

Attunement

There was once a man; he had learned as a child that beautiful tale of how
God tried Abraham, how he withstood the test, kept his faith and for the
second time received a son against every expectation. When he became older
he read the same story with even greater admiration, for life had divided
what had been united in the child's pious simplicity. The older he became
the more often his thoughts turned to that tale, his enthusiasm became
stronger and stronger, and yet less and less could he understand it. Finally it

put everything else out of his mind; his soul had but one wish, actually to see Abraham, and one longing, to have been witness to those events. It was not the beautiful regions of the East, nor the earthly splendour of the Promised Land, he longed to see, not the God-fearing couple whose old age God had blessed, not the venerable figure of the patriarch stricken in years, not the youthful vigour God gave to Isaac – it would have been the same if it had taken place on a barren heath. What he yearned for was to accompany them on the three-day journey, when Abraham rode with grief before him and Isaac by his side. He wanted to be there at that moment when Abraham raised his eyes and saw in the distance the mountain in Moriah, the moment he left the asses behind and went on up the mountain alone with Isaac. For what occupied him was not the finely wrought fabric of imagination, but the shudder of thought.

This man was no thinker, he felt no need to go further than faith. To be remembered as its father seemed to him to be surely the greatest glory of all, and to have it a lot to be envied even if no one else knew.

This man was no learned exegete, he knew no Hebrew; had he known Hebrew then perhaps it might have been easy for him to understand the story of Abraham.

I

And it came to pass after these things, that God did tempt Abraham, and said unto him . . . Take now thy son, thine only son Isaac, whom thou lovest, and get thee into the land of Moriah; and offer him there for a burnt offering upon one of the mountains which I will tell thee of.

It was early morning. Abraham rose in good time, had the asses saddled and left his tent, taking Isaac with him, but Sarah watched them from the window as they went down the valley until she could see them no more. They rode in silence for three days; on the morning of the fourth Abraham said still not a word, but raised his eyes and saw afar the mountain in Moriah. He left the lads behind and went on alone up the mountain with Isaac beside him. But Abraham said to himself: 'I won't conceal from Isaac where this way is leading him.' He stood still, laid his hand on Isaac's head to give him his blessing, and Isaac bent down to receive it. And Abraham's expression was fatherly, his gaze gentle, his speech encouraging. But Isaac could not understand him, his soul could not be uplifted; he clung to Abraham's knees, pleaded at his feet, begged for his young life, for his fair promise; he called to mind the joy in Abraham's house, reminded him of the sorrow and loneliness. Then Abraham lifted the boy up and walked with him, taking him by the hand, and his words were full of comfort and exhortation. But Isaac could not understand him. Abraham climbed the mountain in Moriah, but Isaac did not understand him. Then he turned away from Isaac for a moment, but when Isaac saw his face a second time it was changed, his gaze was wild, his mien one of horror. He caught Isaac by the chest, threw him to the ground and said: 'Foolish boy, do you believe I am your father? I am an idolator. Do you believe this is God's command? No, it is my own desire.' Then Isaac trembled and in his anguish cried: 'God in heaven have mercy on me. God of Abraham have mercy on me; if I have no father on earth, then be Thou my father!' But below his breath Abraham said to himself: 'Lord in heaven I thank Thee; it is after all better that he believe I am a monster than that he lose faith in Thee.'

When the child is to be weaned the mother blackens her breast, for it would be a shame were the breast to look pleasing when the child is not to have it. So the child believes that the breast has changed but the mother is the same, her look loving and tender as ever. Lucky the one that needed no more terrible means to wean the child!

II

It was early in the morning. Abraham rose in good time, embraced Sarah, the bride of his old age, and Sarah kissed Isaac, who had taken her disgrace from her, was her pride and hope for all generations. So they rode on in silence and Abraham's eyes were fixed on the ground, until the fourth day when he looked up and saw afar the mountain in Moriah, but he turned his gaze once again to the ground. Silently he arranged the firewood, bound Isaac; silently he drew the knife. Then he saw the ram that God had appointed. He sacrificed that and returned home . . . From that day on, Abraham became old, he could not forget that God had demanded this of him. Isaac throve as before; but Abraham's eye was darkened, he saw joy no more.

When the child has grown and is to be weaned the mother virginally covers her breast, so the child no more has a mother. Lucky the child that lost its mother in no other way!

III

It was early morning. Abraham rose in good time, kissed Sarah the young mother, and Sarah kissed Isaac, her delight, her joy for ever. And Abraham rode thoughtfully on. He thought of Hagar and of the son whom he had driven out into the desert. He climbed the mountain in Moriah, he drew the knife.

It was a tranquil evening when Abraham rode out alone, and he rode to the mountain in Moriah; he threw himself on his face, he begged God to forgive his sin at having been willing to sacrifice Isaac, at the father's having forgotten his duty to his son. He rode more frequently on his lonely way, but found no peace. He could not comprehend that it was a sin to have been willing to sacrifice to God the best he owned; that for which he would many a time gladly have laid down his own life; and if it was a sin, if he had not so loved Isaac, then he could not understand that it could be forgiven: for what sin was more terrible?

When the child is to be weaned the mother too is not without sorrow, that she and the child grow more and more apart; that the child which first lay beneath her heart, yet later rested at her breast, should no longer be so close. Thus together they suffer this brief sorrow. Lucky the one who kept the child so close and had no need to sorrow more!

IV

It was early morning. Everything had been made ready for the journey in Abraham's house. Abraham took leave of Sarah, and the faithful servant Eleazar followed him out on the way until he had to turn back. They rode together in accord, Abraham and Isaac, until they came back to the mountain in Moriah. Yet Abraham made everything ready for the sacrifice, calmly and quietly, but as he turned away Isaac saw that Abraham's left hand was clenched in anguish, that a shudder went though his body – but Abraham drew the knife.

Then they turned home again and Sarah ran to meet them, but Isaac had lost his faith. Never a word in the whole world is spoken of this, and Isaac told no one of what he had seen, and Abraham never suspected that anyone had seen it.

When the child is to be weaned the mother has more solid food at hand, so that the child will not perish. Lucky the one who has more solid food at hand!

In these and similar ways this man of whom we speak thought about those events. Every time he came home from a journey to the mountain in Moriah he collapsed in weariness, clasped his hands, and said: 'Yet no one was as great as Abraham; who is able to understand him?'

Problema I: Is there a Teleological Suspension of the Ethical?

The ethical as such is the universal, and as the universal it applies to every-one, which can be put from another point of view by saying that it applies at every moment. It rests immanently in itself, has nothing outside of itself that is its *telos* [end, purpose] but is itself the *telos* for everything outside, and when that is taken up into it, it has no further to go. Seen as an immediate being, no more than sensate and psychic, the single individual is the par-ticular [*den enkelte er den enkelte*] that has its *telos* in the universal, and the individual's ethical task is always to express himself in this, to abrogate his particularity so as to become the universal. As soon as the single individual wants to assert himself in his particularity, in direct opposition to the uni-versal, he sins, and only by recognizing this can he again reconcile himself with the universal. Whenever, having entered the universal, the single indi-vidual feels a need to assert his particularity, he is in a state of temptation, from which he can extricate himself only by surrendering his particularity to the universal in repentance. If that is the highest that can be said of man and his existence, then the ethical and a person's eternal blessedness, which is his *telos* in all eternity and at every moment, are identical; for in that case it would be a contradiction to say that one surrendered that *telos* (i.e. sus-pended it *teleologically*) since by suspending the *telos* one would be forfeit-ing it, while what is said to be suspended in this sense is not forfeited but pre-served in something higher, the latter being precisely its *telos*.

If that is the case, then Hegel is right in his 'Good and Conscience' where he discusses man seen merely as the single individual and regards this way of seeing him as a 'moral form of evil' to be annulled in the teleology of the ethical life, so that the individual who stays at this stage is either in sin or in a state of temptation.[7] Where Hegel goes wrong, on the other hand, is in talking about faith, in not protesting loudly and clearly against the honour enjoyed by Abraham as the father of faith when he should really be remit-ted to some lower court for trial and exposed as a murderer.

For faith is just this paradox, that the single individual is higher than the universal, though in such a way, be it noted, that the movement is repeated – that having been in the universal, the single individual now sets himself apart as the particular above the universal. If that is not faith, then Abraham is done for and faith has never existed in the world, just because it has always existed. For if the ethical life is the highest and nothing incommensurable is left over in man, except in the sense of what is evil, i.e. the single individ-ual who is to be expressed in the universal, then one needs no other categories than those of the Greek philosophers, or whatever can be logically deduced from them. This is something Hegel, who has after all made some study of the Greeks, ought not to have kept quiet about.

One not infrequently hears people who prefer to lose themselves in clichés rather than studies say that light shines over the Christian world, while paganism is shrouded in darkness. This kind of talk has always struck me as strange, since any reasonably deep thinker, any reasonably serious artist will still seek rejuvenation in the eternal youth of the Greeks. The explanation may be that they know not what they say, only that they have to say something. There is nothing wrong with saying that paganism did not have faith, but if this is to mean anything one must be a little clearer about what one means by faith, otherwise one falls back into those clichés. It is easy to explain the whole of existence, faith included, and he is not the worst reckoner in life who counts on being admired for having such an explanation: for it is as Boileau says: 'a fool can always find a greater fool who admires him'.[8]

Faith is just this paradox, that the single individual as the particular is higher than the universal, is justified before the latter, not as subordinate but superior, though in such a way, be it noted, that it is the single individual who, having been subordinate to the universal as the particular, now by means of the universal becomes that individual who, as the particular, stands in an absolute relation to the absolute. This position cannot be mediated, for all mediation occurs precisely by virtue of the universal; it is and remains in all eternity a paradox, inaccessible to thought. And yet faith *is* this paradox. Or else (these are implications which I would ask the reader always to bear in mind, though it would be too complicated for me to spell them out each time) – or else faith has never existed just because it has always existed. And Abraham is done for.

That the individual can easily take this paradox for a temptation is true enough. But one should not keep it quiet on that account. True enough, too, that many people may have a natural aversion to the paradox, but that is no reason for making faith into something else so that they too can have it; while those who do have faith should be prepared to offer some criterion for distinguishing the paradox from a temptation.

Now the story of Abraham contains just such a teleological suspension of the ethical. There has been no want of sharp intellects and sound scholars who have found analogies to it. Their wisdom amounts to the splendid principle that basically everything is the same. If one looks a little closer I doubt very much whether one will find in the whole world a single analogy, except a later one that proves nothing, for the fact remains that Abraham represents faith, and that faith finds its proper expression in him whose life is not only the most paradoxical conceivable, but so paradoxical that it simply cannot be thought. He acts on the strength of the absurd; for it is precisely the absurd that as the single individual he is higher than the universal. This paradox cannot be mediated: for as soon as he tries Abraham will have to admit that he is in a state of temptation, and in that case he will never sacrifice Isaac, or if he has done so he must return repentantly to the universal. On the strength of the absurd he got Isaac back. Abraham is therefore at no instant the tragic hero, but something quite different, either a murderer or a man of faith. The middle-term that saves the tragic hero is something that Abraham lacks. That is why I can understand a tragic hero but not Abraham, even though in a certain lunatic sense I admire him more than all others.

Abraham's relation to Isaac, ethically speaking, is quite simply this, that the father should love the son more than himself. Yet within its own compass the ethical has several rankings; let us see whether this story contains any such higher expression of the ethical which might explain his behaviour ethically, justify him ethically for suspending the ethical duty to the son, yet without thereby exceeding the ethical's own teleology.

When an enterprise involving a whole nation is prevented, when such an enterprise is brought to a halt by heaven's disfavour, when divine wrath sends a dead calm which mocks every effort, when the soothsayer performs his sad task and proclaims that the deity demands a young girl as a sacrifice – then it is with heroism that the father has to make that sacrifice. Nobly will he hide his grief though he could wish he were 'the lowly man who dares to weep' and not the king who must bear himself as befits a king. And however solitarily the pain enters his breast, for he has only three confidants among his people, soon the entire population will be privy to his pain, but also to his deed, to the fact that for the well-being of the whole he was willing to offer that girl, his daughter, this lovely young maiden. Oh, what bosom! What fair cheeks! What flaxen hair! And the daughter will touch him with her tears, and the father avert his face, but the hero will raise the knife. And when the news of this reaches the ancestral home all the beauteous maidens of Greece will blush with animation, and were the daughter a bride the betrothed would not be angered but proud to have been party to the father's deed, because the maiden belonged to him more tenderly than to the father.[9]

When that bold judge who saved Israel in the hour of need binds God and himself in one breath with the same promise, then it is with heroism that he is to transform the young girl's jubilation, the beloved daughter's joy, into sorrow, and all Israel will grieve with her maidenly youth; but every free-born man will understand Jephthah, every stout-hearted woman admire him, and every maiden in Israel will want to do as his daughter; for what good would it be for Jephthah to triumph by making his promise but fail to keep it? Would the victory not be taken once more from the people?[10]

When a son forgets his duty, when the State entrusts the father with the sword of judgement, when the laws demand punishment at the father's hand, then it is with heroism that the father must forget that the guilty one is his son. Nobly will he hide his pain, but in the nation there will be not one, not even the son, who fails to admire the father, and every time the laws of Rome are interpreted it will be recalled that many interpreted them more learnedly but none more gloriously than Brutus.[11]

On the other hand, if it had been while his fleet was being borne by wind under full sail to its destination that Agamemnon had sent that messenger who brought Iphigenia to the sacrifice; if unbound by any promise that would decide the fate of his people Jephthah had said to his daughter: 'Sorrow now for two months henceforth over the short day of your youth, for I shall sacrifice you'; if Brutus had had a righteous son and still called upon the lictors to execute him – who would understand them? If to the question, Why did you do it?, these three had replied: 'It is a trial in which we are being tested', would one then have understood them better?

When at the decisive moment Agamemnon, Jephthah, and Brutus heroically overcame their pain, have heroically given up the loved one, and have only the outward deed to perform, then never a noble soul in the world will there be but sheds tears of sympathy for their pain, tears of admiration for their deed. But if at that decisive moment these three men had added to the heroism with which they bore their pain the little words 'It won't happen', who then would understand them? If in explanation they added: 'We believe it on the strength of the absurd', who then would understand them better? For who would not readily understand that it was absurd? But who would understand that for that reason one could believe it?

The difference between the tragic hero and Abraham is obvious enough. The tragic hero stays within the ethical. He lets an expression of the ethical have its *telos* in a higher expression of the ethical; he reduces the ethical relation between father and son, or daughter and father, to a sentiment that has its dialectic in its relation to the idea of an ethical life. Here, then, there can be no question of a teleological suspension of the ethical itself.

With Abraham it is different. In his action he overstepped the ethical altogether, and had a higher *telos* outside it, in relation to which he suspended it. For how could one ever bring Abraham's action into relationship with the universal? How could any point of contact ever be discovered between what Abraham did and the universal, other than that Abraham overstepped it? It is not to save a nation, not to uphold the idea of the State, that Abraham did it, not to appease angry gods. If there was any question of the deity's being angry, it could only have been Abraham he was angry with, and Abraham's whole action stands in no relation to the universal, it is a purely private undertaking. While, then, the tragic hero is great through his deeds being an expression of the ethical life, Abraham is great through an act of purely personal virtue. There is no higher expression of the ethical in Abraham's life than that the father shall love the son. The ethical in the sense of the ethical life is quite out of the question. In so far as the universal was there at all it was latent in Isaac, concealed as it were in his loins, and it would have to cry out with Isaac's mouth: 'Don't do it, you are destroying everything.'

Then why does Abraham do it? For God's sake, and what is exactly the same, for his own. He does it for the sake of God because God demands this proof of his faith; he does it for his own sake in order to be able to produce the proof. The unity here is quite properly expressed in the saying in which this relationship has always been described: it is a trial, a temptation. A temptation, but what does that mean? What we usually call a temptation is something that keeps a person from carrying out a duty, but here the temptation is the ethical itself which would keep him from doing God's will. But then what is the duty? For the duty is precisely the expression of God's will.

Here we see the need for a new category for understanding Abraham. Such a relationship to the divine is unknown to paganism. The tragic hero enters into no private relationship with God, but the ethical is the divine and therefore the paradox in the divine can be mediated in the universal.

Abraham cannot be mediated, which can also be put by saying he cannot speak. The moment I speak I express the universal, and when I do not no one can understand me. So the moment Abraham wants to express himself in the universal, he has to say that his situation is one of temptation, for he has no higher expression of the universal that overrides the universal he transgresses.

Thus while Abraham arouses my admiration, he also appals me. The person who denies himself and sacrifices himself for duty gives up the finite in order to grasp on to the infinite; he is secure enough. The tragic hero gives up what is certain for what is still more certain, and the eye of the beholder rests confidently upon him. But the person who gives up the universal to grasp something still higher that is not the universal, what does he do? Can this be anything but temptation? And if it were something else but the individual were mistaken, what salvation is there for him? He suffers all the pain of the tragic hero, he brings all his joy in the world to nothing, he abandons everything, and perhaps the same instant debars himself from that exalted joy so precious to him that he would buy it at any price. That person the beholder cannot at all understand, nor let his eye rest upon him with confidence. Perhaps what the believer intends just cannot be done, after all it is unthinkable. Or if it could be done and the individual had misunderstood the deity, what salvation would there be for him? The tragic hero, he needs tears and he claims them; yes, where was that envious eye so barren as not to weep with Agamemnon, but where was he whose soul was so confused as to presume to weep for Abraham? The tragic hero has done with his deed at a definite moment in time, but in the course of time he achieves something no less important, he seeks out the one whose soul is beset with sorrow, whose breast cannot draw air for its stifled sighs, whose thoughts, weighed down with tears, hang heavy upon him; he appears before him, he breaks the spell of grief, loosens the corset, coaxes forth the tear by making the sufferer forget his own suffering in his. Abraham one cannot weep over. One approaches him with a *horror religiosus* like that in which Israel approaches Mount Sinai.[12] If then the lonely man who climbs the mountain in Moriah, whose peak soars heaven-high over the plains of Aulis, is not a sleepwalker who treads surefootedly over the abyss, while someone standing at the foot of the mountain, seeing him there, trembles with anxiety and out of respect and fear dares not even to shout to him – for what if he should be distracted, what if he has made a mistake? – Thank you! And thank you again, to whoever holds out to one who has been assaulted and left naked by life's sorrows, holds out to him the leaf of the word with which to hide his misery. Thanks to you, great Shakespeare, you who can say everything, everything, everything exactly as it is – and yet why was this torment one you never gave voice to? Was it perhaps that you kept it to yourself, like the beloved whose name one still cannot bear the world to mention? For a poet buys this power of words to utter all the grim secrets of others at the cost of a little secret he himself cannot utter, and a poet is not an apostle, he casts devils out only by the power of the devil.[13]

But now when the ethical is thus teleologically suspended, how does the single individual in whom it is suspended exist? He exists as the particular in opposition to the universal. Does this mean he sins? For this is the form of sin looked at ideally, just as the fact that the child does not sin because it is not conscious of its own existence as such does not mean that, looked at ideally, its existence is not that of sin or that the ethical does not make its demands of the child at every moment. If this form cannot be said to repeat itself in a way other than that of sin, then judgement has been delivered upon Abraham. Then how did Abraham exist? He had faith. That is the paradox that keeps him at the extremity and which he cannot make clear to anyone else, for the paradox is that he puts himself as the single individual in an absolute relation to the absolute. Is he justified? His justification is, once again, the paradox; for if he is the paradox it is not by virtue of being anything universal, but of being the particular.

How does the single individual assure himself that he is justified? It is a simple enough matter to level the whole of existence down to the idea of the State or to a concept of society. If one does that one can no doubt also mediate; for in this way one does not come to the paradox at all, to the single individual as such being higher than the universal, which I can also put pointedly in a proposition of Pythagoras's, that the odd numbers are more perfect than the even. Should one happen to catch word of an answer in the direction of the paradox in our time, it will no doubt go like this: 'That's to be judged by the outcome.' A hero who has become the scandal of his generation, aware that he is a paradox that cannot be understood, cries undaunted to his contemporaries: 'The future will show I was right!' This cry is heard less frequently nowadays, for as our age to its detriment produces no heroes, so it has the advantage that it also produces few caricatures. Whenever nowadays we hear the words 'That's to be judged by the outcome' we know immediately with whom we have the honour of conversing. Those who speak thus are a populous tribe which, to give them a common name, I shall call the 'lecturers'. They live in their thoughts, secure in life, they have a *permanent* position and *sure* prospects in a well-organized State; they are separated by centuries, even millennia, from the convulsions of existence; they have no fear that such things could happen again; what would the police and the newspapers say? Their lifework is to judge the great, to judge them according to the outcome. Such conduct in respect of greatness betrays a strange mixture of arrogance and pitifulness, arrogance because they feel called to pass judgement, pitifulness because they feel their lives unrelated in even the remotest manner to those of the great. Surely anyone with even a speck of *erectior ingenii* [superiority of mind] cannot become so completely the cold and clammy mollusc as to lose sight altogether, in approaching the great, of the fact that ever since the Creation it has been accepted practice for the outcome to come last, and that if one is really to learn something from the great it is precisely the beginning one must attend to. If anyone on the verge of action should judge himself according to the outcome, he would never begin. Even though the result may gladden the whole world, that cannot help the hero; for he knows the result only when the whole thing is over, and that is not how he becomes a hero, but by virtue of the fact that he began.

But in any case the outcome in its dialectic (in so far as it is finitude's answer to the infinite question) is totally incompatible with the existence of the hero. Or are we to take it that Abraham was justified in relating himself as the single individual to the universal by the fact that he got Isaac by a *marvel*? Had Abraham actually sacrificed Isaac, would that have meant he was less justified?

But it is the outcome that arouses our curiosity, as with the conclusion of a book; one wants nothing of the fear, the distress, the paradox. One flirts with the outcome aesthetically; it comes as unexpectedly and yet as effortlessly as a prize in the lottery; and having heard the outcome one is improved. And yet no robber of temples hard-labouring in chains is so base a criminal as he who plunders the holy in this way, and not even Judas, who sold his master for thirty pieces of silver, is more contemptible than the person who would thus offer greatness for sale.

It goes against my nature to speak inhumanly of greatness, to let its grandeur fade into an indistinct outline at an immense distance, or represent it as great without the human element in it coming to the fore – whence it ceases to be the great; for it is not what happens to me that makes me great, but what I do, and there is surely no one who thinks that anyone became great by winning the big lottery prize. Even of a person born in humble circumstances I ask that he should not be so inhuman towards himself as to be unable to think of the king's castle except at a distance and by dreaming of its grandeur indistinctly, wanting to exalt it and simultaneously destroying its grandeur by exalting it in such a debasing way. I ask that he be human enough to approach and bear himself with confidence and dignity there too. He should not be so inhuman as shamelessly to want to violate every rule of respect by storming into the king's salon straight from the street – he loses more by doing that than the king; on the contrary he should find pleasure in observing every rule of decorum with a glad and confident enthusiasm, which is just what will make him frank and open-hearted. This is only an analogy, for the difference here is only a very imperfect expression of the spiritual distance. I ask everyone not to think so inhumanly of himself as to dare not set foot in those palaces where not just the memory of the chosen lives on but the chosen themselves. He should not push himself shamelessly forward and thrust upon them his kinship with them, he should feel happy every time he bows before them, but be frank and confident and always something more than a cleaning woman; for unless he wants to be more than that he will never come in there. And what will help him are exactly the fear and distress in which the great are tried, for otherwise, at least if there is a drop of red blood in him, they will merely arouse his righteous envy. And whatever can only be great at a distance, whatever people want to exalt with empty and hollow phrases – this they themselves reduce to nothing.

Was there anyone in the world ever as great as that blessed woman, the mother of God, the Virgin Mary? And yet how do people speak of her? To say she was favoured among women doesn't make her great, and if it were not for the odd fact that those who listen can think as inhumanly as those who speak, surely every young girl would ask why am I not favoured too? And had I nothing more to say I should by no means dismiss such a question as stupid; for as regards favours, abstractly considered, everyone is equally entitled. What is left out is the distress, the fear, the paradox. My thought is as pure as the next man's and surely the thought of anyone able to think in this way will be pure; if not, something dreadful is in store; for a person who has once called these images to mind cannot be rid of them again, and if he sins against them, then in their quiet wrath, more terrifying than the clamour of ten voracious critics, they will wreak their awful vengeance on him. No doubt Mary bore the child miraculously, but it went with Mary 'after the manner of women', and such a time is one of fear, distress, and paradox. No doubt the angel was a ministering spirit, but he was not an obliging one who went round to all the other young girls in Israel and said: 'Do not despise Mary, something out of the ordinary is happening to her.' The angel came only to Mary; and no one could understand her. Yet what woman was done greater indignity than Mary, and isn't it true here too that those whom God blesses he damns in the same breath? This is the spirit's understanding of Mary, and she is not at all − it offends me to say, though even more so that people have mindlessly and irresponsibly thought of her thus − she is not at all the fine lady sitting in her finery and playing with a divine child. Yet for saying notwithstanding, 'Behold the handmaid of the Lord', she is great, and it seems to me that it should not be difficult to explain why she became the mother of God. She needs no worldly admiration, as little as Abraham needs our tears, for she was no heroine and he no hero, but both of them became greater than that, not by any means by being relieved of the distress, the agony, and the paradox, but because of these.

Great indeed it is when the poet presents his tragic hero for popular admiration and dares to say: 'Weep for him, for he deserves it'; for there is greatness in meriting the tears of those who deserve to shed them; great indeed for the poet to dare hold the crowd in check, dare discipline people into testing their own worthiness to weep for the hero, for the waste-water of snivellers is a degradation of the holy. But greater than all these is that the knight of faith dares to say even to the noble person who would weep for him: 'Do not weep for me, but weep for yourself.'

One is stirred, one harks back to those beautiful times, sweet tender longings lead one to the goal of one's desire, to see Christ walking about in the promised land. One forgets the fear, the distress, the paradox. Was it so easy a matter not to be mistaken? Was it not a fearful thought that this man who walked among the others was God? Was it not terrifying to sit down to eat with him? Was it so easy a matter to become an apostle? But the outcome, eighteen centuries, that helps; it helps that shabby deception wherein one deceives oneself and others. I do not feel brave enough to wish to be contemporary with such events, but for that reason I do not judge harshly of those who were mistaken, nor think meanly of those who saw the truth.

But now I return to Abraham. In the time before the outcome either Abraham was a murderer every minute or we stay with the paradox which is higher than all mediation.

So Abraham's story contains a teleological suspension of the ethical. He has, as the single individual, become higher than the universal. This is the paradox which cannot be mediated. How he got into it is just as inexplicable as how he stayed in it. If this is not how it is with Abraham, then he is not even a tragic hero but a murderer. To want to go on calling him the father of faith, to talk of this to those who are only concerned with words, is thoughtless. A tragic hero can become a human being by his own strength, but not the knight of faith. When a person sets out on the tragic hero's admittedly hard path there are many who could lend him advice; but he who walks the narrow path of faith no one can advise, no one understand. Faith is a marvel, and yet no human being is excluded from it; for that in which all human life is united is passion,★ and faith is a passion.

Problema III: Was it Ethically Defensible of Abraham to Conceal his Purpose from Sarah, from Eleazar, from Isaac?

The ethical is as such the universal; as the universal it is in turn the disclosed [aabenbare]. Seen as an immediate, no more than sensate and psychic being, the individual is concealed [skjulte]. So his ethical task is to unwrap himself from this concealment and become disclosed in the universal. Thus whenever he wants to remain in concealment, he sins and is in a state of temptation, from which he can emerge only by disclosing himself.

★ Lessing has somewhere made similar remarks from a purely aesthetic point of view. In the passage in question he actually wants to show that sorrow too can express itself with wit. To that end he quotes the words spoken on a particular occasion by the unfortunate English king, Edward II. As contrast he quotes from Diderot: a story of a farmer's wife and a remark of hers, and then continues: 'That too was wit, and the wit of a peasant at that; but the situation made it inevitable. Consequently one mustn't try to find the excuse for the witty expression of pain and of sorrow in the fact that the person who uttered them was superior, well-educated, intelligent, and witty as well, *for the passions made all men again equal* . . . the explanation lies in the fact that in the same situation probably everyone would have said the same thing. The peasant woman's thought is one a queen might just as well have had, just as what the king said on that occasion could, and no doubt would, have been said by a peasant.'[14]

We find ourselves again at the same point. Unless there is a concealment which has its basis in the single individual's being higher than the universal, then Abraham's conduct cannot be defended, since he disregarded the intermediate ethical considerations. If, however, there is such a concealment, then we face the paradox, which cannot be mediated, just because it is based on the single individual's being, in his particularity, higher than the universal, and it is precisely the universal that is the mediation. The Hegelian philosophy assumes there is no justified concealment, no justified incommensurability. It is therefore consistent in its requirement of disclosure, but it isn't quite fair and square in wanting to regard Abraham as the father of faith and to speak about faith. For faith is not the first immediacy but a later one. The first immediacy is the aesthetic [i.e. sensory], and here the Hegelian philosophy may well be right. But faith is not the aesthetic, or if it is, then faith has never existed just because it has existed always.

It will be best here to look at the whole matter in a purely aesthetic way and for that purpose embark on an aesthetic inquiry, which I would ask the reader for the time being to enter wholeheartedly into, while I for my part will adapt my presentation accordingly. The category I would like to examine a little more closely is that of the *interesting*, a category that especially today (just because we live *in discrimine rerum* [at a critical moment]) has acquired great importance, for really it is the category of crisis. Therefore one should not, as sometimes happens, when one has been oneself enamoured of it *pro virili* [as much as one can], disdain the category because it has passed one by; but neither should one be too greedy for it, for what is certain is that to become of interest, for one's life to be interesting, has nothing to do with what you can turn your hand to but is a fateful privilege which, like every privilege in the world of spirit, can only be purchased in deep pain. Thus Socrates was the most interesting person that has lived, his life the most interesting that has been led, but that existence was allotted to him by the deity, and since he had to work for it he was no stranger to trouble and pain. Taking such an existence in vain ill-becomes someone who takes life seriously, and yet such attempts are nowadays not infrequently observed. The category of the interesting is, moreover, a borderline one, it marks the boundary between the aesthetic and the ethical. For that reason in our inquiry we must be constantly glancing over into the territory of ethics, while to give our inquiries weight the problem must be grasped with genuine aesthetic feeling. These days ethics rarely considers such things. The reason is supposed to be that there is no room for them in the System. But then doing so in monographs should be all right; and besides, if one doesn't want to be long-winded about it one can achieve the same results by being brief, so long as one has the predicate in one's power; for a predicate or two can reveal a whole world. Is there no room in the System for little words like these?

Aristotle says in his immortal *Poetics*: *'duo men oun tou muthou meri, peri taut' esti, peripeteia kai anagnōrisis'* ['concerning these things there are then two parts of a plot, peripeteia or reversal of fortune, and anagnorisis or recognition'].[15] Naturally only the second feature, *anagnorisis*, recognition, concerns me here. Whenever there is recognition there is *eo ipso* a question of prior concealment. Just as the recognition is the resolving factor, or the element of relaxation in the life of drama, so is concealment the element of tension. What Aristotle says earlier in the same chapter in respect of the consequences for the worth of tragedy of the question whether *peripeteia* and *anagnorisis* clash, as well as of the 'single' and 'double' recognition, I cannot go into here, even though the sincerity and quiet absorption of Aristotle's discussion have an enviable attraction for one long since tired of the superficial omniscience of the synopticists. A general observation must suffice. In Greek tragedy concealment (and therefore recognition) is a remnant of epic based on a fate in which the dramatic action disappears from view, and from which it acquires its obscure and enigmatic origin. This is why the effect produced by Greek tragedy bears a resemblance to the impression given by a marble statue that lacks the power of the eye. Greek tragedy is blind. Hence it takes a certain abstraction to appreciate it. A son murders his father, but not until later learns it is his father. A sister is about to sacrifice her brother, but at the decisive moment discovers that is who it is. Tragedy of this nature is less apt to interest our *reflective* age. Modern drama has given up the idea of Fate, has in dramatic respects emancipated itself; it observes, it looks in upon itself, takes fate up into its dramatic consciousness. Concealment and disclosure then become the hero's free act, for which he is responsible.

Recognition and concealment are also an essential part of modern drama. It would take us too far to give examples. I am courteous enough to assume that everyone in this so aesthetically voluptuous age – so potent and aroused that conception occurs as easily as with the partridge which, Aristotle says, needs only to hear the voice of the cock or its flight overhead[16] – I am courteous enough to assume that at the mere sound of the word 'concealment' everyone can easily shake a dozen romances and comedies from his sleeve. I can therefore be brief and offer straightaway a fairly broad observation. If the person doing the hiding, i.e. the one who puts the dramatic yeast into the play, hides something nonsensical, we have comedy. But if the concealer is related to the idea, he may come close to being a tragic hero. To give just one example of the comic. A man puts on make-up and wears a wig. The same man wants to have success with the fair sex, and is sure enough of conquests with the help of the make-up and wig, which no doubt make him irresistible. He captures a girl and is on the pinnacle of joy. But now for the point. If he can admit his deception, will he not lose *all* of his powers of fascination once he is revealed as a quite ordinary, in fact even bald-headed male? Doesn't he have to lose the loved one again? Concealment is his free action, for which aesthetics holds him responsible. But that discipline is no friend of bald hypocrites, and will leave him to the mercy of our laughter. Let that suffice as a hint of what I mean, since we cannot include comedy in the terms of this investigation.

My procedure here must be to let concealment pass dialectically between aesthetics and ethics, for the point is to show how absolutely different the paradox and aesthetic concealment are from one another.

A few examples. A girl is secretly in love, though neither party has openly confessed its love to the other. Her parents force her to marry another (she may even be motivated out of considerations of duty). She obeys. She hides her love 'so as not to make the other unhappy, and no one will ever know what she suffers'. – Or a young lad is in a position, just by dropping one word, to possess the object of his craving and restless dreams. But that little word will compromise, yes, even, who knows, ruin an entire family. He nobly chooses to stay in concealment, 'the girl must never know, so that she can perhaps find happiness with another'. What a pity that these two, both concealed from their respective loved ones, are also concealed from one another! For otherwise a remarkable higher unity might have been brought about. – Their concealment is a free act, for which even aesthetically they are responsible. However, aesthetics is a respectful and sentimental discipline which knows more ways of fixing things than any assistant house-manager. So what does it do? It does everything possible for the lovers. By means of a coincidence the respective partners in the respective marriages get wind of the other party's noble decision. Explanations follow. They get each other and as a bonus the rank of real heroes as well; for notwithstanding they have had no time even to sleep on their heroic resolutions, aesthetics sees it as if they had bravely fought for their goal over many years. For aesthetics doesn't bother much about time; it goes just as quickly whether in jest or earnest.

But ethics knows nothing either of this coincidence or this sentimentality. Nor does it have such a rapid concept of time. Thus the matter acquires a different complexion. You can't argue with ethics, because it uses pure categories. It doesn't appeal to experience, which of all laughable things is perhaps the most laughable and, far from making a man wise, if he knows nothing higher it will sooner make him mad. Ethics has no coincidence, so no explanations follow; it doesn't flirt with thoughts of dignity, it puts an enormous burden of responsibility on the hero's frail shoulders; it condemns as presumptuous his thought of wanting to play providence in his action, but also condemns him for wanting to do likewise with his suffering. It enjoins the belief in reality and the courage to contend with all its tribulations, rather than with those bloodless sufferings he has taken on himself by his own responsibility; it warns against putting faith in the calculating shrewdness of reason, more treacherous than the oracles of the ancients. It warns against all misplaced magnanimity. Let reality decide the occasion, that is the time to show courage. But then ethics, too, will offer every possible assistance. If something deeper had been stirring in those two, however, if there had been a seriousness to see the task, to set about it, then no doubt something would have come of them. But ethics cannot help them. Ethics is offended because they are keeping a secret from it, a secret they have incurred on their own responsibility.

Thus aesthetics called for concealment and rewarded it. Ethics called for disclosure and punished concealment.

Sometimes, however, even aesthetics calls for disclosure. When the hero held captive in the aesthetic illusion believes he can save another by his silence, aesthetics calls for silence and rewards it. But when the hero's action involves interfering in another person's life, it calls for disclosure. Now I am talking of the tragic hero. Consider for a moment Euripides's *Iphigenia in Aulis*. Agamemnon is about to sacrifice Iphigenia. Now aesthetics calls for Agamemnon's silence, in so far as it would be unworthy of the hero to seek another's consolation, just as he should keep it quiet for as long as possible for the women's sake. On the other hand the hero, to be that, has also to be tested in the terrible temptation incurred by the tears of Clytemnestra and Iphigenia. What does aesthetics do? It has a way out; it has an old servant standing by who discloses everything to Clytemnestra. And now everything is as it should be.

Ethics, however, has no coincidence, and no old servant standing by. The aesthetic idea contradicts itself as soon as it is applied in reality. Ethics there-fore demands disclosure. The tragic hero demonstrates exactly this ethical courage in that, not himself being captive to the aesthetic illusion, he takes it upon himself to tell Iphigenia her fate. In this the tragic hero is the beloved son of ethics, in whom she is well pleased. If he remains silent, it may be because by doing so he makes it easier for others, or it could also be because it makes it easier for himself. But the tragic hero knows he is free of the latter incentive. In keeping silent here he would be assuming responsibility as an individual, inasmuch as he is impervious to any argument from outside. But this, as tragic hero, he cannot do; for it is just in so far as he continues to express the universal that ethics loves him. His heroic action requires courage, but part of that courage is that he shirks no argument. Now tears, certainly, are a terrible *argumentum ad hominem*,[17] and there are no doubt those whom nothing else touches but who can still be stirred by tears. The play lets Iphigenia weep, in fact like Jephthah's daughter she should have been allowed two months to weep, not in solitude but at her father's feet, to use all her art 'which is but tears', and twine herself instead of the olive branch about his knees.[18]

Aesthetics required disclosure but availed itself of a coincidence; ethics required disclosure and found satisfaction in the tragic hero.

For all the strictness of the ethical requirement of disclosure, it cannot be denied that secrecy and silence, as determinants of inner feeling, really make for greatness in a man. When Cupid leaves Psyche he says to her, 'You will give birth to a child who will be divine if you say nothing, but human if you betray the secret.' The tragic hero, the darling of ethics, is a purely human being, and he is someone I can understand, someone whose every undertaking is in the open. If I go further I always run up against the paradox, the divine and the demonic; for silence is both of these. It is the demon's lure, and the more silent one keeps the more terrible the demon becomes; but silence is also divinity's communion with the individual. [. . .][19]

But now Abraham. How did he act? For I have not forgotten, and the reader may now be pleased to recall, that this was the point to which the whole preceding discussion was intended to lead. Not to make Abraham more intelligible thereby, but in order that his unintelligibility might be seen more in the round, for, as I have said, I cannot understand Abraham, I can only admire him. It was also mentioned that none of the stages described contained an analogue of Abraham, they were elaborated only so as to indicate, from the point of view of their own sphere, the boundary of the unknown land by the points of discrepancy. If there should be any question of an analogy here it would have to be the paradox of sin, but that again belongs to another sphere and cannot explain Abraham, and is itself far easier to explain than Abraham.

So Abraham did not speak. He spoke neither to Sarah, to Eleazar, nor to Isaac. He passed over these three ethical authorities. Because for Abraham the ethical had no higher expression than that of family life.

Aesthetics allowed, in fact demanded, silence of the individual when by remaining silent he could save another. This is already enough to show that Abraham does not lie within the circumference of ethics. His silence is not at all to save Isaac, as in general the whole task of sacrificing Isaac for his own and God's sake is an outrage aesthetically. Aesthetics can well understand that I sacrifice myself, but not that I should sacrifice another for my own sake. The aesthetic hero was silent. Ethics condemned him, however, because it was on the strength of his accidental particularity that he remained silent. His human prescience was what determined that he should be silent. This ethics cannot forgive. All such human insight is only an illusion. Ethics demands an infinite movement which requires disclosure. So the aesthetic hero can indeed speak but will not.

The genuine tragic hero sacrifices himself and everything he has for the universal; his action, his every emotion belongs to the universal, he is revealed, and in this disclosure he is the beloved son of ethics. This does not apply to Abraham. He does nothing for the universal and he is concealed.

We are now at the paradox. Either the individual as the particular can stand in an absolute relation to the absolute, and then the ethical is not the highest, or Abraham is done for – he is neither a tragic hero nor an aesthetic hero.

Here again the paradox might seem the easiest and most convenient thing of all. However, I must repeat that anyone who remains convinced of that is not the knight of faith, for distress and anguish are the only justification conceivable, even though they cannot be conceived in general, for if they could the paradox would be cancelled.

Abraham is silent – but he *cannot* speak, therein lies the distress and anguish. For if when I speak I cannot make myself understood, I do not speak even if I keep talking without stop day and night. This is the case with Abraham. He can say what he will, but there is one thing he cannot say and since he cannot say it, i.e. say it in a way that another understands it, he does not speak. The relief of speech is that it translates me into the universal. Now Abraham can say the most beautiful things any language can muster about how he loves Isaac. But this is not what he has in mind, that being the deeper thought that he would have to sacrifice Isaac because it was a trial. This no one can understand, and so no one can but misunderstand the former. Of this distress the tragic hero knows nothing. In the first place he has the consolation that all counter-arguments have been done justice to, that he has been able to give Clytemnestra, Iphigenia, Achilles, the chorus, every living being, every voice from the heart of humankind, every intelligent, every anxious, every accusing, every compassionate thought an opportunity to stand up against him. He can be sure that all that it is possible to say against him has been said, unsparingly, mercilessly – and to contend with the whole world, is a comfort, but to contend with oneself dreadful. – He need have no fear of having overlooked something, of later having to cry out like King Edward IV at the news of the death of Clarence:

> Who sued to me for him? Who, in my wrath,
> Kneeled at my feet and bid me be advised?
> Who spoke of brotherhood? Who spoke of love?[20]

The tragic hero knows nothing of the terrible responsibility of solitude. Moreover, he has the comfort of being able to weep and wail with Clytemnestra and Iphigenia – and sobbing and crying give relief, while groans that cannot be uttered are torture. Agamemnon can rally himself quickly to the certainty that he will act, and he therefore still has time to bring comfort and courage. This Abraham cannot do. When his heart is stirred, when his words would convey a blessed consolation for the whole world, he dare not console, for would not Sarah, would not Eleazar, would not Isaac say to him: 'Why do you want to do this, you can after all refrain?'? And if in his distress he should want to unburden his feelings and embrace everything dear to him before taking the final step, then this might have the most frightful consequence that Sarah, that Eleazar, that Isaac would be offended by him and believe him a hypocrite. Talk he cannot, he speaks no human language. Though he himself understood all the tongues of the world, though the loved ones understood them too – he still could not talk – he speaks a divine tongue – he 'speaks with tongues'.

This distress I can well understand. I can admire Abraham. I have no fear that anyone should be tempted by this story to want irresponsibly to be the single individual. But I also confess that I myself lack the courage for that, and that I would gladly renounce any prospect of coming further if only it were possible for me to come that far, however late in the day. Abraham can refrain at any moment, he can repent the whole thing as a temptation. Then he can speak, then all will understand him – but then he is no longer Abraham.

Abraham *cannot* speak. What would explain everything, that it is a trial – though note, one in which the ethical is the temptation – is something he cannot say (i.e. in a way that can be understood). Anyone so placed is an exile from the sphere of the universal. And yet what comes next he is even less able to say. For, as was made sufficiently clear earlier, Abraham makes two movements. He makes the infinite movement of resignation and gives up his claim to Isaac, something no one can understand because it is a private undertaking. But then he further makes, and at every moment is making, the movement of faith. This is his comfort. For he says, 'Nevertheless it won't happen, or if it does the Lord will give me a new Isaac on the strength of the absurd.' The tragic hero does at least get to the end of the story. Iphigenia bows to her father's decision, she herself makes the infinite movement of resignation and they now understand one another. She is able to understand Agamemnon because his undertaking expresses the universal. If on the other hand Agamemnon were to say to her, 'Even though the deity demands you as a sacrifice, it's still possible that he didn't – on the strength of the absurd', he would instantly become unintelligible to her. If he could say it on the strength of human calculation, then Iphigenia would surely understand him. But that would mean that Agamemnon had not made the infinite movement of resignation, and then he would not be a hero, and then the seer's utterance is just a traveller's tale and the whole incident a piece of vaudeville.

So Abraham did not speak. Only one word of his has been preserved, his only reply to Isaac, which we can take to be sufficient evidence that he had not spoken previously. Isaac asks Abraham where the lamb is for the burnt offering. 'And Abraham said: My son, God will provide himself a lamb for a burnt offering.'

This last word of Abraham's I shall consider here a little more closely. If it had not occurred the whole incident would lack something. If it had been a different word everything might dissolve in confusion.

I have often pondered on how far a tragic hero, whether suffering or action provides the consummation of his heroism, ought to have a final remark. So far as I can see it depends on what sphere of life he belongs to, on the extent to which his life has intellectual significance, on how far his suffering or action stand in relation to spirit.

It goes without saying that at the moment of consummation the tragic hero, like anyone else, is capable of a few words, even a few appropriate words. But the question is whether it is appropriate for him to say them. If the significance of his life consists in an outward act, then he has nothing to say, since everything he says is essentially idle chat which can only weaken the impact he makes, while the rites of tragedy require on the contrary that he fulfil his task in silence, whether in action or suffering. So as not to go too far afield I shall simply draw on our nearest example. If Agamemnon himself, and not Calchas [the seer], had had to draw the knife on Iphigenia he would only have demeaned himself by wanting to say a few words at the last moment. Everyone knew the significance of his deed, the whole process of piety, pity, feeling, and tears was done with, and besides, his life had no relation to spirit, i.e. he was not a teacher or a witness to the spirit. If on the other hand the significance of the hero's life tends towards spirit, the lack of a remark will weaken the impact he makes. It is not something appropriate he should be saying, not some bit of rhetoric, but something that will convey that he is consummating himself in the decisive moment. An intellectual tragic hero of this kind should allow himself what people often aspire to frivolously, namely having and keeping the last word. We expect of him the same exalted bearing as becomes any tragic hero, but on top of that we expect some word. So if an intellectual tragic hero consummates his heroism in suffering (in death), in this final word he will become immortal before he dies, while the ordinary tragic hero only becomes immortal after his death.

Socrates can be used as an example. He was an intellectual tragic hero. He hears his death-sentence. That instant he dies. Unless you grasp that it requires all the strength of spirit to die, that the hero always dies before his death, you will not come particularly far in your observations on life. So as a hero Socrates is required to stay calm and at ease, but as an intellectual hero he is required to have sufficient spiritual strength at the final moment to fulfil himself. So he cannot, like the ordinary tragic hero, concentrate on keeping himself face to face with death; he has to make this latter movement so quickly that in the same instant he is constantly above that conflict and continues to assert himself. Had Socrates been silent in the crisis of death he would have weakened the effect of his life, aroused a suspicion that the resilience of irony was not, in him, a primitive strength, but only a game whose flexibility he had to exploit in the decisive moment, according to an opposite standard, pathetically to sustain himself.*

What I have been briefly hinting at here doesn't really apply to Abraham, to the extent that one supposes one might find by analogy some appropriate word for Abraham; but it applies to the extent that one sees the necessity of Abraham's fulfilling himself at the final moment not by drawing the knife silently but by having something to say, seeing that as the father of faith he has absolute significance in terms of spirit. As to *what* he is to say, I can form no idea in advance. Once he has said it I can no doubt understand it, even in a sense understand Abraham *in* what is said, yet without thereby coming any nearer him than in the foregoing. If we'd had no remark from Socrates I could have put myself into his position and made one, and if I couldn't do that myself, a poet would have managed. But no poet can reach Abraham.

Before going on to consider Abraham's last word more closely, I must first draw attention to the difficulty of Abraham's coming to say anything at all. The distress and anguish in the paradox consisted, as explained above, precisely in the silence; Abraham cannot speak.† To that extent then it is self-contradictory to demand that he should speak, unless one wants him out of the paradox again, so that in the decisive moment he suspends it, whereby he ceases to be Abraham and brings to naught all that went before. Were Abraham, at the decisive moment, to say to Isaac, 'It is you who are to be

---

* Which of Socrates's remarks is to be regarded as the decisive one can be a matter of controversy, since Socrates has been in so many ways poetically volatilized by Plato. I suggest the following: the death sentence is announced to him, that instant he dies and fulfils himself in the famous rejoinder that he was surprised to have been condemned with a majority of three votes. He could have found no more ironic jest in some market-place flippancy or fool's inanity than in this comment on the death-sentence which condemns him from life itself.

† In so far as there is any question of an analogy, the circumstances of the death of Pythagoras provide one. In his last moments Pythagoras had to consummate the silence he had always maintained, and so he *said*, 'It's better to be killed than to speak.'[21]

sacrificed', this would only be a weakness. For if he could speak at all he should have done so long before, and the weakness then consists in his not having the maturity of spirit and concentration to imagine the whole of the pain beforehand but having pushed some of it aside so that the actual pain proves greater than the imagined one. Besides, with talk of this kind he would fall out of the paradox, and if he really wanted to talk to Isaac he would have to transform his own situation into that of a temptation. Otherwise, after all, he could say nothing. Yet if he does transform his situation in this way he isn't even a tragic hero.

Nevertheless a last word of Abraham's *has* been preserved, and so far as I can understand the paradox I can also understand Abraham's total presence in that word. First and foremost he doesn't say anything, and that is his way of saying what he has to say. His answer to Isaac has the form of irony, for it is always irony to say something and yet not say it. Isaac asks Abraham because he assumes Abraham knows. Now if Abraham had replied, 'I know nothing', he would have uttered an untruth. He cannot say anything, since what he knows he cannot say. So he replies, 'My son, God will provide himself a lamb for a burnt offering.' Here one sees the double movement in Abraham's soul, as it has been described in the foregoing. Had Abraham simply renounced his claim to Isaac and done no more, he would have uttered an untruth. He knows that God demands the sacrifice of Isaac, and he knows that precisely at this moment he himself is ready to sacrifice him. So, after having made this movement, Abraham has at every instant been performing the next, making the movement on the strength of the absurd. To that extent he utters no untruth, for on the strength of the absurd it is after all possible that God might do something quite different. He utters no untruth then, but neither does he say anything, for he speaks in a foreign tongue. This becomes still more obvious when we consider that it was Abraham himself who was to sacrifice Isaac. If the task had been a different one, if the Lord had commanded Abraham to take Isaac out on the mountain in Moriah, and then let his own lightning strike Isaac and take him as a sacrifice in that way, Abraham would in a straightforward sense be right to talk as enigmatically as he did, for in that case he himself could not have known what would happen. But as the task is given to Abraham, it is he who must act, so he must know at the decisive moment what he is about to do, and accordingly must know that Isaac is to be sacrificed. If he doesn't definitely know that, he hasn't made the infinite movement of resignation, in which case his words are not indeed untrue, but then at the same time he is very far from being Abraham, he is less significant than a tragic hero, he is in fact an irresolute man who can resolve to do neither one thing nor the other, and who will therefore always come to talk in riddles. But such a *haesitator* [waverer] is simply a parody of the knight of faith.

Here too it can appear that one can understand Abraham, but only as one understands the paradox. For my part I can in a way understand Abraham, but I see very well that I lack the courage to speak in this way, as much as I lack the courage to act like Abraham. But I do not at all say that what he did is inconsiderable on that account, since on the contrary it is the one and only marvel.

And what did contemporaries think of the tragic hero? That he was great, and they looked up to him. And that noble assembly of worthies, the jury that every generation appoints to pass judgement of its predecessor, came to the same verdict. But none could understand Abraham. And yet think what he achieved! To remain true to his love. But he who loves God has no need of tears, needs no admiration, and forgets his suffering in love, indeed forgets so completely that afterwards not the least hint of his pain would remain were God himself not to remember it; for God sees in secret and knows the distress and counts the tears and forgets nothing.[22]

So either there is a paradox, that the single individual as the particular stands in an absolute relation to the absolute, or Abraham is done for.

Epilogue

Once when the spice market in Holland was a little slack, the merchants had some cargoes dumped at sea to force up the price. That was a pardonable, perhaps necessary, stratagem. Is it something similar we need in the world of spirit? Are we so convinced of having reached the heights that there is nothing left but piously to believe we still haven't come that far, so as at least to have something to fill the time with? Is it this kind of trick of self-deception the present generation needs, is it to a virtuosity in this it should be educated, or has it not already perfected itself sufficiently in the art of self-deception? Or is what it needs not rather an honest seriousness which fearlessly and incorruptibly calls attention to the tasks, an honest seriousness that lovingly fences the tasks about, which does not frighten people into wanting to dash precipitately to the heights, but keeps the tasks young and beautiful and charming to behold, and inviting to all, yet hard too and an inspiration to noble minds, since noble natures are only inspired by difficulty? However much one generation learns from another, it can never learn from its predecessor the genuinely human factor. In this respect every generation begins afresh, has no task other than that of any previous generation, and comes no further, provided the latter hasn't shirked its task and deceived itself. This authentically human factor is passion, in which the one generation also fully understands the other and understands itself. Thus no generation has learned from another how to love, no generation can begin other than at the beginning, the task of no later generation is shorter than its predecessor's, and if someone, unlike the previous generation, is unwilling to stay with love but wants to go further, then that is simply idle and foolish talk.

But the highest passion in a human being is faith, and here no generation begins other than where its predecessor did, every generation begins from the beginning, the succeeding generation comes no further than the previous one, provided the latter was true to its task and didn't betray it. That this sounds wearying is not of course for the generation to say, for it is indeed the generation that has the task and it has nothing to do with the fact that the previous generation had the same task, unless that particular generation or the individuals in it presumed to occupy the position to which only the spirit that governs the world, and which has the endurance not to grow weary, is entitled. If that is the kind of thing the generation begins to do, it is perverted, and what wonder then if the whole of existence should look perverted to it? For surely no one has found life more perverted than the tailor in the fairy-tale who got to heaven in his lifetime and from there looked down on the world? So long as the generation only worries about its task, which is the highest it can attain to, it cannot grow weary. That task is always enough for a human lifetime. When children on holiday get through all their games by noon and then ask impatiently, 'Can't anyone think of a new game?', does this show that they are more developed and advanced than children of the same or a previous generation who could make the games they already know last the whole day? Or does it not rather show that those children lack what I would call the good-natured seriousness that belongs to play?

Faith is the highest passion in a human being. Many in every generation may not come that far, but none comes further. Whether there are also many who do not discover it in our own age I leave open. I can only refer to my own experience, that of one who makes no secret of the fact that he has far to go, yet without therefore wishing to deceive either himself or what is great by reducing this latter to a triviality, to a children's disease which one must hope to get over as soon as possible. But life has tasks enough, even for one who fails to come as far as faith, and when he loves these honestly life won't be a waste either, even if it can never compare with that of those who had a sense of the highest and grasped it. But anyone who comes to faith (whether he be greatly talented or simple-minded makes no difference) won't remain at a standstill there. Indeed he would be shocked if anyone said this to him – just as the lover would be indignant if anyone said he had come to a standstill in his life, for he would reply, 'I'm by no means standing still in my love, for I have my life in it.' And yet he too doesn't come any further, not to anything else. For when he finds that out he has another explanation.

'One must go further, one must go further.' This need to go on is of ancient standing. Heraclitus the 'obscure' who deposited his thoughts in his writings and his writings in the Temple of Diana (for his thoughts had been his armour in life, which he therefore hung up in the temple of the goddess), the obscure Heraclitus has said, 'One can never walk through the same river twice.'[23] The obscure Heraclitus had a disciple who didn't remain standing there but went further and added, 'One cannot do it even once.' Poor Heraclitus to have such a disciple! This improvement changed the Heraclitian principle into an Eleatic doctrine denying movement,[24] and yet all that disciple wanted was to be a disciple of Heraclitus who went further, not back to what Heraclitus had abandoned.

Notes

1 René Descartes, *Principles of Philosophy*, I, §§ 28, 76.

2 See Descartes's *Discourse on Method*, Part I; the words 'of my youth' are not in Descartes's text.

3 Cf. Timothy 4, 7: 'I have fought a good fight, I have finished my course, I have kept the faith.'

4 A reference to an advertisement which appeared in the Copenhagen newspaper, *Berlingske Tidende*.

5 An allusion to a character in J. L. Heiberg's play, *Recensenten og Dyret* (1826), who destroys his own manuscript by tearing it in half.

6 Cf. Luke 14, 28–30: 'For which of you, intending to build a tower, sitteth not down first, and counteth the cost, whether he have sufficient to finish it? Lest haply, after he hath laid the foundation, and is not able to finish it, all that behold it begin to mock him, Saying, This man began to build, and was not able to finish.'

7 See 'The Transition from Morality to Ethical Life [*Sittlichkeit*]' in G. W. F. Hegel, *The Philosophy of Right*, §141.

8 Nicolas Boileau (1636–1711), *The Art of Poetry*, I, 232.

9 A reference to how Agamemnon, encouraged by the prophet Calchas, and ignoring the protests of his wife Clytemnestra, carried out a promise he had made – to sacrifice his daughter Iphigenia in exchange for a fair wind for his fleet at Aulis. See Euripides, *Iphegenia in Aulis*, ll. 448, 107, 687.

10 Cf. Judges 11, 30–40: 'And Jephthah vowed a vow unto the Lord, and said, If thou shalt without fail deliver the children of Ammon into mine hands, Then it shall be, that whatsoever cometh forth of the doors of my house to meet me, when I return in peace from the children of Ammon, shall surely be the Lord's, and I will offer it up for a burnt offering. So Jephthah passed over unto the children of Ammon to fight against them; and the Lord delivered them into his hands. . . . And Jephthah came to Mizpeh unto his house, and, behold, his daughter came out

to meet him with timbrels and with dances. . . . And it came to pass, when he saw her, that he rent his clothes, and said, Alas, my daughter! thou hast brought me very low . . . for I have opened my mouth unto the Lord, and I cannot go back. And she said unto him, My father, if thou hast opened thy mouth unto the Lord, do to me according to that which hath proceeded out of thy mouth. . . . And it came to pass at the end of two months, that she returned unto her father, who did with her according to his vow which he had vowed.'

11 As first consul in Rome, Brutus Junius had his sons executed for plotting against the state c.500 BCE.

12 Cf. Exodus 19, 12: 'whosoever toucheth the mount shall be surely put to death'.

13 Cf. Mark 3, 22: 'And the scribes which came down from Jerusalem said, He hath Beelzebub, and by the prince of the devils casteth he out devils.'

14 In his *Briefe die neueste Literatur betreffend* (letter 81, 7 February 1760), Lessing told a story of Edward II, who explained to his captors that he had no need of hot water to wash his beard, 'and so saying he let two streams of hot tears flow from his eyes and over his cheeks'. Lessing commented: 'the poor man . . . and he was a king.' He followed this with a story from the second of Diderot's *Entretiens sur le fils naturel* (1757), about a peasant woman who had sent her husband on an errand to her family in the next village, where he was murdered by her brothers. When he was laid out, she clung to her dead husband's feet, sobbing and saying 'I never thought when I sent you away that these feet would carry you to your death.' Diderot commented: 'Can you imagine that a woman of higher rank could have spoken more movingly?'

15 See Aristotle, *Poetics* II, 1452b.

16 See Aristotle, *Natural History*, 541a, 27–30 and 560b, 11–17.

17 In classical logical theory, an argument *ad hominem* is one which commits the fallacy of attacking the person rather than the person's opinion.

18 See *Iphigenia in Aulis*, l. 1224.

19 This paragraph is followed by further investigations of the conflict between ethics and silence illustrated by reference to the fate of several 'poetic personages', including a bridegroom from Aristotle's *Politics*, the traditional Scandinavian tale of Agnete and the merman, Shakespeare's Gloucester (from *Richard III*), and Faust and Margarete from Goethe's *Faust*. This discussion, occupying some twenty pages, is not included in this anthology.

20 Shakespeare, *Richard III*, II, i.

21 According to Diogenes Laertius (*Lives of the Philosophers*, VIII, 38), Pythagoras allowed himself to be caught by his enemies, saying he would 'rather be killed than prate about his doctrines'.

22 Cf. Matthew 6, 6: 'But thou, when thou prayest, enter into thy closet, and when thou hast shut thy door, pray to thy Father which is in secret; and thy Father which seeth in secret shall reward thee openly.'

23 This saying is reported in Plato, *Cratylus*, 402a.

24 A reference to the school of Zeno of Elea, which had claimed that movement and change are illusions.

5

Repetition

Fear and Trembling explored the question of faith and knowledge by investigating dozens of different approaches to the story of Abraham and his willingness to sacrifice his son Isaac. In the end the implication was that none of them really makes sense. Despite our best efforts to get an intellectual grip on Abraham, the fact that he was constantly performing faith's 'double movement' − to infinity and back 'on the strength of the absurd' − meant that he would always keep a step or two ahead of our interpretations. The only thing to be understood about 'knights of faith' like Abraham was that they would never be netted by our understandings.

The Epilogue to *Fear and Trembling* transposed the question of faith and knowledge into a different key by connecting it with the question of tradition.[1] Tradition literally means 'passing on' or 'handing down': it is the process by which the spiritual and intellectual wealth preserved and elaborated by one generation forms the inherited capital with which the next generation starts out. Without this general idea of tradition there could be no conception of progress, still less the Hegelian notion of *Aufhebung* (*ophævelse* in Danish), or 'annulment', 'supersession' or 'transcendence' as it is usually expressed in English. *Aufhebung* is a process of continuation-through-negation which ensures that the achievements of our ancestors will be preserved and enhanced in our own cultural world even if we believe ourselves to have jettisoned or forgotten them, and Hegel thought that its ceaseless repetition over the generations would eventually result in a totally inclusive system of thought, absolutely complete and coinciding perfectly with the self-knowledge of God and the Universe.

But if there are such things as 'passions' – movements which lie beyond our control and therefore beyond our comprehension too – then intellectual progress will be unable to pick them up and carry them forward from one generation to the next. Hegel's speculative machine may be a mighty magnet, but passions are like drifting clouds and it can have no influence on them at all. In matters of passion we cannot take over the wisdom of our ancestors, since, as Johannes de Silentio put it in his Epilogue, 'no generation has learned from another how to love', and 'no generation begins other than where its predecessor did, every generation begins from the beginning, the succeeding generation comes no further than the previous one'.[2] Those who speak of historical progress in the understanding of passion demonstrate their hollowness rather than their depth.

The point was epitomized in the final paragraph of *Fear and Trembling*, which took the question of passion and tradition back to one of the very earliest sources of Western philosophy: to Heraclitus the obscure, who attempted to define the incalculable singularity of things by claiming that everything is in a state of continuous fluidity, so that nothing ever comes round again a second time, and 'one can never walk through the same river twice'. But Heraclitus had the misfortune to have a follower, a disciple who wished to make progress by improving his master's wisdom, picking up from where he left off and pressing his insights a little further. Heraclitus's clever disciple was pleased to announce that strictly speaking you cannot even walk through the same river once, presumably because the universe is so unutterably fluid that you would not really be the same person or have the same body once you had dipped your toe in the water. But of course the disciple's improvement is ruinous, for where his master took care to keep different events as clearly separated from each other as stars in a crystalline night, the successor kneaded them together into a smooth paste in which everything blurred indistinctly into everything else. In effect he turned Heraclitus into his opposite – into an 'Eleatic', who believed, with Parmenides and Zeno of Elea, that reality is single and unchanging, and difference and alteration mere illusions.

The novella *Repetition*, which was prepared in parallel with *Fear and Trembling* and published on exactly the same day, is a thorough elaboration of these themes of tradition and progress. One might say that it does for the passion of love what its companion piece did for the passion of faith: it tries to make us feel the weight of its incomprehensibility.

Like *Fear and Trembling*, *Repetition* has a riddling subtitle: *Et Førsog i den experimentierende Psychologi*, which means 'a venture in experimenting psychology', or perhaps – since an earlier draft had 'experimenting philosophy'

– it would be better to translate it as 'some tentative explorations of the human mind'. It also introduces another bizarre pseudonym as its author: Constantin Constantius – who, to judge by his name, ought to be the anti-Heraclitus, a champion of solidity and unity against variousness and flux, and the very foundation stone of the Eleatic principle of permanence. But once he starts telling his story we are bound to notice that Constantin, despite his name, is by nature inconstant – utterly incapable of making up his mind, sustaining an argument, or sticking to a point.

We soon learn that the unreliable Constantin plans to launch a new philosophical system based on the idea of repetition – or rather *gjentagelse*, for as he emphasizes with more patriotism than pertinence, he is not using a 'foreign word' but a 'good Danish one', and 'the Danish language is to be congratulated for giving birth to such a fine philosophical term'.[3] This alone should give us pause, for if everything is repetition then it will be hard to see how anything can really be new, even a newborn Danish philosophical concept. It is strange, too, that Constantin claims that repetition 'expresses the relation between the Eleatics and Heraclitus', since that relation is really one of diametrical opposition rather than harmonious reiteration.

But Constantin's very first paragraph will already have made us wonder whether he is quite the master of his material. His question is 'whether repetition is possible and what significance it has', and he boasts that he has hit upon a perfect method for finding the answer: 'I could take a trip to Berlin', he says, for 'I have been there before'. But the approach is quite obviously hopeless: if there is a problem about the nature of repetition, it is not because it might be impossible for Constantin to go back to Berlin, but because there might be no justification for calling the second trip a 'repetition', given that it could not possibly be exactly the same as the first.

Still we should not conclude that Constantin will have nothing of interest to tell us. Indeed his principal suggestion – that the modern concept of 'repetition' may capture something of what the ancient Greeks meant by *anamnesis* or 'recollection' – seems to have some merit. Plato had argued in the *Meno* and the *Phaedo* that we learn eternal truths not by acquiring them as fresh items of knowledge but by recognizing them like old acquaintances from a previous existence. And Constantin wishes to endorse Plato's conclusion – that great knowledge is never new – while giving it a completely different twist. It is not so much that we travel from the present to the past in a backward movement of recollection, he suggests; more that we travel from the past to the present in a forward movement of repetition. He realizes that the choice between the two concepts may be a matter of subjective attitude rather than objective truth, however, for his principal objection to recollection is that it 'makes us unhappy', whereas 'repetition, if it is possible, will make us happy'. (Readers may well be reminded of the joyful doctrine of eternal return which Nietzsche was to propound some forty years later, though Nietzsche knew nothing about Kierkegaard and certainly never read any of his works.)

After the unwitting display of genial confusion in his first paragraph, Constantin gets to work on the question of love, picking a quarrel with the author of the 'Diapsalmata' in *Either/Or* and hoping to prove that it is better to love in repetition, or into the present, than in recollection, or out of the past. (There is of course a third possibility – loving in hope, with a view to the future – but Constantin dismisses it out of hand: it would be like having a new set of clothes, he says, and never trying them on.) In order to demonstrate that repetition is preferable to recollection, he has conducted a kind of experiment on a friend of his – an unnamed young man who fell in love, but in what Constantin considered to be the wrong way. The man loved, and was loved in return, and naturally he did not wish to put his happiness at risk. Realizing that he could keep his passion out of harm's way by confining it to the past, he decided to recollect it instead of repeating it. But that meant that his present love, despite its poetic intensity, was in danger of becoming an empty pretence and a sham. Constantin has therefore devised a scheme to help his friend out of his faulty happiness: the young man is to deceive his beloved into thinking he is conducting a passionate affair with a pretty young seamstress, which (by Constantin's calculations) should enable all of them – the young man and the girl, and perhaps the seamstress too – to escape the grip of recollection's love, leaving them free to project themselves into repetition. But then the young man leaves Copenhagen without explanation, and Constantin's experiment is left incomplete.[4]

So Constantin begins a second series of experiments, this time with himself as subject: he makes his second journey to Berlin. But he finds the place changed since his last visit, and begins to be persuaded (however illogically) that repetition may be impossible after all. To distract himself he revives his old interest in the theatre, which is of course the home of repetition, in that the same plots, situations and characters are re-enacted there night after night. Constantin likes the metaphor of theatre, because it suggests that we are constituted by the parts we act, as in a 'shadow-play . . . through which we discover ourselves – shadows whose voice is our own voice'.[5] And he likes the physical actuality of theatre too – not so much high tragedies or light comedies as broad, vulgar farces, since they trade on the physical idiosyncrasies of the actors' voices, faces and bodies. Great comedians use their own selves as the material of their work, rather as Socrates was personally present in his philosophizing.

Constantin also notes that the work of the actors and musicians is only half of what goes into the making of a successful performance of a farce: the other essential ingredient is the plebeian audience seated in the gallery, which relates directly and dialectically to the comedians on stage, for 'there is no irony in farce', and nothing can be concealed.

Constantin's description of the theatre is likely to remind a philosophical reader of the allegory of the cave in Plato's *Republic*, where philosophers look on while ordinary mortals, chained and unable to move, watch the shadows cast on a wall by models they cannot directly see. In the Königstadt Theatre in Berlin, Constantin always tries to sit at the back of a box, pretending that the show is being played for himself alone. But he is not unaware of the gallery which juts out over his head 'like the peak of a cap', and then he hears its denizens roar in appreciation of their favourite comedians. 'The vast amphitheatre was like the inside of Jonah's whale, and the noise from the gallery was like the movements of its belly', he recollects.[6] And we readers, meanwhile, may reflect that the situation of the philosopher is much the same, even if Plato and Constantin Constantius will never realize it: not outside in the light of eternal truth, but inside the whale of our clamorous existence.

After that the topic of recollection begins to go sour for Constantin. He is back in Berlin in his delightful old apartment, but it does not appeal to him any more. If this is indeed a repetition, then it seems to him 'repetition of the wrong kind', as it propels him not into further repetition but into recollection: recollection of Berlin last time he was there, and how much he had enjoyed it. He achieves the same results in a coffee house, and then a restaurant; and back in the theatre the following night he becomes convinced that the old magic will never work again: 'the only repetition was the impossibility of repetition', he thought, and the only certainty 'that there is no such thing as repetition' – conclusions he had now established beyond question by 'repeating the experiment in every possible way'. Indeed the whole journey – like Abraham's perhaps – was a complete waste of time, for there was 'no need to travel in order to discover that there is no such thing as repetition'.

But Constantin's readers may now reflect that philosophizing may depend on its audience just as much as farce. He has told us how he noticed a girl who came to the theatre every night, sitting demurely in a box facing his. Though he would never dream of introducing himself to her, she acts as a kind of proxy through whom he can enjoy his evenings inside the whale from a point of view other than his own. Perhaps we can play the same role for Constantin; and he can certainly do it for us.

The second half of *Repetition* consists of an essay called 'Repetition' (not included in this anthology) in which Constantin recollects the boring but reassuring experience of returning to his regular routines in Copenhagen. One day he receives a letter from the young man who had once been both his audience and a subject of his experiments. This 'awoke the recollection living in my soul', he writes, and he begins to realize that 'perhaps I do not fully understand him'.[7] He then transcribes seven letters in which his friend expresses distaste for both recollection and repetition, complaining that each of them is a way of 'knowing so much about everything that nothing is new or unfamiliar', which means that they preclude all novelty and surprise.[8] But at last the young man finds consolation in the lamentations of Job, for 'although I have read the book again and again,' he says, 'every word remains new to me'.[9] Job was lucky enough to have 'received everything *double*', he says, and 'this is called a *repetition*'.[10]

Constantin is disappointed in his student, accusing him of 'total misunderstanding', but then he receives a final letter in which the young man reports that the girl who was the love of his life has married someone else. 'Here I have repetition', he says: 'I understand everything, and existence seems more beautiful to me than ever before . . . I am unified again.'[11]

We may be puzzled by this reasoning, but the book comes to a reassuring end with a letter from Constantin, addressed to his 'dear reader'. He needs a 'good reader', he says, and since such beings do not exist in reality he has created a fictional one in his imagination – an ideal reader who understands 'that there is an art to being a good reader' and who, unlike a literary reviewer, will be capable of appreciating a work like his, which is 'neither comedy nor tragedy, neither novel nor short story, neither epic nor epigram'. And to make sure the communication reaches the right person, he takes the trouble to draw a picture of the envelope or cover in which it is to be sent, properly addressed 'To the honourable Mr N. N., the real reader of this book' (see next page).[12]

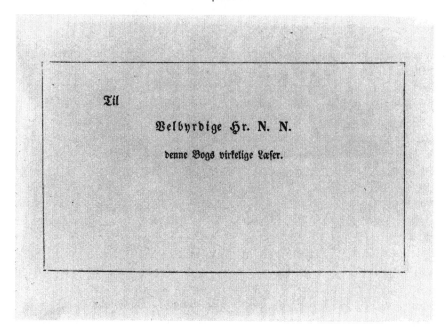

An envelope is both a means of transmitting a message to its proper recipient and a means of concealing it from everyone else: the enclosure of a disclosure. It could of course be addressed to you; and the only question is whether you will care to open it.

Notes

1   See above, pp. 104–6.
2   See above, pp. 104–5.
3   See below, p. 129.
4   See below, pp. 123–7.
5   See below, p. 134.
6   See below, p. 141.
7   Cf. Howard V. Hong and Edna H. Hong, *Fear and Trembling, Repetition*, KW VI, pp. 182, 186.
8   Cf. ibid., p. 189.
9   Cf. ibid., p. 205.
10   Cf. ibid., p. 212.
11   Cf. ibid., p. 220.
12   Cf. ibid., pp. 225, 226, 233.

Repetition: An Essay in Experimental Psychology by Constantin Constantius

The flowers on wild trees are fragrant; on cultivated trees, the fruits.[1]

Everybody knows how, when the Eleatics denied the reality of motion, Diogenes stepped forward to refute them.[2] He *literally* stepped forward, for he said not a word but simply walked backwards and forwards a few times, which he considered sufficient refutation of their doctrine. When I had occupied myself for a long time, at least occasionally, with the problem of whether repetition is possible and what significance it has, and whether things gain or lose by being repeated, it suddenly occurred to me that I could take a trip to Berlin – I had been there before – to find out whether repetition is possible and what its significance may be. As long as I stayed home, I was virtually immobilized by the problem, but say what you will, it is going to play a very important role in modern philosophy, for *repetition* is a decisive word for what the Greeks called 'recollection'. Just as they taught that all knowledge is recollection, modern philosophy will teach that the whole of life is repetition. The only modern philosopher to have had any inkling of this is Leibniz.[3] Repetition and recollection are the same movement, only in opposite directions; for what is recollected is repeated backwards, whereas genuine repetition is recollected forwards. Recollection makes

The first English translation of *Repetition* was made by Walter Lowrie and appeared in 1941; the translation by Howard V. Hong and Edna H. Hong was published in 1983 in *Kierkegaard's Writings*, vol. VI. This translation of the first part (Constantin's 'report') is by Jane Chamberlain and Jonathan Rée and appears here for the first time; copyright © Jane Chamberlain and Jonathan Rée, 2001.

us unhappy, but repetition, if it is possible, will make us happy, provided we give ourselves time to live and do not immediately, at birth, try to find some lame excuse (that we have forgotten something, for example) for creeping out of life again.

I remember reading that recollection's love is the only happy love.[4] This is absolutely true, as long as we recollect that it must first make us unhappy. For in truth, repetition's love is the only happy love. Like recollection's love, it lacks the restlessness of hope, or the anxious adventurousness of discovery, but on the other hand it does not suffer from the wistfulness of recollection. It has the blessed security of the moment [øieblik]. Hope is like a new set of clothes, stiff and starched and splendid, but we have not yet tried them on and do not know whether they will suit us, or even whether they will fit. Recollection is like old clothes which, however beautiful they are, do not fit us any more. But repetition is an everlasting garment that is always soft and comfortable, neither too tight nor too baggy. Hope is a delightful girl who slips through our fingers; recollection is a fine lady, who never quite lives up to the moment; but repetition is a beloved wife who never grows wearisome, for one can only be wearied by the new. We never get tired of what is old, and when we possess it we become happy at last. Only those who avoid the delusion that repetition has to be something new can become truly happy, since otherwise it becomes tiresome. Hope presupposes youthfulness, and so does recollection, but repetition calls for courage. If you live only in hope you are a coward; if you live only in recollection you are a sensualist, but if you will repetition you are a human being, and the more forcefully you achieve it the more deeply human you are. If you do not grasp that life is a matter of repetition, and that this is its beauty, then you are condemned, and you deserve nothing better than what is going to happen anyway – you will die.

For hope is a fruit that tempts but does not satisfy, recollection is paltry pocket-money that does not satisfy, but repetition is the daily bread that satisfies and brings us blessings. Once we have circumnavigated existence, it will become clear whether we really have the courage to acknowledge that life is a repetition and to take delight in the fact. Those who did not circumnavigate life before beginning to live will never have a life; those who circumnavigated it and were sated suffer from a poor constitution; but those who chose repetition – they will truly live. They are not like boys chasing butterflies, or standing on tiptoe to stare at the glories of the world, for they are already familiar with such things. Nor do they resemble the old woman who sits at the spinning-wheel of recollection all day long; they go calmly on their way, cheerful in repetition. Indeed what would life be without repetition? Who would wish to be a memorial volume or a tablet on which time writes something new every moment? Who would want to be at the mercy of everything that is fleeting, new, and gently cheering to the soul? If God himself had never willed repetition, the world would not have come into existence. He would either have followed the insubstantial schemes of hope, or he would have recalled everything and preserved it in recollection. But he did not, and that is why the world endures: it endures because it is a repetition. Repetition is the actuality and seriousness of existence, and those who will repetition are seasoned in seriousness. This at least is my opinion, and it also means that the seriousness of life does not consist in sitting on the sofa and picking our teeth – and being somebody, a Barrister, for instance; or in walking sedately through the streets – and being somebody, such as a Reverend Bishop; any more than the seriousness of life consists in being a royal riding master. It seems to me that all such things are mere jokes, and often rather poor jokes at that.

Recollection's love is the only happy love, according to our author.[5] But from what I know of him, he can sometimes be a little deceitful. It is not that he sets thoughts turning on a spit, so that if we do not grasp them with the same energy they appear in the next instant to mean something else. Rather, he makes his statements in such a way that we can never be sure that he is not really saying something different, and we are easily tempted to assume that he must be right, so that we forget that he was giving expression to the deepest melancholy, and that a profound depression, condensed into a single phrase, could hardly have been better expressed.

It is about a year since I began paying serious attention to a certain young man of my acquaintance. I was attracted by his good looks and the soulful expression of his eyes – he had a characteristic tilt of the head and playfulness of manner, which convinced me that his deeper nature was complex and many-sided, while a certain tentativeness in his tone indicated that he had reached that seductive age when the spirit's maturity first announces itself, just as physical maturity is attested at an earlier age by the breaking of the voice. I had already made use of the informal sociability of a coffee-shop in order to draw him to me and I had managed to make him treat me as a confidant, so that our conversations would bring the melancholy in him bubbling to the surface. My friend was still young and malleable so, like a Farinelli, I could coax the demented king out of his dark refuge, without having to resort to tongs.[6] That was the state of our relationship about a year ago when, as I was saying, he came to me in great distress. He looked even more vigorous and handsome than before, and his large, glowing eyes were staring – in short, he was transfigured. When he told me he was in love, I thought: what a lucky girl to be loved in this way. He had been in love for some time without telling anyone, not even me; but he had now attained his heart's desire – he had declared himself and found his love reciprocated. Even though I am naturally inclined to relate to people as a detached observer, I found it impossible to do so in this case. Say what you will, a young man deeply in love is such a beautiful thing that the mere sight of it makes us abandon observation and surrender to joy. Deep human emotions always disarm those who observe them; the desire to observe arises only when we are confronted by emptiness, or by emotions coyly concealed. Who could be so inhuman as to want to observe people praying with all their soul; who would not be transfixed by an outpouring of devotion in prayer? But if we hear a priest delivering a familiar old sermon, full of artfully contrived passages in which he claims, without any encouragement from the congregation, that he is speaking out of a simple faith – a faith uncomplicated by elaborate phrases, and drawn from prayers which, so he claims and presumably with good reason, provided him with something he had sought in vain in poetry, art and scholarship – then we can calmly put our eye to the microscope: we need not accept everything we hear, and we pull down a blind, a critical screen, so that we can test his every tone and word.

The young man in question was deeply, intensely, beautifully and humbly in love. There was a period when nothing made me happier than seeing him; after all, being an observer is a gloomy business, and it can make one as melancholy as a policeman. But when an observer does his work well, he is like a spy in a higher service, for the art of the observer is to disclose something that has been hidden. The young man talked about the girl he loved, but he used few words, and his talk was not the empty panegyric that lovers often indulge in. There was no self-importance in him – no implication that he must be a clever chap to have caught such a girl. He had no self-confidence either, and his love was wholesome, salubrious and pure. With an engaging frankness he told me he had sought me out because he needed a confidant, someone in whose presence he could talk to himself out loud – the principal reason being that he did not want to spend the whole day with the girl for fear of irritating her. He had already gone to her house many times, and forced himself to come away again.

He now asked me to take a ride with him so as to give him some distraction and help to pass the time. I was happy to oblige, since from the moment he confided in me I had been wholly at his service. I made use of the half-hour before the carriage arrived to write a few business-letters, inviting him to smoke a pipe in the meantime or leaf through an album. He had no need for such occupations, however, since he was sufficiently occupied with himself. Too agitated even to sit down, he paced backwards and forwards across the room. Everything about him was eloquent: his gait, his movement, his gestures. He glowed with love. Just as a grape, at the peak of its perfection, becomes transparent and clear, the juice oozing from its fine veins, just as a fruit bursts its skin when the flesh has fully ripened, so love almost visibly broke forth through his form. I could not help stealing a glance at him now and then, almost besotted, for such a young man is as seductive a sight as a girl.

Just as lovers often do, he used of the words of poets to let love's sweet agitation burst forth in blissful joy. He continued pacing up and down the room, repeating some lines by Poul Møller over and over again:

> From youth a dream comes wafting
> To me in my easy chair,
> A dream of soulful yearning,
> For my radiant damsel fair![7]

His eyes filled with tears, and he threw himself down into a chair, repeating the lines over and over again. The scene made a distressing impression on me. Great God, I thought, never before have I witnessed such dejection. I knew very well that he was prone to melancholia, but not that love could affect him so! And yet every abnormal mental state is consistent if it occurs normally. People often declare that melancholics need only fall in love to be cured. But if they are really afflicted with melancholia, how could they ever avoid being melancholy about what seems to them to be the most important thing in the world?

Despite the evident fact that he was deeply and intensely in love, the young man was able after only a few days to recollect his love. He was already finished, in essence, with the whole relationship. He had taken such an enormous stride at the beginning that he had stepped over life itself. If the girl were to die the next day, it would not really make any difference – he would throw himself into the chair again, and his eyes would fill with more tears as he repeated the poet's words once again. What a strange dialectic! He longs for the girl, and he has to do violence to himself so as to prevent himself from hanging around her all day long; and yet in the very first moment of love he became like an old man about the whole relationship. There had to be a misunderstanding somewhere, and it was a very long time since I had been so moved. It was clear enough that he was going to be unhappy, and it was equally clear that the girl was going to be unhappy too, though it was not so easy to guess exactly how it would come about. This much was certain, though – if anyone was in a position to describe recollection's love, then it was he. Recollection has a great advantage in beginning with loss: it is safe, because it has nothing left to lose.

The carriage had arrived. We drove out along the coast road, and then through the woods. Since I had reluctantly come to relate to him as an observer, I could not resist making various attempts to log, as sailors say, the progress of his melancholy. I tried to strike every possible erotic chord – but to no avail. I plotted the effect of a change of air – but in vain. He was totally absorbed in his melancholy yearning, and nothing could bring him out of it – neither the bold vastness of the sea nor the soothing silence of the forest nor the seductive solitude of twilight. He was not so much drawing the girl towards him as abandoning her. He was making the irretrievable mistake of taking his stand at the end instead of the beginning, and such mistakes can ruin anyone.

And yet I maintain that he was in the correct erotic mood, and no one who has not experienced it at the beginning has ever been in love. But it is necessary to cultivate another mood alongside it. An intensifying recollection like his is the eternal expression of love's beginning, and it is the sign of a real love, but we also need an ironic elasticity in order to be able to make use of it. And this is what he lacked, for his soul was too soft. It may be true that life is over the moment we are born, but there also has to be a life-force to kill this death and transform it into life. In the first dawning of love the present and the future lock horns with each other in order to secure eternal expression, and it is through the recollection of this dawn that eternity flows back into the present – provided, that is, that the recollection is a healthy one.

We turned towards home and when we parted I was almost unbearably moved. I could not shake off the thought that there would be a terrible explosion before long.

Over the next two weeks he visited me occasionally at my house. He was beginning to recognize his mistake – the girl he revered was already becoming something of an annoyance to him. And yet he loved her: she was the only woman he had ever loved, and he could never love another. On the other hand he did not love her; he merely longed for her. Meanwhile he was undergoing a curious transformation. There awoke in him a poetic productivity vaster than I would have thought possible. At last I could understand everything. He did not really love the girl – she was only the occasion that awoke the poetic in him and turned him into a poet. He could never love anyone but her, he would never forget her, never want to love another, and yet still he could only long for her. She had been taken up into his being as a whole, and the memory of her would be eternally fresh. She meant everything to him, and turned him into a poet, thereby signing her own death warrant.

As time passed, his anguish grew more and more acute. Melancholy was gaining the upper hand, and his physical strength was being consumed in mental strife. He realized he had made her unhappy, although he felt no sense of guilt. He was the innocent cause of her unhappiness, and it horrified him and stirred his passions to know that. He knew she would be deeply wounded if he explained how things now stood. It would be like telling her she had become an incomplete being, that he had grown away from her, that he had no more need of that rung of the ladder up which he had climbed. And where would it all lead? Knowing full well that he would never love another, she would become his grieving widow, living purely in the memory of him and their relationship. He could not tell her the truth; he was too proud on her behalf for that. His melancholy imprisoned him more and more, and he decided to carry on with the deception. He now devoted all his poetic creativity to her entertainment and delight; it would have been sufficient to sustain several girls, but he dedicated it entirely to her. She was and remained the one he loved and revered, though he was almost out of his mind with anxiety over the monstrous lie in which he was entangling her. In actuality her existence or non-existence meant virtually nothing to him, though in his melancholy he took delight in making her life enchanting. Of course she was blissfully happy, for she had no idea what he was doing and she drew succulent nourishment from him. He did not want to be productive in any stronger sense of the word, since he would then be obliged to abandon her. He therefore pruned his productivity with shears, as he put it, and presented everything to her like a bouquet. She had no idea of the truth — I am convinced of that. Indeed it would be outrageous if a girl were so narcissistic as to take someone's melancholy in vain. But such things do happen, and I once came very close to discovering such a case. Nothing is more seductive for a girl than being loved by someone with a poetical-melancholic nature. She will have a very easy life, provided she is narcissistic enough to imagine she can love him faithfully by clinging to him rather than giving him up, and she will enjoy not only the honour and good conscience of being faithful, but also a most finely distilled love. God protect us all from such faithfulness!

He came to see me one day, completely overpowered by his dark passions. He cursed his existence, his love, and his beloved girl with uncontrollable savagery. But he never paid me another visit from that moment on. Presumably he could not forgive himself for having told someone that the girl was now a torment to him. He had now ruined his own happiness, even the joy of treating her like a goddess and bolstering her pride. He started avoiding me, and if we chanced to run into each other he would adopt an air of cheerful confidence, but never speak a word. I decided to follow his movements more closely, and − realizing that we tend to be more open in our dealings with servants, housemaids or forgotten old family retainers than with those closer to us in rank and culture − I began to track down some of his associates in inferior stations in life who might know more about his melancholy. There was once a melancholic of my acquaintance who went through life like a dancer. He succeeded in deceiving everybody, including myself, until at last his barber gave him away. This barber was an old man, fallen on hard times, and he attended to all his customers personally. Pity for the barber led our dancer to give vent to his own melancholia, so the barber ended up knowing what no one else had suspected. I was spared this diffi-culty, however, for my young man eventually renewed contact with me, though he was determined never to set foot in my house again. He sug-gested we meet in remote spots at specific times, and I accepted. I purchased two fishing licences for the city moat, and we met there early one morning. At the hour when day does battle with night, when a cold shiver runs through nature even in midsummer, we met in the clammy morning mist amongst the dewy grass, and the birds flew up in alarm at his shrieking. At the hour when night was conquered at last, and every living creature rejoiced in its existence − and when his beloved girl, cocooned in his pain, lifted her head from her pillow and opened her eyes as the god of sleep arose from his seat by her bed, and the god of dreams laid a finger on her eyelids so that she briefly dozed again, while he told her what she had never suspected, but in such a soft whisper that she had forgotten it all when she woke − in that hour we parted again. And whatever the god of dreams may have divulged to her, she never dreamed of what passed between us. No wonder the man turned pale! No wonder that he chose me as a confidant, and he was not the only one!

More time passed. I suffered a great deal for the young man, who was fading day by day. And yet I had no regrets about sharing his suffering, for the Idea was still active in his love. (God be praised that such love can still be found in real life, even though we would seek it in vain in stories and novels.) Love has no meaning without it, and those who are not enthusias-tically convinced that the Idea is the life-principle of love − and that life itself must if necessary be sacrificed for it, or love itself, even if actuality is heaping favours upon it − are forever excluded from poetry. When the Idea is present in love, however, then every movement and fleeting emotion is filled with significance, because this always contains what is essential − namely the poetic collision, which can sometimes, I believe, be even more terrible than in the present case. But serving the Idea (which in the case of love does not make us a servant of two masters) is a hard vocation: no beauty can be so exigent as the Idea, nor can a girl's disapproval be so terrifying as the fury of the Idea, which burns itself into our memory as nothing else can.

If I tried to describe in detail all the moods of the young man as I came to know them, not to mention poetically including a mass of incidental circumstances as well – sitting-rooms and clothes, beautiful surroundings, family and friends – my tale would never end. But I cannot be bothered with things of that kind. I enjoy eating lettuce, but only the heart; as far as I am concerned, the leaves are fit only for pigs. Like Lessing, I prefer the joys of conception to the labour of giving birth. Of course you are welcome to disagree – for my part, I couldn't care less.

Time passed. Whenever I could, I participated in the nocturnal communions where with wild cries he got up his momentum for the rest of the day, which would be devoted to charming his girl. Just as Prometheus, bound to the rock while the vulture pecked at his liver, captivated the gods with his prophesying, so the young man captivated his beloved. Every day the whole thing was raised up to a higher level, because every day was the last. Of course it could not go on forever. He chafed at the chains that bound him, but the more his passion seethed, the more blissful his song, the tenderer his speech – the tighter his chains. It was impossible for him to form a real relationship out of this misunderstanding – that would condemn her to eternal illusion. To explain the mistake to her, to explain that she was merely the visible form, while his thought, his soul, was seeing something else which he projected onto her metaphorically – that would have wounded her so deeply that his pride would not permit it. He despised such a method more than any other, and surely he was right: it is indeed despicable to deceive and seduce a girl, but it is even more despicable to abandon her in such a way that instead of becoming a scoundrel you beat a brilliant retreat by explaining to her that she is not really the ideal, and then consoling her with the thought that she was once your muse. Such a ploy is easy if you are skilled in sweet-talking. In the hour of need she will accept your explanation, and you will escape unharmed as a man of integrity, perhaps even worthy of love. But she will end up even more deeply hurt than if she *knew* she had been deceived. If a love-relationship has started but cannot be consummated, then tactfulness is supremely offensive, and anyone with courage and an understanding of love can easily see that boorish bad behaviour is the only way to save the girl from ruin.

I now urged him to undertake something extremely risky in the hope of putting an end to all his troubles. It was a simple matter of finding a point of unity, and I made the following suggestion to him: *Destroy everything*. Turn yourself into someone so despicable that you can take pleasure in nothing except deception and fraud. This will establish an equality, as there will no longer be any presumption of an aesthetic superiority that gives you rights over her, which people are all too willing to accord to those who are supposedly exceptional in some way. She will then end up victorious, for she will be absolutely in the right, and you absolutely in the wrong. But do not do it too abruptly, as that will merely fan the flames of her love. Start by being just mildly unpleasant to her. Do not tease her – that will upset her too much. Be unreliable and slightly fatuous; do one thing one day and another the next, but without passion, with complete insouciance but never carelessness. Meanwhile, you must be as outwardly attentive as ever, but in a bureaucratic manner, lacking all inwardness. Treat her not with the joy of love itself, but with a certain mawkish *quasi*-love, neither indifference nor desire. Behave unpleasantly, like a man dribbling over his food. But do not embark on the process unless you have the strength to carry it through, otherwise the game will soon be up: for no one is as clever as a girl wondering whether she is loved or not, and nothing is as difficult as performing an extraction on oneself, wielding an instrument that only time really knows how to use. When everything is under way you must contact me, and I will see to the rest. Spread the rumour that you are involved in a new love-affair, and moreover one of a somewhat unpoetic kind, otherwise you will simply encourage her. I know very well that no such thing could ever occur to you, for we both agree that she is your only love, even though you are incapable of translating this purely poetic relationship into genuine love. There will have to be some reality behind the rumour, of course, and I will take care of that: I will find some girl for you in the city, and come to an understanding with her.

It was not merely my regard for the young man that prompted me to suggest this scheme; I cannot deny that I had also conceived a definite dislike for his beloved. It would be disastrous if she ever became aware of our scheme, and she must never have the slightest suspicion of his suffering or the probable reasons for it. And if she did guess something, she should not be allowed to do anything about it: in particular, she must never be given the chance to try and save him by giving him the one thing he needed – namely, his freedom, which no one else could give him, and which would free him precisely because it was her gift, since through this magnanimity she would reassert her hold over him and not be hurt at all! I can forgive girls everything, but I can never forgive them for misunderstanding, in their love, the task of love. Their love must be sacrificial, otherwise they are being masculine rather than feminine, and that is why I always enjoy it when such girls become objects of revenge or ridicule. And what a challenge it is for a comic poet to create such a character – a girl who has sucked the blood out of her lover with her love until he has to break with her in distress and despair, and to allow such a beloved girl to step forward like an Elvira [in Mozart's *Don Giovanni*], who shines in her role, and is wept over by sympathetic relatives and friends – a prima donna amongst the chorus of the deceived, who can speak frankly and forcefully about the faithlessness of men, which is bound to cost her her life, and who speaks with such conviction and aplomb that it never occurs to her that her faithfulness would have meant death to her lover. Great is the faithfulness of women, especially when they have been spurned, and inscrutable and incomprehensible at all times. It would be priceless if her lover, despite his distress, could always maintain sufficient good humour to avoid ever wasting a word of anger on her, confining himself to the more exquisite revenge of duping her by strengthening her impression that she had been disgracefully deceived. I can promise that if the young lady is of this kind, then the revenge will be a terrible blow to her, and it will be poetic justice, provided the young man is able to follow my plan. For he will be conscious of doing the best he can and yet, if she is narcissistic, this will only make her punishment the harsher. He will treat her with the greatest possible loving care but, given her narcissism, her pain will only be intensified.

The young man was happy to go along with my plan. In a little milliner's shop I found just what I needed – an extremely pretty young seamstress whom I promised to protect provided she would go along with the scheme. She was to walk out with him in public places, and he was to pay her visits at appropriate times of day so as to leave no doubt that there was some kind of understanding between them. To that end I secured an apartment for her in a house with two entrances located on different streets, so that he need only pass through the house late at night in order to give the servants and maids sufficient material for the purpose of spreading rumours. Once the arrangements were in place, all I had to do was ensure that his beloved was not left unaware of his new relationship. The seamstress was a nice enough girl, but his beloved would be dumbfounded – quite apart from her jealousy – at being passed over in favour of someone of that type. If I had had no one but his beloved to take into account, I might have chosen a rather different kind of girl, but there were so many other uncertainties, and I did not want to be disingenuous with the young man, so I made my choice entirely for his sake.

The seamstress was engaged for twelve months – the relationship needed to be maintained that long if his beloved was to be completely taken in. During this time he would continue to work on fracturing, so far as possible, his own existence as a poet. If he succeeded, then a *redintegratio in statum pristinum* [restoration of his original state] might be brought about. In the course of the year – and this was very important – the girl would also have the opportunity to work herself out of the relationship; he had not favoured her with any assumptions as to the result of such an operation. And if she had wearied of it, when the moment of repetition came – well, at least he would have acted magnanimously.

All the arrangements were in place. I held all the strings in my hands, but for some reason was extremely apprehensive about the outcome. But in the event he never turned up, and I have not seen him since. He did not have the courage to implement our plan. His soul lacked the elasticity of irony. He was too weak to take irony's vow of silence, or to keep it, and only those who know how to keep silent ever achieve anything. Only those who can really love are truly human, only those who can give expression to their love are genuine artists. In a sense it may have been for the best that he did not embark upon the adventure, for he could hardly have endured its terrors, and from the outset his dependence on me as his confidant had given me some misgivings. Those who know how to keep silent become acquainted with an alphabet with the same number of letters as the ordinary one, and there is nothing they cannot express in its peculiar vocabulary – no sigh so deep that it cannot be uttered in laughter, and no plea so desperate that it cannot be redeemed by a joke. A moment may come when one feels close to losing one's mind but, terrifying as it is, it only lasts an instant. It is like a fever that strikes between half-past eleven and midnight; by one o'clock we may be working more zealously than ever. And if one can withstand this madness, then victory is assured.

Yet here I am, sitting at my desk writing down everything that happened in the hope of proving that recollection's love will always make us unhappy. The trouble with my young friend was that he did not understand repetition: he did not believe in it, and could not will it with conviction. The heavy burden of his fate was that he really did love the girl, but to do so properly he first needed to extricate himself from the poetic confusion he had fallen into. He could have told the girl everything – after all, when one wants to give a girl the push this is a thoroughly decent way of going about it. Yet he was not prepared to do this. He thought it would be immoral, and I could not disagree at all. It would have made it impossible for her ever to exist again on her own terms, and it would have saved him from becoming contemptible in her eyes and from suffering agonies of anxiety about whether he could ever win back what he had squandered.

But consider what the young man could have attained if he had believed in repetition. What inwardness he would then have achieved!

I have pursued the story further than I intended, however. I only wanted to give an account of the very first instant when it became clear that the young man's love was, in a broad sense, the happy love of the wretched knight of recollection. The reader will perhaps allow me to reflect once more on the moment when he burst into my room intoxicated with recollection – when he told me in confidence that he needed to force himself not to spend the whole day with his beloved, while his heart unceasingly 'ging ihm über [overflowed]' in those lines from Poul Møller.[8] On the evening when we finally parted he repeated the same lines. I will never forget the occasion; indeed, the recollection of his disappearance itself would be easier to erase than the memory of that unnerving moment. That is the sort of man I am: in the first shudder of a presentiment my soul runs instantaneously through all the implications, though they may take a long time to manifest themselves in reality. Such a concentration of presentiment is something no one can ever forget. It is a quality that all observers of humanity need, even though it will cause them terrible pain. That first instant can be so overwhelming that we almost faint away, but as we turn pale the Idea takes hold of us, and we enjoy a revelatory rapport with actuality. It appeals to our feminine side, without which it would be impossible for the Idea to take root in us and bear fruit; no one who lacks such femininity will ever make a good observer, for nothing will be revealed by those who cannot reveal the totality.

That evening when we parted he thanked me again for helping him pass the time, which passed far too slowly for someone with his impatience, and I thought to myself: 'Is he perhaps open-hearted enough to tell the girl everything, so that she will end up loving him even more than before?' I do not know what he did, but if he had asked me, I would have advised against it. I had said to him: 'Stand firm in the beginning, from the standpoint of love that is by far the shrewdest course – unless your soul is so serious that you can raise your thoughts to something higher.' If he did tell her everything, he was not handling the affair very shrewdly.

Those who have had some opportunity to observe the behaviour of girls, and eavesdrop on their conversations, will surely have often heard them say things like: 'N.N. is a good man, but he is boring, while F.F. is so interesting and full of wit.' Every time I hear such sentiments from a young maid's mouth I always think: 'She ought to be ashamed of herself; it is deplorable to hear a girl talking like this.' If a man has run wild in the field of the interesting, how can he be saved except by a girl? And will she not therefore be at fault? Either he will not be able to carry it off, in which case he should not be expected to, or he will be able to, and in that case. . . . Girls should always take care not to invoke the interesting, otherwise they will always be losers from the standpoint of the Idea, for the interesting never allows itself to be repeated, and the girl who can avoid it is bound to triumph.

Six years ago I went on a drive of about fifty miles out into the countryside, stopping at an inn for lunch. They served me a fine, hearty meal, and I had done full justice to it and was feeling a little merry. I was standing with a cup of coffee in my hand and savouring its aroma when a pretty girl, radiant and lovely, passed the window and entered the courtyard. I guessed that she was going into the garden, and I was young, so I drank down my coffee, lit a cigar, and was just about to follow the trail of the girl and the sign of fate when there was a knock at the door and who should come in but – the girl. She gave me a respectful curtsy and asked if the carriage in the courtyard was mine, whether I was driving to Copenhagen, and if so whether I would permit her to come with me. The modest and truly feminine dignity with which she uttered her request was enough to make me immediately forget all about the interesting. And yet to drive alone with her in my carriage for fifty miles, accompanied by my coachman and servant, and to have her completely in my power, would of course be far more interesting than meeting the girl in a garden. Nevertheless I am convinced that even if I were more of a fool than I am, I would not have been tempted. The frankness with which she entrusted herself to my care was a far better defence than girlish cunning and wiles. So we travelled together, and she could not have been safer if I had been her father or her brother. I was quiet and reserved – and attentive only when she seemed inclined to make some remark of her own. I told my coachman to drive as fast as possible. At each staging-post we had a break of five minutes, and on each occasion I alighted and asked her with hat in hand if she would care for any refreshment; and my servant also stood behind me, hat in hand. As we approached the city, I told the coachman to drive down a side-road, and there I got out to walk the remaining three miles into Copenhagen. I did not want to embarrass her by a chance encounter with some acquaintance or other. I never asked who she was, where she lived, or what her sudden journey was for, but she has always remained a pleasant recollection for me and I have never allowed myself to corrupt it with even the most innocent curiosity. A girl who yearns for the interesting becomes a trap in which she herself will get caught; but a girl who does not yearn for the interesting will believe in repetition. All honour to those who do so by nature, and also to those who learn to do so by their own efforts.

But I must once more repeat that what I am saying bears only on the theme of repetition. Repetition is a new category and it should now be unveiled. Anyone who knows anything about modern philosophy, and a little about Greek thought, will be able to see without difficulty that repetition is precisely the category which expresses the relation between the Eleatics and Heraclitus, and that it is the same as what has mistakenly been called mediation. Hegelian philosophers have made an extraordinary hullabaloo about mediation, and the phrase has conferred honour and prestige on a great deal of idle talk. It would have been better to think mediation through thoroughly, by giving the Greeks their due. The Greek doctrines of being and nothingness, of 'the moment' and 'non-being', defeat Hegel. And while 'mediation' is a foreign word, 'repetition [gjentagelse]' is a good Danish one, and the Danish language is to be congratulated for giving birth to such a fine philosophical term. In our age it has become unclear how mediation takes place, whether it is a result of the movement of the two different factors and in what sense it is already implicit in them, or whether it is something completely new that intervenes, and if so, how. In this respect Greek reflections on the concept of kinesis – which corresponds to the modern category 'transition' – deserve the closest attention. Nothing could be easier than the dialectic of repetition, for what is repeated has already existed – otherwise it could not be repeated – but it is precisely the fact that it has already existed which makes the repetition something new. When the Greeks said that knowledge is really recollection, they were saying that the whole of existence – everything which is – has already existed. So if we say that life is a repetition we are saying that existence – everything which has already existed – is now coming into existence [bliver nu til]. Without the categories of recollection and repetition, life itself would dissolve into an empty noise, signifying nothing. Recollection is the primitive [ethnisk] world-view, repetition the modern; repetition is the interest of metaphysics and also its undoing; it is the principle behind every ethical opinion, and the conditio sine qua non [necessary condition] of every problem in dogmatics.

Everyone will have their own opinion, both about what I have said concerning repetition and about the way I have said it. I am trying to follow Hamann's example, mit mancherlei Zungen mich ausdrücke, und die Sprache der Sophisten, der Wortspiele der Creter und Araber, Weissen und Mohren und Creolen rede, Critik, Mythologie, rebus und Grundsätze durch einander schwatze, und bald kat anthropon bald kat exochen argumentire ['I speak with many tongues, mixing the language of Sophists with the punning of Cretans and Arabs, whites and blacks and mulattoes, while gossiping indiscriminately about Criticism, mythology, this and that, and first principles, arguing sometimes by human criteria and sometimes by transcendent ones'].[9] Assuming that all this is not simply untrue, perhaps I was right to send off my random notes to a surveyor of the System. They might amount to something after all – perhaps even a footnote in the System. What a grand thought . . . for then I would not have lived my life in vain!

As regards the significance that repetition may have, we can say a great deal without the risk of repeating ourselves. When Professor Ussing[10] was giving an address to the May 28th Society some years ago, he used an expression which displeased the audience. But what did the professor do? He was a strong and awe-inspiring figure in those days, and he banged the table and said: I repeat. At that time he thought that what he said would be enhanced by repetition. A few years ago I heard a priest give exactly the same sermon at two different church services. Had he been of the Professor's opinion, he would have pounded the pulpit on the second occasion and said: I shall repeat what I said last Sunday. But he did no such thing, and made no allusion to it at all. He was not of Professor Ussing's opinion and perhaps – who knows? – perhaps the Professor himself no longer thinks his speech would benefit from being repeated. The Queen once told a story at a formal court occasion, and all the courtiers laughed, including a deaf minister who afterwards stood up, asked permission to tell another story, and then told the same one all over again. Now the question is: what was his view of the meaning of repetition? When a schoolteacher says: for the second time I repeat that Jespersen must sit down and be quiet, and young Jespersen gets a black mark for repeated disobedience, then the meaning of repetition is completely the opposite.

These examples could be multiplied, but I will not dwell on them. Instead I shall describe the voyage of exploration I made in order to investigate the meaning and possibility of repetition. Without anyone's knowledge (rumours would have made the experiment impossible, as well as making the repetition tedious for me) I went to Stralsrund by steamship and then took a seat in the fast coach to Berlin. Scholars differ as to which is the comfiest seat in a stagecoach, but in my opinion all of them are equally unbearable. Last time I had a seat inside the carriage at the front and on the end (some consider this a great prize) and spent the next thirty-six hours being so shaken up with my fellow-passengers that by the time I got to Hamburg I had lost not only my mind but my legs as well. After thirty-six hours the six of us inside the carriage were almost blended into one body, and it gave me a clear idea of what it must have been like for the foolish folk of Mol, who sat together for so long that they could no longer tell which legs belonged to whom. Hoping to remain at least a limb on a smaller body, I chose to sit outside – which made for a change, except that everything was then repeated. I shut my eyes as the postilion blew his horn, and resigned myself to despair while reflecting, as I generally do on such occasions: God knows whether you can stand it, whether you will ever reach Berlin and, if so, whether your

humanity will ever be restored to you, so that you can return to the individuality of isolation, rather than remain forever imprisoned by the memory
of yourself as a limb of a larger body.

Still I reached Berlin eventually. I made straight for my old lodgings in
the hope of establishing how far repetition is possible. I can assure the solici-
tous reader that I had the good luck to procure one of the best apartments
in Berlin last time I was there; and now that I have seen several others, I can
reaffirm it with even greater confidence. Gendarmenplatz is easily the most
beautiful square in Berlin – the *Schauspielhaus* [theatre] and the two churches
look magnificent, especially when glimpsed through a window by moonlight,
and without the recollection of them I might never have undertaken the trip.
There is a house there lit by gas-lamps, and if you go up to the first floor
and open a little door, you find yourself standing in an entrance-hall. To your
left is a glazed door leading to a bedchamber, straight ahead of you a lobby,
and beyond that two rooms, absolutely identical and identically furnished, as
if duplicated in a mirror. The inner room is tastefully lit, with a branched
candelabra on the desk and an elegant armchair upholstered in red velvet,
but the first room is unlit, and here the pale moonlight blends with the
stronger light from the inner room. You sit on a chair by the window looking
down on the great square, as the shadows of passers-by scurry along the walls.
Everything is transformed into a stage set. A dreamy reality begins to dawn
in the depths of your soul, and you feel an impulse to put on your coat and
creep quietly along the streets with your eyes peeled, alert to every sound.
You feel youthfully inspired to do it, though you know you will not. After
finishing your cigar, you withdraw into the inner room and start work. Midnight passes. You put out the lamps and light a night-light. Pure moonlight
reigns, and every shadow seems darker, every footfall takes an age to die away.
The cloudless vault of heaven seems sad and pensive, as if the world had
come to an end and the sky was left entirely to itself. Perhaps you will go
out through the lobby once again, into the entrance-hall and into your little
bedchamber to sleep – if, that is, you are one of those who are blessed with
the ability to sleep.

Sad to say, there was no possibility of repetition here. My landlord was a
chemist, and (to use a pregnant German phrase also used, I believe, in parts
of Copenhagen) *er hatte sich verändert* – he had altered, and was now married.
I would have liked to congratulate him, but my German was not up to it
and the appropriate phrases did not come immediately to mind, so I limited
myself to a little pantomime. I put my hand on my heart, gazed at him with
tender sympathy clearly written on my face, and he shook my hand. After
this display of mutual understanding, he proceeded to expound to me the
aesthetic validity of marriage – which he did extraordinarily well, just as well

as he previously used to expound the perfection of a bachelor's existence. When I speak German I am the most obliging person in the world.

My former landlord was happy to be of service to me, and I was happy to live with him; I therefore took just one room and the entrance-hall. When I came home the first evening and turned on the lights I thought to myself: Alas! Alas! Alas! Can this be repetition? I was utterly dispirited or, if you will, I had entered completely into the spirit of the day, for as fate would have it I had arrived in Berlin on the *allgemeine Buß- und Bettag* [day of universal prayer and repentance]. Berlin was crestfallen. The Berliners may not have thrown dust in each other's eyes with the words '*dust thou art, and unto dust shalt thou return*',[11] but the whole city was covered in a cloud of dust all the same. At first I thought it might have been ordained by the government, but later I became convinced that the inconvenience was due to the wind, which was following its usual malevolent whims with no respect for persons; for in Berlin every other day seems to be Ash Wednesday. But all this is quite irrelevant. The discovery had nothing to do with 'repetition', since I had not noticed the phenomenon on my last visit to Berlin, presumably because it was winter.

Once you have found somewhere to stay and have settled in, you have a fixed point from which you can venture out, a secure hiding-place to which you can retreat in order to enjoy your spoils in private – something I set particular store by, since I resemble those beasts of prey who cannot bear to be watched when they eat – and only then can you start to get acquainted with a city's finer points. Tour guides who go around trying to get wind of what others have sniffed out, or dedicated tourists who want to record the famous sights in their journals and get their names into the family visitors' books in return, can hire a *Lohndiener* [temporary servant] and buy *das ganze Berlin* [All Berlin] for four *Groschen*. Then you will become an impartial observer and your testimony will be as dependable as a police report. But if you are travelling for no particular reason then you will be able to go your own way, occasionally seeing things that no one else notices, disregarding everything that is supposed to be important, and ending up with a random set of impressions which would not mean anything to anyone else. Such carefree drifters often have little to say to others, and any comment they make is liable to damage society's opinion of their manners and morals. Imagine someone who has travelled widely and never taken a railway train – would they not deserve to be expelled from polite society! Or consider a man who went to London and failed to take a carriage through the tunnel under the Thames![12] Or someone who went to Rome, fell in love with a particular district which gave him inexhaustible pleasure, and then left without ever seeing any of the great sights!

There are three theatres in Berlin. The opera and ballet at the Opera House are said to be *grossartig* [magnificent], and the shows at the Theatre are supposed to be instructive and edifying – not merely for pleasure.[13] But I would not know. All I know is that there is a theatre in Berlin called the Königstadt. Dedicated tourists seldom visit it but – and this is also significant – it is even rarer for them to visit those warm, hospitable places of entertainment that lie off the tourist trail, where Danes can get a chance to remind themselves of the restaurants of Mathiesen or Kehlet in Copenhagen. I cheered up at once when, arriving in Stralsund to board the coach to Berlin, I found a newspaper and learned that *Der Talisman* was going to be performed in this theatre.[14] Recollections stirred in the depths of my soul, and even the very first time I was there it was as if my impressions were merely recollections which reached far back into the mists of time.

Every young person with any imagination must at some time or other have been captivated by the magic of the theatre. Surely we have all yearned to be swept into its artificial world so that we could see and hear ourselves like some *Doppelgänger*, splitting ourselves into every possible variation of ourselves, but without ceasing to be ourselves in every variation. Naturally such impulses are not manifested except in early youth, when the imagination has been inspired by this dream of personality but all other faculties remain dormant. In the self-images of imagination the individual is not a real figure but a shadow, or rather, the real figure is invisible and will not content itself with casting a single shadow, for the shadows of the individual are manifold, each of them bearing a certain likeness and all having the same provisional claim to authenticity. The personality itself has not yet been revealed, and its energy is expressed only in the passion of possibility; for it is the same in spiritual life as in plants – the main shoot is the last to emerge. However, our shadow-existence also demands expression, and it is unhealthy not to give it time to live itself out, though it is rather ridiculous if it is lived out as if by mistake. Our claim to be truly human then becomes as doubtful as the claim to immortality of those who do not present themselves in person on Judgement Day, but send a deputation of good intentions instead, together with some fresh resolutions and five-minute plans. The essential point is that everything should happen at its appointed time. Everything has its time in our youth, and what has once had its time will get it again later on; in old age it is just as bad to have nothing in your past that calls for laughter as it is to have nothing that calls for tears.

Up in the mountains we will hear the same wind constantly rehearsing the same unchanging themes, day in and day out, and for a moment we may be tempted to regard it not as an imperfection but as a glorious image of the consistency and reliability of human freedom. But perhaps we are forgetting that there must have been a moment when the wind, which has made its home among these mountains for so many years, made its first entrance to the region and tore through the ravines and into the mountain caverns like a disoriented and bewildered stranger – startling itself with its shrieking, fleeing from its own hollow roar, uttering groans whose source it did not recognize, or a sigh from the abyss of anxiety so deep and terrifying that the wind wondered for a moment whether it dared remain in this new domain, or executing an exuberant and lyrically cheerful jig – until, having become familiar with all its instruments, it brought them together as the symphony which it now rehearses unchangingly day after day. In the same way our own possibility as individuals gets lost in its own possibilities, revealing first one thing and then another. But an individual's possibility is not like the transient wind: it is also formative, and therefore needs to be seen as well as heard. Each of its possibilities is like a noisy shadow. Enigmatic individuals have no more faith in intense and clamorous feelings than in the whispered cunning of wickedness; no more faith in the blissful rapture of joy than in the eternal sigh of sorrow. As individuals we merely want to see and hear with pathos – and what we want to see and hear is ourselves. Yet it is not really ourselves we want to hear; that would not bring us satisfaction. The moment the cock crows and the shapes of twilight withdraw, the voices of the night subside. If they persisted, we would be somewhere else, in the domain where nothing escapes the disconcerting gaze of responsibility, and would find ourselves in the vicinity of the demonic. In order to avoid all sense of our real self, we enigmatic individuals need to surround ourselves with insubstantial and transient shapes, with vaporous clouds of words that can sound without resonance.

The stage provides one such context, and it is particularly appropriate to the *Schattenspiel* [shadow-play] of the enigmatic individual. Amongst the shadows through which we discover ourselves – shadows whose voice is our own voice – the leader of a band of outlaws may be lurking, and we must be able to recognize ourselves reflected in his image. His strong, masculine form, his swift yet penetrating glance, and the passion etched in the lines of his face – everything must be present to us. He must lie in wait in the mountain pass, listening for any sign of travellers approaching, and then sound his horn; his band of outlaws will rush up and join him, and his voice will prevail over the noise; he must show no mercy, and no one can be spared. He turns indifferently away, after tending chivalrously to the frightened girl. Of course the outlaw dwells in the gloomy forest, but if the hero of our imaginations were really abandoned in a forest, even supplied with all he could need, he would not be able to keep calm long enough for us to cover a few miles before giving way completely to a passionate rage which would strike him dumb. He would remind me of a man I knew who some years ago who honoured me with a literary confession. He complained that he was suffering such a superabundance of ideas that it was impossible for him to get anything down on paper – he simply could not write fast enough. He asked me to come to his rescue by acting as his secretary and writing from his dictation. I was immediately suspicious, but assured him that I could write as swiftly as a runaway horse, since I transcribed only one letter of every word and yet could read back everything I had written. My solicitude knew no bounds. A large table was brought out. I laid out several numbered sheets of paper so that I need waste no time on turning pages, prepared a dozen steel pens with their holders, dipped my pen, and the man began to speak as follows: 'Yes, well, you see, gentlemen, what I really wanted to say was. . . .' When he had finished I read his speech to him, and he has never asked me to be his secretary again. It is the same with the outlaw of our imaginations: he would presumably find his task too great for him and yet also too small. But give him a stage-set with a tree, lit by a lamp casting strange shadows, and he will be in the midst of a larger forest than ever existed in reality – larger than the primeval forests of North America – but he will still be able to fill it with his voice without ever growing hoarse. It is the sophistical privilege of the imagination to hold the whole world in a nutshell: the nutshell is larger than the whole world, but the individual fills it completely.

This kind of prepossession for theatrical performances and expectorations is far from being proof of a vocation for the stage. Where there is such a vocation, theatrical talent will manifest itself immediately as a disposition to unified individuality [til det enkelte]. Without it, however, the prepossession is mere immaturity of imagination and even the richest talent will fall short, for it is quite another matter when it is grounded in vanity and a desire for the limelight. Then the whole will be founded on nothing but vanity, though unfortunately this too is a foundation that can run very deep.

Although this aspect of an individual's life will fade with time, it nevertheless reproduces itself in adulthood once the soul has collected itself in mature seriousness. We may then feel that the art of theatre is no longer serious enough for us, but still we may on occasion turn back to it and recapture an old mood. We will want to be comically amused, relating ourselves to theatrical performance in terms of the comical. But since we can no longer take pleasure in the perfection of comedy, or of tragedy for that matter, we turn instead to farce.

The phenomenon is repeated in other spheres. You might for instance come upon someone who is fully mature, and sated with the strong meat of reality, but quite unmoved by even the most highly accomplished paintings. On the other hand he may be captivated by the sight of a Nuremberg print

– a landscape depicting some general country scene – which he found on a market-stall not so long ago.[15] Such abstract generalities do not call for much artistic skill, so the whole effect is achieved through contrasts and fortuitous combinations of circumstances. And yet I suspect that all of us derive our impressions of general country scenes from such landscapes, and that their categories have remained with us ever since we were children. In childhood our categories are so vast that they almost make us dizzy later – in those days we could cut a piece of paper into the shapes of a man and a woman, and they would be man and woman in general in a far stronger sense than Adam and Eve ever were. Landscape painters, whether they strive for faithful representation or ideal reproduction, will sometimes leave us cold, whereas a generalized print may affect us indescribably. We do not know whether we should laugh or cry, for the whole effect depends on the mood in which we perceive it. All of us have surely been through a phase when we could not be satisfied by rich language or passionate oratory, nor by expressions or gestures, and nothing could please us except breaking out into the strangest leaps and somersaults. An individual might learn how to dance, and attend the ballet to admire the artistry of the dancers, but a time might come when ballet no longer touched him. Still there might be moments when he would withdraw to his room and let himself go, deriving an indescribably gratifying feeling of release simply from standing on one leg in some picturesque pose, or wishing the whole world to death and the devil and letting everything depend on the execution of an *entrechat*.[16]

The Königstadt specializes in farce, and its audiences are of course extremely varied. (No one wanting to make a pathological study of the incidence of laughter at different social and temperamental strata should lose an opportunity of attending performances of farce.) The cheers and shrieks of laughter from the gallery and second tier are completely different from the applause of the cultured and critical public lower down; they provide the constant accompaniment without which no farce could ever be successfully performed. On the whole, farces are set amongst the lower social classes, so the gallery and the second tier recognize themselves at once, and their exuberant shouts and *bravos* are not an aesthetic appraisal of individual actors but a pure lyrical eruption of their sense of well-being. They do not think of themselves as an audience, but simply want to take part in what is happening down on the street or wherever the scene is set. But they are too far away, so they behave like children when there is some commotion outside and they are only allowed to watch it from a window. Those in the first tier and the stalls may be roaring with laughter too, but their laughter is essentially different from the Cimbrian-Teutonic howling of the people, and even within this sphere the diverse kinds of laughter are infinitely differentiated in a way quite unlike that found in the audience for a comedy. It may be an imperfection, but that is how it is. The ordinary aesthetic categories founder when confronted by farce, and it is incapable of producing a uniformity of mood in the more cultured part of the audience. The effectiveness of farce depends largely on the spontaneity and creativity of the audience, so it allows us to come into ourselves as single individuals – our enjoyment is not constrained by traditional aesthetic expectations of admiration, laughter or emotion. To a cultured audience, a farce is like the lottery except that one is spared the unpleasantness of winning money. Such uncertainty is not agreeable to the ordinary theatre-going public, however, and they therefore ignore farces or look down their nose at them. It is their loss. Genuine theatregoers usually have a certain straitlaced seriousness; they want to be ennobled and edified at the theatre, or at least they like to think they do; they seek rare artistic experiences, or imagine they do; and they want to know, as soon as they have read the announcement of the show, what the evening will have in store.

No such match between plan and execution is possible in farce, since one and the same farce can produce many different impressions, and indeed it may be least effective when best performed. We cannot rely on the say-so of our neighbours or the newspapers or the man across the street to find out whether we enjoyed it or not. We all have to make up our own individual minds, and no reviewer has yet succeeded in prescribing a rule for sophisticated theatregoers attending farces – in this respect it is impossible to establish the *bon ton*, or a standard of good taste. In farce the reassuring mutual respect between the theatre and its public is suspended. We can find ourselves in the most unexpected moods when watching farces, and we can never be certain that we conducted ourselves in the theatre like a respectable member of society who always laughs and cries in the right places. There are no fine dramatic portrayals for conscientious spectators to admire, since the characters in farces are all judged by the standard of 'the general'. Everything is standardized – situations, actions and lines – and that is why we are just as likely to end up depressed as roaring with laughter.

There is no place for irony in farce. Naïveté is all, and the audience has to be spontaneous both collectively and individually, since the naïveté of farce is so illusory that sophisticates cannot possibly relate naïvely to it. But the pleasure of farce lies largely in how we relate ourselves to it, which is always risky since we will look in vain to left or right or to the newspapers for some confirmation of our enjoyment. On the other hand, farces can have a very singular significance for those sophisticated spectators who are sufficiently relaxed to allow themselves to take pleasure entirely on their own terms, and sufficiently self-confident to know for themselves, without conferring with others, whether they have enjoyed themselves or not. Farces will affect their mood in different ways, sometimes through the remoteness of their abstractions, sometimes through their deployment of tangible realities. In any case, they do not come to the theatre in a firmly settled mood, expecting everything to work its effects in relation to it; rather, they will be so practised in moods that they will hold themselves in a state of readiness, suffused not by one particular mood but by the possibility of all.

The Königstadt puts on farces, and very splendidly too in my opinion. My view is, of course, entirely my own; I force it on no one – I would never dream of using force. Farces must be properly cast if they are going to be a complete success. There should be no more than two actors of exceptional talent or creative genius, or three at most. And they should be creatures of caprice, intoxicated with laughter. They must be dancers of humour, just like anyone else a moment before the performance, and at all other times, but totally transformed the instant they hear the stage-bell, for then they begin to snort and puff like a noble Arab stallion, the distension of their nostrils manifesting the chafing spirit within them: they need to be off at speed and free to gambol wildly. They are not so much reflective artists who have made a study of laughter as lyricists who have dived into the depths of laughter and are now thrust back up on to the stage by its sheer volcanic force. They have not planned their act; they will allow the moment and the forces of nature to take care of everything. They have the courage to behave in public as ordinary folk would not unless they were alone, or as a lunatic might in the presence of everyone; but they have the genius to act with the authority of genius, confident of laughter. Their comic power knows no bounds, their resources are inexhaustible, and they too are surprised by it at almost every moment. They know that they could keep the laughter going all evening, and it would cost them no more effort to do so than it takes me to put all this down on paper.

A theatre with two such geniuses has all it needs for farces; three is the maximum, otherwise the effect will be weakened, just as people can die of overexcitement. The remainder of the cast need not be talented; indeed, it can be a disadvantage if they are. Nor should they be chosen for their beauty; it is better if they are simply brought together by contingent circumstances, as arbitrarily assorted as the crowd who, in the drawing by Chodowiecki, founded Rome.[17] Even physical deformities are no disqualification; indeed, they can be a positive asset. Actors who are bandy-legged or knock-kneed or lanky or stunted, or defective in any another way, can be put to very good use in farces, and the effects they produce are incalculable. Contingency is second only to the ideal. A wit once remarked that the human race can be divided into officers, servant-girls and chimney-sweeps. In my opinion this remark is not only witty but profound, and it would take a great speculative mind to come up with a better classification. If a classification does not conceptually exhaust its object, then we should prefer contingency because at least it sets the imagination in motion. A partially true classification cannot satisfy the understanding, and it means nothing whatsoever to the imagination, so it should by rejected outright, even if it is sanctioned by everyday use; after all, ordinary people are not only extremely stupid but also very short of imagination. Every theatrical portrayal ought to present either a concrete figure which has been thoroughly realized in ideality, or a complete contingency. Theatres that exist for something higher than pleasure offer the former, though even here the public is usually happy as long as the actor is a handsome fellow with an attractive manner, a good stage-face, and a fine voice. But this is not enough for me, as a performance *automatically* awakens my critical faculties, and then I find it impossible to decide what it is to be human, or to fulfil the conditions of humanity. Everyone will agree about this as soon as they reflect that even Socrates, whose particular strength was his self-knowledge and understanding of human nature, 'did not know for certain whether he was a human being, or an even more changeable, complicated and conceited creature than Typhon'.[18] In farces, however, the secondary characters produce their effect through the abstract category 'in general', and by means of contingent particularities. This gets us as far as reality but no further, and it may be regrettable, except that we are comically reconciled to it through the spectacle of contingency, which, simply by stepping onto the artificial world of the stage, pretends to be the ideal. If an exception is to be made for any of the secondary characters, it must be for the young female lead, who must of course be unsophisticated as an actress, and chosen purely for her charm: she must appear friendly and agreeable on the stage, and be pleasant to look at – pleasant, so to speak, to have around.

The players at the Königstadt are almost all I could desire. My only reservation would be in regard to the secondary characters, for I would never utter a word of criticism against Beckmann and Grobecker.[19] Beckmann is undoubtedly a comic genius, and his pure lyricism runs riot in comedy; he distinguishes himself not in the portrayal of character but in sheer exuberance. He may not have any stature in the sphere of artistic commensurability, but he is outstanding in that of individual incommensurability. He has no need for supporting actors or scenery or staging; he delivers the goods himself precisely through his mood. He can be wildly funny at the same time as painting in the scenery around him as deftly as any set-painter. What Baggesen once said about Sara Nickels – that she comes rushing onto the stage pursued by a rural scene – also applies, in a positive sense, to Beck-

mann, except that he always enters walking.[20] At a proper art-theatre you
seldom see an actor who really knows how to walk and stand. Indeed, I have
only ever seen a single example, but nothing to touch what Beckmann is
capable of. He can not only walk, but he can actually *arrive on foot*. Arriving
on foot is a very special thing, and with this stroke of genius Beckmann gives
us an entire setting as well. He not only plays a travelling tradesman, he also
arrives on foot like one, so that we feel everything, catching sight of the
distant smiling village along the dusty road, hearing the hum of its activity,
noticing the little path that turns off by the farrier's shop and runs down to
the village pond, where we see Beckmann arriving on foot, a little bundle
on his back, a stick in his hand, carefree and bold as brass. He can arrive on
the stage on foot followed by a band of street-urchins – whom one does not
see. Even Johan Ryge in *Kong Salomon og Jørgen Hattemager* could not achieve
such an effect.[21] Beckmann is a pure saving for a theatre; with him on stage,
there is no need for street-urchins or stage-scenery. Yet his craft does not lie
in the portrayal of character; it is too truly masterly in its freely sketched
outlines for that. It is an incognito which houses the lunatic demon of
comedy before it extricates itself and sweeps all before it with gay abandon.
In this respect Beckmann is an incomparable dancer. He sings his ditty, and
then the dance begins. Of course he may lack confidence in the effectiveness of his dance-routines in a narrow sense, for he chooses to risk his neck
instead. He dances till he is completely beside himself. The lunacy of laughter in him can no longer be confined by forms or lines, and the only way
he can communicate his mood is by taking himself by the scruff of the neck,
like Münchhausen,[22] and abandoning himself to a crazy caper of joy. Of
course all of us can, as I said before, recognize the relief and relaxation to be
gained by such activity, but actually doing it on stage requires positive genius,
and the authority of genius – otherwise it will merely be distasteful.

Every burlesque comedian needs a voice that can be recognized immediately even when he is off-stage, so that he can prepare the way for himself.
Beckmann has a splendid voice, if not a beautiful one. Grobecker's voice is
even coarser, but one off-stage word from him has the same effect as three
blasts of the trumpets at Dyrehavsbakken[23] – it warns us to be ready to receive
the comical. In this respect I regard him as superior to Beckmann. The
essence of Beckmann is a playful, indomitable good sense through which he
achieves sheer lunacy. Grobecker, by contrast, rises to lunacy through sentimentality and tenderness. For instance, I saw him in a farce in which he was
playing a steward who is devoted to his master and mistress, and so keen to
lay on ceremonies to embellish their lives that he becomes completely
absorbed in the preparations for a rustic celebration to welcome their noble
and distinguished return. Everything is ready. Grobecker has chosen to play

the part of Mercury. He is still dressed as a steward, but has attached wings to his feet and put a helmet on. He adopts a picturesque pose, stands on one leg, and begins to address his master and mistress. Of course Grobecker is not so musical as Beckmann, but he has a special lyrical rapport with laughter. He has a certain tendency to correctness which can make his performances magisterial, especially in dry comedy. He is not such a catalyst as Beckmann, but still he is a genius, and a genius in farce.

You come into the Königstadt theatre, and take your seat in the first tier, since relatively few people sit there – and when you see a farce you need to be comfortable and quite undistracted by that glorification of art which causes people to cram themselves into a crowded theatre as if their salvation depended on seeing the play. The air in the theatre is also fairly pure, untainted by the breath of art-enthusiasts or the sweat of an audience with a passion for art. As a rule you will have no problem getting a box to yourself in the first tier. If not, I would recommend (so that the reader can at least gain a little useful information from me) box five or six on the left. In a corner at the back there is a perfectly positioned seat for just one person. There you sit alone in your box, and it is as if the auditorium were empty. The orchestra plays the overture, and the music echoes rather strangely because the auditorium is deserted. You have come to the theatre not as a tourist or aesthete or critic, but, if possible, as nothing at all, and you are happy to be well and comfortably seated, almost as if you were in your own drawing-room. The orchestra finishes, and the curtain has scarcely begun to rise when a second orchestra strikes up – an orchestra which does not follow the conductor's baton but only its own inner urge, the other orchestra, the sound of nature in the gallery, whose denizens have already sensed that Beckmann is in the wings. It was my habit to sit far back in the box, so that I could see nothing of the second tier or the gallery at all, which jutted out over my head like the peak of a cap. The noise was therefore all the more marvellous in its effect. As far as I could see the theatre was almost empty: the vast amphitheatre was like the inside of Jonah's whale, and the noise from the gallery was like the movements of its belly. From the moment the gallery began to play, no other musical accompaniment was necessary, for Beckmann inspired them as they inspired him.

Oh my unforgettable nursemaid! I shall never forget you – you evanescent nymph who dwells in the little brook that ran past my father's farm. You were always willing to take part in my games, even if you always looked after yourself first! You, my faithful comforter, who never lost your innocent purity, who never aged while I grew old. I turned to you again when I was weary of people, weary of myself, and in need of an eternity of rest; when I was so careworn that I longed for an eternity of oblivion. You never denied me, as humans do, by making eternity just as busy as time and even more terrible. I lay down at your side and escaped from myself into the immense sky above my head, forgetting myself in your soothing murmur! You are my happier self, you evanescent life dwelling in the little brook that runs past my father's farm, where I lie prostrate as if my body were an abandoned pilgrim's staff, while I am redeemed and freed by the melancholy babble! That was just how it was in my box at the theatre. I was cast off like a swimmer's clothing, prostrate by the stream of laughter, playfulness and jubilation that ceaselessly flowed past me. I could see nothing but the expanse of the auditorium, and I could hear nothing but the noise in which I dwelt. Just occasionally I would sit up and glance at Beckmann, which made me laugh so much that I sank down again exhausted beside the flowing stream.

This was pure bliss, but still there was something missing. Then in the desert that surrounded me I spied a figure that gladdened me more than the sight of Friday's footprint gladdened Robinson. There was a girl in a box directly opposite me, sitting in the third row, half hidden by an older couple seated in front of her. Clearly she had not come to the theatre in order to be seen – on the whole one is spared such loathsome feminine display in the Königstadt. She was in the third row, and her dress was modest and simple, almost homely. She was not laden with sable and marten but wrapped in a large scarf, from out of which her humble head bowed like the bell of a lily-of-the-valley leaning out over its great leaves. After glancing at Beckmann again, and letting the laughter convulse my whole body, and after sinking back in exhaustion and allowing myself be carried away again by the stream of jubilation and merriment, I climbed up out of this bath and returned to myself, and my eyes sought her out and the sight of her gentle softness refreshed my whole being. And when a more sentimental scene was being enacted on the stage, I looked at her again and she helped me surrender to it, for she sat calmly through it all, with a quiet smile of childlike wonder on her face. Like me, she was there every evening. Sometimes I wondered why she came, but these thoughts too became just moods in search of her. For a moment it seemed to me that she might be a girl who had suffered much and was now wrapping herself tightly in a shawl, trying to have nothing more to do with the world. But the expression on her face convinced me that she was a happy child who pulled her scarf tight the better to enjoy herself. She had no idea that she was being observed, still less that my eyes were watching her; if she had, it would have been a sin against her and worse for myself, for she was possessed of an innocence and unconsciousness which even the purest thought would have disturbed. We can never discover this for ourselves, but if our guardian angel shows us where such simple concealment hides, then there is no offence, and the guardian spirit is content. If she had merely suspected my mute, half-infatuated pleasure then everything would have been ruined for ever, and nothing could have restored it – not even all her love.

I know a place a few miles from Copenhagen where a young girl lives; I know the large shady garden with its many shrubs and trees. I know a steep slope covered in scrub a short distance away, from which you can look down into the garden from the concealment of the thicket. I have never divulged it to anyone – not even my coachman, for I deceive him by alighting some distance away and walking to the right instead of the left. So when my soul is restless, and the sight of my bed makes me as anxious as the sight of an instrument of torture, even more terrified than a patient at the sight of the operating-table, then I go for an all-night drive. Early in the morning I lie down in the shelter of the thicket. When life begins to stir and the sun opens its eye, the bird flutters its wings and the fox creeps out of its hole, when the peasant stands in his doorway and gazes out over the field, while the milkmaid goes down to the meadow with her pail, and the reaper makes his scythe ring and takes pleasure from the prelude which will be the refrain of his entire day's work – that is when the girl emerges too. Who could sleep? Who could sleep lightly, so that sleep itself does not become a heavier burden than day? Who could rise from their bed as if no one had rested upon it, so that the bed itself was cool and delicious and refreshing to behold, as if the sleeper had not rested upon it but had merely leant over it to straighten it? Who could die in such a way that their deathbed looks more inviting, the instant they are lifted from it, than if a loving mother had puffed up and aired the bedclothes to help her child sleep more soundly? The girl then emerges, and walks around wondering (but who wonders most, the girl or the trees?). She bends down to pick fruit from the bushes, she takes a few light skips, and then stands still, lost in thought. What wonderful eloquence she has! And at last my soul finds repose. Happy girl! If a man should ever win your love, may you make him as happy by being everything to him as you make me by doing nothing for me.

So *Der Talisman* was going to be performed at the Königstadt. The recollection of the piece awoke in my soul, and everything was as vivid to me as it had been long ago. I hurried to the theatre, but there were no boxes available where I could sit on my own – not a single seat in boxes five or six on the left. So I had to take a seat on the right, where I found myself surrounded by people who were not sure whether they wanted to be entertained or to remain indifferent, and such company is always boring. There was hardly a single empty box, and the young girl was nowhere to be seen, or if she was I could not recognize her because she was not alone. Beckmann did not strike me as funny, and after enduring it for half an hour I left the theatre, thinking: There is no such thing as repetition. This made a profound impression on me. I was no longer young, I was not altogether unacquainted with life, and I had cured myself of the habit of counting on uncertainties long before my first visit to Berlin. But still I believed that my experiences in that theatre should have proved more durable, for we must learn to be diminished by existence before we can really appreciate it – and that ought to make it all the more secure. Can existence be even more fraudulent than a bankrupt? He may repay only 50 per cent of what he owes, or 30 per cent, but at least he pays back something. Surely the comical is the least one can ask for – is it possible that it cannot be repeated either?

With these thoughts in mind I went back to my apartment. My desk was where I had left it, and the velvet armchair was still there, but the sight of it was so infuriating that I almost smashed it to pieces – especially as everyone in the house was already in bed and there was no one to take it away. What good is a velvet armchair when nothing else corresponds to it? It is like a naked man in a three-cornered hat! I got into bed, without managing to think a single rational thought, but the room was so bright that, as I drifted between consciousness and dreams, the armchair was constantly before my eyes, and in the morning I acted on my decision to have it thrown out into some neglected corner.

My apartment had become disagreeable to me because it was a repetition of the wrong kind. My thoughts led nowhere, and my troubled imagination kept conjuring up tantalizingly entertaining recollections of how they had presented themselves to me on my previous visit. The hated weed of recollection stifled every new thought at birth. I went down to the coffee-house which I had patronised every day when I had last been in Berlin. There I had always enjoyed the drink which is 'pure and warm and strong and not to be abused', and can therefore stand comparison, as the poet says, with friendship.[24] At least I am in favour of coffee. Perhaps the coffee was just as good as it used to be, and most probably it was; but still I did not like it. The sun was blazing hotly through the windows, the place was as stifling as the inside of a cooking pot. It was practically roasting. There was also a draught which penetrated everywhere like a small trade-wind, and that would have prevented me from thinking of repetition even if the opportunity had arisen.

In the evening I went back to a restaurant where I had often dined on my previous visit, and – through habit perhaps – it still pleased me. I used to go there every evening, and I had grown thoroughly familiar with the place: I knew when the early diners would finish, how they would take leave of their friends, and whether they would don their hats in the inner vestibule or the outer one, or wait till they had opened the door or got outside. Nothing escaped my attention. Like Proserpine [queen of the under-world], I plucked a hair from every head – even the bald ones. And it was still exactly the same: same jokes, same civilities, same fellowship. The place was exactly the same, and with the very same sameness. Solomon compares a contentious woman to rain dripping from a roof;[25] what would he say, I wonder, about this still-life? It is a terrible thought: but here repetition was possible.

The next evening I went back to the Königstadt theatre, but there the only repetition was the impossibility of repetition. The Unter den Linden was unbearably dusty, and my effort to mingle with other people and thus take a human bath met with no success. Twist and turn as I might, it was all in vain. The dancing girl who had previously enchanted me with her grace-fulness, and who always seemed to be about to take a leap, now seemed to have already taken it. The blind man outside the Brandenburg Gate, whom I used to think of as my own harpist – I was probably the only one who ever gave him a thought – was wearing a coat of mottled grey instead of the light green one which I remembered and which had made him look like a weeping willow. He was lost to me and won for humanity in general. The wonderful nose of the beadle had grown dim, and Professor A.A.'s new trousers looked almost military. . . .

After this experience had been repeated for several days running, I was so thoroughly annoyed and tired of repetition that I decided to return to Denmark. My discovery was not particularly remarkable and yet it was very singular: I had discovered that there is no such thing as repetition, and had assured myself of it by repeating the experiment in every possible way.

My only hope lay in going back home. Justinus Kerner tells the story of a man who grew tired of his home and had his horse saddled so that he could ride out into the great wide world. After he had ridden a short distance the horse threw him off. This turn of events was decisive, for when he turned round to remount his horse, his gaze fell once again on the home he wanted to leave – and it looked so beautiful that he immediately turned back.[26] At my home I could be fairly certain of finding everything ready for repetition. I have always greatly disliked upheavals, even to the point of hating household cleaning – especially if it requires soap. I had therefore left the strictest instructions that my conservative principles should be followed even in my absence. But my faithful servant had a different idea. He reckoned that if he began spring-cleaning soon after I left, then he would surely have finished long before I returned, and if you want someone to put everything back exactly where it belongs, then he is your man! On arrival I rang the doorbell, and my servant opened the door. It was a remarkable moment. He turned as pale as death. Through the half-opened door I glimpsed the horror: the world had been turned upside down. I was stunned, and my servant, in his agitation, did not know what to do. Smitten by his bad conscience, he slammed the door in my face, which was altogether too much to bear. My distress had plumbed the depths, and my principles were in ruins. I would have to expect the worst, and be treated as a ghost, like the financial official Grønmeyer [in Heiberg's play, *Kjøge Huskors*]. Now I knew that there is no such thing as repetition, and my earlier view of life had triumphed.

I was mortified to find myself brought to the same point as the young man I had treated so curtly. Indeed, I felt as if I myself were that young man, and as if all my fine words, which I would not now repeat for any price, were only a dream from which I had awoken to discover that life – treacherous life – was constantly taking away all that it gave, but without ever giving *repetition*. And is it not the case that life proves more deceitful the older we become, so that as we get cleverer and better at managing ourselves, things only get worse and our sufferings grow and grow! Little children are utterly helpless, but they always cope very well. I recollect once seeing a nursemaid pushing a pram down the street. There were two children in it, and one of them, scarcely a year old, had fallen asleep and lay there showing no signs of life. The other was a little girl of two, stout and plump and with short arms, like a miniature matron. She had pushed herself forward so that she occupied a good two-thirds of the pram, and the smaller child lay by her side like a little bag she had brought along with her. With glorious egotism she cared for no one, and was only interested in making space for herself. When a cart came hurtling down the street, the pram was in evident danger; people came running up, and with a swift movement the nursemaid pulled it out of harm's way. Everyone who saw the scene was alarmed, myself included. But our little miss remained perfectly calm, and carried on picking her nose without batting an eyelid. Presumably she was thinking, 'this has nothing to do with me – it is the nursemaid's business'. Amongst adults we will seek such heroism in vain.

The older we become, and the more we understand life, the more refined both our taste for pleasure and our capacity to appreciate it. In short, the more competent we get, the less satisfied we are. We can never be satisfied completely, absolutely and in every way – and since more moderate satisfactions are not worth bothering with, it is better to be completely dissatisfied. Anyone who has thought the matter through will surely agree with me that it is never granted to a human being to be absolutely satisfied in every possible way, not even for half an hour in a whole lifetime. It is unnecessary to add that even a fleeting satisfaction requires more than food and clothing.

Once I came very close to it. In the morning I had risen feeling exceptionally well, and my sense of well-being increased disproportionately until midday. At precisely one o'clock I was at the highest peak and had an intimation of a dizzy maximum which is not found on any scale of well-being, no matter how poetic the thermometer. My body had lost its terrestrial weight; it was as if it did not exist – every function was enjoying complete satisfaction, every nerve was delighted with itself and with the whole, and every restless heartbeat of the organism drew attention to the pleasure of the moment and celebrated it. My gait was gliding, not like the flight of a bird that cuts through the air and leaves the earth behind, but like the ripple of wind on corn, the blissful yearning swell of the sea, or the dreamy drift of clouds. My being was as transparent as the depths of the sea, the self-satisfied silence of the night, or the monological stillness of midday. Every chord sounded in my soul with a melodious resonance. My thoughts volunteered themselves with festive gladness, from the most foolish passing fancy to the richest of serious ideas. I had an inkling of my every sensation even before it arrived and awoke within me. It was as if the whole of existence were in love with me, as if everything were vibrating in fateful sympathy with my being. I was all premonition, and everything was enigmatically transfigured in my microcosmic bliss, which transfigured everything in itself, even the unpleasantness – even the most boring remark, the most disgusting sight, the most fatal collision. As I said, I reached the highest peak at precisely one o'clock, and was granted an intimation of the highest of all; but then something in one of my eyes suddenly began to hurt. I shall never know if it was an eyelash, a mote, or a speck of dust, but in that moment I plunged into an abyss of despair – as anyone will understand who has ever climbed as high as I did without losing their curiosity about the question whether, in principle, absolute satisfaction can ever be attained. Since that time I have abandoned all hope of ever being satisfied absolutely and in every way. I have given up my old hopes; not only hopes of absolute satisfaction for ever, but even hopes of a few moments of happiness – so few that a waiter could easily add them up in his head, for 'a tapster's arithmetic may soon bring his particulars therein to a total', as Shakespeare says.[27]

That was how far I had come before I got to know my young man. As soon as I asked myself the question of perfect satisfaction or heard it discussed for even half an hour, I always threw down my cards in disgust. But then I became obsessed and inspired by the idea of repetition, and thus fell prey to my zeal for principles once again. For I am totally convinced that if I had never undertaken the journey which was meant to convince me that repetition is possible, I could have stayed at home and entertained myself enormously with the very same question. Why am I so bad at sticking to the ordinary? Why don't I dress like other people? Why do I need to have principles and walk in stiff boots? Is it not agreed on all sides − amongst preachers and lecturers, poets and writers, sea-captains and undertakers, heroes and cowards − that life is like a stream? How does one come by an idea as foolish as mine, and how can anyone be such a fool as to want to make it into a principle? 'Let it go', my young friend had said to himself, and he was far better off than if he had tried to begin with a repetition. If he had begun with a repetition he would very likely have got his beloved back again. He would have been like the lover in the song about the nun with shaved hair and pale lips − he wanted repetition, and he got it, and it killed him.

> The poor young nun passed by him
> Her habit white as snow,
> Her hair had been hacked by a cruel knife,
> Her lips lacked their burning glow.
>
> The young man sank down sadly,
> Bright tears from his eyes did rain;
> He sat him down upon a stone,
> And his heart it broke in twain.[28]

Long live the post horn! It is my kind of instrument for many reasons, but mainly because you can never be sure of getting the same note out of it twice. A post horn has infinite possibilities, and if you put it to your mouth and place your wisdom in it you will never be guilty of repetition. If you give your friends post horns instead of an answer, you will have told them nothing but explained everything. Praised be the post horn! Let it be my emblem! Just as the ascetics of antiquity used to place a skull on their desk, and derive their life-view from contemplating it, so I shall have a post horn on my table as a constant reminder of the meaning of life. Long live the post horn!

Of course my journey was a waste of time. There was no need for me to travel in order to discover that there is no such thing as repetition. I might just as well have sat quietly in my room, for when vanity has passed away we can move faster than by rail, even though we are sitting still. My entire life shall henceforth be arranged as a reminder of this truth; my servant shall wear the livery of a coach driver, and I shall always be conveyed to dinner parties by post chaise. So farewell at last! Farewell, rich hope of youth! But why are you hurrying so fast? You are chasing something that does not exist, and you, you do not exist either! Farewell, manly strength! Why are you stamping the ground so fiercely; it is only a figment of your imagination! Farewell, imperious resolution! You will come close to your goal, for you cannot take the deed with you without turning back, which you cannot do. Farewell, glorious forest! When I longed to gaze on you, you were blighted! Flow on, you fleeting river! No one knows what you really want, for you want only to flow on and lose yourself in the infinite sea! No one knows whether life is a comedy or a tragedy, because no one knows how it will end, but let it continue anyway! Go on, you drama of existence, in which life, like money, is never returned to us!

Why has no one ever returned from the dead? Because life is less captivating than death, and less convincing. Yes, death is indeed marvellously convincing – if we avoid contradicting it, and let it say its piece, then it will win us over in no time. No one has ever succeeded in making an argument against it, or longed for the eloquence of life. Nothing is more convincing than you, oh death; and next to you there is no one who can speak so beautifully as the philosopher whose eloquence earned him the name of *peisithanatos* [advocate of suicide], because he dedicated his eloquence to you![29]

Notes

1 This epigraph is based on a remark by the Thracian peasant Vinitor in a late Greek dialogue about the Trojan War by Flavius Philostratus (*c.*170–245); see his *Heroicus*, I, 5. In his Journals Kierkegaard described it as a 'little epigram on the relationship between paganism and Christianity'; see Journals and Papers, IV, A 27.

2 This story of Diogenes of Sinope (404–323) is reported in Diogenes Laertius, *Lives of the Philosophers*, VI, 32.

3 G. W. Leibniz (1646–1716), creator of the doctrine of pre-established harmony.

4 A reference to one of the sorrowful 'Diapsalmata' of the first part of *Either/Or*. 'This is my misfortune: an angel of death walks always at my side, but I do not sprinkle blood on the doors of the elect as a sign that he must pass by. No, it is precisely their doors that he enters, for recollection's love is the only happy one.' Cf. KW III, p. 41.

5 i.e. the author of the 'Diapsalmata' in *Either/Or*; see above, n. 4.

6 Carlo Farinelli, the great castrato singer (1705–82) who was said to be the only person who could extricate the Spanish King Philip V from his melancholy; it was to the tongs that he owed his lustrous voice.

7 From 'Den gamle Elsker' ('The Aged Lover') by Kierkegaard's friend Poul Martin Møller (1794–1838).

8 Cf. above, n. 7.

9   Constantin here quotes a macaronic letter written by Johann Georg Hamann (1730–88).
10 Tage Algreen-Ussing (1797–1872), professor of law at Copenhagen University.
11 Cf. Genesis 3, 19.
12 Constantin refers to the first tunnel under the Thames, connecting Wapping and Rotherhithe, which opened in March 1843 and now serves the Whitechapel–New Cross line of the London Underground.
13 The phrase 'not merely for pleasure' (*ikke blot til Lyst*) is inscribed over the stage at the Royal Theatre in Copenhagen.
14 A reference to a farce by the Austrian dramatist Johann Nepomuk Nestroy (1801–62).
15 Nuremberg prints were cheap copper engravings, usually depicting biblical scenes.
16 *Entrechat*: in ballet, clicking the heels together in the course of a leap.
17 Daniel Chodowiecki (1726–1801), an artist who made a satirical engraving of the founding of Rome.
18 See Plato, *Phaedrus*, 230a.
19 Friedrich Beckmann (1803–66) and Philip Grobecker (1815–83) were actors at the Königstadt Theatre in the early and mid-nineteenth century.
20 A reference to the poet Jens Baggesen (1764–1826).
21 Johan Christian Ryge (1780–1842) played Salomon Goldkalb in Heiberg's play *King Solomon and George the Hatter* (1825).
22 Jerom Karl Friedrich, Baron von Münchhausen; see above, p. 26, n. 6.
23 Open ground near Copenhagen used for festivals.
24 The Danish poet Johannes Ewald (1743–81) wrote an 'Inscription for a coffee pot' which included the following lines: 'Your juice, thou noble Mocha fruit, To friendship is closely allied; It must always be pure and hot and strong And never misapplied.'
25 Cf. Proverbs 19, 13: 'The contentions of a wife are a continual dropping.'
26 Justinus Kerner (1786–1862), German doctor and writer.
27 Shakespeare, *Troilus and Cressida*, 1, ii, 115–16.
28 See J. G. Herder, *Volkslieder*, 1825.
29 The philosopher Hegesias, as described in Diogenes Laertius, *Lives of the Philosophers*, II, 86.

6

Philosophical Fragments

On 13 June 1844, eight months after the publication of *Fear and Trembling* and *Repetition*, Kierkegaard brought out a rather more conventional book. It was called *Philosophiske Smuler – eller en Smule Philosophi*, and is usually referred to in English as *Philosophical Fragments – or a Fragment of Philosophy*, though *Scraps*, *Crumbs*, *Chips*, *Bits*, *Morsels* or *Snacks* might be a better translation for *Smuler* than *Fragments*. Either way the title is misleading, since the work is neither scrappy nor fragmentary: it proposes a sustained conceptual argument about truth, history and eternity, set out in five regular chapters, homogeneously academic in style, length and tone: 'A Project of Thought', 'The Deity as Teacher and Saviour: An Essay of the Imagination', 'The Absolute Paradox: A Metaphysical Caprice', 'The Case of the Contemporary Disciple' and 'The Disciple at Second Hand'.

As these chapter titles suggest, *Fragments* revisits the themes of its two predecessors: it takes up the idea of faith as paradox which was proposed by Johannes de Silentio in *Fear and Trembling*, and combines it with the questions of novelty, recollection and repetition which got the better of Constantin Constantius in *Repetition*. *Fragments* is an attempt to rescue the idea of faith by replacing philosophical concepts such as recollection and repetition with the religious idea of the 'moment' (*øieblik*, *Augenblick*) – a word which can be glossed as 'moment of vision' or even 'fullness of time', and which is always anchored in a reference to St Paul's description of resurrection: 'Behold, I shew you a mystery; We shall not all sleep, but we shall all be changed, In a moment, in the twinkling of an eye, at the last trump: for the trumpet shall sound, and the dead shall be raised incorruptible, and we shall be changed.'[1]

Unusually, Kierkegaard attached his name to the book, though only as 'editor'; the authorship itself was attributed to a new pseudonym, 'Johannes Climacus', which literally means 'John (or Jack) the ladder'. There had once been a real Johannes Climacus who lived as a monk in the seventh century and was the author of *Klimax ton paradeison* (*The Ladder to Paradise*), a manual of spiritual education which explained the soul's journey to ascetic virtue in thirty simple steps. In 1839 Kierkegaard had compared Johannes Climacus to Hegel, as another vain Systematic who wanted to get to heaven 'by way of his syllogisms'.[2] But if the Climacus of *Philosophical Fragments* is meant to be a Hegelian, he is not a very successful one. He explains his aims in his opening chapter by presenting two opposing opinions – A and B – between which he hopes to make a decision. The first is the 'Socratic view' that genuine knowledge – the knowledge of eternal verities – is really recollection, so that 'everyone is his own centre, and the entire world centres in him, because his self-knowledge is a knowledge of God'. Opinion A has the implication, as Climacus points out, that teachers are irrelevant to the content of what their pupils learn:

The fact that I have been instructed by Socrates or Prodicus or by a servant-girl is of merely historical concern . . . nor is it of any more than historical interest that Socrates's or Prodicus's doctrine was this or that; for the truth in which I rest was within me all along, and came to light through me, and even Socrates would not have been able to give it to me, any more than the driver can pull the load for the horses, though he may help by applying the whip.[3]

Climacus balances this Socratic conception of teaching against what he calls opinion B, according to which eternal truths come into existence historically.

The moment in time acquires a decisive significance, so that it is impossible for me to forget it, either in time or in eternity; for the Eternal, which did not exist before, came into existence in that moment.[4]

Opinion B is of course religious rather than philosophical, and is particularly deeply rooted in Christianity. The hinge on which Christian faith turns is belief in a specific historical fact: that at a certain date in the past the Deity was born to a life of suffering as an ordinary human inhabitant of particular towns and villages in Palestine. Christians believe, moreover, that Christ taught a gospel which was both eternally true and radically new. His message was not a simple philosophical matter of 'remembering what recollection brings to mind', since it could not be understood except through his existence. Hence Christ was 'more than a teacher': he offered us 'not only the truth, but also the condition for understanding it', by waking us 'not so much to a truth slumbering within us, as to the error, indeed the sin'.[5]

Johannes Climacus now proposes to defend opinion B – the religious notion of eternal truth as residing in the moment rather than in recollection – against its powerful philosophical alternative, opinion A. In his second chapter, which is implausibly described as a 'poetic venture', he presents us with another stark intellectual choice: in order for the moment to have decisive significance, he says, the divine teacher must either (A) raise his disciples up to his own level, or (B) bring himself down to theirs. But (A) is unthinkable, since the teacher would become intolerably anxious lest he bedazzle his disciples rather than getting them to understand; and (B) is unthinkable too, because the disciples would suffer such awful anxieties over their sinfulness that they would be unable to enjoy the peace of love and understanding.

In his third chapter Climacus introduces us to the 'absolute paradox' that lies in the 'attempt to discover something that thought cannot think'. The problem is that it is evidently impossible to conceive of anything that exceeds our intellectual powers: if we succeeded we would have failed, since we would have shown that it was not beyond us after all. And yet God himself must surely surpass our understanding. Admittedly there have been philosophical theologians like Descartes and Spinoza who hold that the definition of God implies necessary existence, and that God must therefore exist in conformity with our conception of him. But Climacus is suspicious of such arguments, believing that they could never be persuasive except to those who were already blessed with faith and hence had no need for them. They remind him, he says, of round dolls which roll over and stand on their heads as soon as you stop holding them upright. He is much more attracted by the idea that God is so strange to us that we cannot begin to comprehend him; but even then, he notes, we still face a dilemma as to 'whether such a paradox can be conceived'.[6]

Climacus sharpens the dilemma in an appendix called 'Paradox and Offence: An Acoustical Illusion'.

If we do not postulate the moment we will be back with Socrates; but we were trying to get away from him and discover something new. But if we do postulate the moment then we are back with the paradox, for the moment is the paradox in its most concentrated form. Because of the moment, the learner becomes untruth: self-knowledge is replaced by self-bewilderment and the consciousness of sin . . . The dialectic of the moment is not difficult: from the Socratic point of view the moment is invisible and undetectable; it does not exist – never has existed and never will.

Hence the learner is truth, and the occasioning moment a joke, like a bastard title-page that does not belong to the book: from this point of view the moment of decision becomes *folly* [*daarskab*].[7]

It is beginning to seem, then, that Climacus's 'project of thought' – his attempt to construct an intelligible concept of the moment – is doomed.

Nevertheless he continues, and in the fourth chapter he wonders whether Christian faith would have come easily to Christ's contemporaries, who had the manifest advantage of knowing him directly, without the mediation of reasoning and hearsay. But he soon realizes that such immediacy would serve no purpose in matters of faith.

Faith is not a form of knowledge, for either knowledge is of the eternal, and excludes the temporal and historical as irrelevant, or it is merely historical. But no knowledge can have as its object the absurdity that the eternal is the historical. If I understand Spinoza's doctrines, then I am concerned with the doctrines and not with Spinoza, though on some other occasion I might be concerned historically with Spinoza himself. But disciples relate to their master in faith, and are eternally concerned with his historical existence. . . . The object of faith is not the *teaching* but the *teacher*.

The 'art and heroism' of Socratic teachers lies in their self-effacement: they seek to absent themselves as they have begun to awaken our souls to eternal truths; and to his contemporaries Christ would have been at best a Socratic teacher, not an object of faith.[8]

In his fifth and final chapter Climacus jumps forward 1843 years, to consider the predicament of those who live long after Christ walked this earth. It might well seem that we have an advantage over our predecessors, since the Christian message will have been clarified and purified in the process of filtering down to us through the intervening generations. But unfortunately knowledge and opinion count for nothing in questions of faith; what matters is decision and conviction, which clearly 'cannot be communicated from one person to another', at least 'not in such a way that the other will believe it'.[9]

If each generation wants simply to bequeath a splendid set of conclusions to the next, will not these conclusions become misunderstandings? Is not Venice constructed over the sea? Suppose it became so densely built up that a generation was born which was no longer aware of this fact – would it not be a terrible misunderstanding if the present generation allowed the piles to rot away so that the city sank? Yet conclusions founded on a paradox are humanly speaking built over a yawning chasm, and their total content, which is handed down to individuals only on the express understanding that they are sustained by a paradox, cannot be inherited like a settled estate, since their entire value trembles in the balance.[10]

Thus it would seem that Johannes Climacus – like Johannes de Silentio and Constantin Constantius before him – has failed to live up to his name. He has found nowhere to fix his ladder of faith, and instead of inducing conviction in us he is more likely to have spread scepticism, in the sense of a principled hesitation before our intellectual choices. We are no nearer an understanding than we were at the beginning – unless of course we say that the solution to our dilemmas lies in recognizing that they are insoluble. And it would appear from Climacus's Preface that he has come to the same conclusion: he cannot decide either way, for 'having an opinion is both too much and too little for me'.[11]

In order to bridge the gap of 1843 years between chapter 4 ('The Case of the Contemporary Disciple') and chapter 5 ('The Disciple at Second Hand'), Climacus offers us the 'Interlude' (*Mellemspil*) printed below. But if the title makes us expect a between-the-acts diversion we will be in for a rude surprise: we are going to be put to work by one of the most demanding pieces of argumentation ever to come from Kierkegaard's pen. Much of the latter part is taken up with a discussion of the power and beauty of Greek scepticism, compared with the glib superficiality of the modern philosophy (especially Hegelianism) which claims to have 'gone further'. But the opening sections of the essay comprise an attempt to discredit the 'modern' view that there is some kind of necessity – natural, social or divine – which shapes the entire course of events in the world.

One obvious modern way of approaching the question of necessity is through the concept of 'will' and 'free will'; another is by way of 'laws of nature', and the question whether they control the entire network of causes and effects. But Johannes Climacus pays no attention to these approaches, preferring to go back to Aristotle's doctrine of possibility (*dynamis*) and its development by the medieval theologians who struggled to reconcile the freedom of our wills with the idea that God must always know in advance what we are going to choose. Their suggestion was that there are throngs of 'possibilities' which are all equally possible even though very few of them will ever have the privilege of coming into existence as 'actualities'. There is nothing in the realm of possibilities which dictates which possibilities will be actualized – no destiny or fate, but merely possibility.

Climacus can therefore argue that 'coming into existence' (*tilblivelse*) is never necessary: the way the world actually goes is only one of indefinitely many possibilities, and there is no prior necessity impelling it one way rather than another. And if he is suggesting that this conception of 'possibility' could do far more damage to the prejudices of 'modern philosophy' than any arguments about free will or laws of nature, he may well be right. For when he affirms that everything is possible, he is not uttering an empty tautology, but contradicting the whole idea of 'prefiguration' – the idea that virtue springs from virtuousness, for instance, and vice from viciousness, and that whatever happens for good or evil can be traced back to good or evil impulses. He is unpicking what might be called the 'obstetric' idea of time – time as a generative process in which the past is constantly 'giving birth' to the future. For if everything is equally possible then nothing is absolutely necessary, and things could always have turned out quite differently.

Climacus's 'Interlude' is exacting and exhausting, but it should not make us forget the five-act structure in which it has its place. Each of his chapters ends with a confessional coda in which he owns up to the most abject sort of repetition, namely plagiarism and the recycling of received ideas. He is a thief; or he has robbed God; his paradox, as he admits, is a tissue of unacknowledged quotations from Shakespeare, Luther, Tertullian and many others, not to mention the Bible. The wretched Johannes Climacus confesses it all, but at least he has the spirit to defend himself by drawing out the moral of his story.

The Moral
There can be no doubt that what is proposed here goes beyond Socrates, as is apparent at every point. Whether it is therefore truer than the Socratic hypothesis is another question entirely, and it cannot be decided in the same breath, since we have here assumed a new organ: faith; a new presupposition: consciousness of sin; a new decision: the moment; and a new teacher: the Deity in time. Without these I would never have dared present myself for inspection before that master of irony who has been admired for thousands of years, and whom I approach with a heartfelt enthusiasm that will yield to none. But going beyond Socrates while nevertheless saying essentially the same things he did, only not nearly so well – that at least is not Socratic.[12]

Notes

1 I Corinthians 15, 51–2.
2 Journals and Notebooks, II A 335; see above, p. 17.
3 *Philosophical Fragments*, I ('A Project of Thought'); cf. KW VII, pp. 11, 12.
4 *Philosophical Fragments*, I; cf. KW VII, p. 13.
5 *Philosophical Fragments*, I; cf. KW VII, pp. 19, 14–15.
6 *Philosophical Fragments*, III ('The Absolute Paradox'); cf. KW VII, pp. 47–8.
7 *Philosophical Fragments*, III, Appendix ('Paradox and Offence'); cf. KW VII, pp. 51–2. (Note that Climacus's remark on the 'folly' of the moment of decision is meant to express not the truth of the moment but Socratic blindness to it.)

8 *Philosophical Fragments*, IV ('The Contemporary Disciple'); cf. KW VII, p. 62.
9 *Philosophical Fragments*, V ('The Disciple at Second Hand'); cf. KW VII, p. 103.
10 *Philosophical Fragments*, V; cf. KW VII, p. 98.
11 See below, p. 160.
12 *Philosophical Fragments*, 'The Moral'; cf. KW VII, p. 111.

Philosophical Fragments, or a Fragment of Philosophy by Johannes Climacus, edited by S. Kierkegaard

Many a good hanging prevents a bad marriage.[1]

Can an eternal consciousness have a historical point of departure? If so, how can such a point of departure be of more than historical interest? And can we base eternal bliss on historical knowledge?

Preface

What is offered here is only a pamphlet, issued in my own cause, on my own responsibility, and at my own expense. It makes no claim to be part of the scholarly industry in which one can acquire legitimacy by serving as a passage or thoroughfare, by leading up to conclusions or preparing the way, by acting as a comrade or as a volunteer, as champion or relative champion, or at least as the absolute fanfare. It is only a pamphlet and would never amount to anything more, even if I were, God willing, to add seventeen further pamphlets to it and produce folios full of half-hour pieces, like Holberg's Magister.[2] My achievement, however, is in keeping with my talents. I am not

The first English translation of *Philosophical Fragments* was the excellent and pioneering work of David Swenson and appeared in 1936; it was revised by Howard Hong and reissued in 1962. A new version by Howard V. Hong and Edna H. Hong appeared in 1985 as part of vol. VII of *Kierkegaard's Writings*. The present translation of the preface and interlude by Jane Chamberlain and Jonathan Rée appears here for the first time, copyright © Jane Chamberlain and Jonathan Rée, 2001.

like the noble Roman who *merito magis quam ignavia* [from talent rather than baseness] declines to serve the System.[3] I am idle from indolence, *ex animi sententia* [from the depths of my soul], and for good reasons. Yet I do not want to be guilty of *apragmosuné* [neglect of public activity], which is an offence against the state in any age and especially in a period of unrest, and was even punishable by death in ancient times. But what if the only effect of political activity were the still greater offence of creating mere confusion? Would it not be better in that case to mind my own business? Not all of us are lucky enough to find our intellectual activities coinciding so happily with the general interest that no one can tell how far we are pursuing them for our own gratification and how far for the public good. For did not Archimedes sit in calm contemplation of his circles while Syracuse was being taken, and did he not address the Roman soldier who was about to murder him in the following beautiful words: *nolite purturbare circulos meos* ['Please do not mess up my circles']? But those of us who are not so fortunate must look for other precedents. When Philip was threatening to lay siege to Corinth, Diogenes − seeing all the inhabitants make themselves busy, cleaning weapons, gathering stones or mending a wall − quickly fastened his cloak and rolled his barrel zealously up and down the streets.[4] When he was asked why, he replied: I keep myself busy by rolling my tub so that no one can accuse me of standing idle amongst so many industrious people. There is nothing sophistical in such behaviour, unless Aristotle was mistaken in saying that sophistry is a means of making money. At least it does not give rise to misunderstandings, since it would be quite impossible for anyone to mistake Diogenes for a saviour or benefactor of his city.

In the same way, it would never enter anyone's head to ascribe world-historical significance to my little pamphlet, which I would regard as a catastrophe anyway. Nor is anyone going to hail its author as the systematic Salomon Goldkalb, who has been so long awaited in our dear city of Copenhagen.[5] That could only happen if the culprit was quite extraordinarily stupid − screaming his endless antistrophic antiphonies whenever anyone told him we were entering some new era or epoch. Presumably he would have yelled his modest sufficiency of common sense so completely out of his head that he would have attained a state of bliss within what might be called the howling madness of the higher lunacy, characterized by endless compulsive shouting of the words 'era', 'epoch', 'era and epoch', 'epoch and era' and 'System'. In this state of bliss his condition is one of irrational exaltation, for he lives as if each day were a leap-year day − the kind that occurs not every four years, but every thousand years − while the Concept itself, like a circus acrobat at festival time, has to execute its perpetual somersaults over and over again, until finally it knocks him flat. May heaven preserve me and my pamphlet from such a fate, and from the meddling of the rowdy louts who would like to spoil my carefree self-satisfaction in being the author of a pamphlet and prevent kind and sympathetic readers from examining it for themselves to see if it contains anything they might find useful. That would put me in the tragicomic predicament of having to laugh at my own misfortune, just as the good citizens of Fredericia must have laughed when they read newspaper reports describing a fire in their town where 'the alarms sounded, and fire-engines tore through the streets', although there is only one fire-engine in Fredericia, and hardly more than one solitary street. The newspaper managed to imply that the fire-engine had made a huge detour instead of going straight to the scene of the fire. My own pamphlet, however, is not going to set off any alarms, nor is its author at all inclined to sound them.

But what, you ask, is my own opinion? . . . Pray do not inquire after that. What my opinions may be is of almost as little interest to others as whether I have any opinions at all. Having an opinion is both too much and too little for me: it presupposes a sense of well-being and security in existence, like having a wife and children in this terrestrial world – something which is not granted to those who have to keep going day and night and still lack a steady income. This is my own condition in the world of spirit, for I have always been trying to teach myself to dance lightly in the service of thought, to the glory of God as far as possible and also for my own enjoyment, renouncing domestic bliss and civic prestige, the communion of the good and harmony of gladness that goes with having an opinion.

Yet what is my reward? May I, like those who serve at the altar, partake of what is laid out on it?. . . . That is up to me. It is a sound investment, as the financiers would say, though not in the sense they would mean. If anyone did me the honour of assuming that I have an opinion, and carried his gallantry to the extreme of subscribing to an opinion because it was mine, I would decline the courtesy as being bestowed on someone unworthy, and I would then reject the opinion as being no better than mine. I can put my own life at risk, and fool around with it in all seriousness; but not someone else's. This is all I can do for the cause of thought, I who have no learning to contribute, 'scarcely enough for the one-drachma course, to say nothing of the big fifty-drachma course'.[6] I have nothing but my life, and I am happy to put it at risk whenever a difficulty appears. Then I can dance lightly, for the thought of death is my amiable dancing partner. Human beings are too heavy for me, and therefore I pray and plead with the Gods: I am no dancer, so let no one invite me to dance.

J. C.

Interlude
Is the Past more Necessary than the Future? Or: Does the Possible become more Necessary by becoming Actual?

Let us now assume, dear reader, that our teacher has lived, died, and been buried, and that some time has elapsed between chapters four and five.[7] It sometimes happens in a comedy, too, that several years are supposed to pass between one act and the next, and the orchestra may play some kind of symphony in order to indicate the passage of time, or to fill and thus foreshorten it. It is in the same spirit that I shall now fill the gap by considering the question set out above. You can decide for yourselves how much time has elapsed, but let us assume, if you will, both in seriousness and in jest, that it is precisely 1843 years. For the sake of the illusion I must therefore allow myself plenty of time, since eighteen hundred and forty-three years is an exceptionally generous amount of time, and it will soon land me in the opposite predicament to that of our philosophers, who never have more than a vague intimation of time. It is also the opposite predicament to that of the historians, for whom it is not the material but time itself that is the problem. If you find me long-winded, therefore, and constantly repeating the same thing 'about the same thing', please bear in mind that I am doing it for the sake of the illusion. Perhaps you will then be able to forgive my long-windedness, and derive satisfaction from realizing that I am far from presuming that it is because you do not understand the matter that you ought to give it your attention. I do not doubt that you have completely understood and accepted the latest [nyeste] philosophy which, like the modern [nyeste] age itself, seems to suffer from a curious absent-mindedness [distraktion] which makes it confuse the performance with the announcement; for who could excel the wonders of modern philosophy and the modern age when it comes to making announcements?

§1   Coming into existence

How are things altered by coming into existence [bliver til], or what kind of change (kinésis) does coming into existence involve? Other kinds of change (alloiōsis) presuppose the existence of that which changes, including the change of ceasing to exist [at være til]. But not coming into existence. For if what comes into existence were changed in itself when it underwent the change of coming into existence, then it would be something else that came into existence, and this would involve a metabasis eis allo genos [shift from one conceptual sphere to another][8] in that we would either be postulating a second change accompanying its coming into existence, which would complicate the question considerably, or we would be mistaken as to what had come into existence, and thus in no position to talk about it. If a plan were to be essentially changed by coming into existence, then it would not itself come into existence; but if it was not changed, then what kind of change does coming into existence involve? Thus the change is not in essence [*væsen*] but in existence [*væren*] – a change from not existing to existing. Yet the non-existence [*ikke-væren*] which is left behind when something comes into existence must also exist, since otherwise 'what comes into existence would not remain unchanged by coming into existence' – unless of course it had never existed, which would be a further reason for regarding coming into existence as absolutely different from every other kind of change. In fact it would not be a change at all, since changes always presuppose something which undergoes change. But of course the being which is also non-being [*ikke-væren*] is nothing other than possibility, while the being which is being is actual being [*væren*] or actuality. Thus coming into existence must be a transition from possibility to actuality.

Can necessity come into existence? Coming into existence is a change, whereas the necessary never changes, since it always relates itself to itself, and always in the same way. Coming into existence is always passivity or *suffering*, but necessity can never suffer – it cannot suffer the suffering of actuality, in which possibilities (not only impossible possibilities but possible possibilities too) are shown to be nothing the moment they become actual, since possibilities are *annihilated* by actuality. Anything that comes into existence thereby demonstrates its own non-necessity, since the only thing which can never come into existence is the necessary, because the necessary already *is*.

So can necessity be defined as the unity of possibility and actuality? But what could this mean? Possibility and actuality differ not in essence but in existence [*væren*]; but how could such a difference constitute a unity that was necessary, given that necessity is a determination not of existence [*væren*] but of essence, and the essence of the necessary is to be? In that case possibilities and actualities would change absolutely in their essence if they became necessary; but a change in essence is not really a change at all. In becoming necessary they would become the one thing that is incapable of coming into existence, and this is as impossible as it is self-contradictory. (The Aristotelian proposition – 'it is possible [to be]', 'it is possible not [to be]', 'it is not possible [to be]'[9] – and the Epicurean doctrine of true and false propositions only confuse the issue here, since it concerns essence rather than existence [*væren*], and therefore has no implications for the determination of the future.)[10]

Necessity stands entirely alone. There is nothing that comes into existence through necessity, any more than necessity itself can come into existence or any more than everything that comes into existence is necessary. There is nothing that exists [er til] because it is necessary; but the necessary exists because it is necessary or because the necessary is. Actuality is no more necessary than possibility, since necessity is absolutely different from both. (Compare Aristotle's theory of the two types of possibility in relation to necessity. His mistake lay in assuming that everything necessary is possible. In order to avoid involving himself in contradictions – and self-contradictions – about necessity, and thus revealing that his original thesis was mistaken, since the possible cannot be predicated of the necessary, he drew a distinction between two kinds of possibility.)

The transition to existence is actuality, and it takes place through freedom. No coming into existence can be necessary before it comes into existence, since it would then be impossible for it to come into existence; nor can it be necessary after it has come into existence, since it would then be impossible for it to have come into existence.

All coming into existence takes place through freedom, not necessity. Things that come into existence do so by virtue of a cause rather than a ground. Every freely acting cause originates in a cause. By postulating intermediate causes we deceive ourselves into thinking that coming into existence is necessary; but the truth is that the intermediate causes, which themselves came into existence, point back to a freely acting cause. Once we have reflected definitively on coming into existence, we will realize that even the consequences of a law of nature are no evidence for a necessary coming into existence. The same applies to freedom, as long as we reflect on its coming into existence rather than allowing ourselves to be misled by its outward manifestations.

§2   The historical

Everything that has ever come into existence is *eo ipso* historical, for even if it has no other historical characteristics, it still has the crucial historical characteristic of having come into existence. When several things come into existence at the same time (*Nebeneinander* [alongside each other], space)[11] this may be all the history they have. But nature itself has a history, even when viewed in this way (*en masse*), and quite apart from the specialized notion of a history of nature.[12]

The historical is the past, and the present is the boundary which has not yet become historical. How then can nature, which is immediately present, be said to be historical, except in the specialized sense? The problem arises because nature is too abstract, in the strictest sense of the word, to be dialectical with respect to time. It is nature's imperfection that it does not have a history in any other sense, but its perfection is that it always retains a trace of history (because it has come into existence, and thus belongs to the past, and because it exists, and thus belongs to the present). On the other hand, it is the perfection of eternity to have no history, and the eternal is the only thing that has absolutely no history.

However, coming into existence can contain within itself a reduplication, in that one coming into existence may contain within itself the possibility of another. This is historical in the stricter sense, in that it is dialectical with respect to time. On the other hand a coming into existence which has something in common with the coming into existence of nature is mere possibility, a possibility which, in the case of nature, exhausts its actuality. It should never be forgotten that any truly historical coming into existence is contained within another coming into existence, and the more specifically historical coming into existence comes into existence through a relatively freely acting cause, which in turn points back to an absolutely freely acting cause.

§3 The past

What has happened has happened and cannot be undone; hence it cannot be changed (Chrysippus the Stoic – Diodorus the Megarian).[13] But is this immutability the same as necessity? The immutability of the past is a result of changes – changes in the sense of comings into existence – but of course it cannot exclude all changes, since it has not excluded this one. Change cannot be excluded (dialectically with respect to time) unless it is excluded at every moment [øieblik]. We can regard the past as necessary only if we forget that it came into existence; but perhaps such forgetfulness is itself necessary?

What happened in the past happened just as it happened; hence it is immutable. But is this the immutability of necessity? The immutability of the past lies in the fact that its actual 'hence' can never be altered, but does it follow that its possible 'how' could not have been different either? The immutability of the necessary, by contrast – the fact that it constantly relates itself to itself, and always in the same way, excluding all change – goes beyond the immutability of the past, which, as we have seen, is dialectical with respect not only to earlier changes, from which it has emerged, but also with respect to a higher change which may supersede it. (Repentance, for example, is always an attempt to supersede an actuality.)

The future has not yet happened, but that does not make it less necessary than the past; after all, the past did not become necessary by happening – on

the contrary, the fact that it happened demonstrated that it was not necessary. And even if the past were necessary, it would not follow that the future
is not – on the contrary, it would follow that the future is equally necessary.
If necessity came into it at all, then we could not speak of past and future
any more. The desire to foretell the future is the same as the desire to understand the necessity of the past, and it is only custom and fashion that makes
one seem more plausible than the other in any given generation. The past
has of course come into existence, and coming into existence is a change,
through freedom, in actuality. If the past were necessary, then it would no
longer belong to freedom – it would no longer belong to that through which
it came into existence. Freedom would then be in a sorry predicament –
laughable at the same time as lamentable – since it would be responsible for
what did not belong to it. Necessity would devour whatever freedom brought
forth, and freedom, like coming into existence, would become an illusion.
Freedom would be a form of witchcraft and coming into existence a false
alarm.*

* A generation given to prophecy will turn its back on the past, and refuse to consider
the testimony of old documents, whereas a generation preoccupied with the necessity of the
past does not like to think about the future. Both of them are entirely consistent, and each
has the opportunity to learn the error of its ways from the other. The Absolute Method in
Hegel's *Logic* is already a difficult matter – a glittering tautology, which decks out scientific
superstition with many signs and wonders. In the historical sciences the method is an obsession, and immediately becomes concrete; history is, of course, the concretion of the Idea, and
this gives Hegel a chance to display his rare erudition and his extraordinary power to impose
shape on his material and stir up movement in it. But it is also a distraction for his readers.
Of course we may forget – perhaps out of respect and admiration for the civilizations of China
and Persia or the thinkers of the Middle Ages, the philosophers of ancient Greece, or the
four world-historical monarchies (which did not escape Gert Westphaler [in Holberg's comedy,
Gert Westphaler], and set the tongue of many a subsequent Hegelian Gert Westphaler wagging)
– we may forget, I say, to ask whether Hegel has succeeded, at the end of his enchanted journey,
in demonstrating what he was promising us at the outset, and in proving the correctness of
the method (which was of course the primary issue which all the world's glory could not
replace, and which alone could excuse the untimely suspense in which we were being held).
But why did we expect to become concrete all at once? Why did we start off by trying to
experiment *in concreto*? Perhaps this question is unanswerable in the dispassionate brevity of
abstraction, lacking as it does any means of diversion or enchantment: what is it for the Idea
to become concrete, or for something to come into existence, or for us to relate ourselves to
what has come into existence, etc.? It is the same in the *Logic*: Hegel of course explained what
transition means, before going on to write the three books which overthrew superstition by
exhibiting transition at work in the determination of categories, thus putting us all in the
embarrassing position of having to acknowledge with gladness the superiority of Spirit, and
give thanks for all we owe it, while never forgetting what Hegel himself must have regarded
as the main point.

§4   The apprehension of the past

Nature, as a determination of space, only exists immediately. But things which are dialectical with respect to time contain a certain doubleness, since after having been present they can be perpetuated as a past. The properly historical is perpetually past (it is over; whether by years or only days makes no difference), and it possesses actuality as past, for it is certain or probable that it occurred. However, the fact that it occurred is also precisely its uncertainty, which will perpetually prevent us from treating the past as if it had always been the same since time began. This conflict between certainty and uncertainty is the *discrimen* [distinguishing mark] of everything that comes into existence and hence also of the past, and it is only through it that the past can be understood. Otherwise our understanding will misunderstand both itself (as understanding) and its object (as the kind of thing that could be an object of understanding). Any understanding which attempted a complete understanding of the past by constructing it would be a complete misunderstanding. (At first glance the concept of manifestation is less compelling than the concept of construction, but the next moment we are back with secondary constructions and necessary manifestations.) The past cannot be necessary, since it came into existence; it did not become necessary by coming into existence (a contradiction), and still less did it become necessary through our understanding of it. (Distance in time gives rise to intellectual illusions, just as distance in space gives rise to sensory illusions.) Contemporaries do not see any necessity in what comes into existence, but when centuries have elapsed since something came into existence it will appear necessary – just as distance can make a square tower look round. If the past became necessary through our understanding of it, then the past's gain would be the understanding's loss, since it would always be an understanding of something else, and hence a misunderstanding. If things are changed by being understood, then understanding becomes misunderstanding. Knowledge does not confer necessity on the present, nor does foreknowledge confer necessity on the future (Boethius);[14] and knowledge of the past does not confer necessity on it, since understanding, like knowledge, never has anything of its own to give.

Those who can understand the past historico-philosophically are therefore prophets in reverse (Daub).[15] They are prophets in that the basis of the certainty of the past lies in an uncertainty which is the same as that of the future, namely a possibility (Leibniz's possible worlds)[16] out of which necessity could never possibly *emerge* – *nam necessarium se ipso prius sit, necesse est* [since necessity necessarily precedes itself]. Historians stand up for the past, moved by a passionate feeling for coming into existence: in other words, by wonder. If philosophers never wonder over anything (and how, except by a new kind of contradiction, could anyone ever come to wonder at a necessary construction?) they have *eo ipso* no contact with the historical, for wherever coming into existence is at stake (and it is of course at stake in the past), the uncertainty of even the most certain coming into existence (the uncertainty of any coming into existence) can express itself only in this worthy and necessary passion of the philosopher (Plato – Aristotle).[17] Even if what has come into existence were the greatest certainty, even if wonderment gave its consent in advance by saying that if it had not existed it would have had to be invented, even then the passion of wonder would be self-contradictory – would be fooling itself – if it ascribed necessity to what had come into existence. Both the word and the concept of Method are sufficient to show that the progress alluded to here is teleological; but every moment [*øieblik*] of a teleological process is also a pause (where wonder stands *in pausa* and waits upon coming into existence) – the pause of coming into existence and of possibility, precisely because the *telos* [end, goal] lies outside the process. If only one path is possible, then the *telos* is not outside the process but is inside and indeed behind it, as with the progress of immanence.

So much for our understanding of the past. But we have so far presupposed knowledge of the past, and must now investigate how this knowledge is acquired. The historical carries within itself the *illusiveness* [*svigagtighed*] of coming into existence, so it cannot be given immediately to our senses. Our immediate impressions of a natural phenomenon or event are not impressions of the historical, since our senses apprehend only presence and never *coming into existence*. But the presence of the historical carries its coming into existence within itself, otherwise it would not be the presence of the historical.

Immediate cognition and sensation can never deceive us, and this shows that the historical cannot be the object of either, since it carries the illusiveness of coming into existence within itself. In relation to the immediate, coming into existence is an illusiveness which casts doubt even on our firmest certainties. When we look at a star, for example, the star will become doubtful the moment we try to understand it as having come into existence. It is as if reflection removed the star from our senses. This much is therefore clear: that the organ with which we apprehend the historical must be formed in conformity with this, and carry within itself a corresponding something by which, in its certainty, it perpetually supersedes the uncertainty that corresponds to the uncertainty of coming into existence – a double uncertainty: the nothingness of non-being and the annihilated possibility, which is also the annihilation of every other possibility. Now this is precisely the nature of faith, for the uncertainty that corresponds in every way to the uncertainty of coming into existence is constantly present as superseded in the certainty of faith. Faith believes in what it does not see: it sees that the star exists, but does not believe it; on the other hand it believes that the star once came into existence. The same is true of events. A happening can be known immediately, but we never immediately know that it has happened, nor even that it is happening, even if it happens, as they say, right under our noses. The illusiveness of a happening consists in the fact that it happened, and this is the transition from nothingness, from non-being, and from the manifoldly possible 'how'. Immediate cognition and sensation have no notion of the uncertainty with which faith must approach its object, but neither do they have any inkling of the certainty that can grow out of uncertainty.

Immediate cognition and sensation can never deceive us. It is important to understand this in order to understand the nature of doubt, and thus assign faith to its proper place. And strange as it may seem, it is this thought that underlies Greek scepticism. This should be clear enough – together with the light it throws on faith – provided we have not been completely confused by Hegelian doubt about everything, against which it is surely not necessary to preach. For what the Hegelians say about doubt may well make us modestly doubt whether they can be said to have doubted anything at all. The scepticism of the Greeks was of a detached kind (*epoché*); they doubted by virtue not of knowledge but of will (withholding assent – *metriopathein*). Now it follows from this that their doubts could only be dispelled through freedom, by an act of will – as every Greek sceptic would have known if he understood himself at all. But they would never give up their scepticism, precisely because they doubted through *will*. That was their choice, and we should not assume that they held the stupid opinion that doubts arise by necessity, nor the even more stupid opinion that they can nevertheless be dispelled. The Greek sceptics did not deny the correctness of sensation and immediate cognition; error, for them, had an entirely different basis – in the conclusions we draw. If we can simply refrain from drawing conclusions, we will never be deceived. If sensation, for example, makes something seem round to us when seen from a distance, but square from closer up, or a stick appear bent in water which can seem to be straight when taken out, then sensation has not deceived us, and we will not be deceived unless we draw some conclusion about the object or the stick. Sceptics therefore hold themselves constantly *in suspenso* [in suspense], and this state of mind is *willed*. The doctrine of Greek scepticism has been divided into three varieties, Zetetic, Aporetic and Sceptic,[18] but these predicates do not express what is peculiar to it, since the sceptics used cognition only as a means of protecting the sceptical state of mind which they prized above everything else. They would not even describe the negative results of their cognition *thétikos* [positively], for fear of being caught out drawing a conclusion. It was the state of mind that was their main concern. ('The end to be realized they hold to be suspension of judgement, which brings with it tranquillity like its shadow', as Diogenes Laertius put it.)[19]★ But it is now perfectly clear that faith is not a form of knowledge but an act of freedom, an expression of will. It believes in coming into existence, and has therefore superseded within itself the uncertainty that corresponds to the nothingness of non-being. It believes in the 'hence' of what has come into existence, and has therefore superseded within itself its possible 'how'. Faith does not deny the possibility of a different 'hence', but for faith the 'hence' of what has come into existence will always be the supreme certainty.

We can never be deceived by what becomes historical through faith, or by what becomes an object of faith as historical (and the two correspond to each other), provided they exist immediately and are directly perceived. Contemporaries may of course use their eyes, but they must be careful of drawing conclusions. They cannot know directly that something has come into existence, and they cannot know it with necessity either, for the first sign of coming into existence is a break in continuity. In the moment when faith believes that things have come into existence, or happened, it casts doubt on the happening and, through their coming into existence, on what has come into existence, as well as on its 'hence' in the possible 'how' of its coming into existence. Faith's conclusion [*slutning*] is really no conclusion at all – it is a resolution [*beslutning*], and therefore it excludes doubt. When faith concludes that something exists, *ergo* it has come into existence, it might seem to be making an inference from effect to cause. But this is not entirely so, and even if it were we would have to remember that the genuine inference runs not from effect to cause but from cause to effect or, more correctly, from ground to consequent (Jacobi).[20] It is not entirely so, since I cannot directly sense or know that what I directly sense or know is an effect, since immediately it only is. I believe that it is an effect, for in order to describe it as an effect I must already have cast it into the doubt and uncertainty of coming into existence. But if faith decides to do this, then doubts are dispelled; and the equilibrium and neutrality of doubt are dispelled in the same moment – not by knowledge, but by will. Thus faith works through

---

★ Both Plato and Aristotle emphasized that immediate sensation and cognition never deceive us. Descartes too, like the Greek sceptics, says that error arises from the will's precipitateness in drawing conclusions. [See Descartes, *Meditations*, 4, and *Principles of Philosophy* XXXI, XLII.] This throws light on faith too. When faith resolves to believe, it runs the risk of error, but it still wants to believe. Otherwise there would be no such thing as faith; wanting to avoid this risk is like wanting to be sure we can swim before we get into the water.

approximations, and is always both supremely disputable (for it unfolds the uncertainty of doubt, which is strong and invincible in multiplying *doubts* [*at tvetyde*, 'making ambiguous'] – *dis-putare* [thinking against]), and supremely secure by virtue of its new quality. Faith is the opposite of doubt. But they are not two varieties of knowledge which can be set alongside each other. Faith and doubt are not different kinds of cognition; they are contrary passions. Faith is a feeling for coming into existence, and doubt is a protest against every attempt to draw conclusions beyond direct knowledge and sensation. Doubters do not deny their own existence, for example, but they never draw conclusions since they want to avoid being deceived. They may make constant use of dialectic in order to make opposites seem equally probable, but scepticism is not constituted by such dialectical arguments, which are no more than arbitrary conventions. Scepticism therefore leads to no results – not even negative ones, since that would imply a recognition of knowledge. It is through sheer will-power that sceptics stop short and abstain from all conclusions.[21]

Those who are not contemporary with a historical event must rely on the testimony of its contemporaries (to which they will relate in the same way as contemporaries relate to immediacy), rather than on the immediacy of cognition and sensation (which can never grasp the historical anyway). But even if the content of such testimony has altered, they still cannot engage with it without assenting to it and thus rendering it historical by making it unhistorical for themselves. The immediacy of the testimony – the mere fact that the testimony exists – is directly present. But the historicity of the present consists in its having come into existence, and the historicity of the past lies in the fact that it became present by coming into existence. When later generations have faith in the past (not in its truth, for that would be a matter of cognition – of essence rather than existence [*væren*] – but in its having been present through coming into existence) they cannot escape the uncertainty of coming into existence. And this uncertainty (the nothingness of non-being [*ikke-væren*] – the possible 'how' of the actual 'hence') will be the same for them as it would have been for contemporaries; their minds must be set *in suspenso* in exactly the same way. They will no longer be confronted by immediacy, or by the necessity of coming into existence, but only by *the 'hence' of coming into existence*. The faith of later generations is of course grounded in contemporary testimony, but only in the same way as the faith of the contemporaries was grounded in direct cognition and sensation. But that was never the basis of contemporary faith, and later generations cannot base their faith on testimony either.

The past was not necessary when it came into existence, nor did it appear necessary to contemporaries who had faith – faith, that is, that it had come into existence – nor will there ever be a moment when it becomes necessary. Faith and coming into existence correspond to each other, and both of them are concerned either with superseded determinations of being – past or future – or with the present considered through superseded determinations of being as something which has come into existence. Necessity, by contrast, has to do with essence, and in such a way that the determination of essence functions precisely to exclude coming into existence. The possibility which eventually became actual belonged to a range of other possibilities which can never be separated from what actually came into existence. However many centuries go by, they will always remain with the past. When later generations, by having faith, repeat its coming into existence, they will always repeat its possibility [its non-necessity] as well, even if they are unaware of doing so.

Notes

1 Shakespeare, *Twelfth Night*, I, v, 19–20.
2 In Holberg's play *Jacob von Tyboe eller den stortalende Soldat* (1725), Magister Stygotius boasts to the beautiful Leonora that he walks 'in the footsteps of the ancients, of which there will be proof, God willing, when I defend my thesis the day after tomorrow', and Climacus is here alluding to her sceptical reply.
3 A reference to the Roman historian Sallust (86–35), who abandoned service to the state in favour of literature.
4 Climacus is referring to Diogenes of Sinope (*c*.404–323), known as the Cynic, who expressed his contempt for the world by living in a barrel.
5 Salomon Goldkalb is a Jewish merchant in Heiberg's play *King Solomon and George the Hatter* (1825), who is mistaken for the long-awaited plutocrat Baron Goldkalb.
6 Plato, *Cratylus*, 384b.
7 These chapters are not included in this anthology.
8 See Aristotle, *Posterior Analytics*, 75a, 38–9.
9 In *On Interpretation*, 21b–23a, Aristotle argues that necessity must imply possibility, since otherwise it would imply either impossibility or the possibility of the opposite.
10 Perhaps a reference to the Epicurean view that an opinion is called true 'if it is subsequently confirmed . . . and false if it is not subsequently confirmed'; see Diogenes Laertius, *Lives of the Philosophers*, X, 33–4.
11 See Hegel, *Philosophy of Nature*, Encyclopaedia, §254.
12 Probably a reference to the *Naturphilosophie* of F. W. J. Schelling (1775–1854).
13 Chrysippus of Soli (*c*.280–207) took issue with the doctrine of Diodorus Cronos (d. 307), who argued that only the actual is possible, since a possibility would prove itself to be impossible if it did not become actual.

14 See Boethius (c.480–524), *The Consolation of Philosophy*, V: 'Just as knowledge of the present does not impart necessity to it, so foreknowledge imparts no necessity to the future.'

15 A reference to an idea of prophesying the past proposed by Carl Daub (1765–1836), who wrote (*Zeitschrift für spekulative Theologie*, 1836): 'Looking into the past, like looking into the future, is an act of divination; and if a prophet can be described as a historian of the future, then a historian is a prophet of the past.'

16 Leibniz (1646–1716) argued that God's foreknowledge did not imply predestination, because he had created only one of an infinite number of possible worlds. See his *Theodicy*, 1710, §§ 406–16.

17 See Journals and Papers, III A 107 (1841): 'Aristotle's thought that philosophy begins with wonder rather than with doubt, as in our day, is a positive point of departure for philosophy.'

18 These terms are explained by Diogenes Laertius as follows: 'All these were called Pyrrhonians after the name of their master, but Aporetics, Sceptics, Ephectics, and even Zetetics, from their principles, if we may call them such – Zetetics or seekers because they were ever seeking truth, Sceptics were inquirers because they were always looking for a solution and never finding one, Ephectics or doubters because of the state of mind which followed their inquiry, namely suspension of judgement, and finally Aporetics or those in perplexity, for not only they but even the dogmatic philosophers were often perplexed.' See *Lives of the Philosophers*, IX, 69–70.

19 The text quotes the Greek, *telos de hoi skeptikoi phasi ton epochon, e skias tropon epakolouthei e ataraxia*; Diogenes Laertius, *Lives of the Philosophers*, IX, 107.

20 A reference to F. H. Jacobi (1743–1819), who argued that causation is a matter of belief rather than knowledge.

21 Climacus here repeats the Greek expression *philosophia ephektiké*; see above, n. 18.

7

The Concept of Anxiety

One of the greatest difficulties for religious belief is the existence of evil and sin: why do they tempt us, what do they mean, and what purpose can they serve in the overall plan of the universe? The issue had already been touched on in the opening chapter of *Philosophical Fragments*, with its distinction between the Socratic teacher, who wishes to recall us to an inborn understanding of truth, and the Christian teacher, who seeks to remind us of our utter erroneousness and unfathomable guilt. As sinners, we cannot hope to reach the truth by a steady process of recollection; instead we have to hope that it will manifest itself to us like a meteor in the night sky, an unexpected arrival from beyond the limits of our world: in other words we depend upon the surprising illumination of 'the moment'.

The Concept of Anxiety (*Begrebet Angest*) – which was published on 17 June 1844, four days after *Philosophical Fragments* – returned to the problem of sin, but approached it from a diametrically different point of view. For one thing, it presented the Socratic method as the essence of truly Christian communication rather than its negation, arguing that by allowing 'the single individual' to speak 'as the single individual to the single individual' it enables us to 'own' or 'appropriate' our thoughts.[1] And secondly, *The Concept of Anxiety* was concerned not with the moment of truth but with what might be called the anti-moment: the point at which sinfulness and error came into existence and insinuated themselves into our lives.

According to Genesis, the world as God first created it was wholly good, and Adam was the best thing in it. God placed Adam in the garden of Eden 'to dress it and to keep it', but he also imposed a curious condition.

The Lord God commanded the man, saying, Of every tree of the garden thou mayest freely eat:

But of the tree of the knowledge of good and evil, thou shalt not eat of it: for in the day that thou eatest thereof thou shalt surely die.[2]

After issuing his warning, God set about creating birds and beasts to keep Adam company, and eventually a woman as well. She became his wife, and in their innocence they 'were not ashamed'. But then Eve had the misfortune to encounter a serpent.

Now the serpent was more subtil than any beast of the field which the Lord God had made. And he said unto the woman, Yea, hath God said, Ye shall not eat of every tree of the garden?

And the woman said unto the serpent, We may eat of the fruit of the trees of the garden:

But of the fruit of the tree which is in the midst of the garden, God hath said, Ye shall not eat of it, neither shall ye touch it, lest ye die.

And the serpent said unto the woman, Ye shall not surely die:

For God doth know that in the day ye eat thereof, then your eyes shall be opened, and ye shall be as gods, knowing good and evil.

And when the woman saw that the tree was good for food, and that it was pleasant to the eyes, and a tree to be desired to make one wise, she took of the fruit thereof, and did eat, and gave also unto her husband with her; and he did eat.

And the eyes of them both were opened, and they knew that they were naked; and they sewed fig leaves together, and made themselves aprons.

And they heard the voice of the Lord God walking in the garden in the cool of the day: and Adam and his wife hid themselves from the presence of the Lord God amongst the trees of the garden.[3]

Adam and Eve hid from God because they were ashamed. They knew they had disobeyed their creator, and perhaps they guessed that through their disobedience they had brought a taint not only upon themselves but on creation itself. Adam blamed the catastrophe on Eve, who in turn blamed the serpent, who no doubt retorted that it was God's fault for setting a trap for them in the first place. But God decided to condemn them all.

The Lord God said unto the serpent, Because thou hast done this, thou art cursed above all cattle, and above every beast of the field; upon thy belly shalt thou go, and dust shalt thou eat all the days of thy life. . . .

Unto the woman he said, I will greatly multiply thy sorrow and thy conception; in sorrow thou shalt bring forth children; and thy desire shall be to thy husband, and he shall rule over thee.

And unto Adam he said, Because thou hast hearkened unto the voice of thy wife, and hast eaten of the tree, of which I commanded thee, saying, Thou shalt not eat of it: cursed is the ground for thy sake; in sorrow shalt thou eat of it all the days of thy life; . . .

In the sweat of thy face shalt thou eat bread, till thou return unto the ground; for out of it wast thou taken: for dust thou art, and unto dust shalt thou return. . . .

Therefore the Lord God sent him forth from the garden of Eden, to till the ground from whence he was taken.[4]

And the punishment was apparently to have no end. Adam and Eve were blessed with two sons, but then they quarrelled: Abel was murdered by Cain, who in turn was banished by God. Sin was released into the world, evil was at large, and innocence irretrievably lost.

Christianity has always presented itself as a solution to the Old Testament riddle of the origin of sin. Early in the fifth century, St Augustine formulated the dogma of the 'fall of man': Adam's disobedience had corrupted the entire human race, he thought, and as a result all of us are born into a state of inherited guilt or 'original sin'; but Christ had suffered pain and humiliation on earth in order to redeem our hereditary debt, allowing all those who believed in him and his resurrection to be saved from evil and admitted to eternal life.

As an explanation of the origin and meaning of sin, however, the Genesis story on its own is liable to leave us unsatisfied, and its Christian sequel does not help much either. Why did God have to create a 'tree of the knowledge of good and evil' in the first place, and why did he forbid Adam to taste its fruit? How could Adam be expected to understand the prohibition when it was only by tasting the forbidden fruit that he would learn the difference between good and evil? How could he shun death when he had no idea what it was? And given that Adam was innocent until the moment he sinned, why did he have to be expelled from Eden – and not only him but his wife as well, and their future children, not to mention the children of every future generation, who would all be condemned to pick up his burden of guilt as if it were their own?

The starting point of *The Concept of Anxiety* was the observation that the biblical account of the origin of sin is hopelessly circular, since it 'boils down to the proposition that *Sin entered the world through a sin*', that is to say 'through Adam's first sin'. A modern understanding will not have much patience with such circular explanations; it will dismiss them as childish myths, preferring to project a hint of incipient sinfulness into paradise to prepare the way for the fall, for in this way 'the circle is interpreted as a straight line, and everything now follows quite naturally'.[5] But from the point of view of *The Concept of Anxiety*, the modern dream of 'eradicating all myths' was itself a myth – a myth of the understanding – and 'no age has been as good as our own at generating myths of the understanding'.[6] We would be better off, in short, if we stuck with the circular idea that the origin of sin is sin.

As the title of the book makes clear, this deliberately circular account of the origin of sin will be elaborated by reference to anxiety, or rather to the 'concept' of anxiety. The Danish for 'concept' is *begreb*, which corresponds to the German *Begriff* – Hegel's word for the ultimate logical systematization of experience and the world. In the beginning, for Hegel, there was 'pure being', and it was utterly featureless, abstract and 'immediate' – immediate in the sense of lacking the 'mediations' which are necessary if its various regions are to be clearly differentiated and properly related to each other. Mediation was the process through which the implicit potentialities of the original state were gradually realized until at last it achieved the infinite concreteness of 'the concept'; and conversely the concept was the explicit elaboration of the inner truth hidden within immediate being, the means through which everything would eventually be given its proper, rational place in the ultimate scheme of things. But if, as Hegel apparently thought, sin is not a genuine entity, but only a misunderstanding of goodness – a misunderstanding which was always going to be redeemed by Jesus and cleared up in the course of humanity's spiritual progress through time – there could be no such thing, strictly speaking, as a 'concept' of sin, still less of 'innocence', which from a Hegelian point of view is sheer undifferentiated immediacy, mere nothingness.[7]

The author of *The Concept of Anxiety* was acutely aware of the paradox of trying to conceptualize what is supposed to be beyond the scope of conceptualization. His name was Vigilius Haufniensis – which, translated out of Latin, means 'the night-watchman of Copenhagen'. Vigilius is no Johannes Climacus, and certainly not a Hegelian; he sees himself simply as a defender of 'dogmatics', or the sector of theology which enunciates the basic standards of orthodoxy (such as the doctrine of original sin), and he takes it for granted that the starting point must be 'to forget what Hegel discovered'.[8] He also likes to pick quarrels with Kierkegaard's other pseudonyms, as of course they often did with each other. And although he is by far the least appealing of them – heavy-handed, irascible, humourless and dryly dialectical – he nevertheless has a substantial argument to make.

In the first of his five chapters he surveys various received interpretations of Adam's disobedience and the origin of sin, complaining that they blur the obvious difference between Adam's situation as the very first sinner and our own as inheritors of a long tradition of sinning. It is no use trying to explain the first sin by treating it as the natural consequence of something else, such as sensuality, for sin would not be sin if it did not come out of the blue – suddenly, through a 'leap' or an act of 'freedom'.[9] And if Adam's first sin was unprecedented and extraordinary, so too, according to Vigilius, are all of ours.

If I were granted just one wish, then I would wish that no reader would be so deep as to ask: What if Adam had not sinned? . . . The foolishness of the question lies not so much in the question itself as in the fact that it is directed to science . . . For sin is precisely the transcendence, the *discrimen rerum* [critical moment] through which sin enters into a single individual as a single individual. Sin never comes into the world differently, nor has it ever done so. So when a single individual is foolish enough to ask about sin as if it were irrelevant to him, he asks only as a fool. . . . In a way it is the simplest thing in the world, but it has been turned into the most difficult. The common people understand it quite correctly, in their own way, because they realize that it was not just six thousand years ago that sin came into the world. But science has promulgated it as a prize problem which has not yet been fully resolved. How sin came into the world, each of us can understand for ourselves; if we try to learn it from someone else, we will *eo ipso* misunderstand it.

Vigilius concludes that if any science can help us understand sin it is psychology – but a special kind of psychology, one which 'confesses that it cannot explain it, and that it *cannot* and *will not* explain more'.[10] The inquiry will be – as the subtitle of *The Concept of Anxiety* puts it – '*a simple psychologically-orienting deliberation*' (*en simpel psychologisk-paapegende Overveielse*), rather than an external and conceptual description. For the difficulty of explaining sin, as the Genesis story makes clear, is that we have to understand what no Hegelian could countenance: that it arises from innocence.

Innocence is ignorance. It is far from the pure being of immediacy, but it *is* ignorance. When ignorance is viewed from outside, it is defined in terms of knowledge; but to ignorance, this is of absolutely no concern.[11]

The observant psychologist must therefore enter into the undifferentiated territory where innocence borders on sin and allow it to come to an understanding of itself on its own terms.

Psychological observers need more agility than tightrope dancers; they must be able to incline and bend themselves towards others, imitating their postures; and their silence in the moment of intimacy should be both seductive and voluptuous, so that what is concealed can have the satisfaction of slipping out to converse with itself in this artificial privacy and silence. They [psychological observers] must therefore have a poetic originality of soul with which they can create both totality and regularity out of materials which are never more than partially and irregularly present in the individual. . . . For that reason they will mimic within themselves every mood and psychic state which they discover in the other. Then they will try to deceive the other by their mimicry; they will see if they can carry the other along into a further development, a development which will be their own creation on the strength of the Idea. . . . If this is done properly, then the other will experience indescribable satisfaction and release, rather as lunatics do when someone understands their obsession, grasps it poetically, and proceeds to develop it further.[12]

Vigilius is apparently claiming that it is through just such an activity of imitative listening that he has arrived at his concept of *angest* or anxiety. Anxiety as he understands it is quite different from fear, since fear is always a definite feeling about a known danger, whereas anxiety is a state of cloudy unknowingness, of baffled apprehensiveness about possibility in general: about everything – or rather about nothing.

But what is the effect of nothing? It gives rise to anxiety. This is the profound secret of innocence, that it is at the same time anxiety. The spirit projects its own actuality as if in a dream, but this actuality is nothing, and innocence always sees this nothing outside itself.[13]

Anxiety or apprehensiveness is an innocent sense of oneself as possibility rather than actuality. 'Anxiety is not a category of necessity, but it is not a category of freedom either: it is entangled freedom, where freedom is not free in itself but entangled – and entangled not by necessity, but by itself.' The origin of sinfulness, Vigilius concludes, is neither absolute necessity nor arbitrary wilfulness, but sheer possibility. Our anxious apprehension of possibility is not the consequence of sin, but its ground: without it, there would be no disobedience and no fall; indeed – he adds rather daringly – there would be no such things as sexuality, or sexual difference, or history.[14]

The trouble with this entire discussion, of course, is that it evidently leaves the problem of the transition from innocence to wickedness as puzzling as ever. From Vigilius's point of view, however, the source of the difficulty is our desire for an explanation of evil, rather than his inability to furnish us with one. Proverbial wisdom may tells us that the 'root of all evil' is cupidity, or alternatively sensuality, covetousness, greed, property or money – or indeed boredom, as the author of 'Crop Rotation' has suggested;[15] but Vigilius insists that the guilty party – the original sinner – is none other than innocence itself.

The biblical story of evil's entry into the garden of Eden is obviously imperfect, because Adam in his innocence could not be expected to understand God's warnings about the consequences of disobedience; indeed it is preposterous to suppose that God would have spoken in the knowledge that he could not be understood. However, the imperfection will be removed, Vigilius says, if we realize that God must have kept his counsel and said nothing. We need to recognize that the story does not trace sin to some external source, but takes place entirely within us, within language, within Adam. 'The imperfection of the tale ... will disappear', Vigilius explains, 'if we realise that the speaker could be language, and that it is Adam himself who is speaking.'[16]

Notes

1 See below, p. 187.
2 Genesis 2, 16–17.
3 Genesis 3, 1–8.
4 Genesis 3, 14, 16–17, 19, 23.
5 *The Concept of Anxiety*, I, §2; cf. KW VIII, p. 32.
6 Ibid., I, §6; cf. KW VIII, p. 46.
7 Ibid., I, §3; cf. KW VIII, p. 37.
8 Ibid., I, §3; cf. KW VIII, p. 35.
9 Ibid., I, §2; cf. KW VIII, p. 32.
10 Ibid., I, §6; cf. KW VIII, pp. 50–1.
11 Ibid., I, §3; cf. KW VIII, p. 37.
12 Ibid., II; cf. KW VIII, pp. 54–6.
13 Ibid., I, §5; cf. KW VIII, p. 41.
14 Ibid., I, §6; cf. KW VIII, p. 49.
15 See above, pp. 59–71.
16 Ibid., I, §6; cf. KW VIII, p. 47.

The Concept of Anxiety: A Simple Psychologically-orienting Deliberation on the Dogmatic Issue of Hereditary Sin by Vigilius Haufniensis

Preface

In my opinion, one who intends to write a book ought to consider carefully the subject about which he wishes to write. Nor would it be inappropriate for him to acquaint himself as far as possible with what has already been written on the subject. If on his way he should meet an individual who has dealt exhaustively and satisfactorily with one or another aspect of that subject, he would do well to rejoice as does the bridegroom's friend who stands by and rejoices greatly as he hears the bridegroom's voice.[1] When he has done this in complete silence and with the enthusiasm of a love that ever seeks solitude, nothing more is needed; then he will carefully write his book

The first English translation of *Begrebet Angest* was by Walter Lowrie, and appeared under the title *The Concept of Dread* on the centenary of the publication of the original, in 1944. (A second edition, revised by Howard A. Johnson, was published in 1957.) These versions have now been overshadowed by the more careful but less relaxed work of Reidar Thomte and Albert B. Anderson, which appeared in 1980, under the title of *The Concept of Anxiety*, as vol. VIII of *Kierkegaard's Writings*. The four selections printed here – 'Preface', 'Introduction', the opening section of chapter 3 ('Anxiety as the Consequence of that Sin which is Absence of the Consciousness of Sin') and the whole of the fifth and final chapter ('Anxiety as Saving through Faith') – are reproduced from this translation.

as spontaneously as a bird sings its song, and if someone derives benefit or joy from it, so much the better. Then he will publish the book, carefree and at ease and without any sense of self-importance, as if he had brought everything to a conclusion or as if all the generations of the earth were to be blessed by his book.[2] Each generation has its own task and need not trouble itself unduly by being everything to previous and succeeding generations. Just as each day's trouble is sufficient for the day,[3] so each individual in a generation has enough to do in taking care of himself and does not need to embrace the whole contemporary age with his paternal solicitude or assume that era and epoch begin with his book, and still less with the New Year's torch of his promise or with the intimations of his farseeing promises or with the referral of his reassurance to a currency of doubtful value.[4] Not everyone who is stoop-shouldered is an Atlas, nor did he become such by supporting a world. Not everyone who says Lord, Lord, shall enter the kingdom of heaven.[5] Not everyone who offers himself as surety for the whole contemporary age proves by such action that he is reliable and can vouch for himself. Not everyone who shouts *Bravo, schwere Noth, Gottsblitz, bravissimo* has therefore understood himself and his admiration.

Concerning my own humble person, I frankly confess that as an author I am a king without a country and also, in fear and much trembling, an author without any claims. If to a noble envy or jealous criticism it seems too much that I bear a Latin name, I shall gladly assume the name Christen Madsen. Nothing could please me more than to be regarded as a layman who indeed speculates but is still far removed from Speculation, although I am as devout in my belief in authority as the Roman was tolerant in his worship of God. When it comes to human authority, I am a fetish worshipper and will worship anyone with equal piety, but with one proviso, that it be made sufficiently clear by a beating of drums that he is the one I must worship and that it is he who is the authority and *Imprimatur* for the current year.[6] The decision is beyond my understanding, whether it takes place by lottery or balloting, or whether the honour is passed around so that each individual has his turn as authority, like a representative of the burghers on the board of arbitration.

Beyond this I have nothing to add except to wish everyone who shares my view and also everyone who does not, everyone who reads the book and also everyone who has had enough in reading the Preface, a well meant farewell.

Respectfully
Vigilius Haufniensis
Copenhagen.

Introduction: The Sense in which the Subject of our Deliberation is a Task of Psychological Interest and the Sense in which, after having been the Task and Interest of Psychology, it Points directly to Dogmatics

The view that every scientific issue within the larger compass of science has its definite place, its measure and its limit, and thereby precisely its harmonious blending in the whole as well as its legitimate participation in what is expressed by the whole, is not merely a *pium desiderium* [pious wish] that ennobles the man of science by its enthusiastic and melancholy infatuation. This view is not merely a sacred duty that commits him to the service of the totality and bids him renounce lawlessness and the adventurous desire to lose sight of the mainland; it also serves the interest of every more specialized deliberation, for when the deliberation forgets where it properly belongs, as language often expresses with striking ambiguity, it forgets itself and becomes something else, and thereby acquires the dubious perfectibility of being able to become anything and everything. By failing to proceed in a scientific manner and by not taking care to see that the individual issues do not outrun one another, as if it were a matter of arriving first at the masquerade, a person occasionally achieves a brilliance and amazes others by giving the impression that he has already comprehended that which is still very remote. At times he makes a vague agreement with things that differ. The gain is always avenged, as is every unlawful acquisition which cannot be owned legally or scientifically.

Thus when an author entitles the last section of his *Logic* 'Actuality', he thereby gains the advantage of making it appear that in logic the highest has already been achieved, or if one prefers, the lowest. In the meantime, the loss is obvious, for neither logic nor actuality is served by placing actuality in the *Logic*. Actuality is not served thereby, for contingency, which is an essential part of the actual, cannot be admitted within the realm of logic. Logic is not served thereby, for if logic has thought actuality, it has included something that it cannot assimilate, it has appropriated at the beginning what it should only *praedisponere* [presuppose]. The penalty is obvious. Every deliberation about the nature of actuality is rendered difficult, and for a long time perhaps made impossible, since the word 'actuality' must first have time to collect itself, time to forget the mistake.

Thus when in dogmatics *faith* is called the *immediate* without any further qualification, there is gained the advantage that everybody is convinced of the necessity of not stopping with faith. The admission may be elicited even from one who subscribes to orthodoxy, because at first he perhaps does not discern the misunderstanding, that it does not have its source in a subsequent error but in that fundamental error (*prōton pseudos*). The loss is quite obvious. Faith loses by being regarded as the immediate, since it has been deprived of what lawfully belongs to it, namely, its historical presupposition. Dogmatics loses thereby, because it does not begin where it properly should begin, namely, within the scope of an earlier beginning. Instead of presupposing an earlier beginning, it ignores this and begins without ceremony, just as if it were logic. Logic does indeed begin with something produced by the subtlest abstraction, namely, what is most elusive: the immediate. What is quite proper in logic, namely, that immediacy is *eo ipso* cancelled, becomes in dogmatics idle talk. Could it ever occur to anyone to stop with the immediate (with no further qualification) since the immediate is annulled [*ophævet*] at the very moment it is mentioned, just as a somnambulist wakes up at the very moment his name is mentioned? Thus when someone finds, and almost solely in propaedeutic investigation, the word 'reconciliation' [*forsoning*] used to designate speculative knowledge, or to designate the identity of the perceiving subject and the object perceived, or to designate the subjective-objective, etc., it is obvious that the author is brilliant and that by means of this brilliance he has explained every riddle, especially to all those who even in matters of science use less care than they do in daily life, where they listen carefully to the words of the riddle before they attempt to guess its meaning. Otherwise he gains the incomparable reputation of having posed by virtue of his explanation a new riddle, namely, how it could ever occur to any man that this might be the explanation. The notion that thought on the whole has reality was assumed by all ancient and medieval philosophy. With Kant, this assumption became doubtful. If it is now assumed that Hegelian philosophy has actually grasped Kant's scepticism thoroughly (something that might continue to remain a great question despite all that Hegel and his school have done with the help of the slogan 'method and manifestation' to conceal what Schelling with the slogan 'intellectual intuition and construction' openly acknowledged as a new point of departure) and now has reconstructed the earlier in a higher form and in such a way that thought does not possess reality by virtue of a presupposition – does it therefore also follow that this reality, which is consciously brought forth by thought, is a reconciliation? In that case, philosophy has only been brought back to where the beginning was made in the old days, when reconciliation did in fact have enormous significance. There is an old, respectable philosophical terminology: thesis, antithesis, synthesis. A more recent terminology has been chosen in which 'mediation' takes the third place. Is this such an extraordinary advance? 'Mediation' is equivocal, for it suggests simultaneously the relation between the two and the result of the relation, that in which the two relate themselves to each other as well as the two that related themselves to each other. It indicates movement as well as repose. Whether this is a perfection must be determined by subjecting mediation to a more profound dialectical test, but, unfortunately, this is something for which we still must wait. One rejects synthesis and says 'mediation'. Very well. Brilliance, however, demands more – one says 'reconciliation', and what is the result? The propaedeutic investigations are not served by it, for naturally they gain as little in clarity as does the truth, as little as a man's soul gains in salvation by having a title conferred upon him. On the contrary, two sciences, ethics and dogmatics, become radically confused, especially when after the introduction of the term 'reconciliation' it is further pointed out that logic and the dogmatical *logos* correspond to each other, and that logic is the proper doctrine of *logos*.[7] Ethics and dogmatics struggle over reconciliation in a *confinium* [border area] fraught with fate. Repentance and guilt torment forth reconciliation ethically, while dogmatics, in its receptivity to the proffered reconciliation, has the historically concrete immediacy with which it begins its discourse in the great dialogue of science. And now what will be the result? Presumably language will celebrate a great sabbatical year in which speech and thought may be at rest so that we can begin at the beginning.

In logic, the *negative* is used as the impelling power to bring movement into all things. One must have movement in logic no matter how it is brought about, and no matter by what means, whether good or evil. The negative lends a hand, and what the negative cannot accomplish, play on words and platitudes can, just as when the negative itself becomes a play on words.* In logic, no movement must *come about*, for logic is, and whatever is logical only *is*. This impotence of the logical consists in the transition of logic into becom-

---

* *Exempli gratia:* '*Wesen ist was ist gewesen*'; *ist gewesen* is a *tempus præteritum* [past tense] of *seyn; ergo,* '*Wesen ist das aufgehobene Seyn*': the *Seyn* that has been. [For example: 'Essence is what has been'; 'has been' is the past tense of 'to be'; *ergo,* 'essence is annulled being': i.e. being that has been. See Hegel, *Science of Logic*, Book 2, 'The Doctrine of Essence', Introduction and opening of chapter 1, A.] This is a logical movement! If anyone would take the trouble to collect and put together all the strange pixies and goblins who like busy clerks bring about movement in Hegelian logic (such as this is in itself and as it has been improved by the [Hegelian] school), a later age would perhaps be surprised to see that what are regarded as discarded witticisms once played an important role in logic, not as incidental explanations and ingenuous remarks but as masters of movement, which made Hegel's logic something of a miracle and gave logical thought feet to move on without anyone's being able to observe them. Just as Lulu [in Friedrich Kuhlau's opera *Lulu* (1824)] comes running without anyone's being able to observe the mechanism of movement, so the long mantle of admiration conceals the machinery of logical movement. To have brought movement into logic is the merit of Hegel. In comparison with this, it is hardly worth mentioning the unforgettable merit that was Hegel's, namely, that in many ways he corrected the categorial definitions and their arrangement, a merit he disdained in order to run aimlessly.

ing, where existence [*tilværelse*] and actuality come forth. So when logic becomes deeply absorbed in the concretion of the categories, that which was from the beginning is ever the same. Every movement, if for the moment one wishes to use this expression, is an immanent movement, which in a profound sense is no movement at all. One can easily convince oneself of this by considering that the concept of movement is itself a transcendence that has no place in logic. The negative, then, is immanent in the movement, is something vanishing, is that which is annulled. If everything comes about in this manner, nothing comes about at all, and the negative becomes an illusion. Nevertheless, precisely in order to make something come about in logic, the negative becomes something more; it becomes that which brings forth the opposition, not negation but a contraposition. And thus the negative is not the stillness of the immanent movement; it is '*the necessary other*', indeed, something that may be very necessary for logic in order to bring about movement, but it is something that the negative is not. Turning from logic to ethics, we find again the same indefatigable negative that is active in the entire Hegelian philosophy. Here one is astonished to discover that the negative is the evil. As a result, confusion is in full swing and there are no limits to cleverness, and what Madame Staël-Holstein has said of Schelling's philosophy, namely, that it makes a man clever for his whole life, applies in every way to Hegelianism.[8] One can see how illogical the movements must be in logic, since the negative is the evil, and how unethical they must be in ethics, since the evil is the negative. In logic they are too much and in ethics too little. They fit nowhere if they are supposed to fit both. If ethics has no other transcendence, it is essentially logic. If logic is to have as much transcendence as common propriety requires of ethics, it is no longer logic.

What has been developed here is probably too complicated in proportion to the space that it occupies yet, considering the importance of the subject it deals with, it is far too lengthy; however, it is in no way extraneous, because the details are selected in order to allude to the subject of the book. The examples are taken from a greater realm, but what happens in the greater can repeat itself in the lesser, and the misunderstanding is similar, even if there are less harmful consequences. He who presumes to develop the System is responsible for much, but he who writes a monograph can and also ought to be faithful over a little.

The present work has set as its task the psychological treatment of the concept of 'anxiety', but in such a way that it constantly keeps *in mente* [in mind] and before its eye the dogma of hereditary sin. Accordingly, it must also, although tacitly so, deal with the concept of sin. Sin, however, is no subject for psychological concern, and only by submitting to the service of a misplaced brilliance could it be dealt with psychologically. Sin has its specific place, or more correctly, it has no place, and this is its specific nature. When sin is treated in a place other than its own, it is altered by being subjected to a nonessential refraction of reflection. The concept is altered, and thereby the mood that properly corresponds to the correct concept★ is also disturbed, and instead of the endurance of the true mood there is the fleeting phantom of false moods. Thus when sin is brought into aesthetics, the mood becomes either light-minded or melancholy, for the category in which sin lies is that of contradiction, and this is either comic or tragic. The mood is therefore altered, because the mood that corresponds to sin is earnestness. The concept of sin is also altered, because, whether it becomes comic or tragic, it becomes in any case something that endures, or something nonessential that is annulled, whereas, according to its true concept, sin is to be overcome. In a deeper sense, the comic and the tragic have no enemy but only a bogeyman at which one either weeps or laughs.

If sin is dealt with in metaphysics, the mood becomes that of dialectical uniformity and disinterestedness, which ponder sin as something that cannot withstand the scrutiny of thought. The concept of sin is also altered, for sin is indeed to be overcome, yet not as something to which thought is unable to give life, but as that which is, and as such concerns every man.

If sin is dealt with in psychology, the mood becomes that of persistent observation, like the fearlessness of a secret agent, but not that of the victorious flight of earnestness out of sin. The concept becomes a different concept, for sin becomes a state. However, sin is not a state. Its idea is that its concept is continually annulled. As a state (*de potentia* [according to possibility]), it is not, but *de actu* or *in actu* [according to actuality or in actuality] it is, again and again. The mood of psychology would be antipathetic curiosity, whereas the proper mood is earnestness expressed in courageous resistance. The mood of psychology is that of a discovering anxiety, and in its anxiety psychology portrays sin, while again and again it is in anxiety over the portrayal that it itself brings forth. When sin is dealt with in this manner, it becomes the stronger, because psychology relates itself to it in a feminine way. That this state has its truth is certain; that it occurs more or less in every human life before the ethical manifests itself is certain. But

★   That science, just as much as poetry and art, presupposes a mood in the creator as well as in the observer, and that an error in the modulation is just as disturbing as an error in the development of thought, have been entirely forgotten in our time, when inwardness has been completely forgotten, and also the category of appropriation [*tilegnelsen*], because of the joy over all the glory men thought they possessed or in their greed have given up as did the dog that preferred the shadow.[9] Yet every error gives birth to its own enemy. Outside of itself, the error of thought has dialectics as its enemy, and outside of itself, the absence or falsification of mood has the comical as its enemy.

in being considered in this manner sin does not become what it is, but a more or a less.

Whenever the issue of sin is dealt with, one can observe by the very mood whether the concept is the correct one. For instance, whenever sin is spoken of as a disease, an abnormality, a poison, or a disharmony, the concept is falsified.

Sin does not properly belong in any science, but it is the subject of the sermon, in which the single individual speaks as the single individual to the single individual. In our day, scientific self-importance has tricked pastors into becoming something like professorial clerks who also serve science and find it beneath their dignity to preach. Is it any wonder then that preaching has come to be regarded as a very lowly art? But to preach is really the most difficult of all arts and is essentially the art that Socrates praised, the art of being able to converse. It goes without saying that the need is not for someone in the congregation to provide an answer, or that it would be of help continually to introduce a respondent. What Socrates criticised in the Sophists, when he made the distinction that they indeed knew how to make speeches but not how to converse, was that they could talk at length about every subject but lacked the element of appropriation.[10] Appropriation is precisely the secret of conversation.

Corresponding to the concept of sin is earnestness. Now ethics should be a science in which sin might be expected to find a place. But here there is a great difficulty. Ethics is still an ideal science, and not only in the sense that every science is ideal. Ethics proposes to bring ideality into actuality. On the other hand, it is not the nature of its movement to raise actuality up into ideality. Ethics points to ideality as a task and assumes that every man possesses the requisite conditions. Thus ethics develops a contradiction, inasmuch as it makes clear both the difficulty and the impossibility. What is said of the law is also true of ethics: it is a disciplinarian that demands, and by its demands only judges but does not bring forth life. Only Greek ethics made an exception, and that was because it was not ethics in the proper sense but retained an aesthetic factor [*moment*]. This appears clearly in its definition of virtue and in what Aristotle frequently, also in *Nicomachean Ethics*, states with amiable Greek naïveté, namely, that virtue alone does not make a man happy and content, but he must have health, friends, and earthly goods and be happy in his family. The more ideal ethics is, the better. It must not permit itself to be distracted by the babble that it is useless to require the impossible. For even to listen to such talk is unethical and is something for which ethics has neither *time* nor *opportunity*. Ethics will have nothing to do with bargaining; nor can one in this way reach actuality. To reach actuality, the whole movement must be reversed. This ideal character of ethics is what tempts one to use first metaphysical, then aesthetic, and then psychological categories in the treatment of it. But ethics, more than any other science, must resist such temptations. It is, therefore, impossible for anyone to write an ethics without having altogether different categories in reserve.

Sin, then, belongs to ethics only insofar as upon this concept it is shipwrecked with the aid of repentance.* If ethics is to include sin, its ideality

---

* In his work *Fear and Trembling* (Copenhagen: 1843), Johannes de Silentio makes several observations concerning this point. In this book, the author several times allows the desired ideality of aesthetics to be shipwrecked on the required ideality of ethics, in order through these collisions to bring to light the religious ideality as the ideality that precisely is the ideality of actuality, and therefore just as desirable as that of aesthetics and not as impossible as the ideality of ethics. This is accomplished in such a way that the religious ideality breaks forth in the dialectical leap and in the positive mood – 'Behold all things have become new' – as well as in the negative mood that is the passion of the absurd to which the concept 'repetition' corresponds. Either all of existence comes to an end in the demand of ethics, or the condition is provided and the whole of life and of existence begins anew, not through an immanent continuity with the former existence, which is a contradiction, but through a transcendence. This transcendence separates repetition from the former existence by such a chasm that one can only figuratively say that the former and the latter relate themselves to each other as the totality of living creatures in the ocean relates itself to those in the air and to those upon the earth. Yet, according to the opinion of some natural scientists, the former as a prototype prefigures in its imperfection all that the latter reveals. With regard to this category, one may consult *Repetition* by Constantin Constantius (Copenhagen, 1843). This is no doubt a witty book, as the author also intended it to be. To my knowledge, he is indeed the first to have a lively understanding of 'repetition' and to have allowed the pregnancy of the concept to be seen in the explanation of the relation of the ethnical [*ethnisk*, pagan] and the Christian, by directing attention to the invisible point and to the *discrimen rerum* [critical moment] where one science breaks against another until a new science comes to light. But what he has discovered he has concealed again by arraying the concept in the jest of an analogous conception. What has motivated him to do this is difficult to say, or more correctly, difficult to understand. He himself mentions that he writes in this manner 'so that the heretics would not understand him'. Since he wanted to occupy himself with repetition only aesthetically and psychologically, everything had to be arranged humorously so as to bring about the impression that the word in one instant means everything and in the next instant the most insignificant of things, and the transition, or rather the constant falling down from the clouds, is motivated by its farcical opposite. In the meantime, he has stated the whole matter very precisely: 'repetition is the *interest* [*interesse*] of metaphysics and also its undoing; it is the principle behind every ethical opinion, and the *conditio sine qua non* [necessary condition] of every problem in dogmatics'. [See above, p. 129.] The first statement has reference to the thesis that metaphysics as such is disinterested, something that Kant had said about aesthetics. As soon as interest steps forth, metaphysics steps aside. For this reason, the word is italicized. In actuality, the whole interest of subjectivity steps forth, and now metaphysics runs aground. If repetition is not posited, ethics becomes a binding power. No doubt it is for this reason that the author states that repetition is the watchword in every ethical view. If repetition is not posited, dogmatics cannot exist at all, for repetition begins in faith, and faith is the organ for issues of dogma. In the realm of nature, repetition is present in its immovable necessity. In the realm of the spirit, the task is not to wrest a change from

comes to an end. The more ethics remains in its ideality, and never becomes so inhuman as to lose sight of actuality, but corresponds to actuality by presenting itself as the task for every man in such a way that it will make him the true and the whole man, the man in an eminent sense [*kat' exokhén*], the more it increases the tension of the difficulty. In the struggle to actualize the task of ethics, sin shows itself not as something that belongs only accidentally to the accidental individual, but as something that withdraws deeper and deeper as a deeper and deeper presupposition, as a presupposition that goes beyond the individual. Then all is lost for ethics, and ethics has helped to bring about the loss of all. A category that lies entirely beyond its reach has appeared. *Hereditary sin* makes everything still more desperate, that is, it removes the difficulty, yet not with the help of ethics but with the help of *dogmatics*. As all ancient knowledge and speculation was based on the presupposition that thought has reality [*realitet*], so all ancient ethics was based on the presupposition that virtue can be realized. Sin's scepticism is altogether foreign to paganism. Sin is for the ethical consciousness what error is for the knowledge of it – the particular exception that proves nothing.

With dogmatics begins the science that – in contrast to that science called ideal *stricte* [in the strict sense], namely, ethics – proceeds from actuality. It begins with the actual in order to raise it up into ideality. It does not deny the presence of sin; on the contrary, it presupposes it and explains it by presupposing hereditary sin. However, since dogmatics is very seldom treated

(*cont'd from p. 188*) repetition or to find oneself moderately comfortable during the repetition, as if spirit stood only in an external relation to the repetition of spirit (according to which good and evil would alternate like summer and winter), but to transform repetition into something inward, into freedom's own task, into its highest interest, so that while everything else changes, it can actually realize repetition. At this point the finite spirit despairs. This is something Constantin has suggested by stepping aside himself and by allowing repetition to break forth in the young man by virtue of the religious. For this reason Constantin mentions several times that repetition is a religious category, too transcendent for him, that it is the movement by virtue of the absurd, and it is further stated that eternity is the true repetition. [See KW VI, p. 221.] All of this Professor Heiberg failed to notice. [J. L. Heiberg had published a review of *Repetition* in 1844.] Instead, through his learning, which like his *New Year's Gift* is superbly elegant and neat, he kindly wished to help this work [*Repetition*] become a tasteful and elegant triviality by pompously bringing the matter to the point where Constantin begins, the point where the aesthetic in *Either/Or* had brought it in 'Crop Rotation'. [See above, pp. 59–71.] If Constantin had actually felt himself flattered by enjoying the singular honour of having been brought into such undeniably select company in this manner, he must, in my opinion, since he wrote the book, have gone stark mad. But if, on the other hand, an author such as he, writing to be misunderstood, forgot himself and did not have ataraxia enough to count it to his credit that Professor Heiberg had failed to understand him, he must again be stark mad. This is something I need not fear, since the circumstance that hitherto he has made no reply to Professor Heiberg indicates sufficiently that he understands himself.

purely, hereditary sin is often brought within its confines in such a way that the impression of the heterogeneous originality of dogmatics does not always come clearly into view but becomes confused. This also happens when one finds in it a dogma concerning angels, concerning the Holy Scriptures, etc. Therefore dogmatics must not explain hereditary sin but rather explain it by presupposing it, like that vortex about which Greek speculation concerning nature had so much to say, a moving something that no science can grasp.

That such is the case with dogmatics will readily be granted if once again time is taken to understand Schleiermacher's immortal service to this science.[11] He was left behind long ago when men chose Hegel. Yet Schleiermacher was a thinker in the beautiful Greek sense, a thinker who spoke only of what he knew. Hegel, on the contrary, despite all his outstanding ability and stupendous learning, reminds us again and again by his performance that he was in the German sense a professor of philosophy on the large scale, because he à tout prix [at any price] must explain all things.

So the new science begins with dogmatics in the same sense that immanental science begins with metaphysics. Here ethics again finds its place as the science that has as a task for actuality the dogmatic consciousness of actuality. This ethics does not ignore sin, and it does not have its ideality in making ideal demands; rather, it has its ideality in the penetrating consciousness of actuality, of the actuality of sin, but note carefully, not with metaphysical lightmindedness or with psychological concupiscence.

It is easy to see the difference in the movements, to see that the ethics of which we are now speaking belongs to a different order of things. The first ethics was shipwrecked on the sinfulness of the single individual. Therefore, instead of being able to explain this sinfulness, the first ethics fell into an even greater and more enigmatic difficulty, since the sin of the individual expanded into the sin of the whole race. At this point, dogmatics came to the rescue with hereditary sin. The new ethics presupposes dogmatics, and by means of hereditary sin it explains the sin of the single individual, which at the same time it sets ideality as a task, not by a movement from above and downward but from below and upward.

It is common knowledge that Aristotle used the term first philosophy [prote philosophia] primarily to designate metaphysics, though he included within it a part which according to our conception belongs to theology.[12] In paganism it is quite in order for theology to be treated there. It is related to the same lack of an infinite penetrating reflection that endowed the theatre in paganism with reality as a kind of divine worship. If we now abstract from this ambiguity, we could retain the designation and by first philosophy [*prote philosophia*]* understand that totality of science which we might call 'ethnical' [or pagan], whose essence is immanence and is expressed in Greek thought by 'recollection', and by *secunda philosophia* [second philosophy] understand that totality of science whose essence is transcendence or repetition.†

The concept of sin does not properly belong to any science; only the second ethics can deal with its manifestation, but not with its coming into existence [*tilblivelse*]. If any other science were to treat of it, the concept would be confused. To get closer to our present project, such would also be the case if psychology were to do so.

The subject of which psychology treats must be something in repose that remains in a restless repose, not something restless that always either produces itself or is repressed. But this abiding something out of which sin constantly arises [*vorder*], not by necessity (for a becoming [*vorden*] by necessity is a state, as, for example, the whole history of the plant is a state) but by freedom – this abiding something, this predisposing presupposition, sin's real possibility, is a subject of interest for psychology. That which can be the concern of psychology and with which it can occupy itself is not that it comes into existence, but how it can come into existence. Psychology can bring its concern to the point where it seems as if sin were there, but the next thing, that sin is there, is qualitatively different from the first. The manner in which this presupposition for scrupulous psychological contemplation and observation appears to be more and more comprehensive is the interest of psychology. Psychology may abandon itself, so to speak, to the disappointment that sin is there as an actuality. But this last disappointment reveals the impotence of psychology and merely shows that its service has come to an end.

That human nature is so constituted that it makes sin possible is, psychologically speaking, quite correct, but wanting to make the possibility of sin its actuality is revolting to ethics, and to dogmatics it sounds like blasphemy, because freedom is never possible; as soon as it is, it is actual, in the same sense as it was said in an older philosophy that if God's existence is possible, it is necessary.

---

* Schelling [in his Berlin lectures of 1844] called attention to this Aristotelian term in support of his own distinction between negative and positive philosophy. By negative philosophy he meant 'logic'; that was clear enough. On the other hand, it was less clear to me what he really meant by positive philosophy, except insofar as it became evident that it was the philosophy that he himself wished to provide. However, since I have nothing to go by except my own opinion, it is not feasible to pursue this subject further.

† Constantin Constantius has called attention [in *Repetition*; see above, p. 129] to this by pointing out that immanence runs aground upon 'interest'. With this concept, actuality for the first time properly comes into view.

As soon as sin is actually posited, ethics is immediately on the spot, and now ethics follows every move sin makes. How sin came into the world is not the concern of ethics, apart from the fact that it is certain that sin came into the world as sin. But still less than the concern of ethics with sin's coming into existence is its concern with the still-life of sin's possibility.

If one asks more specifically in what sense and to what extent psychology pursues the observation of its object, it is obvious in itself and from the preceding that every observation of the actuality of sin as an object of thought is irrelevant to it and that as observation it does not belong to ethics, for ethics is never observing but always accusing, judging, and acting. Furthermore, it is obvious in itself as well as from the preceding that psychology has nothing to do with the detail of the empirically actual except insofar as this lies outside of sin. Indeed, as a science psychology can never deal empirically with the detail that belongs to its domain, but the more concrete psychology becomes, the more the detail attains a scientific representation. In our day, this science, which indeed more than any other is allowed almost to intoxicate itself in the foaming multifariousness of life, has become as abstemious and ascetic as a flagellant. However, this is not the fault of science but of its devotees. On the other hand, when it comes to sin, the whole content of actuality is denied to psychology. Only the possibility of sin still belongs to it. But for ethics the possibility of sin never occurs. Ethics never allows itself to be fooled and does not waste time on such deliberations. Psychology, on the other hand, loves these, and as it sits and traces the contours and calculates the angles of possibility, it does not allow itself to be disturbed any more than did Archimedes.

As psychology now becomes deeply absorbed in the possibility of sin, it is unwittingly in the service of another science that only waits for it to finish so that it can begin and assist psychology to the explanation. This science is not ethics, for ethics has nothing at all to do with this possibility. This science is dogmatics, and here in turn the issue of hereditary sin appears. While psychology thoroughly explores the real possibility of sin, dogmatics explains hereditary sin, that is, the ideal possibility of sin. The second ethics, however, has nothing to do with the possibility of sin or with hereditary sin. The first ethics ignores sin. The second ethics has the actuality of sin within its scope, and here psychology can intrude only through a misunderstanding.

If what has been developed here is correct, it is easily seen that the author is quite justified in calling the present work a psychological deliberation, and also how this deliberation, insofar as it becomes conscious of its relation to science, belongs to the domain of psychology and in turn tends towards dogmatics. Psychology has been called the doctrine of the subjective spirit. If this is pursued more accurately, it will become apparent how psychology, when it comes to the issue of sin, must first pass over [*slaa over*] into the doctrine of the absolute spirit. Here lies the place of dogmatics. The first ethics presupposes metaphysics; the second ethics presupposes dogmatics but completes it also in such a way that here, as everywhere, the presupposition is brought out.

This was the task of the introduction. The introduction may be correct, while the deliberation itself concerning the concept of anxiety may be entirely incorrect. Whether this is the case remains to be seen.

Anxiety as the Consequence of that Sin which is Absence of the Consciousness of Sin[13]

In recent philosophy there is a category that is continually used in logical no less than in historical-philosophical inquiries. It is the category of transition. However, no further explanation is given. The term is freely used without any ado, and while Hegel and the Hegelian school startled the world with the great insight of the presuppositionless beginning of philosophy, or the thought that before philosophy there must be nothing but the most complete absence of presuppositions, there is no embarrassment at all over the use in Hegelian thought of the terms 'transition', 'negation', 'mediation', i.e., the principles of motion, in such a way that they do not find their place in the systematic progression. If this is not a presupposition, I do not know what a presupposition is. For to use something that is nowhere explained is indeed to presuppose it. The System is supposed to have such marvelous transparency and inner vision that in the manner of the *omphalopsychoi* [navel souls, navel gazers] it would gaze immovably at the central nothing until at last everything would explain itself and its whole content would come into being by itself.[14] Such introverted openness to the public was to characterize the System. Nevertheless, this is not the case, because systematic thought seems to pay homage to secretiveness with respect to its innermost movements. Negation, transition, mediation are three disguised and suspicious secret agents (*agentia*) that bring about all movements. Hegel would hardly call them presumptuous, because it is with his gracious permission that they carry on their ploy so unembarrassedly that even logic uses terms and phrases borrowed from transition in time: 'thereupon', 'when', 'as being it is this', 'as becoming it is this', etc.

Let this be as it may. Let logic take care to help itself. The term 'transition' is and remains a clever turn in logic. Transition belongs to the sphere of historical freedom, for transition is a *state* and it is actual.★ Plato fully recognised the difficulty of placing transition in the realm of the purely metaphysical, and for that reason the category of *the moment* [*øieblikket*]† cost him so much effort.

★ Therefore, when Aristotle says that the transition from possibility to actuality is a *kinêsis* [movement], it is not to be understood logically but with reference to historical freedom.

† Plato conceives of the moment as purely abstract. In order to become acquainted with its dialectic, one should keep in mind that the moment is non-being under the category of time. Non-being (*to mé on; to kenon* [that which is not; the empty] of the Pythagoreans) occupied the interest of ancient philosophers more than it does modern philosophers. Among the Eleatics, non-being was conceived ontologically in such a way that what was affirmed about it could be stated only in the contradictory proposition that only being is. If one pursues this further, he will see that it reappears in all the spheres. In metaphysical propaedeutics, the proposition was expressed thus: He who expresses non-being says nothing at all (this misunderstanding is refuted in Plato's *Sophist*, and in a more mimical way it was refuted in an earlier dialogue, *Gorgias*). Finally, in the practical spheres the Sophists used non-being as a means to do away with all moral [*sædelige*] concepts; non-being is not, *ergo* everything is true, *ergo* everything is good, *ergo* deceit etc. are not. This position is refuted by Socrates in several dialogues. Plato dealt with it especially in the *Sophist*, which like all of his dialogues at the same time artistically illustrates what it teaches, for the Sophist, whose concept and definition the dialogue seeks while it deals principally with non-being, is himself a non-being. Thus the concept and the example come into being at the same time in the warfare in which the Sophist is attacked, and which ends not with his annihilation but with his coming into being, which is the worst thing that can happen to him, for despite his sophistry, which like the armor of Mars enables him to become invisible, he must come forth into the light. Recent philosophy has not essentially come any further in its conception of non-being, even though it presumes to be Christian. Greek philosophy and the modern alike maintain that everything turns on bringing non-being into being, for to do away with it or to make it vanish seems extremely easy. The Christian view takes the position that non-being is present [*er til*] everywhere as the nothing from which things were created, as semblance and vanity, as sin, as sensuousness removed from spirit, as the temporal forgotten by the eternal; consequently the task is to do away with it in order to bring forth being. Only with this orientation in mind can the concept of Atonement be correctly understood historically, that is, in the sense in which Christianity brought it into the world. If the term is understood in the opposite sense (the movement proceeding from the assumption that non-being is not), the Atonement is volatilized and turned inside out.

It is in *Parmenides* that Plato sets forth 'the moment'. This dialogue is engaged in pointing out contradictions within the concepts themselves, something that Socrates expressed in so definite a way that while it does not serve to put to shame the beautiful old Greek philosophy, it may well put to shame a more recent boastful philosophy, which unlike the Greek does not make great demands upon itself but upon men and their admiration. Socrates points out that there is nothing wonderful about being able to demonstrate the contrariety (*to enantion*) of a particular thing participating in diversity, but if anyone were able to show contradictions in the concepts themselves, that would be something to admire (*all' ei o estin en, auto touto polla apodeixei kai au ta polla de en, touta ede thaumasomai. Kai peri ton allon apanton osautos.* ['But if anyone can prove that simple unity itself is many or that plurality itself is one, that would be something to admire. The same applies in like manner to everything else', *Parmenides*, 129b–c]).

To ignore the difficulty is certainly not to 'go further' than Plato. To ignore it, and thus piously to deceive thought in order to get Speculation afloat and the movement in logic going, is to treat Speculation as a rather finite affair. However, I remember once having heard a speculator say that one must not give undue thought to the difficulties beforehand, because then one never arrives at the point where one can speculate. If the important thing is to get to the point where one can begin to speculate, and not that one's speculation in fact become true Speculation, it is indeed resolutely said that the important thing is to get to the point of speculating, just as it is praiseworthy for a man who has no means of riding to Deer Park in his own carriage to say: One must

(cont'd from p. 194)

The procedure is that of an imaginatively constructing [experimenterende] dialectic. It is assumed both that the one (to hen) is and that it is not, and then the consequences for it and for the rest are pointed out. As a result, the moment appears to be this strange entity-which-has-no-place (atopon, the Greek word is especially appropriate) that lies between motion and rest without occupying any time, and into this and out from this that which is in motion changes into rest, and that which is at rest changes into motion. Thus the moment becomes the category of transition (metabolē), for Plato shows in the same way that the moment is related to the transition of the one to the many, of the many to the one, of likeness to unlikeness, etc., and that it is the moment in which there is neither hen [one] nor polla [many], neither a being separated nor a being combined (oute diakrinesthai oute sunkrinesthai, Parmenides 157a). Plato deserves credit for having clarified the difficulty; yet the moment remains a silent atomistic abstraction, which, however, is not explained by ignoring it. Now if logic would be willing to state that it does not have the category of transition (and if it does have this category, it must find a place for it within the System itself, although in fact it also operates in the System), it will become clearer that the historical spheres and all the knowledge that rests on a historical presupposition have the moment. This category is of utmost importance in maintaining the distinction between Christianity and pagan philosophy, as well as the equally pagan Speculation in Christianity. Another passage in the Parmenides points out the consequence of treating the moment as such an abstraction. It shows how, if the one is assumed to have the determination of time, the contradiction appears that the one (to hen) becomes older and younger than itself and the many (ta polla), and then again neither younger nor older than itself and the many (151e). The one must nevertheless be, so it is said, and then 'to be' is defined as follows: Participation in an essence or a nature in the present time (to de einai allo ti esti e methexis ousias meta chronon tou parontos, 151e). In the further development of the contradictions [152b–c], it appears that the present (to nun) vacillates between meaning the present, the eternal, and the moment. This 'now' (to nun) lies between 'was' and 'will become', and naturally 'the one' cannot, in passing from the past to the future, bypass this 'now'. It comes to a halt in the now, does not become older but is older. In the most recent philosophy, abstraction culminates in pure being, but pure being is the most abstract expression for eternity, and again as 'nothing' it is precisely the moment. Here again the importance of the moment becomes apparent, because only with this category is it possible to give eternity its proper significance, for eternity and the moment become the extreme opposites, whereas dialectical sorcery, on the other hand, makes eternity and the moment signify the same thing. It is only with Christianity that sensuousness, temporality, and the moment can be properly understood, because only with Christianity does eternity become essential.

not trouble himself about such things, because he can just as well ride in a coffee grinder.[15] This, of course, is the case. Both riders hope to arrive at Deer Park. On the other hand, the man who firmly resolves not to trouble himself about the means of conveyance, just as long as he can get to the point where he can speculate, will hardly reach Speculation.

In the sphere of historical freedom, transition is a state. However, in order to understand this correctly, one must not forget that the new is brought about through the leap. If this is not maintained, the transition will have a qualitative preponderance over the elasticity of the leap.

Man, then, is a synthesis of psyche [*sjel*] and body, but he is also a *synthesis of the temporal and the eternal*. That this often has been stated, I do not object to at all, for it is not my wish to discover something new, but rather it is my joy and dearest occupation to ponder over that which is quite simple.

As for the latter synthesis, it is immediately striking that it is formed differently from the former. In the former, the two factors are psyche and body, and the spirit is the third, yet in such a way that one can speak of a synthesis only when spirit is posited. The latter synthesis has only two factors, the temporal and the eternal. Where is the third factor? And if there is no third factor, there really is no synthesis, for a synthesis that is a contradiction cannot be completed as a synthesis without a third factor, because the fact that the synthesis is a contradiction asserts that it is not. What, then, is the temporal?

If time is correctly defined as an infinite succession, it most likely is also defined as the present, the past, and the future. This distinction, however, is incorrect if it is considered to be implicit in time itself, because the distinction appears only through the relation of time to eternity and through the reflection of eternity in time. If in the infinite succession of time a foothold could be found, i.e., a present, which was the dividing point, the division would be quite correct. However, precisely because every moment [*moment*], as well as the sum of the moments, is a process (a passing by), no moment is a present, and accordingly there is in time neither present, nor past, nor future. If it is claimed that this division can be maintained, it is because the moment is *spatialized*, but thereby the infinite succession comes to a halt – it is because representation is introduced that time can be represented instead of being thought. Even so, this is not correct procedure, for even as representation, the infinite succession of time is an infinitely contentless present (this is the parody of the eternal). The Hindus speak of a line of kings that has ruled for 70,000 years. Nothing is known about the kings, not even their names (this I assume). If we take this as an example of time, the 70,000 years are for thought an infinite vanishing; in representation it is expanded and is spatialized into an illusionary view of an infinite, content-less nothing.* As soon as the one is regarded as succeeding the other, the present is posited.

The present, however, is not a concept of time, except precisely as something infinitely contentless, which again is the infinite vanishing. If this is not kept in mind, no matter how quickly it may disappear, the present is posited, and being posited it again disappears in the categories: the past and the future.

The eternal, on the contrary, is the present. For thought, the eternal is the present in terms of an annulled succession (time is the succession that passes by). For representation, it is a going forth that nevertheless does not get off the spot, because the eternal is for representation the infinitely contentful present. So also in the eternal there is no division into the past and the future, because the present is posited as the annulled succession.

Time is, then, infinite succession; the life that is in time and is only of time has no present. In order to define the sensuous life, it is usually said that it is in the moment and only in the moment. By the moment, then, is understood that abstraction from the eternal that, if it is to be the present, is a parody of it. The present is the eternal, or rather, the eternal is the present, and the present is full. In this sense the Latin poet[16] said of the deity that he is *praesens* (*praesentes dii* [the presence of the gods]), by which expression, when used about the deity, he also signified the powerful assistance of the deity.

The moment signifies the present as that which has no past and no future, and precisely in this lies the imperfection of the sensuous life. The eternal also signifies the present as that which has no past and no future, and this is the perfection of the eternal.

If at this point one wants to use the moment to define time and let the moment signify the purely abstract exclusion of the past and the future and as such the present, then the moment is precisely not the present, because the intermediary between the past and the future, purely abstractly conceived, is not at all. Thus it is seen that the moment is not a determination of time, because the determination of time is that it 'passes by'. For this reason time, if it is to be defined by any of the determinations revealed in time itself, is time past. If, on the contrary, time and eternity touch each other, then it must be in time, and now we have come to the moment.

---

* Incidentally, this is space. The skilful reader will no doubt see herein the proof of the correctness of my presentation, because for abstract thought, time and space are entirely identical (*nacheinander, nebeneinander*), and become so for representation, and are truly so in the definition of God as *omnipresent*.

'The moment' [*øieblik*] is a figurative expression, and therefore it is not easy to deal with. However, it is a beautiful word to consider. Nothing is as swift as the blink of an eye, and yet it is commensurable with the content of the eternal. Thus when Ingeborg looks out over the sea after Frithjof, this is a picture of what is expressed in the figurative word.[17] An outburst of her emotion, a sigh or a word, already has, as a sound, more of the determination of time, and is more present as something that is vanishing; it does not have in it so much of the presence of the eternal, and for this reason a sigh, a word, etc. have the power to relieve the soul of the burdensome weight, precisely because the burden, when merely expressed, already begins to become something of the past. A blink [*blik*] is therefore a designation of time, but mark well, of time in the fateful conflict when it is touched by eternity.★ What we call the moment, Plato calls 'the sudden' [*to exaiphnes*]. Whatever its etymological explanation, it is related to the category of the invisible, because time and eternity were conceived equally abstractly, because the concept of temporality was lacking, and this again was due to the lack of the concept of spirit. The Latin term is *momentum* (from *movere* [to move]), which by derivation expresses the merely vanishing.†

Thus understood, the moment is not properly an atom of time but an atom of eternity. It is the first reflection of eternity in time, its first attempt, as it were, at stopping time. For this reason, Greek culture did not comprehend the moment, and even if it had comprehended the atom of eternity, it did not comprehend that it was the moment, did not define it with a forward

---

★ It is remarkable that Greek art culminates in the plastic, which precisely lacks the glance. This, however, has its deep source in the fact that the Greeks did not in the profoundest sense grasp the concept of spirit and therefore did not in the deepest sense comprehend sensuousness and temporality. What a striking contrast to Christianity, in which God is pictorially represented as an eye.

† In the New Testament there is a poetic paraphrase of the moment. Paul says the world will pass away in a moment, *en atomo kai en ripe opthalmou* ['in the twinkling of an eye', I Corinthians 15, 52]. By this he also expresses that the moment is commensurable with eternity, precisely because the moment of destruction expresses eternity at the same moment. Permit me to illustrate what I mean, and forgive me if anyone should find the analogy offensive. Once here in Copenhagen there were two actors who probably never thought that their performance could have a deeper significance. They stepped forth onto the stage, placed themselves opposite each other, and then began the mimical representation of one or another passionate conflict. When the mimical act was in full swing and the spectators' eyes followed the story with expectation of what was to follow, they suddenly stopped and remained motionless as though petrified in the mimical expression of the moment. The effect of this can be exceedingly comical, for the moment in an accidental way becomes commensurable with the eternal. The plastic effect is due to the fact that the eternal expression is expressed eternally; the comic effect, on the other hand, consists in the eternalization of the accidental expression.

direction but with a backward direction. Because for Greek culture the atom of eternity was essentially eternity, neither time nor eternity received what was properly its due.

The synthesis of the temporal and the eternal is not another synthesis but is the expression for the first synthesis, according to which man is a synthesis of psyche and body that is sustained by spirit. As soon as the spirit is posited, the moment is too. Therefore one may rightfully say reproachfully of man that he lives only in the moment, because that comes to pass by an arbitrary abstraction. Nature does not reside in the moment.

It is with temporality as it is with sensuousness, for temporality seems still more imperfect and the moment still more insignificant than nature's apparently secure endurance in time. However, the contrary is the case. Nature's security has its source in the fact that time has no significance at all for nature. Only with the moment does history begin. By sin, man's sensuousness is posited as sinfulness and is therefore lower than that of the beast, and yet this is because it is here that the higher begins, for at this point spirit begins.

The moment is that ambiguity in which time and eternity touch each other, and with this the concept of *temporality* is posited, whereby time constantly intersects eternity and eternity constantly pervades time. As a result, the above-mentioned division acquires its significance: the present time, the past time, the future time.

By this division, attention is immediately drawn to the fact that the future in a certain sense signifies more than the present and the past, because in a certain sense the future is the whole of which the past is a part, and the future can in a certain sense signify the whole. This is because the eternal first signifies the future or because the future is the incognito in which the eternal, even though it is incommensurable with time, nevertheless preserves its association with time. Linguistic usage at times also takes the future as identical with the eternal (the future life – the eternal life). In a deeper sense, the Greeks did not have the concept of the eternal; so neither did they have the concept of the future. Therefore Greek life cannot be reproached for being lost in the moment, or more correctly, it cannot even be said that it was lost, for temporality was conceived by the Greeks just as naively as sensuousness, because they lacked the category of spirit.

The moment and the future in turn posit the past. If Greek life in any way denotes any qualification of time, it is past time. However, past time is not defined in its relation to the present and the future but as a qualification of time in general, as a passing by. Here the significance of the Platonic 'recollection' is obvious. For the Greeks, the eternal lies behind as the past that can only be entered backwards.* However, the eternal thought of as the past is an altogether abstract concept, whether the eternal is further defined philosophically (a philosophical dying away) or historically.

On the whole, in defining the concepts of the past, the future, and the eternal, it can be seen how the moment is defined. If there is no moment, the eternal appears behind as the past. It is as when I imagine a man walking along a road but do not posit the step, and so the road appears behind him as the distance covered. If the moment is posited but merely as a *discrimen* [division], then the future is the eternal. If the moment is posited, so is the eternal, but also the future, which reappears as the past. This is clearly seen in the Greek, the Jewish, and the Christian views. The pivotal concept in Christianity, that which made all things new, is the fullness of time, but the fullness of time is the moment as the eternal, and yet this eternal is also the future and the past.[18] If attention is not paid to this, not a single concept can be saved from a heretical and treasonable admixture that annihilates the concept. One does not get the past by itself but in a simple continuity with the future (with this the concepts of conversion, atonement, and redemption are lost in the world-historical significance and lost in the individual historical development). The future does not arise by itself but in a simple continuity with the present (thereby the concepts of resurrection and judgement are destroyed).

Let us now consider Adam and also remember that every subsequent individual begins in the very same way, but within the qualitative difference that is the consequence of the relationship of generation and the historical relationship. Thus the moment is there for Adam as well as for every subsequent individual. The synthesis of the psychical and the physical is to be posited by spirit; but spirit is eternal, and the synthesis is, therefore, only when spirit posits the first synthesis along with the second synthesis of the temporal and the eternal. As long as the eternal is not introduced, the moment is not, or is only a *discrimen* [dividing line]. Because in innocence spirit is qualified only as dreaming spirit, the eternal appears as the future, for this is, as has been said, the first expression of the eternal, and its incognito. Just as the spirit, when it is about to be posited in the synthesis, or, more correctly, when it is about to posit the synthesis as the spirit's (freedom's) possibility in the individuality, expresses itself as anxiety, so here the future in turn is the eternal's (freedom's) possibility in the individuality expressed as anxiety. As freedom's possibility manifests itself for freedom, freedom succumbs, and temporality emerges in the same way as sensuousness in its significance as sinfulness. Here

---

* Here one should keep in mind the category that I maintain: namely, repetition, by which eternity is entered forwards.

again I repeat that this is only the final psychological expression for the final psychological approximation to the qualitative leap. The difference between Adam and the subsequent individual is that for the latter the future is reflected more than for Adam. Psychologically speaking, this 'more' may signify what is appalling, but in terms of the qualitative leap it signifies the nonessential. The highest difference in relation to Adam is that the future seems to be anticipated by the past or by the anxiety that the possibility is lost before it has been.

The possible corresponds exactly to the future. For freedom, the possible is the future, and the future is for time the possible. To both of these corresponds anxiety in the individual life. An accurate and correct linguistic usage therefore associates anxiety and the future. When it is sometimes said that one is anxious about the past, this seems to be a contradiction of this usage. However, to a more careful examination, it appears that this is only a manner of speaking and that the future in one way or another manifests itself. The past about which I am supposed to be anxious must stand in a relation of possibility to me. If I am anxious about a past misfortune, then this is not because it is in the past but because it may be repeated, i.e., become future. If I am anxious because of a past offense, it is because I have not placed it in an essential relation to myself as past and have in some deceitful way or other prevented it from being past. If indeed it is actually past, then I cannot be anxious but only repentant. If I do not repent, I have allowed myself to make my relation to the offense dialectical, and by this the offense itself has become a possibility and not something past. If I am anxious about the punishment, it is only because this has been placed in a dialectical relation to the offense (otherwise I suffer my punishment), and then I am anxious for the possible and the future.

Thus we have returned to where we were in Chapter 1.[19] Anxiety is the psychological state that precedes sin. It approaches sin as closely as possible, as anxiously as possible, but without explaining sin, which breaks forth only in the qualitative leap.

The moment sin is posited, temporality is sinfulness.* We do not say that temporality is sinfulness any more than that sensuousness is sinfulness, but

---

* From the determination of the temporal as sinfulness, death in turn follows as punishment. This is a progression, with the analogue, *si placet* [if one wishes], that even in relation to the external phenomenon, death declares itself more terrible the more perfect the organism is. Thus while the death and decay of a plant spread a fragrance almost more pleasing than its spring breath, the decay of an animal infects the air. It is true in a deeper sense that the higher man is valued, the more terrifying is death. The beast does not really die, but when the spirit is posited as spirit, death shows itself as the terrifying. The anxiety of death therefore corresponds to the anxiety of birth, yet I do not wish to repeat here what has been said, partly truly and

rather that when sin is posited, temporality signifies sinfulness. Therefore he sins who lives only in the moment as abstracted from the eternal. But to speak foolishly and by way of accommodation, had Adam not sinned, he would in the same moment have passed over into eternity. On the other hand, as soon as sin is posited, it is of no help to wish to abstract from the temporal any more than from the sensuous.

Anxiety as Saving through Faith

In one of the Grimm fairy tales there is a story of a young man who goes in search of adventure in order to learn what it is to be in anxiety.[21] We will let the adventurer pursue his journey without concerning ourselves about whether he encountered the terrible on his way. However, I will say that this is an adventure that every human being must go through – to learn to be anxious in order that he may not perish either by never having been in anxiety or by succumbing to anxiety. Whoever has learned to be anxious in the right way has learned the ultimate.

If a human being were a beast or an angel, he could not be in anxiety. Because he is a synthesis, he can be in anxiety; and the more profoundly he is in anxiety, the greater is the man – yet not in the sense usually understood, in which anxiety is about something external, about something outside a person, but in the sense that he himself produces the anxiety. Only in this

(cont'd from p. 201) partly cleverly, partly enthusiastically and partly frivolously, that death is a metamorphosis. At the moment of death, man finds himself at the uttermost point of the synthesis. It is as though spirit cannot be present, for it cannot die, and yet it must wait, because the body must die. Because the pagan view of sensuousness was more naïve, its temporality more carefree, so the pagan view of death was milder and more attractive, but it lacked the ultimate. In reading the beautiful essay of Lessing on the presentation of death in classical art,[20] one cannot deny being sadly and pleasurably moved by the picture of this sleeping genius or by seeing the beautiful solemnity with which the genius of death bows his head and extinguishes the torch. There is, if you will, something indescribably persuasive and alluring in trusting oneself to such a guide who is as conciliatory as a recollection in which nothing is recollected. On the other hand, there is something sinister in following this silent guide, because he does not conceal anything. His form is no incognito. Just as he is, so is death, and with that, everything is over. There is an incomprehensible sadness in seeing this genius with his friendly figure bend down over the dying and with the breath of his last kiss extinguish the last spark of life, while all that was experienced has already vanished little by little, and death remains as that which, itself unexplained, explains that the whole of life was a game that came to an end, and in which everyone, the greatest as well as the least, made their departures like schoolchildren, extinguished like sparks of burning paper, and last of all the soul itself as the schoolmaster. And so there is also a muteness of annihilation found in the fact that the whole was merely a children's game, and now the game is over.

sense can the words be understood when it is said of Christ that he was anxious unto death,[22] as well as the words spoken by Christ to Judas: What you are going to do, do quickly.[23] Not even the terrifying verse that made even Luther anxious when preaching on it – 'My God, my God, why hast thou forsaken me?'[24] – not even these words express suffering so profoundly. For the latter signify a condition in which Christ finds himself. And the former signify the relation to a condition that is not.

Anxiety is freedom's possibility, and only such anxiety is through faith absolutely educative, because it consumes all finite ends and discovers all their deceptiveness. And no Grand Inquisitor has such dreadful torments in readiness as anxiety has, and no secret agent knows as cunningly as anxiety how to attack his suspect in his weakest moment or to make alluring the trap in which he will be caught, and no discerning judge knows how to interrogate and examine the accused as does anxiety, which never lets the accused escape, neither through amusement, nor by noise, nor during work, neither by day nor by night.

Whoever is educated by anxiety is educated by possibility, and only he who is educated by possibility is educated according to his infinitude. Therefore possibility is the weightiest of all categories. It is true that we often hear the opposite stated, that possibility is so light, whereas actuality is so heavy. But from whom does one hear such words? From wretched men who never know what possibility is, and who, when actuality has shown that they were not good for anything and never would be, mendaciously revived a possibility that was very beautiful and very enchanting, while the foundation of this possibility was at the most a little youthful giddiness, of which they ought rather to be ashamed. Therefore this possibility that is said to be so light is commonly regarded as the possibility of happiness, fortune, etc. But this is not possibility. It is rather a mendacious invention that human depravity has dressed up so as to have a reason for complaining of life and Governance and a pretext for becoming self-important. No, in possibility all things are equally possible, and whoever has truly been brought up by possibility has grasped the terrible as well as the joyful. So when such a person graduates from the school of possibility, and he knows better than a child knows his ABC's that he can demand absolutely nothing of life and that the terrible, perdition, and annihilation live next door to every man, and when he has thoroughly learned that every anxiety about which he was anxious came upon him in the next moment – he will give actuality another explanation, he will praise actuality, and even when it rests heavily upon him, he will remember that it nevertheless is far, far lighter than possibility was. Only in this way can possibility be educative, because finiteness and the finite relations in which every individual is assigned a place, whether they be small, or everyday, or world-historical, educate only finitely, and a person can always persuade them, always coax something else out of them, always bargain, always escape from them tolerably well, always keep himself a little on the outside, always prevent himself from absolutely learning something from them; and if he does this, the individual must again have possibility in himself and himself develop that from which he is to learn, even though in the next moment that from which he is to learn does not at all acknowledge that it is formed by him but absolutely deprives him of the power.

However, in order that an individual may thus be educated absolutely and infinitely by the possibility, he must be honest toward possibility and have faith. By faith I understand here what Hegel somewhere in his way correctly calls the inner certainty that anticipates infinity. When the discoveries of possibility are honestly administered, possibility will discover all the finitudes, but it will idealize them in the form of infinity and in anxiety overwhelm the individual until he again overcomes them in the anticipation of faith.

What I am saying here probably strikes many as obscure and foolish talk, because they pride themselves on never having been in anxiety. To this I would reply that one certainly should not be in anxiety about men and about finitudes, but only he who passes through the anxiety of the possible is educated to have no anxiety, not because he can escape the terrible things of life but because these always become weak by comparison with those of possibility. If, on the other hand, the speaker maintains that the great thing about him is that he has never been in anxiety, I will gladly provide him with my explanation: that is because he is very spiritless.

If an individual defrauds possibility, by which he is to be educated, he never arrives at faith; then his faith will be the sagacity of finitude, just as his school was that of finitude. But men defraud possibility in every way, because otherwise every man, if he had merely put his head out of the window, would have seen enough for possibility to use in beginning its exercises. There is an engraving by Chodowiecki that represents the surrender of Calais as viewed by four persons of different temperaments, and the task of the artist was to mirror the various impressions in the facial expressions of the four.[25] The most commonplace life no doubt has experiences enough, but the question is that of the possibility in the individual who is honest with himself. It is told of one Indian hermit who for two years lived on dew that he once came to the city, tasted wine, and became addicted to drink. This story, like similar stories, can be understood in different ways. It may be regarded as comic, it may be regarded as tragic. But the individuality who is educated by possibility needs but one such story. In that very moment, he is absolutely identified with the unfortunate man; he knows no finite evasion by which he may escape. Now the anxiety of possibility holds him as its prey until, saved, it must hand him over to faith. In no other place can he find rest, for every other place of rest is mere chatter, although in the eyes of men it is sagacity. Therefore possibility is absolutely educative. In actuality, no man ever became so unhappy that he did not retain a little remnant, and common sense says quite correctly that if one is cunning, one knows how to make the best of things. But whoever took possibility's course in misfortune lost all, all, as no one in actuality ever lost it. Now, if he did not defraud the possibility that wanted to teach him and did not wheedle the anxiety that wanted to save him, then he would also receive everything back, as no one in actuality ever did, even though he received all things tenfold, for the disciple of possibility received infinity, and the soul of the other expired in the finite. In actuality, no one ever sank so deep that he could not sink deeper, and there may be one or many who sank deeper. But he who sank in possibility – his eye became dizzy, his eye became confused, so he could not grasp the measuring stick that Tom, Dick, and Harry hold out as a saving straw to one sinking; his ear was closed so he could not hear what the market price of men was in his own day, did not hear that he was just as good as the majority. He sank absolutely, but then in turn he emerged from the depth of the abyss lighter than all the troublesome and terrible things in life. However, I will not deny that whoever is educated by possibility is exposed to danger, not that of getting into bad company and going astray in various ways as are those educated by the finite, but the danger of a fall, namely, suicide. If at the beginning of his education he misunderstands the anxiety, so that it does not lead him to faith but away from faith, then he is lost. On the other hand, whoever is educated [by possibility] remains with anxiety; he does not permit himself to be deceived by its countless falsifications and accurately remembers the past. Then the assaults of anxiety, even though they be terrifying, will not be such that he flees from them. For him, anxiety becomes a serving spirit that against its will leads him where he wishes to go. Then, when it announces itself, when it cunningly pretends to have invented a new instrument of torture, far more terrible than anything before, he does not shrink back, and still less does he attempt to hold it off with noise and confusion; but he bids it welcome, greets it festively, and like Socrates who raised the poisoned cup, he shuts himself up with it and says as a patient would say to the surgeon when the painful operation is about to begin: Now I am ready. Then anxiety enters into his soul and searches out everything and anxiously torments everything finite and petty out of him, and then it leads him where he wants to go.

When one or another extraordinary event occurs in life, when a world-historical hero gathers heroes about him and performs deeds of valour, when a crisis occurs and everything gains significance, then men want to have a part in it, because all of this is educative. Possibly so. But there is a simpler way in which one may become more thoroughly educated. Take the pupil of possibility, place him in the middle of the Jutland heath, where no event takes place or where the greatest event is a grouse flying up noisily, and he will experience everything more perfectly, more accurately, more thoroughly than the man who received the applause on the stage of world-history if that man was not educated by possibility.

So when the individual through anxiety is educated unto faith, anxiety will eradicate precisely what it brings forth itself. Anxiety discovers fate, but just when the individual wants to put his trust in fate, anxiety turns around and takes fate away, because fate is like anxiety, and anxiety, like possibility, is a 'magic' picture.[26] When the individuality is not thus transformed by himself in relation to fate, he will always retain a dialectical remnant that no finitude can remove, just as no man will lose faith in the lottery if he does not lose it by himself but is supposed to lose it by continually losing when he gambles. Even in relation to the most insignificant things, anxiety is promptly at hand as soon as the individuality wants to sneak away from something or stumble upon something by chance. In itself, it is of no significance; from the outside, from the finite, the individual can learn nothing about it. But anxiety takes swift action, instantly plays the trump card of infinity, of the category, and the individuality cannot take the trick. Such an individuality cannot in an outward way fear fate, its vicissitudes and defeats, because the anxiety within him has already fashioned fate and has taken away from him absolutely all that any fate could take away. In the dialogue *Cratylus*, Socrates says that it is terrible to be deceived by oneself, because one always has the deceiver present;[27] similarly, one may say that it is fortunate to have present such a deceiver who piously deceives and always weans the child before finitude begins to bungle him. Even if in our time an individuality is not educated by possibility in this manner, our age nevertheless has an excellent characteristic for each one in whom there is a deeper nature and who desires to learn the good. The more peaceful and quiet an age is and the more accurately everything follows its regular course, so that the good has its reward, the easier it is for an individuality to deceive himself about whether in all his striving he has a beautiful but nevertheless finite goal. In these times, one does not need to be more than sixteen years old to recognize that whoever performs on the stage of the theatre of life is like the man who travelled from Jericho and fell among robbers.[28] Whoever does not wish to sink in the wretchedness of the finite is constrained in the most profound sense to struggle with the infinite. Such a preliminary orientation is analogous to the education by possibility, and such an orientation cannot take place except through possibility. So when shrewdness has completed its innumerable calculations, when the game is won – then anxiety comes, even before the game in actuality has been lost or won, and anxiety makes the sign of the cross against the devil, and shrewdness becomes helpless and its most clever combinations vanish like a witticism compared with the case that anxiety forms with the omnipotence of possibility. Even in the most trifling matters, as soon as the individuality wants to make a cunning turn that is merely cunning, wants to sneak away from something, and the probability is that he will succeed – because actuality is not as sharp an examiner as anxiety – then anxiety is there at once. If it is dismissed because it is merely a trifle, then anxiety makes this trifle as prominent as the little place Marengo became in the history of Europe, because there the great battle of Marengo was fought.[29] If an individuality is not weaned away from shrewdness by himself, it will never be thoroughly accomplished, because finitude always explains in parts, never totally, and he whose shrewdness always fails (and even this is inconceivable in actuality) may seek the reason for this in his shrewdness, and then strive to become still more shrewd. With the help of faith, anxiety brings up the individuality to rest in providence. So it is also in relation to guilt, which is the second thing anxiety discovers. Whoever learns to know his guilt only from the finite is lost in the finite, and finitely the question of whether a man is guilty cannot be determined except in an external, juridical, and most imperfect sense. Whoever learns to know his guilt only by analogy to judgements of the police court and the supreme court never really understands that he is guilty, for if a man is guilty, he is infinitely guilty. Therefore, if such an individuality who is educated only by finitude does not get a verdict from the police or a verdict by public opinion to the effect that he is guilty, he becomes of all men the most ridiculous and pitiful, a model of virtue who is a little better than most people but not quite so good as the parson. What help would such a man need in life? Why, almost before he dies he may retire to a collection of models. From finitude one can learn much, but not how to be anxious, except in a very mediocre and depraved sense. On the other hand, whoever has truly learned how to be anxious will dance when the anxieties of finitude strike up the music and when the apprentices of finitude lose their minds and courage. One is often deceived this way in life. The hypochondriac is anxious about every insignificant thing, but when the significant appears he begins to breathe more easily. And why? Because the significant actuality is not after all so terrible as the possibility he himself has fashioned, and which he used his strength to fashion, whereas he can now use all his strength against actuality. Yet the hypochondriac is only an imperfect autodidact when compared with the person who is educated by possibility, because hypochondria is partly dependent on the somatic and is consequently accidental.* The true autodidact is precisely in the same degree a theodidact, as another author has said,† or to use an expression less reminiscent of the intellectual, he is one who on his own cultivates philosophy [*autourgos tis tés philosophias*]‡ and in the same degree one who tends the things of God [*theourgos*]. Therefore he who in relation to guilt is educated by anxiety will rest only in the Atonement.

Here this deliberation ends, where it began. As soon as psychology has finished with anxiety, it is to be delivered to dogmatics.

*   It is therefore with a higher meaning that Hamann employs the word 'hypochondria' when he says: 'However, this anxiety in the world is the only proof of our heterogeneity. If we lacked nothing, we should do no better than the pagans and the transcendental philosophers, who know nothing of God and like fools fall in love with lovely nature, and no homesickness would come over us. This impertinent disquiet, this holy hypochondria is perhaps the fire with which we season sacrificial animals in order to preserve us from the putrefaction of the current century.'[30]

†   Cf. *Either/Or*. ['Balance Between the Aesthetic and the Ethical', KW IV, pp. 270–1.]

‡   See Xenophon's *Symposium* [I, 5; written *c*.380 BCE], where Socrates uses this expression about himself.

Notes

1   Cf. John 3, 29: 'the friend of the bridegroom, which standeth and heareth him, rejoiceth greatly because of the bridegroom's voice'.

2   God's words to Abraham at Genesis 12, 3: 'in thee shall all families of the earth be blessed'.

3   Cf. Matthew 6, 34: 'Sufficient unto the day is the evil thereof.'

4   When a work of speculative theology ('a currency of doubtful value') by H. L. Martensen (1808–84) was published in Danish in 1841, the introduction declared that it 'marked an epoch'. (Cf. KW VIII, p. 223, n. 6.)

5   Cf. Matthew 7, 21: 'Not every one that saith unto me, Lord, Lord, shall enter into the kingdom of heaven.'

6   Holberg's comedy *Erasmus Montanus* (1731) features a foolish clerk who thinks that 'imprimatur' – which signifies permission to print – is the name of a high office.

7   In ethics and philosophical theory generally, *logos* refers to reasons and definitions, as in *Republic*, 343a, where Plato speaks of *ho tou dikaiou logos* ('the definition of justice'). In Christian dogmatics, however, *logos* is closely related to God, as in John 1, 1: 'In the beginning was the Word [*logos*], and the Word was with God, and the Word was God.'

8 Anne Louise Germaine, Madame de Staël (1766–1817), author of an influential book on German thought, *De l'Allemagne* (1814).

9 Kierkegaard refers to Aesop's story of a dog which was carrying a delicious piece of meat in its mouth: it came to a river, and mistaking its own reflection for another dog carrying another piece of meat, it lunged for it, thus losing its meal in its effort to snatch a shadow.

10 Cf. Plato, *Gorgias*, 448d–e: 'he is skilled in rhetoric rather than dialogue'.

11 F. E. D. Schleiermacher (1768–1834), German theologian and philosopher, author of *Der Christliche Glaube* (1821–2).

12 See Aristotle, *Metaphysics*, 6, 1, 1026a 29.

13 The following extract is from the third chapter, where it is preceded by these words: 'In the two previous chapters, it was maintained continually that man is a synthesis of psyche [*sjel*] and body that is constituted and sustained by spirit. In the individual life, anxiety is the moment – to use a new expression that says the same as was said in the previous discussion, but that also points toward that which follows.'

14 A reference to the Greek monks who gazed at their own navels in order to achieve divine ecstasy. In November 1837 Kierkegaard wrote in his journal: 'there is nothing more dangerous or more paralysing than the kind of self-isolating gazing at ourselves which makes everything else vanish – world history, human life, society – so that in an egoistic circle we see only our own navel, like the *omphalopsychitai*' (II A 187).

15 *Kaffemølle* – coffee grinder – was a standard comical term for a public coach.

16 A reference to the Roman comic poet Terence (*c*.195–158), who is also reputed to have died of grief when his translations from Greek were lost at sea.

17 An allusion to an engraving on the title page of Esaias Tegner's *Frithjof's Saga* (1825).

18 Cf. Galatians 4, 4: 'But when the fullness of the time was come, God sent forth his Son.'

19 Not included in this anthology.

20 Gotthold Ephraim Lessing (1729–81), 'Wie die Alten den Tod gebildet' ('How the Ancients Pictured Death'), 1769.

21 See 'Märchen von einem, der auszog, das Fürchten zu lernen' ('The Story of a Boy who Went Forth to Learn the Meaning of Fear'), a story collected by the Brothers Grimm.

22 Cf. Mark 14, 34: 'My soul is exceeding sorrowful unto death.' See also John 12, 27, and Matthew 36, 37.

23 Cf. John 13, 27: 'Then said Jesus unto him, That thou doest, do quickly.'

24 See Mark 15, 34.

25 The painter Daniel Chodowiecki (1726–1801).

26 Literally 'witches' letter' [*Hexebrev*]: an ambiguous picture as described in *Either/Or*, which 'shifts from one thing to another, depending how one shifts and turns it.' (Cf. KW IV, p. 258.)

27 Cf. Plato, *Cratylus*, 428d: 'Nothing is worse than self-deception; the deceiver is always at home and always with you.'

28 Cf. Luke 10, 30: 'A certain man went down from Jerusalem to Jericho, and fell among thieves, which stripped him of his raiment, and wounded him, and departed, leaving him half dead.'

29 Napoleon's forces won a decisive victory over the Austrian army at Marengo, just outside Alessandria in northern Italy, in 1800.

30 This note refers to the collected works of J. G. Hamann (1730–88), vol. 6, p. 194.

8

Prefaces

The great works of ancient or medieval philosophy are likely to strike modern readers as peculiarly unattractive. They are dry, forbidding and obscure, and they make no apology for it. They make no effort to welcome us and put us at our ease. Instead of throwing open their doors to us they keep them bolted and boarded up, as if they would prefer not to be approached at all. They do not even have the explanatory titles we have learned to expect from modern philosophical books, let alone their subtitles and chapter-headings and running heads, and the reassuring apparatus of epigraphs, dedications, acknowledgements, forewords and prefaces with which modern books introduce themselves and allow us to place them amongst our previous literary acquaintances.

It all began to change in the seventeenth century, as philosophers started to bring out small books attractively printed in vernacular languages, and sought to ingratiate themselves with a book-buying public which might refuse to read anything that did not promise them immediate comfort and pleasure. The so-called modern philosophers may have believed that their philosophies constituted self-contained systems of immaculate truth, but they nevertheless undertook to make themselves attractive to potential readers who might be nervous about getting started. Francis Bacon's *Advancement of Learning* (1605) began with his elaborate presentation of himself and his work to King James; Descartes's entire *Discourse on Method* (1637) was written as a preface, in the form of an autobiographical sketch, to three scientific treatises; Hobbes's *Leviathan* (1651) opens with a letter of dedication to a friend, followed by an introduction summarizing the plan and intention of the entire book; and Locke's *Essay Concerning Human Understanding* (1690) has not only a dedication and an introduction but also an *Epistle to the Reader*. 'I here put into thy hands, what has been the diversion of some of my idle and heavy hours', he begins, thus sounding a keynote of self-deprecation and informality before he sets us down to the serious business of epistemology.

There was perhaps something a little ridiculous in the efforts of seventeenth-century philosophers to step outside their philosophical works and converse informally with non-philosophical readers: after all, if the invitations and enticements they offered were really consistent with their philosophy then they should have been built into the main work, and if not they were misleading if not downright dishonest. But that would not prevent Immanuel Kant from writing prefaces on a very grand scale: to the first and second editions of the *Critique of Pure Reason* (1781, 1787), the *Prolegomena* (1783), the *Groundwork* (1785), the *Critique of Practical Reason* (1788), the *Critique of Judgement* (1790), *Religion within the Boundaries of Mere Reason* (1793) and *The Metaphysics of Morals* (1797). Indeed Kant's prefaces could be collected into a substantial volume to serve as a summary of the entire range of his work.[1] With prefaces like these, the books themselves begin to seem superfluous.

Hegel was perhaps the first to treat philosophical prefaces as a philosophical problem. The whole of his *Phenomenology of Spirit* (1807) was intended as an introduction to a promised 'System of Science', but it was itself preceded by an introduction explaining how ordinary consciousness needs to raise itself up to a state of absolute knowledge. Moreover the introduction was itself introduced by a preface – a monumental essay which Hegel opened with a disquisition on the oddity of philosophical prefaces. He began by recalling that a preface usually provides authors with a platform for explaining the aim of their book and their motive in writing it, and for staking their claim to have filled a gap in contemporary literature or carried forward an urgently needed argument. Hegel conceded that such initial declarations of intent could serve a useful purpose in books dealing with specific ranges of facts or historical events; but they could never be justified, he argued, in works of universal philosophy, whose ambition was nothing less than to offer an all-embracing statement of the whole truth about everything. But a book has to begin somewhere, and Hegel's solution was to open all his publications – not only the *Phenomenology*, but also the *Science of Logic* (1812, 1816), the *Encyclopedia* (1817, 1827, 1830) and the *Philosophy of Right* (1821) – with prefaces exploring the impossibility of philosophical prefaces.

From Kierkegaard's point of view, however, the Hegelian approach to prefaces was merely glib and insincere: – a clumsy attempt to cover up the fact that even the most impersonal system of thought has to be learnt and taught and discussed by particular individuals. For Kierkegaard, philosophical prefaces were like comedies in which philosophers bid farewell to individuality and try to hide inside their systems, though we know they are bound to fail. They were like a thumbprint left by the historical actuality of a teacher, and they provided a natural focus for the passions of the individual learner.

This applied even to *The Concept of Anxiety*, whose glum preface had a certain winsome charm in spite of itself.[2] And the effect was strengthened by the appearance, on the very same day – 17 June 1844 – of a zany volume called *Prefaces: Light Reading for Certain Classes According to Time and Occasion*, whose author was named as Nicolaus Notabene. The book is what its title suggests – an anthology of prefaces. It contains eight possible prefaces to eight non-existent books, each exemplifying the various kinds of bond between philosophers and their readers that philosophical prefaces may seek to establish. The first of them is a shameless statement of the real message of every preface: that the book we are about to read is 'what the times demand'.[3] Then we come to the task of creating a reputation, and ensuring that the book becomes the talk of the town even if no one gets round to reading it. ('That friend out in the country has not read the book but received a letter from a man in the capital who has not read the book either but read the review that in turn was written by a man who had not read the book but heard what the trustworthy man said who had flicked through the pages at Reitzel's bookshop.')[4] There is also the need to appeal to the Christmas and New Year market, while catching the eye of the great reviewer who will be kind enough to 'tally the votes' of public opinion.[5] In the fifth preface Nicolaus notes the advantage to an author of building a reputation as a speaker who can rouse a crowd to ecstatic applause, and in the sixth he asks his readers to take care to see his various works as forming a 'totality'.[6] In the seventh he alludes to the reassuring technique of taking ten books on a given subject and synthesizing them into an eleventh, and he begs for our tenderness and mercy as he explains that he cannot face the rigours of philosophical authorship even on such attenuated terms: 'an eleventh book is still a labour and therefore too much trouble for . . . the individual who is intent on absolute importance and immortal merit'. He knows very well that modern philosophy began with Descartes, and he has heard all about how Hegel conjured Becoming out of a blend which mediates Being and Nothingness; but for some reason he begins to feel a little unwell whenever he hears people talking about mediation.[7]

Nicolaus has therefore decided to start a journal for philosophical outsiders like himself, who find themselves not quite equal to the labour of doubting absolutely everything, and who would prefer 'the more human task of doubting whether all the philosophers understood what they said' – an enterprise to which his eighth preface is to serve as an introduction. Of course he is sure that his doubts about the wisdom of the philosophers will eventually be dispelled, provided he can wait long enough. But in the meantime his whole project threatens to collapse before it has even got under way, for how can he relate himself to philosophy at all when he admits he does not understand it? He cannot even define himself as a philosophical outsider unless he already understands 'the boundary that limits me and thereby excludes me from philosophy'; and 'by defining my boundary negatively I am still defined in continuity with the other'. So it seems he is doomed to be incorporated into philosophy despite his clear inability to understand it: 'I become an infinitely, infinitely, infinitely small bit of a philosopher,' he notes; 'but I am still included.'[8] It seems therefore that Nicolaus can find nowhere to hide from the terrible power of systematic philosophy – not even the modest privacy of a personal preface.

The eight prefaces in *Prefaces* are prefaced by a preface, in which Nicolaus tries to engage our sympathies by presenting an autobiographical explanation of his obsession with prefacing. He tells a tragicomic story of his everyday domestic life in a way which may or may not seduce us, but which, we may be sure, can have no bearing on the serious and impersonal tasks of philosophy itself.

Notes

1   See Immanuel Kant, *Vorreden*, edited by Eberhard Günter Schulz (Munich: Langen Müller, 1996).
2   See above, pp. 180–1.
3   *Prefaces* I; cf. KW IX, pp. 13–14.
4   *Prefaces* II; cf. KW IX, pp. 16–17.
5   *Prefaces* III, IV; cf. KW IX, pp. 22, 24.
6   *Prefaces* V, VI; cf. KW IX, pp. 27, 31.
7   *Prefaces* VII; cf. KW IX, pp. 38, 45.
8   *Prefaces* VIII; cf. KW IX, pp. 49, 51, 58.

Prefaces: Light Reading for Certain Classes according to Time and Occasion
by Nicolaus Notabene

Preface

It often happens that an insignificant trifle, a thoughtless remark, an unguarded outburst, an accidental look or an involuntary gesture gives us the opportunity to get inside a person and discover things about them which have escaped more careful observation. Yet this insignificant remark could itself become distorted and conceited, so I renounce it for the moment and hasten to pursue my real project. In relation to a book a preface is a triviality, but surely we might get an opportunity for bargain-price observation through a more meticulous, comparative study of prefaces. Much effort is spent in the scholarly world trying to organize literature – to assign every work to its place in the age, and define that age in terms of the progress of the human race – yet no one has explored what could be gained if a *literatus* [literary type] were trained to read nothing but prefaces, and to read them systematically from the earliest times down through the centuries to the present day. Prefaces are characterized by the accidental, like dialects, idioms and provincialisms. They are more subject to fashion than the works themselves, and they change like styles of dress. Sometimes they are long, sometimes short; sometimes bold, sometimes demure; sometimes rigid, sometimes

The first English translation of *Prefaces* was by William McDonald (Tallahassee: Florida State University Press, 1989); a second, by Todd W. Nichol, appeared in vol. IX of *Kierkegaard's Writings* (1997). The present translation of the preface to *Prefaces* is by Jane Chamberlain and Jonathan Rée and appears here for the first time. Copyright © Jane Chamberlain and Jonathan Rée, 2001.

careless; sometimes worried and shamefaced, sometimes self-confident and brash; sometimes not entirely blind to the weaknesses of the book, sometimes totally oblivious, sometimes more conscious of defects than anyone else. Sometimes the preface is a first sample of a production, sometimes an aftertaste. And all this is purely ceremonial. Even an author who sets out to denounce his age will conform to common practice in insignificant matters – that is, in his prefaces – and the reader can then observe a very droll collision between the how and the how far. The more I think about it, the more the study of prefaces seems to promise. Just consider the opposite case: the Greek simplicity that makes an excellent basis for the presentation of results. I stop this thought in its flight, however; I am not equipped to pursue it and it would probably lead me astray.

Modern scholarship has dealt prefaces a mortal blow. The authors of the past can easily cut a pitiful figure: we do not know whether to laugh or cry as we observe their comical awkwardness in getting to the point, while their naïveté in expecting anyone to care is quite touching. But such a situation cannot occur nowadays, for when a book begins with the topic and the System with nothing, there does not seem to be anything left over to say in a preface. This has made me realize that prefaces are a quite unique kind of literary production, and since they have been marginalized it is high time they emancipated themselves like everything else. In this way something good can still come of them. The incommensurable, which in earlier times would have been consigned to the preface of a book, can now be expressed in prefaces detached from any particular book. This should, I think, resolve the conflict to mutual pleasure and satisfaction; if the preface and the book cannot become a couple, then let them get a divorce.

The latest methods of scholarship have made me realize that it is time to make a new start. At present there is merely a phenomenon which hints at a deeper reason; if I deserve any credit it is only for making the break in earnest. There must have been times in the life of every aesthetically developed author when he did not feel like writing a book but was keen to write a preface – either to a book of his own or to someone else's. This suggests that prefaces are essentially different from books, and that writing them is a very different matter, otherwise – or so it would seem at first sight – the urge to write prefaces would make itself felt only when the author had finished a book or was planning one, thus raising the question whether the preface should be written first or last. If we are in this kind of predicament, however, then we must either already have found our topic, or at least be imagining that we have. But since we may also feel like writing a preface without having found a topic, it is easy to see that it cannot have a topic, since if it did the preface would itself become a book, and the whole question of preface and book would become irrelevant. Thus a preface as such – an emancipated preface – must have no topic: it must not discuss anything, and insofar as it appears to be about something, it must be only an appearance and a kind of pretence.

There is no other way to define prefaces purely lyrically, and according to their concept, for in the common traditional sense they are mere ceremonies of time and custom. A preface sets a mood, and writing a preface is like sharpening a scythe, tuning a guitar, chatting with a child, or spitting out of the window. No one knows how it comes about, but the desire takes one by surprise, the desire to write a preface, the desire to do it *leves sub noctem susurri* [in light nocturnal murmurs].[1] Writing a preface is like ringing a doorbell to tease someone, or passing a young girl's window and gazing at the cobblestones, like shaking your stick in the air at the wind or tipping your hat when there is no one to be greeted. Writing a preface is like making a claim on public attention, or having something on your conscience that you are tempted to confess; it is like bowing as an invitation to a dance though you do not move, like a rider pressing his horse's flank with his left leg, pulling the reins to the right, hearing the horse go 'Pst', and not caring about the rest of the world; it is like joining in without suffering the least inconvenience, or standing on the hill at Valby and gazing at wild geese. Writing a preface is like arriving at a staging post on a coach, waiting in the dark, anticipating what is about to appear, seeing the gate open and with it the sky, gazing at the country road which is constantly receding before you, glimpsing the secret of the forest, the seductive disappearance of the path, or hearing the sound of the post horn and the beckoning invitation of Echo. It is like hearing the crack of the coachman's whip, the forest's confused repetition, and the cheerful conversation of your fellow travellers. And then writing a preface is like arriving at your destination, standing in a cosy living-room, greeting the object of your longing, sitting in an armchair, filling a pipe, lighting it – and having an endless amount to say to each other. Writing a preface is like beginning to fall in love – the soul sweetly troubled, a riddle abandoned, each event a clue to the explanation. Writing a preface is like bending aside a branch at the jasmine-covered cottage and gazing at the girl who sits there unaware: my beloved. Yes indeed: this is what it is like to write a preface.

But what of the writer of prefaces? He goes amongst people like a jester in winter or a fool in summer, he is hello and goodbye rolled into one, always happy, carefree and contented. He is an irresponsible good-for-nothing, indeed immoral, for he goes to the Stock Exchange not to scrape money together but only to stroll around; he does not give addresses to general assemblies, because the air is too close, and he does not propose toasts because

he would have to give notice several days in advance. He does not run errands
for the System or pay his instalments on the national debt – he does not
even take it seriously. He goes through life like a cobbler's apprentice who
ambles down the street whistling, while a customer is waiting for his boots
and will have to wait as long as there is a single slide left or a remotely
interesting sight to be seen. Ah yes, this is your writer of prefaces.

Everyone else can ponder all this at leisure, as and when they please. But
for me it is quite different. I am bound by a promise and an obligation to
devote myself exclusively to this kind of writing. How it all hangs together
I will tell the reader at once, for this is precisely the right place: just as slander
belongs in a coffee-house, this is the sort of thing that belongs in a preface.

Although I am unusually happy in my married life, and perhaps unusually grateful for my happiness too, it is not without its problems. It was my
wife who first noticed them, however, and at first I suspected nothing. Several
months had passed since our wedding. I was gradually becoming practised in
the methods of the married state, when slowly but surely I once more became
aware of a desire which I had always nurtured and which in my innocence
I thought I could still indulge: engagement in some kind of literary work. I
chose my topic, laid out all the relevant books in my possession, borrowed a
few more from the Royal Library, and arranged my notes synoptically. My
pen, so to speak, was already dipped. My wife, however, sensed that some
such thing was in the wind and began observing me closely. Occasionally
she dropped an ambiguous comment, or hinted that she did not quite approve
of what I was doing in my study, my extended stays there, my literary labours.
I kept my wits about me, though, and pretended not to understand – indeed
at first I really did not know what she was doing. But one day she took me
by surprise and wrung from me a formal admission that I was on my way
to wanting to be an author. If her behaviour had hitherto been like a recon-
naissance exercise, she now concentrated her forces until finally she declared
war, and so openly that she tried to confiscate everything I had written and
use it as a backing for her embroidery or for curlers, etc. An author's position can hardly be more desperate than this; even one who is subject to
special censorship can still hope to get his work into a state in which it can
be approved for publication, but my creation was constantly being smothered
at birth. And there were other ways in which it was becoming clearer and
clearer to me how desperate my predicament was, for I had scarcely discovered that I was the object of a campaign in the press before I grasped what
I should have realized earlier: that it would do irreparable harm to humanity if my writings did not see the light of day. Now what could be done
about this? Unlike a banned author, I could not appeal to the Chancery, to
provincial consultative assemblies, to the esteemed public or to the remem-

brance of posterity. I had to live and die, or stand and fall with my wife. Now, I am certainly regarded by my contemporaries as a good and experienced debater who can plead my case rather well, but this proficiency is no use to me here: I can argue with the devil himself, but I cannot argue with my wife. She has, you see, only one syllogism, or more correctly not even one. Learned people would call it sophistry but she, who is not interested in being learned, calls it teasing. The method is quite simple, at least for anyone who knows how to follow it. If ever I say something that does not please her – whether in the form of a syllogism or a long speech or a short remark (the form does not matter) – when it fails to please her, she gives me a look that is lovable, charming, good-natured and enchanting, but also triumphant and devastating, and she says: You are only teasing. Thus all my debating skill becomes otiose: it serves no purpose at all in my domestic life. If I, as an experienced dialectician, can represent the course of justice – which according to the poet is very long[2] – then my wife is like the Royal Danish Chancery, *kurz und bündig* [brief and to the point], except that she differs from that august body in being very lovable. It is precisely this lovableness which endows her with an authority she can exercise at any moment in a most enchanting way.

That is how the matter stands. I have never got further than my opening paragraph. Since this was of a general nature, and to my mind so successfully composed that she would find it quite amusing if only it were written by someone else, it occurred to me that I might be able to win her over by reading it out to her. I was prepared for her to reject my request and use the opportunity to say that 'things have come to quite a pass when you not only occupy yourself with writing all the time but force me to listen to your lectures'. But it was not like that at all. She accepted my suggestion with great kindness; she listened, laughed, and admired. I thought that victory was mine. She came over to the table where I was sitting, put an arm intimately around my neck and asked me to repeat a passage once again. I began to read, holding the manuscript high enough for her eye to follow me. It was wonderful! I read further, but was still not quite beyond that passage when the manuscript burst into flames. Without my noticing it, she had pushed the candle underneath the manuscript. The fire prevailed, there was nothing to be done, and my introductory paragraph went up in flames – to general rejoicing, for my wife rejoiced for us both. Like a high-spirited child she clapped her hands and then threw herself around my neck with a passion, as if I had been separated from her or even lost. I could not get a word in edgeways. She begged my forgiveness for having fought for her love in this way. She implored with such emotion that she almost convinced me that I had been on the way to becoming a prodigal husband. She explained that she could not bear to see me changed in this way. 'Your thought', she said, 'belongs to me; it has to belong to me. Your attentions are my daily bread; your approval, your smile, your jokes are my life, my inspiration. Do not with-hold them – oh, do not deny me my due – for my sake, for the sake of my happiness, so that I may joyfully do my only joy: to think of you and find all my satisfaction in continuing to woo you, day in and day out, as you once wooed me.'

Now what justifies a wife in such behaviour, a wife who is lovable in the eyes of all who know her, and above all lovable to me, as delicious as the day is long? Her view *in contento* [in brief] is as follows: a married man who is an author is little better than a married man who goes to his club every night. Indeed, he is even worse, for a man who goes to his club is absent only as long as he is absent, whereas an author: 'Well, presumably you are not aware of it, but you have changed completely. You cocoon yourself in your thoughtfulness from morning till night, and especially at dinner. You sit and stare like a ghost or like Nebuchadnezzar reading the invisible writing.³ When I myself have made your coffee, put it on the tray and come happily to stand before you and curtsey – well, I nearly drop the tray out of fright, and above all I have lost my cheerfulness and joy and I cannot curtsey to you any longer.'

Just as my wife on every occasion knows how to add her Catonian *præterea censeo* ['let me also say'], though she does not do it as boringly as Cato, so too everything can be made to serve her for argument.⁴ Her reasoning is like an invocation of nature [*naturbesværgelse*]. If, at the defence of a doctoral dissertation, my opponent came out with similar arguments, I would proba-bly turn my back on him and denounce him as the *Magister* does in Holberg: he is an ignoramus who does not know how to distinguish between an *ubi prædicamentale* [a predicative place] and an *ubi transcendentale* [a transcenden-tal place].⁵ With my wife it is a different matter. She reasons straight from the hand – and straight to the heart, where it really comes from. She has thus taught me to understand how Catholics can find edification in a service conducted in Latin, since her reasoning is like Latin to the uneducated, but still she always edifies and moves and touches me.

'For a married man to be an author', she says, 'is sheer infidelity: it flies in the face of what the pastor told us, for the validity of marriage lies in this, that the man holds fast to his wife and to nothing else.' She is not troubled in the least if I respond by saying that she may not have paid sufficient atten-tion to the pastor's words, that one could almost think that she has been so forgetful that she needs to go to the pastor again to learn that marriage is a special and 'particular' duty – and that all duties can be divided into general and particular, and are duties either to God, or to ourselves and our neighbours. She dismisses the whole thing as teasing, and she has 'not forgotten, by the way, what it says in the textbook about marriage – that it is especially the man's duty'. In vain I try to explain her linguistic error – that she has construed the words illogically, ungrammatically, against all principles of interpretation, since this passage is indeed about the special duties of the husband, while the special duties of the wife are dealt with in the following paragraph. But all in vain. She takes her stand on her previous 'For a married man to be an author is the worst kind of infidelity.' Now it has even become the 'worst' infidelity. If I then remind her that the man, according to all divine and human laws, is the master, and that otherwise my position in life would be quite insignificant, since I become only an *encliticon*[6] to her, which is still claiming too much, she will reproach me for my unfairness, 'for I know very well that she asks for nothing, that her only wish is to be absolutely nothing in relation to me'. I protest that if I am ultimately only an *encliticon*, then it is important to me that she become as great as possible, so that I do not become even less by being an *encliticon* to nothing, but she simply looks at me and says: just teasing.

My wife is consistent, fixed in her idea. I have tried to flatter her, saying it would be delightful for us if my – our – name became famous; that she is the muse who inspires me. But she will have none of it. She regards fame as a terrible calamity, my complete ruin, and she hopes with all her heart that I will run into some severe criticism and that it will at last bring me to my senses. As for being my muse, she does not believe it, still less want it, and she prays with all her soul that God will save her from thus bringing upon herself the end of her wedded bliss. She is unyielding, and *summa summarum* [in a word], 'let us hear the conclusion of the whole matter':[7] 'either', she says, 'a proper husband – or else . . . well, the rest is not important'.

Now while the reader may find her argument rather weak, as I confess I do, since she entirely ignores the real issues at stake – namely, the boundaries between marital and personal duty, which would be more than enough to occupy a head as profound as it is acute – nevertheless she still has an argument *in subsidio* [in reserve], to which the reader will perhaps give more weight. One day, after we had battled over our differences and the quarrel had transformed itself, as it always does, into a *redintegratio amoris* [restoration of love], she took me intimately by the arm, gave me an utterly disarming look, and said: 'My love! I did not want to say it so bluntly. I was hoping to find another way to persuade you to renounce your project and thus save you from disappointment. But that is not succeeding, so I am obliged to tell you with all the probity that befits a wife: I do not think you are capable of being an author. But on the other hand – yes, you may laugh at me a little – but on the other hand, you have the genius and talent and an extraordinary gift for being my husband in such a way that I will never cease to admire you, while showing all my grateful love and revelling in my inferiority.' She did not attempt to develop the argument any further, however. When I tried to ask her whether, how far, and how, she came up with another explanation, saying that 'one day I would come to regret becoming an author and thus betraying her, but by then it would be too late to shrug off the regret and I would have to endure its bitterness instead'.

And how did the quarrel end? Who won – the *hostis domesticus* [enemy within] or the author? It is not hard to guess – though the reader who reads this and thus knows that I became an author may have a momentary difficulty. The outcome was that I promised not to try to be an author. But it was like a defence of an academic thesis, when the candidate has triumphed over all objections, and the opponent finally raises some linguistic scruple in order at least to be in the right about something, and the candidate politely concedes in order to agree that there is at least one thing that he is right about: I reserved for myself permission to write prefaces. I appealed in this respect to various analogies, for instance that men who have promised their wives that they will give up snuff may be allowed to collect as many snuffboxes as they like in compensation. She accepted the proposal, perhaps believing that it is impossible to write a preface without writing a book (which of course I would not dare to do) unless one is already a famous author who may provide such things on request, but of course this could not possibly apply to me.

So much for my promise and my obligation. The small and trifling things I publish here have been written *salva conscientia* [with a clear conscience]. My wife knows nothing about them, however, since I wrote them when I was away in the country. I beg the critics to be gentle with me – for what if they discovered that my wife was right all along, and that I was not capable of being an author? What if they were to tear me to pieces and my wife found out? Then I would surely look in vain for encouragement and consolation from my life's companion. She would probably cry with joy at having carried her point, at having taught me a lesson, finding confirmation of her faith in a just Providence and corroboration of her idea that for a married man to be an author is the worst kind of infidelity.

Notes

1   An allusion to and slight misquotation of Horace, *Odes* I, ix; see above, p. 26, n. 1.
2   A reference to a line in *Kallundborgs-Krøniker – eller Censurens Oprindelse* by Jens Baggesen: 'Thi saare lang er Rettens Vei' ('Since so long is the way of justice').

3   An allusion to the 'writing on the wall' at Belshazzar's feast; see Daniel 5, 5.

4   The elder Cato (234–149) was said to end all his speeches to the Roman Senate with the phrase 'let me also say that Carthage ought to be destroyed'.

5   An allusion to the pedant Stygotius in Ludvig Holberg's play, *Jacob von Tyboe* (1725).

6   An *encliticon* is an expression which occurs only as a suffix to other words.

7   Cf. Ecclesiastes 12, 13: 'Let us hear the conclusion of the whole matter: Fear God, and keep his commandments: for this is the whole duty of man.'

9

Concluding Unscientific Postscript

With its elaborate discussions of paradox, possibility, eternity and time, *Philosophical Fragments* had been one of the most demanding philosophical works ever published in Danish, or indeed any other language; but its pseudonymous author, Johannes Climacus, did his best to make light of it. He was of course trying to offer a serious philosophico-theological argument, to the effect that individuality should not be subsumed into collectivity, and that religious faith needs to be shielded from the glare of self-evident truths and systematic certitudes. But he realized he would be falling into a kind of contradiction if he presented his case in a coercively argumentative form, so he chose to pass it off as a collection of random borrowings loosely assembled into a pamphlet (*piece*). 'An author of pamphlets such as I am has no seriousness of purpose,' he added, so 'why should I feign a seriousness I do not have?'[1]

But Johannes closed *Philosophical Fragments* with a teasing promise: 'in the next section of this pamphlet, if I ever write it, I propose to call the problem by its true name, and clothe it in its historical costume'. In other words he would try to reduce the relations between philosophy and faith to a kind of system – a system which would reveal Christianity in all its indelible oddity, focusing on the indissoluble paradox that the birth, life and death of Jesus Christ were contingencies which brought eternity into the world.

For it is a frivolous matter to write a pamphlet – but to promise the System is a serious thing; many a man has become extremely serious both in his own eyes and in those of others by making such a promise. However, what the historical costume of the following section will be is not hard to see. It is well known that Christianity is the only historical phenomenon which in spite of the historical, indeed precisely because of it, has sought to provide a point of departure for the eternal consciousness of the single individual: Christianity has tried to interest the individual but not merely historically; it has attempted to build the individual's eternal happiness on a relationship to something historical.[2]

Two years later the Copenhagen public would discover that Johannes's promise was serious, even if its fulfilment was characteristically skittish. The sequel to *Philosophical Fragments* appeared on 28 February 1846 under the title *Concluding Unscientific Postscript to the Philosophical Fragments* ('by Johannes Climacus, edited by S. Kierkegaard'), and it proved to be rather more than a short, systematic supplement to a little pamphlet. In fact *Postscript* was more than five times as long as the text it was meant to comment on, and it contained prose of such monumental difficulty that the reader is left wondering if Johannes the humorist has changed out of all recognition, into an insufferable professorial bore in desperate need of a lighter heart and a heavier editor.

Postscript was also adorned with two fateful subtitles. The first – *A Mimical-Pathetical-Dialectical Compilation* – gave readers a now-familiar warning that they were about to witness an exercise in generic promiscuity. The second, on the other hand – *An Existential Contribution* (*Existentielt Indlaeg*) – contains a message that no one would have been able to decipher at the time, since it involved a decisive alteration in the vocabulary of Western philosophy. For it was mainly through *Postscript* that the idea of 'existence' was narrowed down so that instead of applying to all categories of entities, human or non-human, it would refer specifically to our lives as finite human beings, or rather as *enkelte* (usually translated as 'individuals' or 'single individuals').

Approximately fifty copies of *Postscript* were sold in the first three years, so it was a notable failure even by Kierkegaard's own standards. But in retrospect it has come to be seen as the first work of 'existential' thought, or the founding text of the twentieth-century 'existentialism' of Jaspers, Heidegger and Sartre. As such it can be read as an early attempt to draw philosophical attention to the distance that separates our *Existenz* as individuals from the 'abstract thought' of tradition and the 'pure thought' of modernity – an appeal to us to be true to the terms of our finite historical existences instead of yearning for some otherworldly purity outside time.

The concept of existentialism is a rather inexact way of defining the themes of the *Postscript*, as well as an anachronistic one; but still it highlights some of the book's studied grotesqueness. Johannes opens with a cheerful preface in which he expresses the hope that 'fate will smile upon his enterprise' and save him from earnest fools who might try to 'persuade the public that there is something in it'.[3] This is followed by an introduction which mocks, yet again, the Hegelians who say that they have completed their System, or almost, if as yet not quite.[4] But when he starts to formulate the issues he will confront in the *Postscript*, Johannes grows more sombre: he will first discuss the 'objective problem' of whether Christianity is true, he says, and then the 'subjective problem' of the 'relationship of the individual to Christianity'; for the essential question is utterly serious: 'How can I, Johannes Climacus, share in the happiness promised by Christianity?'[5]

Book one despatches the Objective Problem at high speed. The argument is that neither the direct and immediate knowledge furnished by the history of Christianity, nor the mediated knowledge provided by speculative theology, can have anything to say to those of us who understand what is at stake in religion. We realize that we come to religious questions not as disinterested observers but – to use a phrase that will be often repeated – as existing individuals with an 'infinite interest' in the outcome. And beliefs which concern us so closely need to be handled, according to Johannes, with the lightest possible touch: it is like trying to saw through a piece of wood, and we will never succeed unless we refrain from applying pressure.[6]

The Subjective Problem is dealt with in book two, whose subtitle includes the vital Kierkegaardian catchphrase: 'becoming a Christian'. From a truly Christian point of view, Johannes says, merely being a Christian is no better than not being one; the problem is how to *become* a Christian. His treatment of this issue is divided into two sections, the main one a vast and variegated discussion of 'becoming subjective', the other, which precedes it, a relatively brief engagement with the eighteenth-century German dramatist and critic Gotthold Ephraim Lessing.

Lessing had once been under the spell of the idea of the 'Reasonableness of Christianity' as expounded by John Locke and the English deists; but later he came to think that the passionate significance of religious beliefs meant that they reached far beyond sweet reasonableness. Johannes therefore presents us with a sequence of four 'theses' (three of them reproduced below, pp. 231–62) about subjectivity, folly, and the limits of systematicity and 'direct communication' – theses which Johannes, as an incorrigible plagiarist, would have liked to borrow from Lessing, even if Lessing had never uttered them.

Afterwards Johannes tries to offer his own account of the problem of 'subjectivity'. Other philosophers (Kant and Hegel for example) had used the term to designate a supposed inner correlative of outward objectivity, but for Johannes it was the name of a duty which is forced on us by our singular existences: what he calls the task of 'becoming subjective'.[7] For it is not a matter of telling an impersonal truth about the nature of subjectivity, but of trying to believe that 'truth is subjectivity'. The phrase occurs in the title of a chapter in which Johannes describes walking in the countryside and coming upon a freshly covered grave flanked by two grief-stricken mourners – a fragile old man and a little boy, evidently his grandson. Johannes realizes that the person who has died was the man's son, and father to the boy, and he hears the grandfather lamenting a double loss: for it seems that his dead son had succumbed to the death-in-life of speculative thought before succumbing to death itself. 'That he, my unhappy son, should have allowed himself to be so deceived', he cries. 'What was the point of all his learning, if it meant he could never explain himself to me, and I could not discuss his error with him because it was too elevated?'[8]

On witnessing this terrible scene, Johannes swears a solemn vow – so secret that not even his landlady would get to know of it – to dedicate himself to 'discovering where the misunderstanding between speculative thought and Christianity lies'.[9] But in a long appendix in the middle of the book he tells the story of how he began to lose heart. It was in February 1843 that he made his resolution; and just then a book appeared in the shops which performed exactly the task he had in mind: Victor Eremita's *Either/Or: A Fragment of Life*. And Johannes's uncanny experience of *déjà lu* was to be repeated again and again for the best part of three years: he would have a new literary thought, and 'lo and behold, a pseudonymous book appeared which did exactly what I was planning to do'. After Eremita's *Either/Or* he was confronted with Magister Kierkegaard's *Two Edifying Discourses*, Constantin Constantius's *Repetition*, and *Fear and Trembling* by Johannes de Silentio, to mention only a few. Johannes's inchoate private thoughts were finding expression before he even set pen to paper: so many 'elements in the realisation of the idea which I had formulated', as he put it, 'but was ironically exempted from realising'.[10]

Of course I have no idea whether my own understanding coincides with that of the authors, since I am only a reader. On the other hand, I am delighted that the pseudonymous authors – presumably aware of the relation of indirect communication to truth as inwardness – have never said anything or abused a preface in order to take an official position on their output, as if authors were by right the best interpreters of their own words, or as if it could profit a reader to know that an author 'intended such and such' when it had not in fact been carried out.[11]

Of course Johannes has to admit that he eventually asserted his independence and published something of his own: the 'pamphlet' called *Philosophical Frag-*

ments. But he now thinks it was a rather questionable production, based on unjustified assumptions about its readers. *Fragments*, he says, was an attempt to say something not merely about knowledge, but about existence, and for that reason its message had to be communicated indirectly.

Indirect communication makes communication into an art of a very different kind than it is ordinarily assumed to be – that is, when the communicator is thought of as offering something to his audience: either to those who already know, so that they may judge it, or to those who are ignorant, so that they can gain knowledge. But no one notices the next problem, which is what makes communication so difficult dialectically: that the recipient is an existing individual, and that this is the heart of the matter. It is much easier to stop people in the street and talk to them while standing still than to speak to passers by while keeping walking and not delaying them or forcing them to go out of their way. But such is the relation between one existing individual and another when the communication concerns the truth as existence-inwardness.

But the more he thinks about it, the more he realizes that his theory of 'communication through books' is not only unusual but also problematic, and he finds himself foundering on the question of whether his indirect communications could not in fact be directly communicated, in the form of the direct thesis that 'Subjectivity, inwardness is truth.'[12]

Concluding Unscientific Postscript is a book which grows like a snowball: part two is almost twenty times as long as part one, and section two of part two is ten times longer than section one. And whilst the elegant appendix in which Johannes Climacus tries to take revenge on Søren Kierkegaard would have constituted a neat finale, in fact it barely gets us halfway through the book. It is followed by a chapter on 'Actual Ethical Subjectivity', attacking the ideal of disinterestedness, especially in matters concerning our own existence, in which of course we have an 'infinite interest'. (The first section of 'Actual Ethical Subjectivity' is reproduced below, pp. 262–75.) The chapter concludes by sketching a portrait (not included here) of those rare thinkers who are so devoted to 'understanding themselves in existence' that they refuse to partake in the pleasures of speaking on behalf of others, of 'being part of the human race and saying "we", "the age we live in" or "the nineteenth century"'. Dedicating themselves to the task of becoming an 'existing individual in existence' they take care not only with their conclusions, but with the form of their communications – their 'style' – as well.[13]

Ironically enough, this injunction is followed by a long chapter containing 200 pages of general conclusions, presented with very little style at all. It is intended as a condensed summary of *Fragments*, but turns out to be twice its length. The first half – section A – expounds a relatively brief definition of 'existential pathos' (*existentielle pathos*) in three dialectical stages, and the second – section B – enlarges systematically on three dialectical contradictions between eternal truth and historical fact: the two essential aspects of Christianity. At the hinge between section A and section B Johannes introduces a distinction between the kinds of religiousness which correspond to each of them: 'Religiousness A', as he calls it, which is a jumble of high-minded ethical precepts, not specifically Christian; and 'Religiousness B', or 'paradoxical religiousness', which has the courage to face up to the absurdities of Christian faith without flinching.[14]

The distinction between religiousness A and religiousness B is eminently communicable, and it has often been removed from its original niche amongst Johannes's meditations on indirect communication and treated as a portable epitome of Kierkegaardian theology. Within *Postscript*, however, it led on to a chapter called 'Conclusion' in which the difficulty of becoming a Christian is summed up in a parable about an English highwayman who disguised himself with a large wig before attacking a gentleman and running off with his purse. A wandering pauper who passed along the road shortly afterwards took a fancy to the discarded wig and put it on his head before walking to the next town. There he was noticed by the gentleman, who took him to the magistrate's court and denounced him as his assailant. But the true highwayman happened to be sitting in the courtroom, observing the passing scene, and he took it into his head to suggest that the accuser might be mistaken. To prove the point he donned the wig himself, whereupon the gentleman realized his error, but too late: he could not unswear the oath with which he had identified the wrong person, so he came away empty handed, and the robber got off scot free. With this edifying little parable, and its strange equation of Christ with a highway robber, Johannes abruptly decides to 'end the whole book'.[15]

But the conclusion does not bring *Concluding Unscientific Postscript* to an end. It is followed by an appendix called 'Towards an Understanding with My Reader' (see below, pp. 275–80), in which Johannes declares that he is not in fact a Christian, but a 'humorist'. He has done his best to ensure that the book he has written will be wholly superfluous, and has addressed it exclusively to a reader who is a pure fiction, a mere figment of Johannes's imagination. But even after this final confession, the *Postscript* is still not over. Just before publication, a brief final appendix was added to *Postscript*, in small print but over Kierkegaard's own name. It was called 'A First and Last Explanation',[16] and it sought to place it beyond doubt that, whatever the pseudonymous authors might think, the *Concluding Postscript* really did mark a conclusion: an end to Kierkegaard's meteoric three-year career as an author.

After an almost complete confession of his authorship of the pseudonymous works, and a further account of indirect communication, Kierkegaard bids his pseudonyms a final farewell.

Notes

1 See *Philosophical Fragments*, chapter 5; cf. KW VII, p. 109.

2 Ibid.; cf. KW VII, p. 109.

3 *Concluding Unscientific Postscript to the Philosophical Fragments*, preface; cf. KW XII.1, p. 8.

4 Ibid., introduction; cf. KW XII.1, p. 13.

5 Ibid.; cf. KW XII.1, p. 17.

6 Ibid., part one, chapter II ('The Speculative Point of View'); cf. KW XII.1, p. 57.

7 Ibid., part two, §2, chapter I ('Becoming Subjective'); cf. KW XII.1, p. 129.

8 Ibid., part two, §2, chapter II ('Subjective Truth, Inwardness: Truth is Subjectivity'); cf. KW XII.1, p. 238.

9 Ibid.; cf. KW XII.1, p. 241.

10 Ibid., part two, §2, chapter II, appendix ('A Glance at a Contemporary Effort in Danish Literature'); cf. KW XII.1, pp. 251, 269.

11 Ibid.; cf. KW XII.1, p. 252.

12 Ibid.; cf. KW XII.1. pp. 274–6, 277, 278.

13 Ibid., part two, §2, chapter III, 4 ('The Subjective Thinker: His Task, his Form, his Style'); cf. KW XII.1, pp. 351, 355, 357.

14 Ibid., part two, §2, chapter IV ('Intermediate Clause between A and B'); cf. KW XII.1, pp. 555–7.

15 Ibid., part two, §2, chapter V, conclusion ('Subjective Determination of Being a Christian'); cf. KW XII.1, pp. 615–16; see also p. 69.

16 See below, pp. 280–4.

Concluding Unscientific Postscript to the Philosophical Fragments: A Mimical-pathetical-dialectical Compilation; an Existential Contribution by Johannes Climacus, edited by S. Kierkegaard

Possible and Actual Theses by Lessing

I would not presume to appeal to Lessing or invoke his authority, nor am I trying to use his fame to make my readers feel obliged to understand me (or at least to claim to), while at the same time they are embarrassed by my obscurity (which is of course as repellent as Lessing's fame is attractive). Nevertheless I now propose – and why not? – to present some theses which I shall attribute to Lessing even though I cannot be sure he would agree with them. In teasing high spirits, I might have been tempted to suggest that he uttered them himself, though perhaps not directly, or, in sentimentality

Concluding Unscientific Postscript first appeared in English in a translation by David Swenson, completed by Walter Lowrie (Princeton, 1941). A version by Howard V. Hong and Edna H. Hong was published (in two books) as vol. XII of *Kierkegaard's Writings* in 1992. The six selections printed below are all from book two: the first, second and fourth of the 'Possible and Actual Theses by Lessing'; the opening section of chapter 3; and the two concluding appendices. The translations are by Jane Chamberlain and Jonathan Rée and appear here for the first time, copyright © Jane Chamberlain and Jonathan Rée, 2001.

and admiration, that he is in some way responsible for them, or that I am ascribing them to him purely out of generosity, with proud discretion and self-esteem; or again, that I fear he might be offended or troubled if his name were associated with them. Very few authors are such good company as Lessing. Why? I think it is because he has such confidence. There can be no question here of the trivial and easy association between a distinguished genius or master and a less distinguished student, messenger or journeyman. I could not become Lessing's disciple even if I was determined to do so at all costs, for he has made discipleship impossible. Just as he is himself free, so, I think, he wants to make everyone else free in relation to him. He cannot abide the puffed-up ambitions of the student, and he fears being made ridiculous by those who, like babbling echoes, slavishly parrot whatever they have heard.

Thesis 1: The subjective existing thinker is aware of the dialectic of communication

Whereas objective thinking is indifferent to the existence of the thinking subject, subjective thinkers, as existing, are essentially interested [*interesseret*] in their own thinking. They exist in it, and it is thus subjected to a further kind of reflection – the reflection of inwardness, of ownership – which makes it the subject's exclusive possession. Objective thinkers stake everything on results, encouraging us all to become like a cheat – who copies out the answers and reels them off by rote; subjective thinkers, on the other hand, stake everything on the process and ignore results – partly because they possess the results as soon as they get under way, and partly because (like everyone else who has avoided being duped into objectivity, and thus turning inhumanly into Speculations) they are, as existing, in a constant process of becoming.

The reflection of inwardness is the double-reflection of subjective thinkers. In thinking, they think the universal, but they become more and more subjectively isolated through existing in this thinking and engaging with it in their inwardness.

The difference between subjective and objective thinking must find expression not only in the content of communication but also in its form.★

★ Double-reflection is already implicit in the very idea of communication. In the isolation of inwardness, the existing subject wants to communicate himself – that is, he wants to maintain his thinking in the inwardness of his subjective existence and yet at the same time to communicate himself. (Moreover, through his inwardness he also wants to express the life of eternity, in which the existence-category of movement is inconceivable, and therefore sociality and

In other words, subjective thinkers will always be aware that the form of their communication needs to be artistically characterized by as much reflection as they themselves have when they exist in their thinking. I emphasize *artistically*, since the secret lies in not giving direct expression to the double-reflection – doing so would indeed be a contradiction.

Ordinary communication between one person and another is wholly immediate, because people ordinarily exist in immediacy. If one person makes a statement, and someone else acknowledges it by reiterating it word for word, we might be tempted to assume that they understand each other and are in agreement. But if they are not aware of the doubleness of thought-existence, they will not understand the double-reflection of communication, and they will have no idea that this kind of agreement could also be an immense misunderstanding. Nor will they ever suspect that just as the subjective existing thinker achieves freedom through doubleness, so the secret of communication depends on freeing the other, which is why one should never communicate oneself directly, and indeed it would even be impious to do so. This is all the more true, of course, when what is essential is the subjective, and hence it applies first and foremost in the religious sphere – unless, of course, the communicator is God himself or someone who appeals to the miraculous authority of an apostle, rather than a mere human being who hopes to give his words and deeds some meaning.

(*cont'd from p. 232*) fellowship as well, and hence essential communication is also inconceivable because it is assumed that everyone essentially possesses everything.) It is not possible (barring thoughtlessness, to which of course nothing is impossible) for this contradiction to be expressed in a direct form. Yet it is not so difficult to see that such existing subjects might want to communicate themselves all the same. A man who falls in love, for example, and whose love is his very inwardness, may very well want to communicate himself – but not directly, because it is precisely the inwardness of his love that is important to him. He is essentially concerned with continually appropriating the inwardness of love, so he will never have a result or reach a conclusion. Whilst he may very much want to communicate, therefore, he can never make use of a direct form of communication, since that would presuppose results and finality. It is the same in the God-relationship. Anyone who is in this relationship is constantly in a process of inward becoming – in inwardness – and can never communicate himself directly, for the movement here goes in precisely the opposite direction. Direct communication demands certainty, but certainty is impossible for anyone in a process of becoming – indeed, it would be a deception. It is analogous with human love: if a girl is in love and longs for marriage, because of the secure certainty it would give her, if she wants to settle herself in legal security as a spouse, if she would exchange maidenly yearning for marital yawning, then her lover could rightly complain of her unfaithfulness, for even if she would never love anyone else, she would have let go of the Idea and would no longer really love him. That is the meaning of essential unfaithfulness in human love; whereas contingent unfaithfulness is simply a matter of loving someone else.

We can never become subjective religious thinkers, therefore, without grasping the doubleness of existence, and understanding that direct communication would amount to an attempt to swindle both God (perhaps cheating Him of another person's worship in truth)[1] and ourselves (by pretending we had ceased to be existing human beings), and indeed to swindle other human beings too (by limiting them to a merely relative God-relationship). Direct communication would be a swindle and a contradiction of our entire thought. But to state this directly would also be a contradiction, because the form would be direct despite the double-reflection of the utterance. To expect a thinker to contradict his entire thinking and world-view through the form of his communication, and console him with the suggestion that he can at least accomplish something that way, and that no one will mind – indeed, that no one will even notice in this objective age, when such exquisite consistency has become a scruple which every systematic journeyman holds in contempt – this is certainly sound advice, and pretty inexpensive too. Imagine a religiously existing subject who believed that no one should have disciples, and that having disciples would be a betrayal of both God and humanity. Suppose he was also rather stupid (for if we need more than honesty to make our way in the world, we certainly need a bit of stupidity in order to be really successful and widely understood) and stated his belief directly and with unction and pathos – what then? Well, he would be understood – and before long ten people would come forward to offer their services in preaching this doctrine, asking no more than a free shave once a week in return. The lucky man would have his doctrine further reinforced, that is to say, by acquiring disciples who accepted and broadcast his disapproval of discipleship.

Objective thinking is completely indifferent to subjectivity and therefore to inwardness and inward appropriation; its method of communication is therefore direct. Of course it may not be simple, but it is direct: it has none of the art and artfulness of double-reflection, the God-fearing and humane solicitude about communicating itself which is characteristic of subjective thinking. It can be understood directly and reeled off by rote, is aware only of itself, so it is not really communication at all★ – or at least not artistic

---

★ This is always the case with the negative: wherever it is unconsciously present, it transforms the positive into the negative. Here it transforms communication into illusion, because no thought is given to the negative in the communication: the communication is regarded as purely and simply positive. In the artfulness of double-reflection, the negativity of communication is taken into consideration, and it is this form of communication – which may seem not to be communication at all compared with that other communication – which is communication indeed.

communication, since that always requires consideration of its recipient and care in adapting the form of the communication to the recipient's misunderstanding. Like most people, objective thinkers* are fiercely kind and communicative; they communicate without reserve, grasping at any testimonials to the truth of objective thinking, and recommendations and promises about how one day everyone will come to accept it, since it is so certain. Or perhaps so uncertain, since testimonials and recommendations and promises which are intended to persuade those who do not yet accept the truth may also express a need on the part of the teachers for the security and reassurance of majority approval. If their contemporaries withhold it, then they will appeal to the future instead, so great is their certainty. Their certainty is like the independence of those who need the world to acknowledge their independence from the world so that they can be sure of it.

The form of a communication is by no means the same as its expression. A first reflection gives a thought its proper expression in words, but it is followed by a second reflection, which concerns the relation between the communication and its communicator, and reflects [*gjengiver*] the existing communicator's own relation to the Idea. Allow me to give a few examples; there is plenty of time, after all, since what I am writing is far from being the much-anticipated final paragraph that is destined to complete the System. Suppose, then, that someone wanted to communicate the following conviction: truth is inwardness; there is no objective truth, for truth consists in inward appropriation.† Suppose he spoke with inspired fervour because he was convinced that his message would be the salvation of all who heard it. Suppose he reiterated it at every opportunity until he got through not only to those who perspire easily but to the thick-skinned as well – what then? Well, the labourers standing idle in the marketplace would go straight to work in the vineyard on hearing what he said, proclaiming the doctrine to one and all. And what then? Well, he would have contradicted himself still further, just as he had done from the beginning, since his fervour and inspi-

---

* Please bear in mind that I am speaking of the religious sphere, in which objective thinking is arrant irreligiousness if it is supposed to rank as the highest. Wherever objective thinking is not supposed to have anything to do with subjectivity, however, direct communication is in order.

† I say 'suppose', since in this form I may be permitted to spell out both the most certain and the most preposterous. This means that the most certain is not proposed as the most certain, but only as a hypothesis which may shed light on the relationship; and in the same way the preposterous is not proposed essentially, but only hypothetically, so as to shed light on logical relationships.

ration for communicating his message was in itself a misunderstanding. The only thing that mattered, of course, was that he should make himself understood, and the inwardness of the understanding would consist precisely in each individual understanding it for himself. But he ended up as a town-crier of inwardness – and a town-crier of inwardness is certainly a creature worth seeing.

Convictions of this kind cannot be really communicated without art and self-discipline. They require the discipline of inwardly grasping that the individual's God-relationship is the most important thing, and that the bustling activity of others expresses a lack of inwardness and a superabundance of amiable stupidity. They call for the art of inexhaustibly varying the doubly-reflected form of the communication, just as inwardness is itself inexhaustible. The greater the art, the greater the inwardness; indeed, if we had sufficient artistry we could even allow ourselves to admit that we were using it; we could be confident that our infinite concern to preserve our own inwardness would enable us in the next moment to ensure the inwardness of our communication. And such concern saves us from every kind of positive idle talk.

Suppose someone wanted to communicate that the truth is not the truth, since it is the way which is the truth – that the truth exists only in a process of becoming, of inward appropriation, so that it does not issue in results. Suppose he was a philanthropist who could not bear to withhold this knowledge from others. Suppose he tried the artistic method, but, despite his best endeavours, was never able to tell whether he had helped anyone, and suppose he decided to take the splendid shortcut of communicating directly through *Adressavisen* [a Copenhagen newspaper], thus gaining masses of followers – what then? Well, his statement would of course turn into a result. Or suppose someone wanted to communicate that every reception is a creation, and repeated it so often that the statement even came to be a standard exercise in children's copy-books – then it would certainly have been confirmed. Suppose there was a kindly gentleman who wanted to communicate the conviction that every individual's God-relationship is a secret. Suppose he cared so much for other people that he simply could not keep quiet about his conviction, but he nevertheless had enough sense to grasp that communicating it directly might perhaps involve him in contradiction, and therefore only communicated it to others under a vow of secrecy – what then? Well, either he was assuming that the disciple was wiser than the teacher, and really could keep silent whereas the teacher could not (what an excellent satire on being a teacher!), or he was so blissfully swamped in gobbledygook that he lost sight of the contradiction altogether. These good-hearted people are very strange: it is touching that they cannot keep quiet about such things, but it is very vain of them to believe that other people need assistance in their God-relationship – as if God did not already have the power to help both himself and anyone else who cared to be helped. Yet it requires a strenuous effort to hold fast to the thought, while existing, that we are nothing before God, and that our efforts never amount to more than a joke. It is no easy matter to learn enough respect for others to stop dreaming of poking our nose into their God-relationship, both because we have quite enough on our hands in dealing with our own, and because God is no friend to impertinence.

Wherever subjectivity is of importance in knowledge, so that inward appropriation becomes all-important, communication must be a work of art; it is doubly-reflected, and its first form is the subtle precept that subjective individuals must be kept devoutly separate from each other, and prevented from fusing together in objectivity. This is objectivity's farewell to subjectivity.

Only doubly-reflected subjective thinking has secrets; ordinary communication and objective thinking have none. The essential content of subjective thinking has to be essentially secret because it cannot be communicated directly; this is the meaning of its secrecy. What is essential for such knowledge is inward appropriation, which means that it cannot be directly expressed, and this keeps it concealed from those who are not doubly-reflected in the same way within themselves. But it cannot be said in any other way, since this is the essential form of the truth.* Those who try to communicate it directly are therefore fools, and so are those who expect them to do so. Confronted with such cunning artistic communication, everyday human stupidity will always denounce it as 'egotism'. So when stupidity prevails, and communication becomes direct, stupidity will have prevailed by having made a fool of the communicator too.

A distinction can be made between essential secrets and contingent ones. What is said at a secret meeting of a Council of State, for example, can be directly understood once it is made publicly known, and is therefore only a contingent secret. What will happen in a year's time is also a contingent secret, because no one knows it yet; but when it has happened it will be possible to understand it directly. But when Socrates distanced himself from every

---

* In our age, anyone with a well-developed subjectivity, and therefore a good sense of the art of communication, is bound to have a gloriously high old time. He will be thrown out on his ear for being incapable of objectivity, until at last some kind-hearted objective fellow, a systematic sort of chap, will take pity on him and help him halfway into his paragraphs. For what was once regarded as impossible, such as depicting Mars in the armour that made him invisible, can now be achieved extremely well. And indeed – this is even more peculiar – he will half succeed.

external relationship by appealing to his *daimon*, apparently expecting everyone else to do the same, then we have a life-view which essentially becomes a secret (or becomes an essential secret) because it cannot be communicated directly. The most Socrates could do was help others negatively, through maieutic artistry, to arrive at the same point of view. Subjectivity, which through dialectical inwardness eludes direct forms of expression, is always an essential secret.

The inexhaustible artistry of such forms of communication corresponds to and reflects the existing subject's relationship to the Idea. Perhaps this can be clarified (without presupposing that anyone has actually been conscious of it and existed in this way) by sketching this existence-relationship in the form of an experiment.

Thesis 2: In his existence-relation to truth, an existing subjective thinker is negative and positive in equal measure; he has as much humour as essential pathos, and is constantly in the process of becoming – of striving

Since the existing subject exists (and this is the fate of all of us – except those who are so objective that they have pure being to be in), he is of course in the process of becoming. And just as the form of his communication must conform essentially to his own existence, so his thinking must correspond to the form of existence. Everyone is now familiar, thanks to Hegel, with the dialectic of communication. In processes of becoming, the alternation between being and non-being (still a somewhat obscure determination, given that being itself is also the continuity of the alternation) is later described as negativity and positivity.

Nowadays we hear a great deal of talk about negativity and about negative thinkers, and those who are positive are forever preaching, and offering prayers of grateful thanks to God and Hegel that they are positive rather than negative. In relation to thinking, positivity can be classified under the following categories: sense-certainty, historical knowledge, and speculative result. Yet this positivity is also untrue. Sense-certainty is deceptive (as we learn both from Greek scepticism and from modern philosophy), historical knowledge is illusory (since it is mere approximation-knowledge), and the speculative results are a muddled mishmash. Hence positive knowledge cannot express the situation of the knowing subject in existence, since it deals only with a fictitious objective subject – and to mistake ourselves for such a thing is to fool ourselves. Every subject is an existing subject, and we must express this essentially in our knowing by abstaining from the illusory closure of sense-certainty, of historical knowledge, and of illusory results. Historical knowledge can teach us a great deal about the world, but nothing about ourselves, for it does not take us beyond the sphere of approximation-knowledge. We may fancy that we have attained a certainty in our supposed positivity that can only be achieved in the infinite, but as existing we can never be in the infinite, we can only constantly arrive. Nothing historical can become infinitely certain to me except this: that I exist. And this is not historical, nor can any other individual become infinitely certain of it, for we can have infinite knowledge only of our own existence. The speculative result is an illusion which arises from existing subjects seeking to abstract, in thought, from their existing and thus become *sub specie æterni* [from the point of view of eternity].

Negative thinkers are therefore always better off, since their awareness of the negative gives them something positive, while positive thinkers are simply deluded and therefore have nothing at all. Because the negative is present in existence, and present everywhere (since existence [*tilværelse, existents*] is constantly in the process of becoming), our only escape is to become constantly aware of it. Any attempt to become positively assured is mere foolishness.

The negativity in existence, or rather the negativity of existing subjects (which must be essentially reflected in their thinking in an adequate form) has its ground in the subject's synthesis as an existing infinite spirit. The only certainty is the infinite and the eternal, but since this is in the subject it is also in existence, and its first expression is therefore its illusiveness and the enormous contradiction that the eternal becomes in coming into existence.

And this must be reflected in the form of the existing subject's thinking. To state it directly would be to speak an untruth, since direct statements leave out the illusiveness, making the form of communication become as confusing as when the wrong word comes out of the mouth of an epileptic, although the problem may not be as obvious to the confused speaker as it would be to an epileptic. Let me give an example. As existing subjects we are eternal, but as existing we are temporal. Now, the illusiveness of the infinite lies in the fact that the possibility of death is present in every moment, and every kind of positive stability is therefore suspect. If we are not conscious of this at every moment, then our positive confidence in life is simply speculative childishness, an arrogant swaggering about in systematic buskins. But if we become conscious of it, then the thought of infinity will grow so infinite that our existence will seem to vanish into nothing. But how are existing subjects to reflect it in their thought-existence? Everyone knows what it is like to exist, but those who are positive know it positively, which means that they do not know it at all – but then of course they are extremely busy with the whole of world history. Once a year on a special occasion they may grasp this thought and declare, in the form of an assurance, that this is how things are. But the fact that they only notice it now and then on special occasions just confirms how extremely positive they are, and their putting it in the form of stable reassurances only shows that, although they can state it, they do not know what they are talking about, and can therefore forget it again a moment later.

The only adequate form for such negative thoughts is an elusive one, because direct communication relies on steady continuity, whereas the elusiveness of existence isolates us whenever we grasp it. Those who are aware of this will avoid every kind of direct statement. Content with being human, they have an impassive strength that saves them from being tempted to make pronouncements about world history in its entirety, which would gain them the admiration of the like-minded – and the ridicule of existence. Socrates was something of an idler, as everyone knows. He never troubled himself with either world history or astronomy – Diogenes tells us he gave up astronomy, so it would be presumptuous to guess what he was doing when he stood still and stared at the stars.[2] But he always had time on his hands, and was eccentric enough to be concerned about the simply *human* – a concern which, oddly enough, is regarded as eccentric among *human beings*, whereas it is considered perfectly normal to be concerned about world history, astronomy, and other such things. I read a wonderful article in the *Fyenske Tidsskrift* which said that Socrates was something of an ironist.[3] This really ought to be better known by now, and I am glad to appeal to this article since I wish to make a similar point. When evoking the infinite, Socrates's irony sometimes takes the form of speaking like a lunatic. His words are as cunning as existence itself, and perhaps (I say 'perhaps' because I do not claim to be as wise as the positive writer in the *Fyenske Tidsskrift*) this could be because he does not want to acquire an impressionable and faithful audience which would listen to his statements about the negativity of existence and appropriate them positively. Socrates's lunacy may also have meant that when he was discussing a question with other people he was conferring about it privately with the Idea as well. Those who can only speak in direct forms will not understand this. Nor is there anything to be gained by trying to spell it out once and for all, since its secret is precisely that it must always be present in the thought and its reflection, just as it is present everywhere in existence. It is always best when we are not understood, therefore, since we are thereby protected from misunderstanding. Socrates really speaks like a lunatic when he remarks on how very strange it was that the sea-captain who ferried people from Greece to Italy took their money on arrival, and then calmly walked up and down on the beach as if he had done them all a service, though he could not really be sure that he had done them a kindness, since it might have been better for all of them if they had lost their lives at sea.[4]* Perhaps one or two of those present really thought he was mad (for according to Plato and Alcibiades, he was generally considered rather weird [atopos]), though others may simply have thought he had a funny way of expressing himself. Perhaps. But perhaps Socrates was also keeping a rendezvous with his Idea – with ignorance – and having grasped the infinite in the form of ignorance he had to keep it by him wherever he went. Assistant professors do not care about such matters, however – they deal with them with pathos once a year in the fourteenth paragraph, and they are quite right to leave it at that if they have wives and children to support, good prospects to nurture, and no good sense to lose.

Subjective existing thinkers who have the infinite in their soul have it constantly, and their form will always be negative. When the form of existence is reflected in their own existence as actually existing, then, as existing, they will always be just as negative as they are positive, their positivity consisting in the ever-deepening inwardness of their response to negativity. Among so-called negative thinkers there will always be some who, having caught a glimpse of negativity, yield completely to the positive and go out into the streets noisily peddling their sanctifying negative wisdom – and of course the result can be cried up as easily as herring from Holstein. Street-traders of this negative kind are not much cleverer than their positive rivals, but they have no right to get angry with them, since they themselves are essentially positive. They are not existing thinkers; they may have been once, before they discovered their result, but from that moment on they no longer existed as thinkers – only as street-traders and auctioneers.

Genuine subjective existing thinkers are always negative and positive in equal measure, and vice versa. They do not achieve this state all at once in a chimerical mediation, but are in it as long as they exist, and they always communicate accordingly. They are not extraordinarily communicative: if they were, they would be treating those who desire to learn as if they did not participate in ordinary human existence. They are aware of the negativity

---

* If anyone were to speak like this today, he would be universally regarded as mad. But those who are positive know that Socrates was a wise man, and they know with positive conviction that it is quite definitely so: ergo.

of the infinite in existence, and constantly keep the wound of negativity open, which may of course sometimes bring salvation. (Those who allow the wound to heal will become positive . . . and the more deceived.) And they express the same thing in their communication: they are always learners, never teachers, and when they are as negative as they are positive they are constantly striving.

Such subjective thinkers do, of course, miss out on something because of this: they forfeit a certain positive, plump satisfaction in life. Most people's lives change when they reach a certain stage in their journey: they get married, enter a profession, and feel they must therefore accomplish something and have results. (This desire for results is a consequence of their shame before others, rather than any consideration of the consequences of modesty before the deity.) And so they believe, for the sake of custom and convention, that they have actually accomplished something, or else they moan and groan about all the things that have got in their way. But it is a terrible insult to the deity if the groans are meant for Him! And it is another terrible insult to the deity if the moans are merely a matter of custom and convention! How contradictory it is for them to moan that they are too busy chasing after worldly things to have time for higher things, since they could simply give up worldly things and stop moaning! And if they do apply themselves to a little striving from time to time, it never amounts to more than a cursory annotation to a text completed long ago. In this way they evade all active awareness of the enormous difficulties involved in even the simplest statements about existing as a human being, but as positive thinkers they retain their confident knowledge of the whole of world history and the secret thoughts of our Lord.

Those who exist are in a constant process of becoming. Actually existing subjective thinkers constantly reproduce their own existence in their thinking, and transpose their thinking into becoming. This is similar to having a style: only those who never complete anything have genuine style, for they 'trouble the waters of language'[5] with every beginning, and for them even the most everyday expressions come into existence with utterly fresh originality.

To be thus constantly in the process of becoming constitutes the illusiveness of the infinite in existence. It could drive ordinary sensualists to despair, for we all like to get things finished. But this is an evil inclination, and we should try to renounce it. The perpetual process of becoming is the uncertainty of earthly life, where everything is uncertain. Of course everyone knows this, and speaks about it from time to time, particularly on special occasions though never without sweat and tears. But by speaking about it directly and thus upsetting themselves as well as others, they demonstrate in practice what they had already made clear by the form in which they expressed themselves – that they do not understand what they are talking about.*

The following story was told by Charon in the underworld, according to Lucian.[6] There was once a man who invited a friend to come and dine with him. He promised a rare dish, and the friend thanked him kindly. 'Be sure to come', said the man. 'You can certainly count on it', said his friend. But as they took leave of each other a tile fell from a roof and killed him. 'You would have died laughing', Charon says. But suppose the friend had been an orator who had just given a touching speech about the uncertainty of everything! For that is indeed how people talk: they know everything, and at the same moment they do not. And that is why it is considered fatuous and eccentric to bother with such things and all the difficulties they entail – they are all too well known. It is considered a very fine thing to be concerned with special or distinctive knowledge, known exclusively to the few, and a waste of time to bother with what everyone already knows, where the only possibility of distinction lies in the inane triviality of *how* it is known, which is no way to get famous. Suppose the friend had replied in terms of uncertainty – what then? Well, people would have thought him mad, though many might not have noticed; for uncertainty can be expressed so illusively that only those who are already familiar with such thoughts can detect it. Of course they would not regard it as madness – and they would be right, since while the reply might wend its cheerful way drolly through the rest of the good-humoured conversation, the speaker could have kept a private rendezvous with the deity, who is present whenever the uncertainty of everything is thought infinitely. Those who actually have an eye for the deity can therefore see him everywhere, whereas those who see him only on special occasions do not really see him at all; they are superstitiously deceived by a phantom.

---

* A thoroughly cultivated individual can be recognized by the degree of dialectical thinking in which he lives his everyday life. The art lies in living our daily lives in the decisive dialectic of the infinite, but carrying on living none the less. Most people rely on comfortable categories for everyday use, and resort to those of infinity only on special occasions, so that they never really possess them. Of course it takes tremendous effort to exist and make daily use of the dialectic of the infinite, just as it takes tremendous effort to prevent it from swindling us out of existence instead of training us in it. It is well known that the sound of cannons may at first deafen us, but it is also well known that if we stay put we will grow accustomed to the noise and be able to hear every word of a conversation just as clearly as if the guns had fallen silent. It is similar for those whose spiritual existence is intensified by reflection.

Subjective existing thinkers are positive and negative in equal measure. This can also be expressed by saying that they are as alive to comedy as to pathos. In ordinary existence, pathos and comedy are distributed in such a way that some people have one and others the other, or that they sometimes have a little more or less of the one or the other. But the proportions are always equal for those who exist in a double-reflection: they have exactly as much sense of comedy as of pathos. This equality is a matter of mutual assurance, for pathos will become mere illusion if it is not secured by comedy, and comedy which is not secured by pathos is mere childishness. Those who cannot create this equality for themselves will never understand it. What Socrates said about the sea voyage may have sounded like a joke, but it was uttered with deep seriousness. If he had meant it as a joke, it might have been accepted, though it would certainly have worried anyone of a nervous disposition if he meant it seriously. But suppose Socrates did not mean it in this way at all? And what if the friend had responded to the invitation by saying: 'I will most certainly come, unless of course I accidentally get killed by a falling roof-tile, since then I will have to disappoint you'? That might also have sounded like a joke. And yet it could have been spoken with the greatest seriousness, and the speaker could have been joking with his friends at the same time as addressing the deity.

Suppose there was a girl expecting her lover to arrive on the ship Socrates mentioned. Suppose she hurried to the harbour, came upon Socrates and, bursting with a lover's passion, asked after her beloved. Suppose the jesting Socrates ignored her question and simply said: 'Well the skipper is walking up and down the beach with a smug expression, and jingling his payment in his pocket, though he cannot really know for sure whether it might have been better for all of them if they had lost their lives at sea.' What then? If she had any sense she would have realized that Socrates was telling her, in his roundabout way, that her lover had arrived safely, and once she was sure of that – what then? She would laugh at Socrates, since she was not so carried away as to forget how wonderful it was that her lover had arrived. The girl cared for nothing except her rendezvous with her lover, and a loving embrace on the safe seashore – she was not mature enough for a Socratic rendezvous with the deity in the Idea, on the boundless seas of uncertainty.

But let us now suppose that our young lady was a little more experienced – what then? She would of course know exactly the same as Socrates – the only difference would be in the way each of them knew it. Yet Socrates presumably lived the whole of his life in this difference, and even at the age of 70 he had not finished striving to practice ever more inwardly what every 16-year-old girl knows. He was not like someone who has learned Hebrew – he could not turn to the girl and say 'You know nothing about this, and it takes a very long time to learn.' Nor was he like a skilled sculptor, whom the girl could easily admire because she can see that he can do what she cannot. The problem is that Socrates knows nothing that she does not know. So it is hardly surprising if he was indifferent to death: presumably the poor fellow realized that he had wasted his life, and that it was now too late to start learning the sorts of things that only special people know. No wonder he did not raise any objections to his death sentence – after all, he knew the state would not lose anything irreplaceable when he died. He may perhaps have said to himself, 'If only I had been a professor of Hebrew, or a sculptor, or a great dancer – not to say a world-historical genius bestowing blessings on humanity as a whole – then the state would never recover from losing me, as its citizens would never learn the lessons I could have taught them! But as it is, why should anyone care about me, for I know nothing that is not already known to everyone.' What a joker Socrates was! He joked about Hebrew, and sculpture, and dance, and world-historical bliss, but he was also so concerned about the deity that – even though he practised unrelentingly all his life (as a great dancer in honour of the deity) – he never had any confidence that he would be able to pass the deity's ultimate test; and anyway, what could that be?

There is an apparent difference between comedy and tragedy at the level of immediacy, but it vanishes in double-reflection where the difference becomes infinite and thus establishes their identity. From a religious point of view, therefore, devotion can be expressed as piously through comedy as through pathos. The basis of both comedy and tragedy lies in the disparity – in the contradiction between infinity and finitude, eternity and the process of becoming. A pathos that excludes humour or comedy is therefore a mis-understanding; it is not pathos at all. Subjective existing thinkers are there-fore as double-faced as the existence-relation itself. When we look at a disparity with the Idea in front of us, we see it with pathos; when we look at it with the Idea behind us, we see it with humour. When subjective exist-ing thinkers turn to face the Idea, they will interpret the disparity with pathos, but when they turn their back and let it illuminate disparity from behind, then they will interpret it with humour. There is thus an infinite reli-gious pathos in addressing God as 'Thou', and infinite humour in turning our backs on Him and seeing, within finitude, how finitude may be infil-trated from beyond. We will never have the pathos of infinity until we have completely exhausted comedy; but if we have the pathos of infinity, we will immediately be given comedy too.

Prayer is thus the highest pathos of infinity,* but it is also comical† because its inwardness makes it incommensurable with every kind of external expression – especially if we follow the scriptural injunction to anoint our heads and wash our faces when we are fasting.[7] Comedy can be present here in two different ways. The inappropriate form would be exemplified if, say, a mighty fellow tried to express the inwardness of his prayers by coming forward as he prayed, twisting and turning in various athletic postures so that an artist studying the musculature of the arm would find it all very instructive – especially if the man had left his arms bare. The inwardness of prayer and its 'groanings which cannot be uttered' are not commensurable with the muscular.[8] But the true form of comedy occurs when the infinite is at work in someone while no one – absolutely no one – realizes it. In relation to the perpetual process of becoming, comedy and pathos are both simultaneously present in the repetition of a prayer; its inward infinitude seems to make it unrepeatable, so the repetition calls for both laughter and lamentation.

Subjective existing thinkers exist in this way too, and it is reflected in the way they express their arguments. Hence it is impossible for others simply to appropriate their pathos without further ado. Comedy keeps cropping up in Lessing's arguments rather like comic episodes in a romantic drama, some-

---

* The Socratic gaze is another way of expressing the highest pathos, and is therefore equally comic. Let us try an experiment. Socrates is standing gazing into space. Two passers-by come along. One of them says: 'What is that man doing?' and the other one answers: 'Nothing.' Let us suppose, however, that one of them has some understanding of inwardness, and interprets Socrates's behaviour as an expression of religion, saying: 'He is praying; he is immersed in the divine.' Let us now focus on the 'praying'. Is Socrates using many words, or any words at all? No – for Socrates understood his God-relationship in such a way that he would not dare to say anything at all for fear of talking gobbledygook and having a bad wish granted. It was said to have happened before, when a man approached the oracle and it prophesied that his sons would prosper and grow famous, and he anxiously asked: 'And then presumably they will all come to a miserable end?' To which the oracle replied: 'This wish will also be granted.' The oracle was making the perfectly reasonable assumption that those who consult it are petitioners, and from this point of view it was perfectly reasonable to say 'granted' – but it was a sad irony for the father. And so Socrates did nothing whatsoever. He did not even speak inwardly with God, and yet he did the highest thing possible. Presumably he understood this perfectly well, and knew how to emphasize it teasingly. Judging from his dissertation, on the other hand, Magister Kierkegaard has hardly understood this at all. He mentions Socrates's negative attitude to prayer, quoting the [spurious] dialogue *Alcibiades II*, but, as is to be expected of a positive theology student in our age, he could not resist trying to rebuke Socrates, in a footnote, telling him that this negativity is true only up to a certain point. [Cf. *The Concept of Irony*, KW II, pp. 176–7.]

† I do not mean the contingent comedy, as when a praying man is holding a hat in front of his face without realizing that its crown is missing, so that he can accidentally be seen face to face.

times in the wrong place, perhaps: or perhaps not – I cannot say for sure. The *ergötzlich* [amusing] figure of Hauptpastor Götze was comically preserved for posterity when Lessing incorporated him into his arguments.[9] This is of course unsettling, for unfortunately we cannot entrust ourselves to Lessing's exposition with the same confidence as we would to the arguments of the truly serious speculators, who have at last completed their work and reduced everything to a single principle.

Existing subjective thinkers are constantly striving; but this does not mean that they have a finite goal, and that their striving will be finished when they reach it, for they strive infinitely in a constant process of becoming. They guarantee it by constantly being negative and positive in equal measure – and equally alive to essential comedy and essential pathos, which in its turn is based in their existing and in the reflection of their existing in their think-ing. The existence of a thinker is itself the process of becoming, though of course it is easy to abstract from it and become unthinkingly objective. It makes no essential difference how far we progress along this path, since however far we go (and it is, of course, only a finite comparison) we will remain in the process of becoming as long as we exist.

Existence itself, or existing, is a striving, and it contains pathos and comedy in equal measure. It has pathos because its striving is infinite – that is to say, directed towards the infinite in an infinitization which is the highest pathos; and it has comedy because the striving is self-contradictory. From the stand-point of pathos, every single second has infinite value; but from the stand-point of comedy, ten thousand years are but a joke – a yesterday. And yet the time in which we exist is composed of just such parts. If someone plainly stated that ten thousand years are but a joke, many fools would agree, and regard the remark as very wise – while forgetting that a single second has infinite value too. There are those who will be baffled by the thought that a single second could have infinite value; they would think it makes more sense to say that ten thousand years have infinite value. But in fact both are equally difficult to understand, provided we take the time to understand what needs to be understood, or allow ourselves to be so infinitely gripped by the thought of there being no time to waste – not even a second – that every second acquires infinite value.

This feature of existence recalls the Greek conception of Eros as expressed in Plato's *Symposium*, and elaborated in Plutarch's 'Isis and Osiris'.[10] The par-allels between Isis, Osiris and Typhon do not concern me, but we would be right to be reminded of Plato when Plutarch recalls that Hesiod regarded Chaos, Earth, Tartarus and Eros [*Elskov*] as first principles [*grundvæsener*].[11] For here Eros clearly means existence, or the ways in which life – as a synthesis of infinity and finitude – enters into everything. Eros, according to Plato, was begotten of Poverty and Wealth, and its nature is a combination of the two. But what is existence itself? It is the child of infinity and finitude, eternity and temporality, and that is why it is a constant striving. This was Socrates's opinion. Love [*Kærligheden*] is therefore a constant striving – or in other words, the thinking subject exists. No one but an objective Systematic who has turned into a Speculation and ceased to be human could dwell in the realm of pure being. A Socratic existence cannot of course be understood finitely, as if it were a perpetual and steady striving towards a goal that is never reached. But to the extent that subjects encompass the infinite and exist through it, they will be in the process of becoming.

We will never be able to explain existence if we forget, in our thinking, to think of our existing – in other words if we try to stop being human and become a book or something objective instead – which only a Münchhausen can do. Objective thinking does of course have its own reality, but if our topic is subjectivity then objectivity is always a misunderstanding. Even those who devote their entire lives to logic do not actually become logic; they have their existence in entirely different categories. They may not consider it worth thinking about, and in that case there is no more to be said; but they would not be happy to learn that existence makes fun of those who want to become purely objective.

> **Thesis 4: Lessing said: If God were holding complete truth in his right hand and in his left a singular and always restless striving after truth, a striving in which I would err for ever and a day, and if he directed me to choose between them, I would humbly ask for his left hand and say, Father, grant me this, for pure truth belongs to you alone**[12]

Presumably the System had not been finished when Lessing spoke these words; and now, alas, he is dead! If he were alive today, when the System is virtually finished – or at least is well under way and should be finished by next Sunday – he would have grabbed it with both hands, believe me. He would have had neither the time, nor the good manners, nor the high spirits to play a game with God, so to speak, by opting in all seriousness for the left hand. But then the System already has more to offer us than God holds in both his hands, to say nothing of next Sunday, when it will quite definitely be finished.

Lessing's words are taken from his little essay *Eine Duplik* (1778), which he wrote in response to a pious critic who had defended the story of the Resurrection following an attack which had appeared in Lessing's *Fragments*.[13] Of course no one was quite sure why Lessing published these fragments, and not even the venerable scholar Hauptpastor Götze[14] could find a passage in the Apocalypse which applied to Lessing, or a prophecy which he fulfilled. Lessing somehow forced his readers, through their relation to him, to accept his principle. Although plenty of results and conclusions were available even in those faraway days, no one managed to dispense with Lessing or have him butchered, preserved, and packaged in a world-historical paragraph. He remained a mystery, and no one invoking him now would have much hope of getting any further.

First of all, though, an assurance concerning my own humble self. I am as willing as anyone to bend a knee and worship the System, if only I could catch sight of it. But so far I have had no success and, though I have young legs, I have grown tired of running back and forth from Herod to Pilate.[15] Once or twice I have come very close to kneeling, but the moment I spread my handkerchief on the ground to stop my trousers getting dirty, I have addressed an innocent question to one of the initiates. 'Tell me frankly,' I ask, 'is it now completely finished – because if it is, I will kneel down before it, even if it means ruining my trousers (the road having become rather muddy from the heavy traffic to and from the System)?' And they always reply 'No, I'm afraid it's not quite finished yet.' So once again the System is late and my act of worship has to be postponed.

System and completion are pretty much the same thing: if the System is not finished, then there is no System. Elsewhere I have pointed out that a not-quite-finished System is a hypothesis, whereas a half-finished System is a nonsense. If anyone accuses me of nit-picking here, since the Systematics themselves admit that the System is not finished, I can only reply: 'why call it a System, then; why speak with a forked tongue?' When they recite the sum and substance of their knowledge, why do they never mention the fact that something is missing? They thereby encourage those who are less knowledgeable than them to assume that everything is finished – unless of course they are writing only for readers even more knowledgeable than themselves, something which one might have expected the Systematics to find inconceivable. As soon as anyone approaches the structure, therefore, one of the architects will come along – an extremely pleasant man, very polite and welcoming – and say: 'Yes indeed, the building work is still under way, and the System is not quite finished yet.' Did he not know that already, then, when he sent out his heart-warming invitation to the whole of humanity? And if he knew it, why did he not say so himself – why did he describe the fragment he had created as a System? For as I have already said: a fragment of a System is a nonsense.

To be constantly striving towards a System, by contrast, is truly to be striving; and striving, perpetual striving, was of course what concerned Lessing –

and certainly not a striving after nothing! On the contrary: Lessing was concerned with a striving after truth, and used a strange phrase to describe it: *den einzigen immer regen Trieb* [a 'singular and always restless striving']. The word *einzig* [singular] can only mean the infinite, just as having but a single thought is greater than having many. So both Lessing and the Systematics are concerned with perpetual striving, but Lessing is stupid or truthful enough to call it perpetual striving, whereas the Systematics are clever or dishonest enough to call it a System. How would this difference between them be judged in parallel situations? When Behrend lost his silk umbrella, he announced that he had lost a cotton one, calculating that anyone who found it would be less likely to return it if it were described as silk.[16] Perhaps the Systematics think along the same lines: 'Alas, if the newspapers or the title-page described my creation as a perpetual striving, then surely no one would ever admire me or buy a copy? But if I call it the System, the Absolute System – well, then people will be queuing up to buy it.' Unfortunately, the problem remains that what the Systematic is selling is not in fact the System!

Let us go further then, though we must be careful not to make fools of each other. I, Johannes Climacus, am no more and no less than a human being, and I take it that those I have the honour of addressing are human beings too. If they want to be Speculations, pure speculative thoughts, then I will have to break off the conversation, since from that moment they become invisible to me, and no longer impinge on the feeble mortal eyes of an ordinary human being.

Let us now explore two propositions: (A) a logical system is possible; but (B) a system of existence is not possible.

A

a) Those who want to construct a logical system must take care not to include anything which is subject to the dialectic of existence – that is, anything that is only through existing or having existed, rather than through simply being. It follows from this that Hegel's unique and uniquely admired invention – the introduction of movement into logic (not to mention the fact that he never even tried to justify it) – can only cause confusion in logic.* Of course it is also rather odd to make movement fundamental in a

---

* The insouciance with which the Systematics concede that Hegel did not manage to introduce movement into every department of logic is rather like the grocer who thinks that a few raisins more or less are of no importance when making up a large order. But this farcical complaisance is of course a form of contempt for Hegel which even his severest critics would avoid. There were of course logical investigations prior to Hegel, but in his case method was supposed to be everything. For him, and for anyone sharp enough to understand what it means

sphere where movement is inconceivable, or to expect movement to explain logic when logic cannot explain movement. On this point, however, I am fortunately in a position to refer to a sound thinker who – a rarity in our age! – has happily been schooled by the Greeks; a thinker who has freed himself and his thinking from any servile, snivelling relation to Hegel (from whose fame everyone seeks to profit, if only by trying to absorb him or go further). The Trendelenburg of the *Logische Untersuchungen* is content with Aristotle and himself; he has the merit of having understood, amongst other things, that movement is the inexplicable presupposition and common feature which unites thinking and being as their continual reciprocity.[17] I shall not attempt to show here how his views relate to those of the Greeks, and to Aristotle in particular; or how – strange as it may seem, at least to ordinary folk – his exposition resembles a small section of Plutarch's 'Isis and Osiris'.[18] Far be it for me to suggest that Trendelenburg learned nothing from Hegel's philosophy, but fortunately he has understood that it is pointless to try to go further than Hegel or make improvements to his structure. This is the dishonest way in which many a bungler in our age has helped himself to Hegel's celebrity and now fraternizes with him like a lazzarone, whereas Trendelenburg, by contrast, stays as sober as a Greek. Without promising us the world or offering complete bliss to humanity as a whole, he achieves a great deal and bestows blessings on all who can profit from his guidance in studying the Greeks.

A logical system should not include anything which has any relation to existence, anything which is not indifferent to existence. But the infinite advantage of logical, objective thinking over every other kind of thinking is limited by the fact that, from a subjective point of view, it is only a hypothesis, precisely because it is indifferent to existence in the sense of actuality. This doubleness distinguishes the logical from the mathematical, which has absolutely no relation either to or from existence since its medium is pure objectivity, rather than objectivity combined with the hypothetical as the contradictory unity through which it is negatively related to existence.

(cont'd from p. 250) to will something great, the question of whether movement is or is not present at this or that particular point cannot be a matter of indifference, as when the grocer has an argument with his customer about an order which is a little over- or under-weight. Hegel staked his entire reputation on the question of method. But methods have the strange characteristic that they are nothing at all when viewed in the abstract; they are not methods unless they are applied or implemented. If they are not implemented then they are not methods, and in the absence of any other method, there is no method at all. We can leave it to Hegel's admirers to treat him like a bird-brain; his critics, however, will always revere him as one who willed something great, even if he never achieved it.

A logical system should not be a mystification, or a ventriloquism in which the content of existence shows up surreptitiously and in disguise, so that logical thought is astonished when it sees what the Herr Professor or Magister has up his sleeve. A stricter discrimination between the two would be possible if we could decide in what sense the category is an abbreviation of existence, or whether logical thinking is an abstraction from existence or an abstraction which has no relation to existence. I would like to deal with this question at a little more length elsewhere, and even if I could never settle it completely, at least it will have been worth posing it in this way.

b) The dialectic of beginnings needs to be clarified. It is quite amusing that a beginning is, and yet also is not, precisely because it is a beginning, and swapping true dialectical remarks of this kind has long been one of the games they play in Hegelian circles.

The System begins, so it is said, with immediacy; indeed, in the absence of dialectics, there are those who become so rhetorical that they claim that the System begins with the most immediate of all, even though the comparative reflection implied here could ultimately prove dangerous for the beginning.* The System begins with the immediate, and therefore without presuppositions, and therefore absolutely; the beginning of the System, that is to say, is the absolute beginning. This is of course entirely correct, and has been rightly admired. But before the System begins, we ought surely to explore and clarify the implications of an equally important question: *How does the System begin with the immediate – that is, does it begin with it immediately?* The answer must of course be an unconditional 'No'. Assuming that the System comes after existence (which could cause it to be mistaken for a System of existence) it will of course come behind it, and it will not begin immediately with the immediacy with which existence began, although in another sense existence did not begin with immediacy, since immediacy never exists as such, but is superseded as soon as it comes into being. Hence the beginning of the System which begins with immediacy *is itself attained through reflection*.

That is the problem. If we hang on to this thought, and do not let it slip away from us, either through evasiveness or thoughtlessness or through breathless haste to get the System finished, then it will be sufficient, in all its

---

* It would be tedious to try to show precisely how. Such matters are usually a waste of time anyway, since we may take great pains to construct an objection, only to discover from the philosopher's reply that he has been the victim of a misunderstanding – not so much our failure to understand his sanctified philosophy, more our mistaken presumption that he meant the whole thing to mean something, rather than being an exercise in slack thinking concealed by extremely pretentious words.

simplicity, to demonstrate that there can never be a system of existence, and that a logical system should never lay claim to an absolute beginning, since such a beginning, like pure being, is a pure chimera.

If it is impossible to make an immediate beginning with immediacy (it would have to be thought of as an event or as a miracle – in other words it cannot be thought at all) and if beginnings are attained through reflection, then we must ask the simple question (and I hope I will not be forced to stand in the corner for being so simple that everyone can understand my question and must therefore be embarrassed by my exhibition of common knowledge): How can I call a halt to the reflection that had to be set in motion in order to reach the beginning? Reflection has the peculiar quality of being infinite. This means that it cannot stop itself, because it would have to use itself to stop itself, and the only way it can be brought to a halt is the way a disease can be cured if it is itself allowed to prescribe its own treatment – that is, if it is succoured and nourished. Perhaps the infinity of reflection is a bad infinity, in which case we will of course be finished very soon, since the bad infinity [*slette Uendelighed*][19] is said to be so despicable that we must abandon it forthwith, the sooner the better. But may I be permitted to ask a question? Why is it that Hegel and the Hegelians, who are supposed to be dialecticians, get so angry at this point – and angry as only Germans can be? Is 'bad' a dialectical term? How does such a word enter into logic? Can scorn and contempt and threatening behaviour be legitimate means of effecting logical movement, so that individuals consent to the idea of the absolute beginning simply because they are afraid of what the neighbours will say? Is 'bad' not an ethical category?★ What am I saying if I speak of the bad infinity? I am accusing individuals of not wanting to bring the infinity of reflection to an end. But am I not then placing a demand on them? On the other hand I have to assume, if I am in genuinely speculative mode, that reflection will itself put an end to itself, so why place demands on anyone? And what exactly am I demanding? I am requiring a deliberate decision [*beslutning*]. In one respect I am right to do so, since this is indeed the only way reflection can be halted, but on the other hand it cannot be right for a philosopher to provoke people by at one moment assuming that reflection itself puts an end to itself in the absolute beginning, and at the next moment deriding those who are stupid enough to believe him – deriding them, in order to help them towards the absolute beginning, which is then attained in two ways. But if we demand a decision, then we have abandoned presuppositionlessness. A beginning can only happen when

★ Even if it is not an ethical category, it is certainly an aesthetic one. Plutarch (in *The Obsolescence of Oracles*, xxii [*Moralia* 421f–422a]) says that it was for reasons like this that philosophers refused to countenance a plurality of worlds: the oppressive infinity frightened them.

reflection has been halted, and reflection can only be halted by something else – and something very different from the logical, namely a decision. And the beginning cannot be presuppositionless unless the beginning at which reflection comes to an end is a breakthrough, so that the absolute beginning itself breaks through the perpetual infinity of reflection. If, on the other hand, it is a break in which reflection is broken off in order to allow a beginning to emerge, then this beginning cannot be absolute, since it has been effected by a *metabasis eis allo genos* [shifting of genus, category mistake].[20]

If reflection can attain a beginning in immediacy, then immediacy cannot mean what it usually means. Hegelian logicians have understood this quite correctly, and they therefore define the immediate, with which Hegel's *Logic* begins, as the most extreme abstraction left behind by an exhaustive process of abstraction. There is nothing objectionable in their definition, though we can certainly object to their failure to adhere to their own principle, since the definition indirectly implies that there is no such thing as an absolute beginning. 'How so?' you may ask: 'how could there be anything further if we have abstracted from everything?' Indeed – *if* we really have abstracted from everything. But let us suppose for a moment that we are human beings. The act of abstraction is infinite, like the act of reflection, so how – since every x leads to a y – can I bring it to a halt? Let us try our luck at a thought-experiment. Suppose the infinite act of abstraction to be *in actu* [real or actual]. Of course, the beginning is not the act of abstraction, since that comes afterwards. So what do I begin with, if I have abstracted from everything? Alas, at this point a Hegelian, overcome with emotion, might throw his arms around me and sob with blissful relief, saying: 'You begin with nothing.' And this of course is what the System says – that it begins with nothing. But now I must ask my second question: How can I begin with nothing? If the infinite act of abstraction is not one of those tricks that allows us to do two things at once – if it is in fact the most strenuous activity we could undertake – what then? Well, it would then take all my strength to maintain it, and if my strength faltered in any way, I would no longer be able to abstract from everything. If I make my beginning on this presupposition, I will not begin with nothing, precisely because I will not have abstracted from everything in the moment of beginning. This means that if it were possible for human beings to abstract from everything in their thinking, it would be impossible for them to do any more than that: if it is not completely beyond our human powers, it most certainly exhausts them. To make a beginning simply because one has grown weary of the act of abstraction would not satisfy anyone, except perhaps a grocer who was not too scrupulous about small inaccuracies.

The expression – 'to begin with nothing' – is itself deceptive, regardless of its relation to the infinite act of reflection. 'To begin with nothing' is neither more nor less than a paraphrase of the dialectic of beginning. A beginning is, and yet also is not, precisely because it is a beginning, and this could also be expressed by saying: 'The beginning begins with nothing.' But this is merely an alternative formulation, and does not get us any further forward. In the first case I merely think the beginning *in abstracto*; in the second case, I think of the relation of the equally abstract beginning to something with which it begins. It then becomes perfectly clear that this something – the only thing that could correspond to such a beginning – is a nothing. But this is merely a tautological paraphrase of the other statement: 'the beginning is not'. 'The beginning is not' and 'the beginning begins with nothing' are completely identical statements, and we have not made any progress.

What if, instead of speaking or dreaming about an absolute beginning, we spoke about a leap? To content ourselves with 'mostly', 'as good as', 'perhaps you could say that', 'you could well say that, but sleep on it overnight', would simply show our kinship with Trop, who slowly but surely came to assume that having almost come close to taking an examination in law was the same as being qualified to practise as a lawyer.[21] Everyone can see that Trop is ridiculous, but in the kingdom of truth and the sanctuary of science those who reason speculatively in his fashion are regarded as good philosophers – as genuine speculative philosophers. Lessing was no speculative philosopher, and therefore he assumed the opposite – that an infinitely small distance can make the chasm infinitely wide, since it is the leap itself that constitutes the width of the chasm.

The strange thing about the Hegelians is that they know in logic that reflection itself brings itself to an end, and that universal doubt changes into its opposite by itself (a true fisherman's yarn this – that is, truly a fisherman's yarn), but they also know in their everyday lives, where they are pleasant enough and just like you and me (though far more learned and talented and so on, as I am perfectly willing to concede), that the only thing that can bring reflection to a halt is a leap. Let us dwell on this oddity for a moment. If the individual does not bring the reflection to a halt – that is to say, if no decision intervenes – then he will be infinitized by reflection.* Running wild in reflection in this way will make individuals truly objective – less and less capable of the decision of subjectivity and a return into themselves. They assume that reflection can bring itself objectively to an

---

* The reader will perhaps remember that when the matter becomes objective there can be no question of eternal bliss, since bliss lies precisely in subjectivity and decision.

end, but really the opposite is the case; reflection does not stop objectively, and if it is stopped subjectively it does not stop itself, since it is the subject that stops it.

To take an example, when Rötscher (whose book on Aristophanes shows a good understanding of the necessity of transition in world-historical development, and who surely must also have understood the passage of reflection through itself to the absolute beginning in logic)[22] set himself the task of explaining Hamlet, he knew that nothing could bring reflection to an end except a resolute decision.[23] He did not assume (shall I say 'strangely enough'?), strangely enough, that by continuing to reflect Hamlet finally arrived at an absolute beginning. But in logic he assumes (shall I say 'strangely enough'?), strangely enough, or at least he probably assumes, that the passage of reflection through itself comes to an end at an absolute beginning. I cannot understand this – which pains me because I admire Rötscher's talent, his classical education, and his tasteful yet original conception of psychological phenomena.

What I have said here about beginnings in logic – which also shows that there could never be an existential system, as I will explain in detail below in (B) – is very plain and simple. I am almost ashamed to say it, or ashamed that I have to say it – ashamed of my situation as a poor pamphleteer who finds himself compelled to say this kind of thing, though he would prefer to worship the System on his knees. What I have said could also have been put in a different way, which might perhaps make an impression on someone or other in that the exposition would specifically recall certain scholarly controversies of the recent past. The question would then turn on the significance of Hegel's *Phenomenology of Spirit* for the System[24] – whether it should be regarded as an introduction which stands outside it, and, if so, whether the introduction can then be incorporated into the System; furthermore, whether Hegel should be credited with the remarkable achievement of having written not merely the System but two or even three systems, which would of course require a miraculously systematic head, which it seems he really must have had, since he finished the System more than once, and so on. All this has been said often enough, of course, but it has usually been said in a most confusing way. A large book has been written about it, which first summarizes everything Hegel said, and then considers this or that later contribution – all of which simply distracts the reader, smothering in bewildering long-windedness what should have been stated succinctly.

c) In order to shed some light on logic, it may be worth orienting ourselves psychologically towards the state of mind of those who think logically – so as to explore what kind of dying away from oneself it requires and what part, if any, the imagination plays in it. This again is a plain and humble remark, but that need not make it untrue or superfluous: philosophers are such extraordinary creatures that even the most extravagant imagination could scarcely invent anything so fabulous. How, in general, does the empirical I relate to the pure I = I? Those who wish to be philosophers will surely want to know; they will not want to become a laughing stock when they are transformed – through an *ein, zwei, drei kokolorum* [one, two, three, hey presto!] – into Speculations. As long as those who concern themselves with logical thought remain sufficiently human to remember that they are existing individuals then, even if they were to complete the System, all the fantasy and charlatanry would eventually disappear. It would take an exceptionally logical head to remodel Hegel's theory of logic, but those who have been inspired by the great things that Hegel claimed to have achieved – and who show their enthusiasm by believing it, and their enthusiasm for Hegel by believing it of him – need nothing more than sound common sense in order to realize that Hegel often behaved irresponsibly: not towards grocers, who never believe half of what they are told anyway, but towards all the young enthusiasts who believed him. When such youngsters come to themselves again after having enthusiastically believed the highest, as of course Hegel has been said to be; and when in a questionable moment they have enthusiastically despaired of themselves because they refuse to abandon Hegel, then even if they are not particularly talented, they have every right to demand that the nemesis of laughter devour everything in Hegel that it legitimately can. And such youngsters have indeed elevated Hegel, but in a completely different way than the devotees whose insincere asides make either too much of Hegel, or too little.

B

No system of existence is available to us. But neither this nor anything else that has been said should be taken to mean that no such system exists. Existence itself is a system for God, but not for an existing spirit. System and completion correspond to each other, but existence is the opposite of them both. From an abstract point of view, system and existence cannot be thought together, because in order to think existence, systematic thought must think it as superseded, and therefore not as existing. Existence is the spacing that opens things out; system is the closure that consolidates.

A mirage and illusion now intervenes in actuality, as I tried to show in *Philosophical Fragments*. I must refer to this now, in connection with the question whether the past is more necessary than the future.[25] When an existence belongs wholly to the past, it is of course over and done with, and to that extent it can be grasped systematically. This is quite right – but for whom?

Those who are themselves existing can never attain a closure outside existence, of a kind that might correspond to the eternity into which the past has entered. Good-natured thinkers may be so *distrait* [distracted] that they forget their own existences; but Speculation and Distraction are not quite the same thing. On the contrary, the mere fact that these thinkers exist testifies to the claim of existence on them, and their contemporary existence – if they are great – may, when it is over and past, acquire the validity of a conclusion for a systematic thinker. But who is this systematic thinker? He is in existence yet outside it, and in his eternity he is eternally closed while also enclosing existence within himself. In short – he is God. So why the deception? Now that the world has lasted 6000 years, existence surely makes the same demands on those who exist as it always did: and its claim is that we should become not contemplating spirits in fantasy, but existing spirits in actuality. Understanding always comes after the event. Individuals who exist now obviously come after the 6000 years that preceded them, and if we assume that they can understand these years systematically, then the strangely ironical consequence will be that they can never understand themselves as existing because they themselves would never have existed, so they would have left nothing that needed to be understood. It follows that such a thinker would have to be either our Lord or a fantastical something-I-know-not-what. Anyone can see that this is immoral, and will surely also recognize the truth in what another author has said about the Hegelian System: that Hegel has given us the completed System, the Absolute System – but without an ethics.[26] We may well smile at the ethico-religious fantasies of medieval ascetics, but we should never forget that farcical, speculative extravagances about becoming an I = I (but such a philistine that no enthusiast could ever bear such a life) are equally ludicrous.

Let us then ask, with the simplicity with which a Greek boy might have asked his teacher (and if the higher wisdom can explain everything but cannot answer a simple question, then the world is clearly out of joint): 'Who shall write or complete such a System?' Surely a human being, unless we go back again to that strange talk of human beings becoming Speculations and subject-objects. A human being, then, and surely a living – that is, existing – human being. Or if the Speculation which constructs the System is the combined effort of several different thinkers, in what final conclusion does this fellowship consolidate itself? How does it come to light? Surely through a human being? How do the several individual thinkers relate themselves to this combined effort, and what are the determinations which mediate between the individual and world history? And what kind of creature must one be in order to string it all together on a systematic thread – a human being or a Speculation? If one is a human being, then of course one exists.

In general, there are two different paths that existing individuals may take. Either they can do their best to forget that they exist, in which case they become comical, since existence has the remarkable characteristic that those who exist do so whether they want to or not. (The comical contradiction of wanting to be what we are not – a bird, for example – is no more comical than that of not wanting to be what we are, in this case an existing individual. It is the same in the realm of language: we find it comical if someone forgets his own name, since he thereby forgets not just what he is called, but the very singularity of his essence.) Or alternatively they can focus all their attention on the fact that they exist. It is on this ground, in the first instance, that we must criticize modern [*moderne*] speculation – not so much because it proceeds from mistaken presuppositions, but because it has become comical through having forgotten, in a fit of world-historical absentmindedness, what it is to be human: and not what it is to be human in general, since even the Speculators might consent to consider that, but what it is for you or me or him or her to be human, each of us for ourselves and on our own.

Existing individuals who focus all their attention on the fact that *they* exist will also endorse Lessing's beautiful comment on continual striving – not as something which will earn its author immortal fame (it is too simple for that), but as something which everyone who pays attention will recognize as true. But existing individuals who forget their existence will become increasingly *distrait*, and just as some people preserve the fruits of their leisure by writing, so we may expect, as the fruit of their distraction, the long-awaited system of existence – well, not all of us of course, but only those who are almost equally *distrait*. The more the Hegelian System carries on distractedly becoming a system of existence and, moreover, nears completion – though without having an ethics (which is where existence properly belongs) – the more the simple philosophizing performed by existing individuals for other existing individuals will call attention to the ethical.

Philosophizing does not address itself fantastically to phantasms; it is concerned with existing individuals – and the question whether continual striving is inferior to systematic closure cannot be answered fantastically and *in abstracto*, since it concerns the capacities of existing beings in so far as they exist. Once we recall this we will realize that continual striving is the only thing that never disappoints. The repetition with which we have to fill out our existence (if we are to avoid going backwards or turning into phantasms) will again be a continual striving because – even if we achieve the highest – here closure will elude us again and be postponed once more. This recalls the Platonic conception of love as a lack – as a lack which is felt not only by those who desire something they do not have, but also by those who want to keep what they already possess. Fantastico-speculatively we can have positive closure inside the System, and fantastico-aesthetically we can have it in the fifth act of a play; but such closures are fit only for phantasms.

Continual striving is an expression of the ethical life-view of existing subjects, and must not be understood metaphysically. But then of course individuals never exist metaphysically either. On the basis of a misunderstanding, we could then develop an opposition between systematic closure and a continual striving after truth, and we might even try to follow the Greek ideal of being a perpetual learner. In this sphere, however, that would be a complete misunderstanding. From an ethical point of view, perpetual striving is the consciousness of being an existing individual, and this constant learning expresses a perpetual becoming-real which will never be finished as long as the subject exists; and the subject knows it and so is not deceived. But Greek philosophy was constantly related to ethics, and the principle of constantly being a learner was not regarded either as a great discovery or as the task of a few exceptional, inspired individuals, since it was neither more nor less than our understanding that we exist. We deserve no credit for knowing this, and it is sheer thoughtlessness to forget it.

So-called pantheistic systems of philosophy have often been criticized for obliterating [at de hæve] both freedom and the distinction between good and evil. But perhaps we could express ourselves just as definitely by saying that such systems fantastically dilute the concept of existence. It would be wrong to restrict this criticism to pantheistic systems, however; we could demonstrate that systems are always essentially pantheistic precisely on account of their closure. Existence has to be superseded by eternity before the system can be completely closed – no remnant of existence can be left behind, not even a tiny dingle-dangle like the existing Herr Professor who writes the System. But that is not how the question is usually approached: pantheistic systems are criticized partly by torrents of aphorisms endlessly promising a new system, and partly by supposed new systems which are churned out complete with special paragraphs emphasizing the concepts of existence and actuality. It makes no difference to the restless Systematics that these paragraphs make a mockery of the whole system – that rather than being parts of the system they are really absolute protests against it. In reality, the concept of existence cannot be directly presented in a paragraph of a system, and earnest oaths and devils-take-me only make the didactic topsy-turviness more ludicrous. An actual emphasis on existence has to be expressed in an essential form, and given the illusiveness of existence this must be indirect – system is quite alien to it. But this cannot be allowed to become another reassuring formula [blanquet] in its turn, since the indirect expression will be constantly rejuvenated in its form. It is quite acceptable for records of committee meetings to include dissenting votes, but systems which contain dissenting votes as paragraphs are extraordinary monstrosities. No wonder the System persists. It haughtily ignores objections, and if a particular objection attracts a little attention, then the systematic entrepreneurs get a copyist to copy it out so that it too can be entered into the System; and in the end the book will be bound and the system complete.

The systematic Idea is the unity of subject and object, of thought and being; but existence is precisely their separation. It does not follow of course that existence is thoughtless, only that it is the spacing which constantly keeps subject separate from object, and thought separate from being. From the objective point of view, thought is pure thought, and corresponds abstract-objectively to its object, which is therefore itself, so that truth is the correspondence of thought with itself. Thus objective thought has no relation to existing subjectivity, and while we are always left with the difficult question of how an existing subject can enter into an objectivity for which subjectivity is pure and abstract (which again is an objective determination and does not relate to any existing human being), existing subjectivity is bound to continue evaporating until at last − if a human being can really become such a thing, rather than just imagining it − this existing subjectivity becomes a purely abstract contributor and witness to this pure relation between thought and being, this pure identity, indeed this tautology, which strictly implies not that the thinker exists, but only that he is a thinking thing.

Existing subjects, on the other hand, exist, as indeed does every human being. It would therefore be an injustice to call this objective tendency an impious and pantheistic self-idolization; we should rather treat it as an essay in comedy, since the idea that we should do nothing between now and the end of the world except suggest further improvements to the nearly-finished system − this is merely a systematic consequence for Systematics.

It would be a further injustice to try to set up ethical categories in direct opposition to the objective tendency − and pointless too, since we would have no common ground with those we want to criticize. But if we remain within the sphere of metaphysics, we can use comedy, which also belongs in the metaphysical sphere, in order to catch out our transfigured Professor. If a dancer could leap extremely high, then we would admire him, but if he pretended to fly, then − even if he could leap higher than any dancer before him − he would deservedly become a laughing stock. The act of leaping essentially means belonging to the earth and obeying the law of gravity, so a leap can only be momentary. But the act of flying would mean liberation from earth-bound conditions; it is the privilege of creatures with wings and perhaps of those who live on the moon; indeed it may be there that the System will eventually find its true readers.

Being a human being has been abolished, and every Speculator confuses himself with humanity in general, thus becoming both infinitely grand and an absolute nothing. He confuses himself with humanity in a fit of sheer distraction, rather as the opposition press uses the royal 'we' and sailors like to say 'Devil take me.' But when we have been cursing for a long time, we finally return to direct utterance, because swearing always nullifies itself. When we have learned that any fool can say 'we', we realize how much it means to be just one. When we see that any fool can play at being humanity in general, we finally realize that simply living a human life means far more than playing this kind of party game. And one more thing: everyone can see that it is utterly ludicrous for a fool to play this game, but it is no better when it is played by the grandest of the grand, and we can happily laugh at him too, whilst also, as is fitting, paying all due respect to his talents and his learning and so forth.

Actual Ethical Subjectivity and the Subjective Thinker: Existence and Actuality

The difficulty of existence and existing can never really be explained or expressed in the language of abstraction. Abstract thinking is conducted *sub specie æterni* [from the point of view of eternity], and therefore disregards the concrete and the temporal, the becoming of existence, and the awkward circumstance that those who exist are a compound of eternity and temporality and somehow situated in existence.* If we assume that there is nothing higher than abstract thinking, then we shall have to accept that not only scientific thought but scientific thinkers too must arrogantly turn their back on existence, leaving the rest of us to fend for ourselves. And this has consequences for the abstract thinker as well – he is condemned to a state of distraction, since he himself is still, in spite of everything, an existing individual.

---

* Trendelenburg has brilliantly demonstrated how Hegel, in his *Logic*, helps himself to ideas which are already imbued with concretion, and happen to be informed by exactly those items which the Professor will need for his next supposedly necessary transition. To take the first example which comes to mind, how is the transition from existence (*die Existenz*) to existents (*Existierenden*) supposed to be accomplished? 'Existence is the immediate unity of reflection-into-self [*Reflexion in sich*] and reflection-into-another [*Reflexion in Anderes*]. Thus (?) [*daher*, Johannes's emphasis and query] it follows that existence is the indefinite multitude of existents.' [Hegel, *Logic* (part one of the *Encyclopaedia*), §123.] But why exactly should existence, as a purely abstract determination, divide itself up in this way?

There is nothing wrong with raising abstract questions about actuality – individuals and contingency are, after all, clearly constituents of actuality and directly opposed to abstraction – but it is far easier to answer them abstractly than to say what it means for a given determinate thing to be an actuality. Abstraction neglects all determinate things, but the difficulty lies in combining them with the Ideality of thought in an act of thinking. Abstraction prevents this contradiction from arising, so it cannot possibly concern itself with it.

The fraudulence of abstraction becomes clear in connection with existential questions, where abstraction avoids the difficulty by leaving it out, and then boasts that everything has been explained. It explains immortality in general, for instance, and everything goes quite splendidly, because immortality becomes identical with eternity – with eternity as essentially the medium of thought. But abstraction does not care whether existing human individuals are immortal, which is precisely the difficulty. Abstraction is disinterested, but existing individuals are infinitely interested in existing, and the difficulty of existence is precisely their interest. Abstract thinking therefore gives our immortality a helping hand by killing us off as particular existing individuals and then making us immortal; it assists us in the same way as the doctor in Holberg whose medicine cured the fever but killed the patient.[27] Even the most distinguished abstract thinkers look ridiculous when they refuse to acknowledge or make clear to themselves the relationship between their abstract thinking and the fact that they are existing individuals – for then they are on the point of ceasing to be human altogether. Actual human beings are compounds of infinity and finitude, and their actuality consists precisely in holding them together. They are infinitely interested in existing, unlike abstract thinkers, who are double-beings: on the one hand, fantastic creatures who live in the pure being of abstraction, and on the other pitiful professorial figures whom abstract beings can cast aside like an unwanted walking stick. The biographies of such thinkers (who may well have written some excellent books) will sometimes make us shudder at the thought of what it is to be a human being.* It is sad to think of the poor, ailing lacemaker with her exceedingly beautiful lace, but it is comic to observe a thinker who, for all his flamboyance, exists personally as a numbskull: he may have been personally married, but he knew so little of the power of love that his marriage was as impersonal as his thought; apart from

---

* And when we read in their writings that thought and being are one and the same, and consider how they lived their lives – we may reflect that the being with which thought is identical is certainly not the human kind.

his philistine concern about which university would offer him the best career, his personal life lacked all pathos and pathological struggle. We might have expected that such a misrelation would be impossible in the field of thinking – that such things take place only in the wretched external world in which people are forced to slave away for others and we cannot admire the lace without shedding a tear for the lacemaker. We would like to believe that the life of a thinker must be as rich as a human life can be – just as it was in Greece long ago.

But the lives of abstract thinkers are another matter entirely. They have not understood either themselves or the relation between abstract thinking and existence, and they are either following the inclination of their talents or complying with some kind of instruction. Of course most of us can admire those artists whose existence consists in following their talents without ever caring what it may mean to be human, so that we forget the artist in our admiration for the work of art. But I also know that the tragedy of such existing individuals is that their anomalousness has no personal reflection in the ethical; and I also know that the thinkers of ancient Greece were themselves works of art in their existence rather than sickly individuals who happened to have created works of art. Being a thinker should not imply being an anomaly, or an exception to being human. Abstract thinkers lack all sense of comedy, and it follows that while their thinking may testify to exceptional talents, it is not that of people who have in an eminent sense existed as human beings. Yet the pedants are constantly telling us that there is nothing higher than thinking, that thinking includes everything within itself, and no one demurs when the thinker is made to exist as an anomalous or exceptional talent rather than as essentially human. But their proposition about thinking is not reduplicated in their ideas, so their existence contradicts their thinking, which just goes to show that it is all mere pedantry. Thinking is higher than either feeling or imagination – or so we are told by pedantic thinkers who do not have an ounce of pathos or passion in them. Thinkers with absolutely no sense of comedy inform us that thinking is higher than irony and humour. How hilarious! In relation to Christianity and every problem of existence, abstract thinking is nothing but an essay in comedy, and so-called 'pure' thinking is generally a psychological curiosity, an admirable ingenuity in combining and constructing in the fantastic medium of pure being. Those thinkers who seek to sanctify the supremacy of pure thought simply demonstrate that they have never existed as human beings, and, amongst other things, that they have never acted in the eminent sense – in the sense of inwardness, that is to say, rather than achievement. But action in the eminent sense is essential to human existing. And when we act – when we risk something decisive in extreme subjective passion and in full consciousness of eternal responsibility, as any of us may do – then we learn some-thing very different, and come to know that being human has nothing to do with endlessly stitching things together into a system. By existing essentially as humans, we also acquire a sense of comedy. Of course not all those who actually exist as human beings are going to become comedians or comic poets, but they will at least have a sense of comedy.

I shall now illustrate the impossibility of expressing the difficulty of exis-tence and existing in the language of abstraction by reference to a decisive problem about which a great deal has already been said and written. It is well known that Hegelian philosophy has annulled the principle of contradiction, and Hegel himself has more than once sat in judgement on the kind of thinkers who are unable to get beyond the sphere of understanding and reflection, and therefore keep insisting on their either/or. It has now become quite a popular game – as soon as anyone suggests an *aut/aut* [either/or], some Hegelian will ride in clippety-clop on horseback (like Jens Skovfoged in *Kallundborgs-Krøniken*),[28] sort out the problem, and ride off home again. The Hegelians have been on our trail as well – espe-cially against Bishop Mynster – and they have notched up many a splendid victory for Speculation. More than once Bishop Mynster has been reduced to a mere vanquished standpoint, though he seems to be holding up rather well under the circumstances; and perhaps we should be more worried about unvanquished heroes, and the strain to which their triumphs must subject them.[29]

But it is possible that both the conflict and the victory rest on a misun-derstanding. Hegel is completely and absolutely right to say that there is no *aut/aut* from the point of view of eternity, or in the language of abstraction, or in pure thought and pure being. How on earth could there be, when all contradictions have been removed by abstraction? But Hegel and the Hegelians ought perhaps to offer us an explanation of the masquerade through which contradiction, movement, transition and so on are supposed to find their way into logic. The champions of the *aut/aut* will never succeed if they try to invade the territory of pure thought in order to defend their cause. Just as the giant who battled with Hercules lost all his strength when lifted off the ground, so the *aut/aut* of contradiction is automatically annulled when lifted out of existence and swept up into the eternity of abstraction. But Hegel is mistaken when he forsakes abstraction, plunges down into exis-tence, and uses all his might to try and annul the double *aut*. This cannot be done within existence, since it would annul existence as well. If we remove existence (that is, if we abstract), then there is no more *aut/aut*; but if the *aut/aut* is removed from existence, then existence is removed as well, and then of course it is not annulled in existence. There may be no truths in theology which are not truths in philosophy too, but there are certainly truths concerning existing individuals which are not true in abstraction. It is also ethically true that pure being is a fantasy, and that it is wrong for existing individuals to try to forget that they exist.

We need to be very careful, therefore, in all our dealings with Hegelians; above all, we must establish what it is exactly that we have the honour of conversing with. Is it a human being, an existing human being? Does he exist *sub specie æterni*, even when eating, sleeping, blowing his nose, or whatever else human beings do? Is he himself the pure I = I? Surely that could never happen to a philosopher, but how else could he, as existing, relate to the middle term through which he can discharge his ethical responsibility in existing, with existing, and through existing? Does he exist? And if so, is he not in a process of becoming? And if he is in a process of becoming, must he not then relate himself to the future? And will he not relate himself to the future through action? If he never acts, he will surely forgive an ethical individual who, with passion and dramatic truth, denounces him as a fool. But if he does act *sensu eminenti* [in an eminent sense], will he not relate himself to the future in infinite passion, and thus confront an *aut/aut*? To existing individuals, eternity is not eternity but the future, since eternity is only eternity for the eternal, for those who are not in a process of becoming. To such beings we might pose the following question (if such a question can be addressed to them at all): in so far as it is possible for us to abandon existence in order to be *sub specie æterni*, is it something that just happens to us, or is it the result of a resolute decision, or even something that we are under some obligation to do? For if we are obliged to do it, then an *aut/aut* must have been established *sub specie æterni*. Or perhaps he was born *sub specie æterni* and has lived *sub specie æterni* ever since, so that he cannot even understand my question, since he has never had anything to do with the future or had any experience of making decisions? In that case it will be quite clear that whatever I have the honour of conversing with, it is not a human being. Yet this is not quite the end of the matter for me, because it strikes me as a very remarkable thing that these mysterious beings have started appearing. There is a very rare kind of fly that has often been observed before outbreaks of cholera, and I wonder if these fabulous pure thinkers may not be a similar omen of an impending catastrophe for humanity − perhaps even the loss of the ethical and the religious?

We must therefore be wary of abstract thinkers and their wish to remain for ever in the pure being of abstraction, which they regard as the highest of human attainments, while abstract thought − which leads to neglect of the ethical and misunderstanding of the religious − is treated as the highest form of human thinking. But we must also avoid hankering after an *aut/aut sub* *specie æterni*, in which, as the Eleatics thought, 'everything is and nothing comes into being [*opkommer*]'.* Absolute disjunction is found only where everything is in a process of becoming, and eternity is present as a constraint on the passion of decision – the passionate decision through which *eternity* relates to *the individual in a process of becoming* as *futurity*. For when I link becoming to eternity my reward is not rest but futurity. And this of course is the reason why Christianity preaches the eternal as futurity: it is bound to assume an absolute *aut/aut* simply because it is addressed to existing individuals.

Logical thinking always takes place *sub specie æterni* and in the language of abstraction. But any attempt to think existence in this way overlooks the difficulty of thinking eternity in the process of becoming – a difficulty we cannot avoid, however, since as thinkers we are always in a process of becoming. Hence it is easier to think abstractly than to exist, unless existing is understood in a very loose and vulgar sense, like the loose and vulgar sense of being a subject. Here we have another example of how the simplest tasks are the most difficult. There is nothing extraordinary about existing, or so we tell ourselves, and it is certainly not an art: anyone can exist, after all, whereas abstract thinking is said to be something very special. But to exist in truth, so that our existence becomes saturated with consciousness – to be eternal, as if far beyond existence, at the same time as being present in it and yet in a process of becoming – that really is difficult. If thinking had not become alien in our time, and artificial, then thinkers would make a very different impression – as in ancient Greece, where thinkers were existing individuals passionately inspired by thinking, and as in Christendom long ago, when thinkers were believers ardently seeking to understand themselves in an existence of faith. If this were to be attempted by thinkers in our time, then pure

---

* Misled by constant talk about a perpetual process in which opposites are synthesized into higher and higher unities, some have drawn parallels between Hegel's doctrine and the Heraclitan claim that all is flux and nothing abides. This is a misunderstanding, however, since everything Hegel said about process and becoming is illusory. This is why the System lacks an ethics, and has nothing to say to the living when they inquire seriously into becoming with a view to knowing how to act. Despite all his talk about process, therefore, Hegel understood world history not in terms of becoming, but – with the assistance of the illusoriness of the past – in terms of a closure from which becoming was entirely excluded. It is therefore impossible for Hegelians to understand themselves through their philosophy; they may be able to understand what is over and done with, but those who are still alive have not yet passed away. Presumably they comfort themselves with the thought that if they can understand China and Persia and six thousand years of world history, then a single individual scarcely matters, even if it happens to be oneself. I myself do not see it that way; in fact I find it easier to think of it the other way round: those who cannot understand themselves are going to have a very strange understanding of China and Persia.

thought would lead to one suicide after another. For when pure thought is supposed to be everything, or the highest thing in relation to human existence, rather than a partial fragment which can reach some accommodation with personal existence in its ethical and religious mode, then its implication for existence must be suicide. We may not approve of suicide, but we can certainly praise the passion. Nowadays, however, we can enjoy the spectacle of thinkers regularly putting their extraordinary ingenuity on display at certain times of day, even if they have nothing else in common with human beings.

To think existence in abstraction and *sub specie æterni* is essentially to supersede it. This has more or less the same merit as the much-trumpeted act of annulling the principle of contradiction. Existence cannot be conceived without movement, and movement cannot be conceived *sub specie æterni*. Leaving movement out of account was not exactly a masterpiece, but the attempt to bring it back into logic, along with time and space, in the guise of transition only added to the confusion. If all thought is eternal, then the existing individual is in difficulty. Existence, like movement, is a very difficult thing to get round. We cannot think it without annulling it; therefore we cannot think it. So there seems to be something – namely existing – that cannot be thought. But the difficulty remains, because existence combines the two in the existence of the thinker.

The philosophers of ancient Greece were not too distracted to focus their continual dialectical efforts on movement. They never forgot that they were existing individuals, and therefore took refuge in suicide, or in dying in the Pythagorean sense, or in being dead in the Socratic sense, in order to think.[30] They were conscious of being thinkers, but were also conscious that the medium of existence frustrated their attempts to sustain continuity in their thinking, because it constantly brought them back to the process of becoming. Hence they had to do away with themselves in order to think truly. Modern philosophy smiles condescendingly at such childishness, for whilst all modern thinkers acknowledge that thought and being are one, they also know that it is not worth the effort to try to be what one thinks.

When abstract philosophy and pure thought try to explain everything by explaining away what is decisive, we must cling to the issue of existing and the demands placed on existing individuals by the ethical. All we have to do is fearlessly dare to be human, refusing to let ourselves be frightened or embarrassed or tricked into becoming some kind of phantom. It would be different if pure thought were to explain its relation to the ethical or to ethically existing individualities; but it never does. It does not even pretend to do so, since if it did it would have to involve itself in another kind of dialectic – the Greek dialectic or the dialectic of existence. Every existing individual has the right to expect that anything that presumes to call itself wisdom should have an ethical character. Once people have embarked on the process (imperceptible to them) of gradually forgetting to exist, so that they can begin to think *sub specie æterni*, our objection has to be of a different kind. There are no doubt many objections that could be directed against Hegelianism from within pure thought, but they would leave everything essentially as it was. But while I am perfectly willing – as a humble reader who would never presume to be a judge – to admire Hegel's logic, and while I am sure I would learn a great deal if I studied it some more, I remain sufficiently defiant, proud and obstinate to continue insisting that Hegelian philosophy confuses existence – both by failing to determine its relation to existing individuals and by neglecting the ethical.

Scepticism is at its most dangerous when it appears most innocuous, and the idea of pure thought as the positive truth for existing individuals is itself a form of scepticism, since such positivity is entirely chimerical. It is wonderful to be able to explain the past and the whole of world history, but if understanding the past is regarded as the highest aspiration for one still living, then this positivity is a form of scepticism – and a very dangerous form, because the enormous amount we thought we had understood does not live up to our expectations. Hence Hegel's philosophy is terribly vulnerable, and the danger comes from indirect attacks. Imagine an existing doubter with a boundless and attractive youthful confidence in the heroes of scientific knowledge, and imagine him setting out to seek the truth, the truth for existence, that lies in Hegelian positivity: he will end up writing an appalling epigram about Hegel. Please do not misunderstand me: I am not saying that every young man is capable of overcoming Hegel – far from it. If he is sufficiently bumptious and obnoxious to attempt such a thing, then his attack will misfire. He must never even dream of attacking Hegel; on the contrary, he should be prepared to submit to him with complete feminine devotion, though with sufficient tenacity to hold fast to his question. In that case he will become a satirist without knowing it. The young man is an existing doubter; he is constantly suspended in doubt, and reaches out for truth because he longs to exist in it. Hence he is negative, whereas Hegel's philosophy is of course positive – no wonder he places his trust in it! But pure thought is always a chimera for existing individuals seeking a truth in which they can exist. Existing under the guidance of pure thought is like travelling through Denmark and relying on a small map of Europe, on which Denmark is no larger than a little dot – indeed, it is even more impossible. The satire lies precisely in the young man's admiration and enthusiasm for Hegel, his boundless faith in him.

This would have been realized long ago if pure thought had not been borne up by an awe-inspiring public reputation, so that no one would dare question its magnificence, or admit that they do not understand it –

though it is in a sense impossible to understand, since no one can come to understand themselves through it, and understanding oneself is surely an absolute condition for understanding anything else. Socrates said ironically that he was not sure that he was human rather than something else, but Hegelians can claim with all the solemnity of the confessional: 'I do not know if I am human, but at least I have understood the System.' I myself would prefer to say: 'I know that I am human, and I know that I have not understood the System.' Having made that very clear, I would add that if any of our Hegelians were prepared to take me under their wing and guide me towards an understanding of the System, I would co-operate in every possible way. I would try to make myself as stupid as possible, divesting myself of every presupposition except my ignorance so as to become all the more capable of learning; and I would try to make myself as indifferent as possible to accusations of scientific amateurism, in order to be sure at least of learning something.

There is no existing without passion, unless of course existing is taken to mean just any sort of existing. That is why the thinkers of ancient Greece were all essentially passionate thinkers. I have often pondered the question of how to provoke people into passion. I considered getting them to sit on a horse and then startling the horse into the wildest gallop, or, in order to bring the passion out more clearly, finding someone who is in a terrible rush to get somewhere (and is therefore in something of a passion already) and giving him a lame horse that can hardly walk. But in fact existing is always like this provided we are conscious of it. Or if we took a driver who was not much given to passion and harnessed his carriage to Pegasus on one side and a broken old nag on the other, and ordered him to drive – I think that might do the trick. And yet existing is like this too, provided we are conscious of it. Eternity is like a winged horse, galloping at infinite speed; but temporality is an old nag, and the existing individual is the driver – provided existing is not understood too loosely, since in that case the individual might not be a driver but a drunken peasant dozing in his cart and letting the horses go wherever they please. Of course he could drive if he wanted, for he is also a driver – just as there are perhaps many of us who . . . also exist.

If existence is movement then there must be some continuity that holds the movement together, since otherwise it would not be movement. Just as the proposition that everything is true really implies that nothing is true, so the proposition that everything is in movement implies that nothing is.*

---

*   This was undoubtedly what Heraclitus's disciple meant when he said that it was impossible to walk through the same river even once. Johannes de Silentio referred to this disciple's remark in *Fear and Trembling*, though with more rhetorical flamboyance than truth. [See above, p. 106.]

Immobility belongs to movement as its goal, in the sense both of *telos* [end] and of *metron* [measure]; otherwise the proposition that everything is in movement – if we also take time away and assert that everything is movement – is also automatically an affirmation of stasis. That is why Aristotle, who made so much of movement, said that God, the unmoved mover, moves everything.[31] And whilst pure thought annuls all movement, or meaninglessly introduces it into logic, the difficulty for existing individuals lies in giving existence the continuity without which everything would disappear. An abstract continuity is no continuity at all, and the existence of existing individuals essentially prevents continuity, while passion is the momentary continuity which simultaneously restrains movement and impels it. For existing individuals the goal of movement is both decision and repetition. Eternity provides the movement with continuity, but abstract eternity lies beyond movement, and concrete eternity in existing individuals is simply maximum passion. Idealizing* passion, that is to say, is always the anticipation of the eternal in existence, which enables existing individuals to exist.† The eternity of abstraction is achieved only by disregarding existence, and the only way existing individuals can enter into pure thought is through a devious beginning, whose deviousness will be avenged by reducing the existence of existing individuals to insignificance, and infecting their discourse with a measure of delirium. This applies to the vast majority of people in our time, who seldom if ever speak as if they were conscious of being singular, existing individuals, but prefer to become pantheistically dizzy and go along with everyone else in holding forth about the masses and the nations and the unfolding of world history. But passion's anticipation of eternity cannot quite give existing individuals the absolute continuity they desire, even if it offers the possibility of an approximation to the only true continuity that existing individuals can have. This recalls my thesis that subjectivity is truth, since to existing individuals objective truths are like abstract eternities.

Abstraction is disinterested, but as existing individuals we have no higher interest than existing. Hence we always have a *telos*, and it is this *telos* that Aristotle refers to when he distinguishes between *nous theoretikos* [pure, theoretical thought] and *nous praktikos to telei* [practical thought in its end].[32] But pure thought is surely utterly detached. Abstraction tries to disregard exis-

---

* Earthly passion hinders existing by transforming existence into the momentary [*øieblikkelige*].

† Poetry and art have been called anticipations of eternity. If we want to say this, however, we should note that they are not essentially related to existing individuals, since the contemplation of poetry and art – 'pleasure in the beautiful' – is supposed to be disinterested, taking us contemplatively outside of ourselves as existing individuals. [Cf. the doctrine of disinterested aesthetic pleasure in Kant's *Critique of Judgement*.]

tence, while still maintaining a relation to it, but pure thought hovers in a mystical detachment which bears absolutely no relation to existing individuals. It explains everything within itself except itself – explains everything within itself in such a way that a decisive explanation concerning the real question becomes impossible. Thus if an existing individual asks how pure thought relates itself to existing individuals, and how he should set about gaining admittance into it, pure thought will have nothing to say – it merely explains existence within the terms of its own pure thinking so that everything becomes confused. Existence, in a weak and etiolated sense, has a place allotted to it within pure thought; but existence is the reef on which pure thought runs aground, and anything that pure thought can say about it is essentially revoked in advance. When pure thought talks about the immediate unity of reflection-into-itself and reflection-into-another, and dreams of superseding it, then something else must interpose itself between the elements of the immediate unity. What is this something else? It is *time*. But time has no place allotted to it within pure thought. So what do supersession, transition and the new unity mean? What can it possibly mean to think, but without taking thought seriously, since everything that can be said will have been absolutely revoked in advance? And what can it mean when pure thinkers refuse to acknowledge this, devoting themselves to trumpeting the positive truth of their thinking instead?

Existing individuals are also thinking individuals, and just as existence combines thinking with existing, so there are two different media: that of abstraction and that of actuality. But pure thought confronts us with yet a third medium – a medium of very recent invention. It begins, so we are told, after a most exhaustive abstraction. Pure thought is – how shall I put it? – piously or thoughtlessly ignorant of the relation which abstraction constantly maintains with that from which it abstracts. Within pure thought every doubt is laid to rest: we can have eternal positive truth as well as anything else we might care to mention. Pure thought is therefore a pure phantom. And if Hegelian philosophy has emancipated itself from all presuppositions, it could not have done so without the insane presupposition of the beginning of pure thought.

The highest interest of existing individuals is existing, and this interest is their actuality. But actuality cannot be described in the language of abstraction. Actuality is an *inter-esse* [between-being] within abstraction's hypothetical unity of thought and being. Abstraction treats the question of possibility and actuality, but its conception of actuality is a misrepresentation: its medium is not actuality but possibility. Abstraction grasps actuality only by superseding it, which simply transforms it into possibility. Within abstraction and the language of abstraction, actuality cannot be described except in terms of possibility. In the language of actuality, on the other hand, abstraction is merely a possibility relative to actuality itself, and not a possibility relative to an abstract or possible actuality. Actuality or existence is the dialectical element in a trilogy which has neither beginning nor end for existing individuals, who exist only in the dialectical element. Abstraction brings the trilogy to a close. But how? Is abstraction something real rather than the act of an abstractor? But abstractors must be existing individuals, who exist in a dialectical element which they can neither mediate nor bring to a conclusion – least of all an absolute conclusion – as long as they exist. Their activity must relate itself to actuality – to their own existence – as a possibility. They must explain how, as existing individuals, they can set about it – or alternatively, how they manage to give up being existing individuals, and how they acquire the right to do so.

The moment we begin to ask such questions, we are speaking ethically and asserting the claim of the ethical over existing individuals. And whatever else it may mean, this claim must require them to exist, which is also their highest interest, rather than to abstract from existence.

Existing individuals cannot cling absolutely to the supersession of the dialectical element; that would require a medium other than existence, which is of course precisely the dialectical element. If existing individuals can grasp this supersession at all, they can grasp it only as possibility, and possibility cannot constrain us when interest is in play. This is why their knowledge of it must be disinterested, though of course as existing individuals they can never be completely disinterested, and from an ethical point of view they have no right to think of becoming disinterested, even *approximando*, since the ethical makes the interest of existence infinite for them – so infinite that the principle of contradiction gains absolute validity.

Here again it becomes clear, as we have already seen, that abstraction can never engage with the difficulty of existence and existing. Thinking actuality in the medium of possibility does not present the same difficulty as thinking it in the medium of existence. This is because existence, as a process of becoming, hinders the thinking of existing individuals; it is almost as if actuality were impossible to think – though of course existing individuals also think. Even if we are drowning in the profundity of pure thought, we may still get the feeling *mitunter* [occasionally] that there is something *distrait* about the whole business, since pure thinkers are never very clear about what it means to exist as a human being.

All knowledge of actuality is possibility; and the only actuality which we, as existing individuals, can grasp with more than mere knowledge is our own actuality – the fact that we exist. This actuality is our absolute interest, and if abstraction requires us to become disinterested in order to acquire knowledge, then the ethical requires us to have an infinite interest in existing.

The only actuality for us as existing individuals is our own ethical actuality; other kinds of actuality are merely objects of knowledge for us, while true knowledge translates actuality into possibility.

The evidence of the senses can always be deceptive, as the Greek Sceptics knew, and more recently the modern Idealists. And knowledge of the historical is equally deceptive, at least if it claims to have the reliability of actuality, since we cannot have knowledge of historical actualities except by dissolving them in possibility. (This point is further developed below.) Abstraction is possibility – either a preceding possibility or a subsequent one – and pure thought is but a phantom.

As actual subjectivities we are ethically existing subjectivities rather than knowing subjectivities, since through knowledge we transpose ourselves into the medium of possibility. Of course abstract thinkers also exist, but their existing is a kind of satire against them. Their attempt to demonstrate their existence on the basis of their thinking is a bizarre contradiction, since they could not think abstractly unless they had already abstracted from their existence. It thus becomes clear that whilst they seek to break away from the presupposition of their existence, their act of abstraction is itself a bizarre proof of it, since if it succeeded they would cease to exist. The Cartesian *cogito ergo sum* has been repeated often enough, but if the 'I' in 'I think' is understood as an individual human being, then the argument proves nothing: 'I *am* thinking *ergo* I am', but if I *am* thinking then no wonder I am – the point has already been made, and the conclusion says no more than the premise. But if the 'I' in 'I think' is understood as an individual existing human being, then the philosophers will say: 'stuff and nonsense, it has nothing to do with my individual I or with yours, but only with the pure "I"'. Yet surely this pure 'I' has no existence beyond thought-existence, so why is it presented as the conclusion of an argument? It cannot be a conclusion, since the argument is no more than a tautology.

It might be said that abstract thinkers do not demonstrate through their thinking that they exist, but merely show that their abstractions can never entirely prove the opposite. But it would be a wilful misunderstanding to try to draw the opposite conclusion – that as existing individuals in our actual existence we never think at all. Of course we think, but we think everything in a kind of converse relation to ourselves, because we have an infinite interest in existing. Socrates was surely a thinking individual of this sort; he gave infinite emphasis to ethical knowledge, which is concerned with existing subjects who have an infinite interest in existence, and was indifferent to all other knowledge.

Any attempt to derive existence as a conclusion from thinking is bound to be contradictory, since thinking does exactly the converse: it subtracts existence from actuality, and thinks it by superseding it and translating it into possibility. (This point is further developed below.) The only way we can know an actuality is by thinking it – except in the case of our own. But can our thought ever abstract entirely from our actuality? Abstract thinkers try to do so, of course; but always in vain, since they do not cease to exist, and their continuing existence as 'a sometimes pitiful professorial figure'[33] is both an epigram on abstract thinkers and the reproach of the ethical against them.

The Greeks, by contrast, never forgot what it means to exist. The ataraxia of the sceptics may have been an attempt to abstract from existing, but at least it was an existence-attempt. In our own time, by contrast, abstraction takes place only in books, just as everything is doubted once and for all only in books. One cause of the confusions of modern philosophy is that the philosophers issue lots of little maxims about infinite tasks, and they all take this paper-money seriously. It hardly ever occurs to anyone to try to fulfil the demands of the task for themselves in their own existing. That is why it has become so easy to finish with everything and begin without presuppositions. Consider, for example, the old presupposition that doubting everything is the task of an entire lifetime: nowadays it is no sooner said than done.

Appendix: Towards an Understanding with my Reader

The undersigned author of this book, Johannes Climacus, does not claim to be a Christian, though he is wholly preoccupied with how difficult it must be to become one. Still less is he one of those who was once a Christian, but has ceased to be one by going further. He is a humorist, happy with the circumstances of the moment while always hoping for something better. He feels particularly fortunate that, even if everything else goes wrong, he was born in the century of speculative theocentrism, an age of speculative thinkers and great men of extraordinary insight. Yet I do not believe that any of these esteemed gentlemen could ever be so happy as a private humorist, privately beating his breast or roaring with laughter in his secluded retreat. A private humorist can easily become an author, of course – as long as he takes care never to write except for his own gratification, and as long as he keeps himself to himself, neither fraternising with the mob nor yielding to the self-importance of the age. He is not like the man who came to gawp at a fire and ended up being set to work at the pumps; nor does he have the embarrassment of thinking that he might be standing in the way of all those fine gentlemen who are important, or who should be and must be and will be important.

This work has been written in experimental seclusion, and is not concerned with anything other than myself, purely and simply myself alone. 'I, Johannes Climacus, now thirty years of age, native of Copenhagen, and a plain man like any other, have been informed of the existence of a highest good: it is known as eternal bliss, and Christianity sets the terms of our relation to it. I now ask myself the question: How am I to become a Christian?' I ask it entirely on my own account; yes, that is what I am doing, or rather have already done, since the question is at the heart of the whole work. No one need bother to tell me that the book is completely superfluous and entirely irrelevant to the present age – unless of course they feel they must at all costs say something – for this is precisely the response the author hopes for, and the judgement he himself has already pronounced. He knows perfectly well how fatuous it will seem to write such a book in our time, assuming anyone should notice. Therefore as soon as anyone . . . but what am I saying? Oh, how you do get carried away, vain heart! But no – it is wrong to allow oneself to be led into temptation. Otherwise I would say that as soon as anyone tells me how to apply for permission to write as a single individual, or to set up as an author in the name of humanity, or the century, or the age, or the public, the many, the majority, or (and this is perhaps an even rarer privilege) to write as a single individual against the public but in the name of 'the many', to take issue with the majority in the name of another majority, or in the name of the majority even while admitting that one belongs to a minority – while also, as a single individual, enjoying both the polemical elasticity of being in a minority and the kudos of being, in the eyes of the world, part of a majority – if anyone could let me know the cost of obtaining such a licence (since even if the fee does not have to be paid in cash, it might still be exorbitant) then, assuming I could afford it, I might find it impossible to resist the temptation of writing, as soon as possible, an exceedingly important book which will speak out on behalf of millions and millions and billions and billions. Till that time no one has any right to object to my book for being superfluous – at least not unless they can explain what is at stake – though from my point of view superfluousness is no objection at all.

So my book is superfluous, and no one should bother deferring to it: anyone who does so has *eo ipso* misunderstood it. To be an authority is far too onerous an existence for a humorist like me, for whom it is one of life's special pleasures that there is always a sufficiency of great men who are willing and able to serve as authorities. We have the advantage of being able to adopt their opinions without question, provided we are not so foolish as to try patronizing them, which would of course do no one any good. And above all, may heaven preserve me, and my book too, from the violence of popularity, and from bellowing sectarians who will want to quote it approvingly and add my name to some list or other. They may not be able to grasp the fact that experimental humorists can never serve their sectarian purposes, but we humorists will be glad to have it confirmed that we do not serve the purposes which in any case we wanted to elude. I have no qualifications as a sectarian, for I hold no opinions except this – that becoming a Christian must be the very hardest thing. This is not really an opinion, however, and it does not have any of the qualities that usually characterize opinions: it does not flatter me, since I do not pretend to be a Christian; but neither does it offend Christians, since they can have no objection to my regarding what they do as the very hardest thing; and it does not offend the enemies of Christianity either – indeed, it magnifies their magnificence, implying that they have gone even further . . . than the very hardest thing. I have never wanted actual confirmation that I hold an opinion – I have not sought out hangers-on, applause, or public execution. In truth I hold no opinions, nor do I desire any, and I am perfectly content. Roman Catholic books, especially old ones, often have a note at the back informing the reader that everything is to be understood in accordance with the doctrine of the holy universal mother Church; in just the same way I give notice that everything I have written should be understood as having already been revoked: my book boasts not only a conclusion but a recantation as well. No one can ask for a better bargain, either before or hereafter.

It is of course an innocent pastime and amusement to write and publish a book, provided one does not have a publisher who would get into difficulties if it did not sell. It is a permissible private enterprise within a well-ordered state where luxury is tolerated and citizens are permitted to spend their time and money as they please – building houses, buying horses, going to the theatre, or writing superfluous books and having them printed. But in that case, could it not also be considered one of life's innocent and permissible quiet pleasures – which poses no threat to the keeping of the Sabbath or to any other precept of duty and propriety – to imagine a reader whom our book might now and then address, provided, of course, we never make any attempt whatsoever to persuade any actual person to become our reader? 'Only the positive is an infringement of the personal freedom of another';[34] the negative is a courtesy that cannot be said to cost money, since only the printing does that, and even if one were so ill-mannered as to impose the book on others as a gift, at least no one would have been forced to buy a copy. In a well-ordered state it is perfectly permissible to be silently in love, and the more profound the silence, the more permissible the love. Yet it is not permissible for a man to make overtures to all the girls, and swear to each of them that she is his one true love. And those who actually have a sweetheart already are forbidden by considerations of fidelity and propriety from hankering after an imaginary one, no matter how silently they do so, whereas it is permitted to those who do not have an actual sweetheart. In the same way, an author with no actual readers should be allowed an imaginary one – he should even be allowed to proclaim it, since no one could possibly take offence. Let the well-ordered state be praised! All happiness to those who know how to appreciate it! How could anyone want to reform the state and change the form of government? Of all forms of government, the monarchical is the best – it is the best at encouraging and protecting the quiet fancies and innocent delusions of private citizens. But democracy is the most tyrannical form of government, since it demands positive participation from every citizen, as the societies and general assemblies of our day remind us all too insistently. Is it tyranny if one person wants to rule and thus set the rest of us free? No; but it is tyranny when everyone wants to rule, and we are all obliged to participate in government into the bargain – even those who make it very clear that they want no part of it.

If an author wants to have an imaginary reader as a quiet fiction and altogether private pleasure then it is no one's business but his own. Let this be said as a civic apology and defence for what should need no defence, since its silence should shield it from attack: the innocent and harmless pleasure of having an imaginary reader is an infinite delight, though disdained and unappreciated by many. It is the purest expression of freedom of thought, precisely because it renounces freedom of speech. I do not feel competent to honour and praise such a reader; but no one who knows him will deny that he is the most agreeable of readers by far. He understands everything both all at once and bit by bit. He has the patience not to skip over subordinate clauses and jump from the woof of the individual chapters to the warp of the table of contents; he can hold out just as long as the author. He understands that all understanding is renunciation, and that our understanding with him as our sole reader amounts to a renunciation of the whole book. He understands that writing a book and renouncing it is quite different from not writing it at all; that writing a book which does not pretend to have any significance for anyone is quite different from leaving it unwritten. And even though he always approves and never demurs, we still respect him far more than all the noisy opponents in a lecture theatre – but then we can always talk to him in complete confidence.

Even if I say so myself, dear reader, I am quite something when it comes to philosophy. It is my vocation to create a new trend. I am a poor, single, existing individual with sound natural faculties, a certain dialectical proficiency and some culture too. Yet I have been tried and tested in life's *casibus* [calamities] and I confidently appeal to my sufferings – not as a matter of apostolic honour (they have too often been self-inflicted wounds), but as my teachers, and I do so with more pathos than Stygotius when he appealed to all the universities where he had studied and debated.[35] I insist on maintaining a sincerity which forbids me to parrot things I do not understand, or to appeal to Hegel except in special cases (and this has caused me great pain ever since I forsook him). It also means having to relinquish fame through association, whilst remaining what I myself concede is infinitely little – an unrecognizable, vanishing atom like every other single individual. I cultivate a kind of sincerity which both comforts me and equips me with an extraordinary sense of comedy and an ability to ridicule the ridiculous. (Strangely enough, I cannot ridicule what is not ridiculous – presumably that calls for different aptitudes.) I now feel that thanks to my own thinking, I have educated myself sufficiently through reading, and oriented myself through existing until I have reached the point where I am ready to be a pupil or apprentice, which is of course a task in itself. I am now in a position to begin to learn, in a higher sense, though I do not pretend to be capable of anything else.

If only I could find a teacher! I do not mean a teacher of the classics, since we have plenty of them, and if that was the kind of learning I wanted, I could start as soon as I had acquired the basics. Nor do I mean professors of the history of philosophy, although I certainly have much to learn and could do with a good teacher. I do not mean teachers of the difficult art of religious oratory either, since I am lucky enough to have a very distinguished one and I have certainly done my best to put his earnest advice to good use – though this is something I know on the basis of the respect I feel for His Reverence, rather than from any particular benefit I have derived from his instruction, and I would not like to claim cunning credit for anything that was not mine or to measure his importance by the yardstick of my own incidental achievements. And I am not speaking of teachers of the fine art of poetry and the secrets of language and taste, for we have such an initiate amongst us, as I know very well – and I hope I shall never forget him and all I owe him. But the teacher I am looking for – in a different way, ambiguously and doubtfully – is one who will teach the ambiguous art of thinking about existence and existing. And I dare swear that if such a teacher could be found, and if he undertook to teach me, slowly, step by step, letting me ask questions as a good teacher should, and not moving on to the next topic till the last had been completely mastered, then something remarkable would come of it. Of that I have no doubt at all. For I cannot believe that such a teacher would content himself with the practice of the dull theologians in our schools, who assigned me a paragraph or two every day and made me recite it by rote the next.

By good or bad fortune, I have never yet set eyes on a teacher who could offer me precisely what I seek, so these efforts of mine must *eo ipso* lack importance. They are for my enjoyment only – and it could not be any other way. No student of existence could want to give instruction to others (and I for one would never entertain the vain and empty desire of becoming such a teacher). It is the most that can be expected of a learner who essentially knows neither more nor less than what pretty much everyone knows – except that he knows it more definitely or, when it comes to things which everyone knows or thinks they know, knows definitely that he does not know them. If I were to say this to anyone but you, dear reader, it is possible that I would not even be believed. In our age anyone who says 'I know everything' will be believed, whereas anyone who says 'There is much I do not know' will be accused of lying. You may remember the play by Scribe, in which a dissolute character who has had many love-affairs explains how, when he tires of a girl, he simply sends her a note saying 'I know everything.' The method, he says, has never failed him.[36] In our age, too, I believe, saying 'I know everything' has never failed a speculative thinker. But the liars and miscreants who say 'There is much I do not know' will get their just deserts in this, the best of worlds – the best of worlds, that is, for those who know how to poke fun at it either by knowing everything . . . or by knowing nothing at all.

J. C.

A First and Last Explanation

Just for the sake of form and order, I would like to make a confession. Though hardly anyone can really be interested to *know* it, it happens that I am what is called the real author of the following works: *Either/Or* (Victor Eremita), Copenhagen, February 1843; *Fear and Trembling* (Johannes de Silentio), 1843; *Repetition* (Constantin Constantius), 1843; *The Concept of Anxiety* (Vigilius Haufniensis), 1844; *Prefaces* (Nicolaus Notabene), 1844; *Philosophical Fragments* (Johannes Climacus), 1844; *Stages on Life's Way* (Hilarius Bookbinder: William Afham, the Judge, Frater Taciturnus), 1845; *Concluding Postscript to the Philosophical Fragments* (Johannes Climacus), 1846; an article in *The Fatherland*, No. 1168, 1843 (Victor Eremita); and two articles in *The Fatherland*, January 1846 (Frater Taciturnus).

My pseudonymity or polyonymity has nothing to do with any fear of legal penalty, since as far as I am aware I have never committed any offence, and both the printer and the Censor, as an officer of state, have always been properly notified of the true identity of the author of each publication. Nor is it a matter of personal whim. It is *essential* to the nature of my output itself which, for purely poetic reasons – in order to express the various psychological differences between individualities – called for a total indifference to matters of good and evil, heartbreak or high spirits, bumptiousness or despair, suffering or triumph, and so on; and this indifference is limited only by ideal considerations of psychological consistency, which no real and actual person would ever dream of adopting given the moral restrictions of actuality. What I have written is therefore undeniably mine, but only in so far as I have put a life-view into the mouth of a poetically actual creative individual by making his words audible. My relation is even more external than that of a poet, who makes up his characters *poetically* yet writes the preface personally. For I am impersonally, or personally in the third person, a prompter whose poetic creations include *authors* whose *prefaces*, indeed whose very *names*, are their own creation.

Hence the pseudonymous books do not contain a single word of my own; I have no opinion of them except as a third party, no knowledge of their meaning except as a reader, and not even the most tenuous private connection to them, as no such thing is possible in a doubly-reflected communication. A single word from me personally and in my own name would be a piece of presumptuous self-forgetfulness which, from a dialectical point of view, would annihilate the essence of the pseudonyms. I am not the editor Victor Eremita any more than I am the Seducer or the Judge in *Either/Or* – the poetically actual subjective thinker whom we meet again in 'In Vino Veritas'.[37] I am not Johannes de Silentio any more than I am the knight of faith he portrays in *Fear and Trembling*, or the author of the preface to that book, which is the individual creation of a poetically actual subjective thinker. I am not the Quidam of the experiment in the story of suffering 'Guilty?/Not Guilty?'[38] any more than I am the experimenter – precisely as little, in fact, since the experimenter is a poetically-actual subjective thinker and the object of the experiment is his own psychologically consistent creation. Indifference is what I am – it is a matter of indifference what and how I am, simply because it is absolutely irrelevant to this creation whether in my innermost being it is a matter of indifference to me what and how I am. Anything which can have a happy significance that agrees beautifully with the distinguished person who undertakes it, in relation to undertakings which are not dialectically reduplicated, could only be a tiresome distraction in relation to the altogether indifferent foster-father of a perhaps not undistinguished creation.

Portraits or likenesses of me, and questions as to whether I wear a hat or a cap, are of interest only to those for whom the indifferent has become a matter of importance – perhaps because matters of importance have become indifferent to them. In a legal and a literary sense the responsibility is mine, in that I have made these creations audible in the world of actuality, but dialectically it is easy to understand that this has nothing to do with any poetically-actual author, so it is wholly consistent from a legal and literary point of view that it should be entirely my responsibility. I say 'legal and literary' because poetic creation would immediately become impossible, or meaningless and unbearable, if every word had to be regarded as literally the creator's own. So if people ever want to quote from my books, I hope and pray that they will be good enough to cite the relevant pseudonym rather than my own name, so as to make it clear that the passage belongs, in a feminine sense, to the pseudonym, even if the civil responsibility is mine. I have always been aware that my personal actuality is an inconvenience which the sentimentally self-assertive pseudonyms would prefer to do away with as soon as they can. They would like to reduce its significance to zero, and yet with ironic attentiveness they also wish to make use of it as a diametrical contrast. For my relationship to the author or authors seamlessly combines that of secretary with – ironically enough – that of a dialectically reduplicated author. Anyone who has taken an interest in these matters has always assumed that I am the author of the pseudonymous books, but now that I have explained myself the explanation may at first give the strange impression that I, who of course must know best, am the only one who sees any uncertainty or ambiguity in my authorship, because in these cases I am the figurative author, whereas I am quite literally and straightforwardly the author of, for example, every word of the *Edifying Discourses*.[39] The poetized author has his own definite life-view, but views which may be meaningful, witty and refreshing when understood in that way might well sound strange, ludicrous or even repulsive in the mouth of some single, definite, real individual. It is not my fault if readers unacquainted with the educative use of distantiating idealities have gained a distorted impression of the pseudonymous books by intruding into my real personality, and thus deluded themselves – *actually* deluded themselves – by dragging in my personal actuality instead of dancing with the doubly-reflected, light ideality of a poetically-real author. It is not my fault if, though paralogistic impudence, they have been led astray by senselessly bringing my private singularity into the dialectical doubleness of qualitative contrasts, since I have always done everything I could to protect the proper purity of the relationship, and to guard and defend it from an inquisitive section of the reading public who – in whose interest, God knows – have always tried their hardest to get their hands on it.

The opportunity seems to offer itself now, and if I were reluctant it would almost demand it of me, so I shall give an open and direct confession – not in my capacity as author, since I am not an author in the ordinary sense of the word, but as a collaborator who has helped the pseudonyms to become authors. First I want to give thanks to Providence, which has favoured my efforts in so many ways without resting so much as a single day in four and a quarter years, and which has been far more bountiful than I ever expected, although I can honestly testify that I have dedicated my whole life to it too, far beyond what I at least had expected, even if my achievements may strike others as nothing more than long-winded trivialities. So I thank Providence from the bottom of my heart, and do not much care that I cannot really be said to have achieved anything, particularly in the external world. I find it ironically appropriate, considering the nature of my output and the ambiguity of my authorship, that my fees have always been, at best, somewhat Socratic.

After begging pardon and forgiveness in advance, as is fitting, in case it should seem improper for me to speak in this way (though some might also object if I failed to do so) I next want to honour the memory of my poor father, who is of all men the one to whom I owe most, and not least with regard to my work. Herewith I bid farewell to the pseudonyms with doubtful good wishes for their future, hoping that fate will be favourable to them, and precisely as they would wish. I know them intimately, of course, and I am sure they would neither expect nor desire to have a large readership; but I hope they will be blessed with one or two good individual readers. From my own readers, if I may speak of such a thing, I tentatively request a forgetful remembrance as a token of their recognition that I am, as the relationship requires, irrelevant to the books, and I here offer my thanks for it at the moment of parting, as I also heartily thank everyone who has kept silent, as with profound veneration I also thank the firm of Kts – for having spoken.[40]

If the pseudonyms have ever offended respectable persons, or indeed anyone else I admire in any way, or if they have disturbed or undermined any actual good in the established order – then no one is more ready to apologize than I, as the one responsible for holding their careful pen. My knowledge of the pseudonyms, such as it is, does not of course entitle me to have the last word about them, as they would undoubtedly agree, since their significance (whatever that may eventually turn out to be) certainly does not consist in offering new proposals or astonishing revelations, or in establishing a new party and hoping for further progress. Their real significance consists in precisely the opposite: in wanting to signify nothing and, at the distance of a double-reflection, to read more inwardly the original text of individual human existence-relationships – the familiar old text handed down to us from our forefathers.

Let us hope that this work will be spared the attentions of apprentice dialecticians, and that it will always be left just as it is.

Copenhagen, February 1846
S. Kierkegaard

Notes

1   Cf. John, 4, 23: 'But the hour cometh, and now is, when the true worshippers shall worship the Father in spirit and in truth.'
2   See Diogenes Laertius, *Lives of the Philosophers*, II, 21.
3   A reference to an article on 'Orestes and Oedipus or the Collision', by Hans Friedrich Helweg (1816–1901), which appeared in 1845.
4   See Plato, *Gorgias*, 511d–512h.
5   Perhaps an allusion to John 5, 4: 'whosoever then first after the troubling of the water stepped in was made whole'.
6   Charon relates the tale which amused him so much in Lucian's *Charon, or the Inspectors*, §6.
7   Cf. Matthew 6, 17: 'But thou, when thou fastest, anoint thine head, and wash thy face.'
8   An allusion to Romans 8, 26: 'the Spirit itself maketh intercession for us with groanings which cannot be uttered'.
9   Johann Melchior Götze (1717–86).
10   See Plato, *Symposium*; 203b–204a, and Plutarch, *Isis and Osiris*, §57, *Moralia*, 374c.
11   See Hesiod, *Theogony*, ll. 116–22.
12   'Wenn Gott in seiner Rechten alle Wahrheit, und in seiner Linken den einzigen immer regen Trieb nach Wahrheit, obschon mit dem Zusatze, mich immer und ewig zu irren, verschlossen hielte, und spräche zu mir: wähle! Ich fiele ihm mit Demuth in seine Linke, und sagte: Vater, gieb! die reine Wahrheit ist ja doch nur für dich allein!' (G. E. Lessing, *Eine Duplik*, 1778).
13   An allusion to Hermann Samuel Reimarus, *Fragmente des Wolfenbüttelschen Ungennanten*, published anonymously under Lessing's auspices in 1777.
14   See above, n. 9.
15   Cf. Luke 23, 1–12.
16   A reference to Israel Joachim Behrend (1761–1821), a Copenhagen eccentric.
17   Friedrich Adolf Trendelenburg (1802–72), professor of philosophy at Berlin; in his *Logical Investigations* (1840), he tried to undermine Hegelianism by promoting the idea of 'movement' at the expense of 'dialectic'.
18   See Plutarch, *Isis and Osiris*, §60; *Moralia*, 375d.
19   An allusion to Hegel's *schlechte Unendlichkeit* or 'bad infinity'.
20   Cf. Aristotle, *De Caelo*, 268a30.
21   A reference to the perpetual student in J. L. Heiberg's play, *Recensenten og Dyret* (1826).

22 An allusion to Heinrich Theodor Rötscher, author of *Aristophanes und sein Zeitalter* (1827).

23 Heinrich Theodor Rötscher discussed Hamlet in his *Die Kunst der Dramatischen Darstellung* (1841–6).

24 Hegel's *Phenomenology of Spirit* (1807) antedates his elaboration of his System.

25 See above, pp. 161–71.

26 The reference is to Frater Taciturnus, one of the pseudonymous authors of *Stages on Life's Way*.

27 An allusion to Ludwig Holberg's play *Barselstuen*.

28 An allusion to a character in *Kallundborgs-Krøniken eller Censurens Oprindelse*, by Jens Immanuel Baggesen.

29 Jakob Peter Mynster (1772–1854), bishop primate of the Church of Denmark, was a spiritual inspiration to Kierkegaard, but after his death in 1854 Kierkegaard tactlessly criticized him in the journal *Fædrelandet*. See 'Was Bishop Mynster a "Truth-Witness"', in KW XXIII, pp. 3–8.

30 An allusion to Pythagorean disciplines of purification, and Socratic attempts to free the soul from the body.

31 Cf. Aristotle's *Metaphysics*, 1072b.

32 Cf. Aristotle, *On the Soul*, 433a.

33 See above, pp. 261, 263.

34 A partial quotation from the preface to *Concluding Unscientific Postscript* (not included in this anthology); cf. KW XII.1, pp. 7–8.

35 An allusion to a character in Ludwig Holberg's play *Jacob von Tyboe* (1725).

36 A reference to the play *Une chaine* (1841) by the French dramatist Eugène Scribe (1791–1861).

37 'In Vino Veritas' is a section of *Stages on Life's Way*, 'related' by William Afham, who is here identified with the author of the second part of *Either/Or*.

38 Another reference to *Stages on Life's Way*.

39 Six sets of *Edifying Discourses* (or *Upbuilding Discourses*) were published in Kierkegaard's own name between 1843 and 1845.

40 'Kts' was a pseudonym of Jakob Peter Mynster, formed from the first letter of the second syllable of each of his names.

10

My Work as an Author

In the three years following the publication of *Either/Or* in February 1843, Kierkegaard's literary productivity was extraordinary. *Repetition* and *Fear and Trembling* came out later that year, and *Philosophical Fragments*, *The Concept of Anxiety* and *Prefaces* in 1844. In 1845 there was the bulky *Stages on Life's Way*, which became famous for explicitly adding a third option – the religious way of life – to the 'aesthetic' and 'ethical' alternatives considered in *Either/Or*.[1] Then there were the even more extensive explorations of the limits of philosophy in *Concluding Unscientific Postscript*, which appeared in February 1846. And apart from all these pseudonymous works, Kierkegaard had also published more than a dozen religious *Discourses* in his own name. By the time of his thirty-third birthday in May 1846, he was becoming recognized as an extremely prolific author; but a very enigmatic one too.

In 1847 Kierkegaard's publisher suggested issuing a second edition of *Either/Or* (the only one of his books to have sold its entire run). The prospect of repeating his beginning seems to have encouraged Kierkegaard to look back on his life's work and start composing an essay describing 'The Point of View for My Work as an Author', which would in effect be an exact negation of *Prefaces*: not a set of stammering false starts designed to mock the very idea of authoritative interpretations, but an attempt at a definitive vindication of all his writings and a lesson to his readers in how his works ought to be interpreted.

Kierkegaard hoped to expand on the literary confessions he had appended to *Concluding Unscientific Postscript*[2] and combine them with the concept of the religious from *Stages on Life's Way* so as to reveal a religious purpose behind all his writings. From *Either/Or* to *Concluding Unscientific Postscript*, he claimed, his works had described a single movement, a journey towards the recognition of the ultimate value of simple Christianity. Despite outward appearances, therefore, his works had never been anything but 'religious' in intention – 'religious from first to last'. They had moved from poetry and aesthetics towards religion, and from philosophy and dialectics towards Christianity, and as a consequence they had also moved from indirectness and pseudonymity towards direct communication in his own name. And the complex movement had been necessary as a matter of 'strategy' – a strategy to outwit Christianity's greatest enemy, which for Kierkegaard was 'Christendom' (*Christenhed*).[3] Christendom was a system which removed the religiousness from Christianity by treating religion as a public institution which could be taken for granted, rather like banking or the legal system; and Kierkegaard's writings had always been designed, he claimed, to break through the defences of Christendom in order to bear witness to the unnerving difficulties of 'becoming a Christian'.

At first Kierkegaard contemplated publishing his apologia as a book; then he proposed presenting it in the form of 'a short series of lectures on the organizing theme throughout my entire work as an author'. (No more than twenty people would be admitted to the course, and they would all be given a solemn warning in advance: though the lectures would be laborious and very boring, those who heard them would find the rest of their lives far more difficult to live.)[4] But he could not settle on either of these options, and in any case he was also at work on the manuscripts which would eventually become *The Sickness Unto Death*, *Practice in Christianity* and *The Book on Adler*. He remained preoccupied with 'The Point of View' throughout 1848, thinking that he might use it as the preface to a second edition of *Either/Or*, should he decide to produce one. But he hesitated, playing with the idea of publishing his confession pseudonymously, or perhaps withholding it till after his death. Alternatively, he contemplated publishing three volumes of his most recent work under the title 'The Collected Works of Completion', with 'The Point of View' as their climax and epitome.

He hesitated again. The second edition of *Either/Or* appeared in May 1849, almost identical to the first. *The Sickness Unto Death* came out in July 1849, and *Practice in Christianity* in September 1850 (both of them 'by Anti-Climacus, edited by S. Kierkegaard'). Then in August 1851 he at last published a synopsis of 'The Point of View' as a pamphlet in his own name entitled *On my Work as an Author*. After that Kierkegaard never wrote any more pseudonymous works. He steered clear of 'aesthetic' and 'ethical' themes, confining himself exclusively to 'the religious'. He also adopted an increasingly polemical tone, and his productivity declined until it reached an almost human scale. He died on 11 November 1855, apparently secure in the thought that his real work had been completed several years before. He had prepared a final text of *The Point of View for my Work as an Author* – subtitled 'A Direct Communication, Report to History' – and Peter Kierkegaard saw to its publication in 1859, hoping to put the lid on his brother's literary coffin at last.

On the face of it at least, *On my Work as an Author* and *The Point of View* are amongst the simplest works Kierkegaard ever wrote. They seem to mark a moment of truth in which the comedian removes his mask and, with tender solemnity, offers us the true explanation of all his elaborate and dazzling routines; and most readers have clutched at them with gratitude, hailing them as Kierkegaard's masterpiece, comparing them with the *Confessions* of St Augustine or Cardinal Newman's *Apologia pro Vita Sua*, and treating them as more significant than his enigmatic primary works themselves.

On the other hand they are undoubtedly distressing documents as well. Kierkegaard's comments on the political events of 1848 – Germany's victory over Denmark in the struggle over Schleswig-Holstein and the revolution which placed constitutional constraints on the Danish monarchy – are merely peevish,[5] and his splenetic fury at Copenhagen's popular comic weekly the *Corsair*, which had lampooned him in a series of features about the thinness of his legs and the unequal length of his trousers, is manifestly disproportionate and hysterical.[6] Moreover his descriptions of himself as a 'spy in a higher service', a 'martyr' and a 'sacrifice' involve a measure of self-dramatization, not to say self-delusion, mitigated only by the banality of an anonym called 'my poet', who wrote that 'the martyrdom this author suffered may be briefly described thus: He suffered from being a genius in a market town.'[7]

Perhaps there are moments, however, when Kierkegaard's confessions still flicker with irony. When he offers 'my judgement of this age . . . that it lacks religious education', we can hardly fail to think of the bantering Johannes Climacus in the preface to *Philosophical Fragments*: 'Having an opinion is both too much and too little for me: it presupposes a sense of well-being and security in existence, like having a wife and children in this terrestrial world . . .'[8] Readers with a taste for irony will also cleave to the passages where Kierkegaard concedes that his statements about his writings have no special authority, and that he is presenting them to us not in his capacity as an author, but simply, like us, as reader.[9] 'With this present little book,' he writes, 'I conclude my whole previous authorship.'[10] But if the authorship was coming to an end, his readership had hardly begun.

Notes

1   *Stages on Life's Way: Studies by Sundry Persons* ('collected and sent to the press and published by Hilarius Bookbinder') comprises (a) an account by 'William Afham' (perhaps to be identified with the Judge William of *Either/Or*) of a drunken banquet attended by, amongst others, Constantin Constantius, Victor Eremita and Johannes the Seducer, followed by (b) an enormous diary of a love affair, by 'Quidam', and (c) a commentary on the diary by 'Frater Taciturnus', who claims to have fished it up from the bottom of a lake. Johannes Climacus was to comment that the three stages 'are not abstract, as immediacy, mediation, and unity; they are concrete in existence-categories [*existents-bestemmelse*] as pleasure-perdition, action-victory, and suffering'. See 'A Glance at a Contemporary Effort in Danish Literature' in *Concluding Unscientific Postscript*; cf. KW XII.1, p. 294.

2   See above, pp. 280–4, 'A First and Last Explanation'.

3   See *On my Work as an Author*, appendix: 'My Position as a Religious Author within "Christendom" and my Strategy'; cf. KW XXII, p. 15.

4   See Journals and Notebooks, VIII[2] B 186; cf. KW XXII, p. 159.

5   See for example pp. 314–15 below.

6   See for example pp. 315–16 below.

7   See for example pp. 339–41 below.

8   See above, p. 160.

9   See for example p. 302 below.

10   See p. 339 below.

On my Work as an Author
by S. Kierkegaard

He who believes he has stature and riches,
God and the Kingdom of Heaven are his.
He who believes he is poor and small,
'Lord have mercy' is his only call.[1]

The Accounting

Copenhagen, March, 1849

When a land is little the proportions are in every respect small in the little
land. So in respect to literature: the honorarium and all that goes with it will

The selections printed here comprise the main text of *On my Work as an Author*, but without
the long appendix 'My Position as a Religious Author within "Christendom" and My Strategy'. This is followed by several passages from *The Point of View*: the introduction; both sections ('A: The ambiguity' and 'B: The explanation') of part one; and, from the much longer
part two, the later parts of chapter one, on the aesthetic works, both parts of chapter two, and
all of chapter three (except a few paragraphs on Kierkegaard's childhood), including the epilogue and conclusion, but not the 'Two Notes concerning My Work as an Author' which
Kierkegaard added in March 1855. Both *On My Work as an Author* and *The Point of View* have
been translated by Howard V. Hong and Edna H. Hong as vol. XXII of *Kierkegaard's Writings*
(1998), but what is printed here is the familiar and readable version by Walter Lowrie, which
was published in 1939 and had a decisive impact on the reception of Kierkegaard in the
English-speaking world. The translation has been thoroughly checked against the original and
corrected where necessary.

be insignificant. If one is not a poet, and more particularly a dramatist, and does not write textbooks or is not supported in some other way by one's profession, then the business of being an author is about the most wretchedly rewarded, the least secure, and to that extent the most thankless occupation. If there live a man possessed of the talents requisite for authorship, who in addition to that is so fortunate as to have some property, he can then become an author more or less at his own expense. However, this is fitting enough and therefore constitutes no ground for complaint. It is becoming for the individual in his particular calling to love his idea, the nation to which he belongs, the cause which he serves, and the language in which as an author he has the honour to write. Such indeed will be the case when there is harmony of understanding between the individual and the people, which in turn (if such be the case) will treat the individual rather handsomely.

Whether my experience has been in any respect the contrary of this, whether I may have been treated unhandsomely by one or many – that is, properly speaking, something which does not concern me, but is very properly their concern. On the other hand, what does concern me, and what I so gladly acknowledge as my concern, is to have the duty and privilege of rendering thanks for what favour, goodwill, friendliness, and appreciation have been shown me in general or by particular individuals.

The movement described by the authorship is this: *from* the poet (from aesthetics), *from* philosophy (from speculation), *to* the indication of a more inward definition of what Christianity is – *from* the *pseudonymous* 'Either/Or', *through* 'The Concluding Postscript' *with my name as editor*, *to* the 'Discourses at Communion on Fridays',★ two of which were delivered in the Church of

---

★   Later, however, there appeared a new pseudonym, Anti-Climacus [author of *The Sickness Unto Death* (1849) and *Practice in Christianity* (1850)]. On the other hand the very fact that it is a pseudonym indicates (as the name *Anti*-Climacus itself indicates) that he signifies a coming to a halt. All the earlier pseudonyms are lower than the 'edifying author'; the new pseudonym represents a higher pseudonymity. It is to be understood, however, that the 'coming to a halt' is accomplished by pointing out something higher, with the consequence of forcing me back within my limitations, condemning me because my life does not correspond to so lofty a claim, so that the communication has to be poetic. And somewhat earlier the same year [1849] there appeared a little book, *Two Minor Ethico-Religious Treatises*, by H. H. Without going further into the question, it is not easy to explain the significance of this little book, which does not belong *in* the authorship so much as *to* the authorship as a whole, and hence was made anonymous for the sake of keeping it quite outside. It is like a nautical beacon *towards* which one steers, but in such a way, be it observed, that the navigator understands he *has to keep a certain distance away from it*. It defines the limitations of the authorship. 'The Difference between a Genius and an Apostle' (Treatise No. 2) is that 'the genius is without authority'. But just because genius as such is without authority, it lacks entirely the ultimate concentration in itself which bestows power and title to emphasize the

our Lady. This movement was accomplished or described *uno tenore*, in one breath, if I may use this expression, so that the authorship, regarded *as a whole*, is religious from first to last – something that anyone who has eyes to see must see, if he wants to see. Just as the natural scientist at once recognizes by the way the strands are crossed in the spider's web what artful little animal it is who made the web – so the discerning mind will recognize that corresponding to this authorship there is an originator who, as author, 'has only willed one thing'.[2] The discerning mind will at the same time recognize that this one thing is the religious, but the religious altogether and utterly transposed into reflection, yet in such a way that it is altogether and utterly withdrawn from reflection and restored to simplicity – that is to say, he will see that the road travelled has the aim of *approaching, of attaining* simplicity.

And this, moreover, is the *Christian* movement (a movement in *reflection*, as in fact it originally was). In a Christian sense simplicity is not the point of departure from which one goes on to become interesting, witty, profound, poet, philosopher, etc. No, the very contrary. One begins *here*, and then becomes simpler and simpler, *attaining* simplicity. This, within 'Christendom', is the *Christian* movement of reflection: one does not reflect oneself into Christianity, but reflects oneself out of something else and becomes, more and more simply, a Christian. If the author had been a richly gifted spirit, or (supposing him to be that) if he had been twice as gifted a spirit, he would have needed more time, perhaps twice as much, to follow this path in literary production and reach this point.

But just as that which has been communicated (the religious thought) has been entirely transposed into reflection and taken back out of reflection again, so the *communication* has also been decisively marked by reflection; in other words, use has been made of the kind of communication proper to reflection. 'Direct communication' means communicating the truth directly. 'Communication in reflection' means deceiving into the truth. But since the aim of the movement is to attain simplicity, the communication must, sooner

---

(*cont'd from p. 291*) duty of 'letting oneself be put to death for the truth' (Treatise No. 1). Genius as such remains in the sphere of reflection. That again is the category of my whole authorship: to *call attention* to the religious, to Christianity – but *without authority*. – And finally [in 1849], to take account of even the least things, there appeared later *The Lilies of the Field and the Birds of the Air*, three godly discourses which served as the accompaniment to the second edition of *Either/Or*, and also *The High Priest – The Pharisee – The Woman that was a Sinner*, three discourses at communion on Fridays, which served as the accompaniment to Anti-Climacus's *Sickness Unto Death* – and the prefaces to both these little works repeat that first preface, the preface to the *Two Edifying Discourses* of 1843. ([Note added in] *October* 1849.)

or later, end in direct communication. It began *maieutically*, with aesthetic works* and all the pseudonymous works are *maieutic*. That indeed is the reason why these works were pseudonymous – whereas the directly religious (which was present from the very first as a glinting suggestion) bore my own name. The directly religious was present from the first, for the *Two Edifying Discourses* of 1843 were actually simultaneous with *Either/Or*.† And in order to establish the directly religious as contemporaneous, the publication of each new pseudonymous work was accompanied almost simultaneously by a little collection of *Edifying Discourses* – until the appearance of the *Concluding Postscript*, which set the problem, which is the problem *kat' exochén* [in an eminent sense] of the whole authorship, namely, 'how to become a Christian'.‡ From that moment the glinting hints of direct communication cease and there begins the purely religious productivity: *Edifying Discourses in Divers Spirits*; *The Works of Love*; *Christian Discourses*. But as a reminder of the beginning (and corresponding to the position occupied by the *Two Edifying Discourses* at the beginning, when the majority of the writings were aesthetic) there came at the conclusion (when for a long time the productivity had been exclusively and voluminously religious) a little aesthetic article by Inter et Inter in *Fædrelandet*, for July 1848.[3] Coming at the beginning, the *Two Edifying Discourses* had hinted, like a preliminary flash, that this was really what was to come out of it all, what it was all leading to. The flash of the little aesthetic article, coming as it does at the conclusion, by reflecting as it were

---

* The maieutic lies in the relationship between aesthetic works as a beginning and religion as *telos* [end, goal]. The point of departure was the aesthetic, wherein possibly the majority live their lives; and then the religious is introduced so unexpectedly that those who had been enticed by the aesthetic suddenly found themselves in the midst of decisive definitions of Christianity and were at least obliged to take notice.

† At the same time this disposes of the illusion that religion is something one has recourse to as one grows older. 'One begins as an aesthetic writer, and then, when one has grown older, and no longer possesses the vigour of youth, one becomes a religious writer.' But when an author begins *simultaneously* as an aesthetic and a religious author, it surely is not possible to explain the religious works from the casual circumstance that he has grown older; for simultaneously one surely cannot be older than oneself.

‡ The *situation* (i.e. becoming a Christian in 'Christendom', when one is a 'Christian' as a matter of course) – a situation which, as any dialectician can perceive, transposes everything into reflection – requires indirect communication, because the aim in this case is to dispel the illusion which consists in calling oneself a Christian and perhaps even believing it, without being any such thing. And so whoever raised the problem did not describe himself *directly* as a Christian and others as not being any such thing. *On the contrary*, he denied that he was a Christian and conceded that others were. This is what Johannes Climacus does. In a case of pure receptivity, as with an empty vessel which is to be filled, direct communication is appropriate; but where illusion enters in, that is to say, where there is something that must be removed, direct communication is out of place.

the hint given at the beginning of the authorship, draws attention to the fact that from the very beginning the aesthetic was merely the point of departure, a position which had to be left behind. The *Concluding Postscript* is the middle point, so precisely (though this is not worthy to be mentioned except as a curiosity) that even the quantities of material presented before and after it are roughly equal – provided that the *Eighteen Edifying Discourses* are included, as is only reasonable, in the purely religious work;[4] and even the periods of time occupied by the authorship before the *Concluding Postscript* and after it are about the same.

Finally, in another respect also the movement of the authorship is decisively marked by reflection, or rather it is the movement of reflection itself. The direct way of beginning is with individuals, some few readers; and then the task – or rather the movement – is to gather a crowd and win for oneself an abstraction, the public. Here, however, the beginning was made *maieutically*, sensationally, and therefore with a public – which is always at hand when there is something going on – and the movement was, maieutically, to stir up the 'crowd' in order to get hold of 'the individual',★ understanding this word in a religious sense. At precisely the moment when the sensation awakened by *Either/Or* was at its height, the *Two Edifying Discourses* of 1843 appeared, which employed the formula subsequently repeated as a stereotyped phrase: 'It seeks that single individual whom with joy and gratitude I call my reader.' And precisely at the critical moment when the *Concluding Postscript* (which, as I have said, poses the problem) was delivered to the printer, with instructions to begin the work as soon as possible, and the publication presumably was bound to follow shortly after – just at that moment one of the pseudonyms made the greatest possible effort to repel the public,† in a

---

★   This again, (corresponding to the fact that a religious author *begins* with aesthetic production, and to the fact that, instead of loving himself and his own advantage, and forwarding his effort by creating illusion, he hates himself and removes the illusions) – this again, I say, is the dialectic, or the dialectical movement, that is to say, to *counteract* oneself in one's *actions*, which is what I call reduplication, and it is an example of the heterogeneity which distinguishes every true godly effort from worldly effort. To strive or to work *directly* is to work or strive in immediate connection with a factually given condition. The dialectical is the exact *converse*, that is to say, counteracting one's effort by one's own action. This duplication is 'seriousness', like the pressure upon the plough which determines the depth of the furrow, whereas the direct effort is a smoothing over, which not only goes more quickly and easily, but is by far a more thankful task, for it is worldliness and homogeneity.

†   Only one thing more. The literary despicableness of the press was broadcasting itself far and wide. To speak in all sincerity, I believed that I was also doing a charitable deed. It was rewarded (even by some of those for whose sake I exposed myself to such treatment) . . . as a work of love commonly is rewarded in this world, and by help of such reward it became a truly Christian work of love.

newspaper article directed at the spot where it would be most effective.[5] Then the decisive religious production began. Once again I dedicated myself religiously to 'that individual', to whom the next essential work (after the *Concluding Postscript*)* was dedicated. I refer to the *Edifying Discourses in Divers Spirits*, or rather the first part of that book which is an exhortation to confession. Perhaps nobody noticed it the first time I employed the category 'that individual', and nobody paid much attention to the fact that it was repeated in stereotyped form in the prefaces to each volume of *Edifying Discourses*. When for the second time I repeated the message, and multiplied it by itself, standing firmly by my first pronouncement, I had done everything I could to put the whole weight of emphasis on that category. Here again the movement tends towards simplicity: it is from the public to the individual. *Religiously* speaking, there is no such thing as a public, but only individuals;† for religion is seriousness, and seriousness is . . . the individual – in the sense, however, that absolutely every human being can be, and indeed must be, an individual. To me, the edifying author, it was and is, therefore, a joy that from this moment this matter of 'the individual' began to receive some attention. This was and is a joy to me; for though it is true enough that I have faith in the correctness of my thought against all the world, yet almost the last thing for me to relinquish is my faith in human individuals. And this is my faith, that despite all that is confused, evil, and detestable in those who have become an irresponsible and unrepentant 'public' or 'crowd', there is also truth, goodness, and loveliness in them provided they become individuals. Oh, how lovable and human they become if they become individuals before God!

That is how I *now* understand everything as a whole. Hitherto I was unable thus to survey what has in fact been my own development. Nothing would be more out of place here than long-windedness. What is required is to be able to fold together in simplicity what is unfolded in the many books, and which as unfolded constituted the many books. And this brief communication is more particularly occasioned by the fact that the first-fruit of authorship now appears a second time – the new edition of *Either/Or*, which I was unwilling to publish earlier.

---

* For the little literary review of the novel *Two Generations* followed so immediately upon the *Concluding Postscript* that it is all but contemporaneous. As a matter of fact, it is one of the things I produced *qua* critic, not *qua* author; yet in the last section it contains, from the point of view of 'the individual', a sketch of the future which the year 1848 did not belie. [Kierkegaard refers to *Two Ages: A Literary Review*, published in his own name in 1846.]

† And in so far as there is, in a religious sense, such a thing as a 'congregation', this is a concept which does not conflict with 'the individual', and which is by no means to be confounded with what may have *political* importance: the public, the crowd, the numerical, etc.

Personally – when I bethink me of my inward sufferings, which I may well have brought upon myself – one thing concerns me absolutely. It is more important to me than the whole authorship, and lies closer to my heart: to express, as sincerely and strongly as possible, what I can never be sufficiently grateful for, and what I shall unalterably recollect for ever, even if I forget the whole authorship – that Providence has done infinitely more for me than I ever expected, could have expected, or might have dared to expect.

Without authority to *call attention* to the religious, to Christianity, is the category for my entire authorship, regarded as a whole. From the very first moment I have asserted clearly that I am 'without authority', and have repeated it as a stereotyped phrase. I prefer to regard myself as a *reader* of the books, rather than their *author*.

'Before God', religiously, when I converse with myself, I regard the entire authorship as my education and development – which is not, however, to imply that I am now complete or completely finished so as to need no more upbringing and development.

Notes

1   'Wer glaubet, der ist groß und reich, / Er hat Gott und das Himmelreich. / Wer glaubet, der ist klein und arm, / Er schreiet nur: Herr Dich erbarm.' From 'Der Frommen Lotterie' by Gerhard Tersteegen (1697–1769), poet, mystic and wandering preacher.

2   A reference to 'An Occasional Discourse' of 1847; cf. KW XV, pp. 24–5.

3   Kierkegaard here refers to his *The Crisis and a Crisis in the Life of an Actress*, published in the Journal *Fædrelandet*, 188–91, July 1848.

4   *Eighteen Edifying Discourses* (1845) brought together the six sets of *Edifying Discourses* published in 1843 and 1844.

5   Kierkegaard refers to his 'The Activity of a Travelling Aesthetician and How he Still Happened to Pay for the Dinner', published in *Fædrelandet*, 2078, December 1845.

The Point of View for my Work as an Author: A Direct Communication, a Report to History by S. Kierkegaard

In everything the purpose must weigh with the folly.[1]

What shall I say?
My words weigh nothing,
O God, how great thy wisdom is,
Thy kingdom, power and goodness.[2]

Introduction

In my career as an author, a point has now been reached where it is permissible to do what I feel a strong impulse to do and so regard as my duty – namely, to explain once and for all, as directly and frankly as possible, what is what: what I as an author declare myself to be. The moment (however unpropitious it may be in another sense) is now appropriate; partly because (as I have said) this point has been reached, and partly because I am about to encounter for the second time in the literary field my first production, *Either/Or*, in its second edition, which I was not willing to have published earlier.

There is a time to be silent and a time to speak.[3] So long as I considered the strictest silence my religious duty I strove in every way to preserve it. I have not hesitated to counteract, in a *finite* sense, my own effort by the enigmatic mystery and *double entente* which silence favours. What I have done in that way has been misunderstood, has been explained as pride, arrogance, and

God knows what. So long as I considered silence my religious duty I would not do the least thing to obviate such a misunderstanding. But the reason I considered silence my duty was that the authorship was not yet at hand in so complete a form that the understanding of it could be anything but misunderstanding.

The contents of this little book affirm, then, what I truly am as an author, that I am and was a religious author, that the whole of my work as an author is related to Christianity [*Christendommen*], to the problem 'of becoming a Christian', with a direct or indirect polemic against the monstrous illusion we call Christendom [*Christenheden*], or against the illusion that in such a land as ours all are Christians of a sort.

I would beg of every one who has the cause of Christianity at heart – and I beg the more urgently the more seriously he takes it to heart – that he make himself acquainted with this little book, not curiously, but devoutly, as one would read a religious work. How far a so-called aesthetic public has found or may find enjoyment in reading, attentively or casually, the productions of an aesthetic character, which are an incognito and a deceit in the service of Christianity, is naturally a matter of indifference to me; for I am a religious writer. Supposing that such a reader understands perfectly and appraises critically the individual aesthetic productions, he will nevertheless totally misunderstand me, inasmuch as he does not understand the religious totality in my whole work as an author. Suppose, then, that another understands my works in the totality of their religious reference, but does not understand a single one of the aesthetic productions contained in them – I would say that this lack of understanding is not an essential lack.

What I write here is for orientation. It is a public attestation; not a defence or an apology. In this respect, truly, if in no other, I believe that I have something in common with Socrates. For when he was accused, and was about to be judged by 'the crowd', his daemon forbade him to *defend* himself.[4] Indeed, if he had done that, how unseemly it would have been, and how self-contradictory! Likewise there is something in me, and in the dialectical position I occupy, which makes it impossible for me, and impossible in itself, to conduct a defence for my work as an author. I have put up with a great deal, and I hope to put up with more without suffering the loss of my self – but who knows? Perhaps the future will deal more gently with me than the past. The one thing I cannot put up with – not without suffering the loss of my self and of the dialectical character of my position (which is just what I cannot put up with) – this only thing is to *defend* myself *qua* author. That would be a falsehood, which, even if it were to help me finitely to gain the whole world, would eternally be my destruction.[5] With humility before God, and also before men, I well know wherein I personally may have offended; but I know also with God that this very work of mine as an author was the prompting of an irresistible inward impulse, a melancholy man's only possibility, the honest effort on the part of a soul deeply humbled and penitent to do something by way of compensation, without shunning any sacrifice or labour in the service of truth. Therefore I know also with God, in whose eyes this undertaking found favour and still finds it, as it rejoices also in His assistance, that with regard to my authorship it is not I that need to defend myself before my contemporaries; for, if in this case I have any part, it is not as counsel for the defence but as prosecutor.

Yet I do not indict my contemporaries, seeing that I have religiously understood it as my duty thus to serve the truth in self-denial, and as my task to do everything to prevent myself becoming esteemed and idolized. Only the man who knows in his own experience what true self-denial is can solve my riddle and perceive that it is self-denial. For the man who in himself has no experience of it must rather call my behaviour self-love, pride, eccentricity, madness – for which opinion it would be unreasonable of me to indict him, since I myself in the service of the truth have contributed to form it. There is one thing unconditionally which cannot be understood either by a noisy assembly, or by a 'highly esteemed public', or in half an hour – and that one thing is the character of true Christian self-denial. To understand this requires fear and trembling, silent solitude, and a long interval of time.

That I have understood the truth which I deliver to others, of that I am eternally certain. And I am just as certain that my contemporaries, in so far as they do not understand it, will be compelled, whether by fair means or foul, to understand it some time, in eternity, when they are exempted from many distracting cares and troubles, from which I have been exempted. I have suffered under much misunderstanding; and the fact that I voluntarily exposed myself to it does not indicate that I am insensible to *real* suffering. As well deny the reality of all Christian suffering, for the mark of it is that it is voluntary. Neither does it follow as a matter of course and as a direct inference that 'the others' have no blame, seeing that it is in the service of truth I suffer this. But however much I have suffered from misunderstanding, I cannot but thank God for what is of infinite importance to me, that He has granted me understanding of the truth.

And then only one thing more. It goes without saying that I cannot explain my work as an author wholly, i.e. with the purely personal inwardness in which I possess the explanation of it. And this is in part because I cannot make public my God-relationship. It is neither more nor less than the generic human inwardness which every man may have, without regarding it as an official distinction which it would be a crime to hide and a duty to proclaim, or which I could appeal to as my legitimation. In part because I cannot wish (and no one can desire that I might) to obtrude upon others something that concerns only my private person – though naturally there is much in this which for me serves to explain my work as an author.

Part One

A: The ambiguity or duplicity in the whole authorship:* – whether the author is an aesthetic or a religious author

It remains, then, to be shown that there is such a duplicity from first to last. This is not an instance of the common case where the assumed duplicity is discovered by someone else and the person concerned is obliged to prove that it *does not exist*. Not that at all, but quite the contrary. In case the reader should not be sufficiently observant of the duplicity, it is the business of the author to make as evident as possible the fact that it is there. That is to say, the duplicity, the ambiguity, is a conscious one, something the author knows more about than anybody else; it is the essential dialectical distinction of the whole authorship, and has therefore a deeper reason.

But is this a fact, is there such a pervading duplicity? May one not explain the phenomenon in another way, by supposing that there is an author who first was an aesthetic author, and then in the course of years *changed* and became a religious author? I will not dwell upon the consideration that, if this were the case, the author would not have written such a book as the present one, and surely would hardly have undertaken to give a survey of the whole work – least of all would he have chosen the moment which coincides with the republication of his first book. Neither will I dwell upon the fact that it would be strange if such a change were to be accomplished in the course of only a few years. In other instances where an originally aesthetic author becomes a religious author, it is usual for many years to elapse, so that the hypothesis which explains the change by pointing to the fact that he has actually become considerably older does not lack plausibility. But this I will not dwell upon; for though it might seem strange and almost inexplicable, though it might prompt one to seek and find any other explana-

---

* In order that the titles of the books may be readily available they are given here. First group (aesthetic work): *Either/Or*; *Fear and Trembling*; *Repetition*; *The Concept of Dread* [*Anxiety, Angest*]; *Prefaces*; *Philosophical Fragments*; *Stages on Life's Way* – along with eighteen edifying discourses which were published successively. Second group: *Concluding Unscientific Postscript*. Third group (religious works): *Edifying Discourses in Divers Spirits*; *The Works of Love*; *Christian Discourses* – along with a little aesthetic article, *The Crisis and a Crisis in the Life of an Actress*.

tion, nevertheless it would not be absolutely impossible for such a change to occur in the space of only three years. I will show rather that it is impossible to explain the phenomenon in this way. For when one looks closer it will be seen that nothing like three years elapsed before the change occurred, but that the change is simultaneous with the beginning – that is, the duplicity dates from the very start. For the *Two Edifying Discourses* are contemporaneous with *Either/Or*. The duplicity in the deeper sense, that is, in the sense of the authorship as a whole, is not at all what was a subject of comment in its time, viz. the contrast between the two parts of *Either/Or*. No, the duplicity is discovered by comparing *Either/Or* and the *Two Edifying Discourses*.

The religious is present from the beginning. Conversely, the aesthetic is present again at the last moment. After two years, during which only religious works were published, there follows a little aesthetic article.* Hence assurance was provided both first and last against an interpretation of the phenomenon which supposes an aesthetic author who with the lapse of time has changed and become a religious author. Just as the *Two Edifying Discourses* came out between two and three months after *Either/Or*, so this little aesthetic article came out between two and three months after the purely religious writings of the two years. The *Two Edifying Discourses* and the little article correspond to one another conversely and prove conversely that the duplicity is both first and last. Although *Either/Or* attracted all the attention, and nobody noticed the *Two Edifying Discourses*, this book betokened, nevertheless, that the edifying was precisely what must come to the fore, that the author was a religious author, who for this reason has never written anything aesthetic, but has employed pseudonyms for all the aesthetic works, whereas the *Two Edifying Discourses* were by Magister Kierkegaard. Conversely, although the purely edifying works produced during the two years have possibly attracted the notice of others, no one, perhaps, in a deeper sense, has remarked upon the significance of the little article, which indicates that now the whole dialectical structure of the authorship is completed. The little article serves as a testimony in the confrontation of witnesses, in order to make it impossible at the end (as the *Two Edifying Discourses* did at the beginning) to explain the phenomenon by supposing that there was an author who first was an aesthetic author and later *changed* and became subsequently a religious author – for he was a religious author from the beginning and was aesthetically productive even at the last moment.

The first group of writings represents aesthetic productivity, the last group is exclusively religious: between them, as the turning point, lies the *Conclud-*

---

* *The Crisis and a Crisis in the Life of an Actress*, in *Fædrelandet*, July 1848. [See KW XVII, pp. 301–25.]

ing Postscript. This work concerns itself with and sets 'the Problem', which is the problem of the whole authorship: how to become a Christian. So it takes cognizance of the pseudonymous work, and of the eighteen Edifying Discourses as well, showing that all of this serves to illuminate the Problem – without, however, affirming that this was the aim of the foregoing production, which indeed could not have been affirmed by a pseudonym, a third person, incapable of knowing anything about the aim of a work which was not his own. The *Concluding Postscript* is not an aesthetic work, but neither is it in the strictest sense religious. Hence it is by a pseudonym, though I add my name as editor – a thing I did not do in the case of any purely aesthetic work.[†] This is a hint for anyone who is concerned about such things and has a flair for them. Then came the two years during which nothing but religious works came out, all bearing my name. The period of the pseudonyms was past, the religious author had developed himself out of the aesthetic disguise – and then, as a testimony and as a precaution, came the little aesthetic article by a pseudonym, *Inter et Inter.*[6] This is calculated to make one conscious all at once of the authorship as a whole. As I have remarked, it reminds one inversely of the *Two Edifying Discourses.*

B: The explanation: that the author is and was a religious author

It might seem that a mere protestation to this effect on the part of the author himself would be more than enough; for surely he knows best what is meant. For my part, however, I have little confidence in protestations with respect to literary productions and am inclined to take an objective view of my own works. If as a third person, in the role of a reader, I cannot substantiate the fact that what I affirm is so, and that it could not but be so, it would not occur to me to wish to win a cause which I regard as lost. If I were to begin *qua* author to protest, I might easily bring to confusion the whole work, which from first to last is dialectical.

So I cannot make any protestation – at least not before I have tried in another way to make the explanation so evident that a protestation of the sort here contemplated would be entirely superfluous. When that has been accomplished, a protestation might be *permissible* as a lyrical satisfaction to me, in case I were to feel an impulse to make it, and it might be *required* as a religious duty. For *qua* man I may be justified in protesting, and it may be

---

[†] The literary review *Two Ages* is no exception; partly because it is not aesthetic in the sense of poetic production, but is critical; and partly because it has a wholly religious background in the interpretation of the 'present age'.

my religious duty to make a protestation. But this must not be confounded with authorship: *qua* author it does not avail much that I protest *qua* man that I have intended this or that. But everybody will admit that when one is able to show with respect to a phenomenon that it cannot be explained in any other way, and that in this particular way it can be explained in every detail, or that the explanation fits at every point, then this explanation is substantiated as evidently as it is ever possible to establish the correctness of an explanation.

But is there not a contradiction here? It was established in the foregoing section that the ambiguity was present up to the last, and in so far as this was successfully proved, it becomes impossible to prove what the explanation is; so that a declaration, a protestation, seems in this case to be the only means of releasing the dialectical tension and untying the knot. This reasoning appears to be *acute*, but really it is *sophistical*. In case a sophistical person should find it necessary in a given contingency to resort to a mystification, it would be perfectly natural for him to do it in such a way that the comical situation results that he cannot get himself out of it. But this, too, is due to a lack of seriousness, which prompts him to fall in love with mystification for its own sake, instead of using it for a purpose. Hence when a mystification, a dialectical reduplication, is used in the service of a serious purpose, it will be so used as merely to obviate a misunderstanding, or an over-hasty understanding, whereas all the while the true explanation is at hand and ready to be found by him who honestly seeks it. To take the highest example: the whole life of Christ on earth would have been mere play if He had been incognito to such a degree that He went through life totally unnoticed – and yet in a true sense He was incognito.

So it is in the case of a dialectical reduplication; and the mark of a dialectical reduplication is that the ambiguity is maintained. As soon as the requisite seriousness grasps it, it is able also to release it, but always in such a way that seriousness itself vouches for the fact of it. For as a woman's coyness has a reference to the true lover and yields when he appears, but only then, so, too, dialectical reduplication has a reference to true seriousness. To one less serious the explanation cannot be imparted, for the elasticity of the dialectical reduplication is too great for him to grasp: it takes the explanation away from him again and makes it doubtful to him whether it really is the explanation.

Let the attempt be made. Let us try to explain the whole of this literary production on the assumption that it is written by an aesthetic author. It is easy to perceive that from the beginning it is incongruous with this explanation, which breaks down when it encounters the *Two Edifying Discourses*. If, on the contrary, one will experiment with the assumption that it is a religious author, one will perceive that, step by step, the assumption corresponds at every point. The only thing that remains inexplicable is how it could occur to a religious author to employ aesthetics in such a way. That is to say, we are confronted again by the ambiguity or the dialectical reduplication. Only the difference now is that the assumption of his being a religious author will have taken firm hold, and it remains only to explain the ambiguity. How far it may be possible for a third person to do this I do not venture to determine; but the explanation is that contained in the Second Part of this little book.

Here only one thing more – a thing which, as I have said, may be a lyrical satisfaction to me *qua* man, and *qua* man is my religious duty; namely, a direct protestation that the author is and was a religious author. When I began *Either/Or* (of which, be it said parenthetically, there existed beforehand literally only about a page, viz. a few Diapsalmata, whereas the whole book was written in the space of eleven months, and the Second Part first) I was potentially as deeply under the influence of religion as ever I have been. I was so deeply shaken that I understood perfectly well that I could not possibly succeed in striking the comforting and secure *via media* [middle way] in which most people pass their lives: I had either to cast myself into perdition and sensuality, or to choose the religious absolutely as the only thing – either the world in a measure that would be dreadful, or the cloister. That it was the second I would and must choose was at bottom already determined: the eccentricity of the first movement was merely the expression for the intensity of the second; it expressed the fact that I had become thoroughly aware how impossible it would be for me to be religious only up to a certain point. Here is the place of *Either/Or*. It was a poetical catharsis, which does not, however, go farther than the ethical. Personally, I was very far from wishing to summon the course of existence to return comfortingly to the situation of marriage for my sake, who religiously was already in the cloister – a thought which lies concealed in the pseudonym *Victor – Eremita* [the hermit].

Such is the situation; strictly speaking, *Either/Or* was written in a monastery, and I can assure the reader (the assurance being especially addressed, if it should chance to fall under his eyes, to him who has no capacity or leisure to survey such a productivity as mine, yet has possibly been disturbed by the strange amalgamation of the religious and the aesthetic in my writings) – I can assure the reader that the author of *Either/Or* devoted a definite time each day, regularly and with monastic precision, to reading for his own sake edifying books, and that in fear and in much trembling he reflected upon his responsibility. Among other things, he reflected especially (how wonderful!) upon 'The Diary of a Seducer'.[7] And then what occurred?

The book had an immense success – especially (how wonderful!) 'The Diary of a Seducer'. The world opened its arms in an extraordinary way to the admired author, whom all this, however, did not 'seduce' – for he was an eternity too old for that.

Then followed *Two Edifying Discourses* – things of the most vital importance often seem insignificant. The big work, *Either/Or*, which was 'much read and more discussed' – and then the *Two Edifying Discourses*, dedicated to my deceased father, published on my birthday (May 5th), 'a little flower hidden in the great forest, not sought out either for its beauty, or for its scent, or because it was nourishing'.* No one took serious notice of the two discourses or concerned himself about them. Indeed I remember that one of my acquaintances came to me with the complaint that in good faith he had gone and bought the book with the notion that, since it was by me, it must be something witty and clever. I remember, too, that I promised him that if he wished, he should get his money back. I held out *Either/Or* to the world in my left hand, and in my right the *Two Edifying Discourses*; but all, or as good as all, grasped with their right what I held in my left.†

I had made up my mind before God what I should do: I staked my case on the *Two Edifying Discourses*; but I understood perfectly that only very few understood them.‡ And here for the first time comes in the category 'that *individual* whom with joy and gratitude I call *my* reader', a stereotyped formula which was repeated in the Preface to every collection of Edifying Discourses. No one can justly lay it to my charge that I have changed, that perhaps at a later moment, perhaps for the reason that I was not in the good graces of the public, I judged differently about this matter than I had before. No. If ever I stood in the good graces of the public, it was two or three months after the publication of *Either/Or*. And this very situation, which to many perhaps would be a temptation, I regarded as the one favourable moment for doing what I had to do to assert my position, and I employed

---

* Cf. Preface to the *Two Edifying Discourses* of 1843. [See KW V, p. 5.]

† Cf. Preface to the *Two Edifying Discourses* of 1844: 'It seeks *my* reader, who receives in his right hand what is offered with the left.' [See KW V, p. 179. This phrase also alludes to Lessing's *Eine Duplik*, as discussed in *Concluding Unscientific Postscript*; see above, p. 248.]

‡ Hence the tone of sadness in the Preface where it is said of the little book: 'Inasmuch as it may be said in a figurative sense that on its publication it starts out as it were upon a journey, I let my eye follow it a little while. I saw then how it went its way along lonely paths, or alone on the highways. After one or other little misunderstanding, due to the fact that it was deceived by a casual likeness, it finally encountered that individual whom with joy and gratitude I call *my* reader, whom it seeks, to whom as it were it stretches out its arms', etc. Cf. Preface to the *Two Edifying Discourses* of 1843 [KW V, p. 5.]. This first Preface had and still has for me a very intimate and personal significance, such as it would hardly be possible for me to communicate.

it in the service of the truth to introduce my category 'the individual' – it was then that I broke with the public, not out of pride and arrogance, etc. (and certainly not because at that moment the public was unfavourable to me, since on the contrary it was entirely favourable), but because I was conscious of being a religious author and as such was concerned with 'the individual' ('the individual' – in contrast to 'the public'), a thought in which is contained an entire life-view and world-view.

From now on, that is, as early as the publication of *Fear and Trembling*, the serious observer who himself disposes of religious presuppositions, the serious observer to whom it is possible to make oneself intelligible at a distance, and to whom one can talk in silence (cf. the pseudonym Johannes – *de silentio*), [8] was in a position to discern that this, after all, was a very singular sort of aesthetic production. And this was justly emphasized by the most reverend signature Kts., which delighted me greatly.[9]

Part Two, in which the Whole Work of Authorship is Construed from the Point of View that the Author is a Religious Author

Chapter One

A: The aesthetic works: why the beginning of the work was aesthetic, or what this signifies, understood in relation to the whole. ★ *[. . .]*[10]

That the whole of the aesthetic work, viewed in relation to the work as a whole, is a deception – understanding this word, however, in a special sense.
Anyone who considers the aesthetic work as the whole and then considers the religious part from this point of view, could only consider it as a falling away, a falling off. I have shown in the foregoing that the assumption upon which this point of view is based is not tenable. There it was established that from the very beginning, and simultaneously with the pseudonymous work, certain signals, displaying my name, gave telegraphic notice of the religious.

But from the point of view of my whole activity as an author, integrally conceived, the aesthetic work is a deception, and herein is to be found the deeper significance of the use of pseudonyms. A deception, however, is a rather ugly thing. To this I would make answer: One must not let oneself be

---

★   Once and for all I must earnestly beg the kind reader always to bear *in mente* [in mind] that the thought behind the whole work is: what it means to become a Christian.

deceived by the word 'deception'. One can deceive a person for the truth's sake, and (to recall old Socrates) one can deceive a person into the truth. Indeed, it is only by this means, i.e. by deceiving him, that it is possible to bring into the truth one who is in an illusion. Whoever rejects this opinion betrays the fact that he is not well-versed in dialectics, and that is precisely what is especially needed when operating in this field. For there is an immense difference, a dialectical difference, between these two cases: the case of a man who is ignorant and is to have a piece of knowledge imparted to him, so that he is like an empty vessel which is to be filled or a blank sheet of paper upon which something is to be written; and the case of a man who is under an illusion and must first be delivered from that. Likewise there is a difference between writing on a blank sheet of paper and bringing to light, by the application of caustic fluid, a text which is hidden under another text. Assuming then that a person is the victim of an illusion, and that in order to communicate the truth to him the first task, rightly understood, is to remove the illusion – if I do not begin by deceiving him, I must begin with direct communication. But direct communication presupposes that the receiver's ability to receive is undisturbed. But here such is not the case; an illusion stands in the way. That is to say, one must first of all use the caustic fluid. But this caustic method is negativity, and negativity understood in relation to communication is precisely the same as deception.

What then does it mean, 'to deceive'? It means that one does not begin *directly* with the matter one wants to communicate, but begins by accepting the other man's illusion as good money. So (to stick to the theme with which this work especially deals) one does not begin thus: I am a Christian; you are not a Christian. Nor does one begin thus: It is Christianity I am proclaiming; and you are living in purely aesthetic categories. No, one begins thus: Let us talk about aesthetics. The deception consists in the fact that one talks thus merely to get to the religious theme. But, on our assumption, the other man is under the illusion that the aesthetic is Christianity; for, he thinks, I am a Christian, and yet he lives in aesthetic categories.

Even if ever so many parsons were to consider this method unjustifiable, and just as many were unable to get it into their heads (in spite of the fact that they all of them, according to their own assertion, are accustomed to using the Socratic method), I for my part tranquilly adhere to Socrates. It is true, he was not a Christian; that I know, and yet I am thoroughly convinced that he has become one. But he was a dialectician, he conceived everything in terms of reflection. And the question which concerns us here is a purely dialectical one, it is the question of the use of reflection in Christendom. We are reckoning here with two qualitatively different magnitudes, but in a formal sense I can very well call Socrates my teacher – whereas I have only believed, and only believe, in One, the Lord Jesus Christ.

B: Concluding Unscientific Postscript

The *Concluding Postscript* constitutes, as I have already said, the turning-point in my whole work as an author. It presents the 'Problem', that of becoming a Christian. Having taken the whole pseudonymous, aesthetic work as the description of *one* path by which a person may become a Christian (viz. *away* from the aesthetic in order to become a Christian), it undertakes to describe the other path (viz. *away* from the System, from speculation, etc., in order to become a Christian).

C: The religious works

I could express myself very briefly even with regard to the *Concluding Postscript*, since that book does not present any difficulties when the point of view for the literary work as a whole is that the author is a religious author. The only thing that required explanation was the question how, on this assumption, the aesthetic work was to be conceived. And what, on this assumption, requires no explanation at all is the last section, the purely religious work, which of course establishes the point of view.

Conclusion. What does all this come to, when the reader puts together the points dwelt upon in the foregoing paragraphs? It means that this is a literary work in which the whole thought is the task of becoming a Christian. But it is a literary work which understood from the very first and consistently followed out the dialectical implication of the fact that the situation is Christendom – a reflective modification – and hence transformed into reflection all the relationships of Christianity. To become a Christian in Christendom means either to become what one is (the inwardness of reflection or becoming inward through reflection), or it means that the first thing is to be disengaged from the toils of one's illusion, which again is a reflective modification. Here there is no room for vacillation or ambiguity of the sort one commonly experiences elsewhere when one does not know and cannot make out whether one is situated in paganism, whether the parson is a missionary in that sense, or whereabouts one is. Here one does not miss what is generally lacking, viz. a decisive categorical definition and a decisive expression for the situation: to preach Christianity . . . in Christendom. Everything is put in terms of reflection. The communication is qualified by reflection, hence it is indirect communication. The communicator is characterized by reflection, therefore he is negative – not one who says that he himself is a Christian in an extraordinary degree, or even lays claim to revelations (all of which answers to immediacy and direct communication); but, on the contrary, one who even affirms that he is not a Christian. That is to say, the communicator stands behind the other man, helping him negatively – for whether he actually succeeds in helping someone is another question. The problem itself is a problem of reflection: to become a Christian . . . when one is a Christian of a sort.

Chapter Two: The difference in my personal mode of existence corresponding to the essential difference in the works

In this age, and indeed for many ages past, people have quite lost sight of the fact that authorship is and ought to be a serious calling implying an appropriate mode of personal existence. They do not realize that the printed word in general, as an expression of the abstract and impersonal communication of ideas, and the daily press in particular, because of its formal indifference to the question whether what it reports is true or false, contributes enormously to the general demoralization, for the reason that the impersonal, which for the most part is irresponsible and incapable of repentance, is essentially demoralizing. They do not realize that anonymity, as the highest expression for the abstract, the impersonal, the irresponsible, the unrepentant, is a fundamental source of the modern demoralization. On the other hand, they do not reflect that anonymity would be counteracted in the simplest possible way, and that a wholesome corrective would be furnished for the abstractness of printed communication, if people would but turn back again to antiquity and learn what it means to be a single individual, neither more nor less – which surely even an author is too, neither more nor less. This is perfectly obvious. But in our age, which reckons as wisdom that which is truly the mystery of unrighteousness [onde], viz. that one need not inquire about the communicator, but only about the communication, the objective only – in our age what is an author? An author is often merely an x, even when his name is signed, something quite impersonal, which addresses itself abstractly, by the aid of printing, to thousands and thousands, while remaining itself unseen and unknown, living a life as hidden, as anonymous, as it is possible for a life to be, in order, presumably, not to reveal the too obvious and striking contradiction between the prodigious means of communication employed and the fact that the author is only a single individual – perhaps also for fear of the control which in practical life must always be exercised over anyone who wishes to teach others, to see whether his personal existence comports with his communication. But all this, which deserves the most serious attention on the part of one who would study the demoralization of the modern state – all this I cannot enter into more particularly here.

A: The personal mode of existence in relation to the aesthetic works
I come now to the first period of my authorship and my mode of existence. Here was a religious author, but one who began as an aesthetic author; and this first stage was one of incognito and deceit. Initiated as I was very early and very thoroughly into the secret that *mundus vult decipi* [the world wants to be deceived], I was not in the position of being able to wish to follow such tactics. Quite the contrary. With me it was a question of deceiving inversely on the greatest possible scale, employing every bit of knowledge I had about men and their weaknesses and their stupidities, not to profit thereby, but to annihilate myself and weaken the impression I made. The secret of the deceit which suits the world which wants to be deceived consists partly in forming a coterie and all that goes with that, in joining one or another of those societies for mutual admiration, whose members support one another with tongue and pen in the pursuit of worldly advantage; and it consists partly in hiding oneself from the human crowd, never being seen, so as to produce a fantastic effect. So I had to do exactly the opposite. I had to exist in absolute isolation and guard my solitude, but at the same time take pains to be seen every hour of the day, living as it were upon the street, in company with Tom, Dick, and Harry, and in the most fortuitous situations. This is truth's way of deceiving, the everlastingly sure way of weakening, in a worldly sense, the impression one makes. It was, moreover, the way followed by men of a very different calibre from mine to make people take notice. Those reputable persons, the deceivers who want the communication to serve them instead of serving the communication, are on the look-out only to win repute for themselves. Those despised persons, the 'witnesses for the truth', who deceive inversely, have ever been wont to suffer themselves to be set at naught in a worldly sense and be counted as nothing – in spite of the fact that they labour day and night, and suffer besides from having no support whatever in the illusion that the work they perform is their career and their 'living'.

So this had to be done, and it was done, not now and then, but every day. I am convinced that one-sixth of *Either/Or*, together with a bit of coterie, and then an author who was never to be seen – especially if this was carried on for a considerable time – must make a much more extraordinary effect. I, however, had made myself sure of being able to work as laboriously as I pleased and as the spirit prompted me, without having to fear that I might get too much renown. For in a certain sense I was working as laboriously in another direction – against myself. Only an author will be able to understand what a task it is to work *qua* author, i.e. with spirit and pen, and yet be at the beck and call of everybody. Although this mode of existence enriched me immensely with observations of human life, it is a standard of conduct which would bring most men to despair. For it means the effort to dispel every illusion and to present the idea-relation in all its purity – and verily, it is not truth that rules the world but illusions. Even if a literary achievement were more illustrious than any that has yet been seen – if only the author were to live as is here suggested, he would in a brief time have insured himself against worldly renown and the crowd's brutish adulation. For the crowd possesses no ideality, and hence no power of retaining impressions in spite of contrary appearances. It is always the victim of appearances. To be seen again and again, and to be seen in the most fortuitous situations, is enough to make the crowd forget its first impression of the man and become sick and tired of him. And, after all, to keep oneself perpetually in view does not consume a great deal of time, if one employs one's time shrewdly (i.e. in a worldly sense insanely) and to the best effect, by going back and forth past the same spot – the most frequented spot in the city. Every one who husbands his reputation, in a worldly sense, will not return by the same way he went, even if it is the most convenient way. He will avoid being seen twice in so short a time, for fear people might suppose he had nothing to do, whereas if he sat in his room at home three-quarters of the day and was idle, such a thought would never occur to anybody. On the other hand, an hour well spent, in a godly sense, an hour lived for eternity and spent by going back and forth among the common people . . . is not such a small thing after all. And verily it is well pleasing to God that the truth should be served in this way. His spirit witnesseth mightily with my spirit that it has the full consent of His Divine Majesty.[11] All the witnesses of the truth indicate their approval, recognizing that one is disposed to serve the truth, the idea, and not to betray the truth and profit by the illusion. I experienced a real Christian satisfaction in venturing to perform on Monday a little bit of that which one weeps about on Sunday (when the parson prates about it and weeps too) . . . and on Monday one is ready to laugh about. I had real Christian satisfaction in the thought that, if there were no other, there was definitely one man in Copenhagen whom every poor man could freely accost and converse with on the street; that, if there were no other, there was one man who, whatever the society he more commonly frequented, did not shun contact with the poor, but greeted every maidservant he was acquainted with, every manservant, every common labourer. I felt a real Christian satisfaction in the fact that, if there were no other, there was one man who (several years before existence set the human race another lesson to learn) made a practical effort on a small scale to learn the lesson of loving one's neighbour and alas! got at the same time a frightful insight into what an illusion Christendom is, and (a little later, to be sure) an insight also into how the simpler classes suffered themselves to be seduced by paltry newspaper-writers, whose struggle or fight for equality (since it is in the service of a lie) cannot lead to any other result but to prompt the privileged classes in self-defence to stand proudly aloof from the common man, and to make the common man insolent in his forwardness.

The description of my personal existence cannot be carried out here in any greater detail; but I am convinced that seldom has any author employed so much cunning, intrigue, and shrewdness to win honour and reputation in the world with a view to deceiving it, as I displayed in order to deceive it inversely in the interest of truth. On how great a scale this was carried out I shall attempt to show by one single instance, known to my friend Giødwad, the proof-reader of *Either/Or*.[12] I was so busy when I was reading the proofs of *Either/Or* that it was impossible to spend the usual time sauntering back and forth on the street. I did not get through the work till late in the evening, and then I hastened to the theatre, where I remained literally only for five to ten minutes. And why did I do this? Because I feared the big book would create for me too great a reputation.* And why did I do this? Because I knew human nature, especially in Copenhagen. To be seen every night for five minutes by several hundred people sufficed to substantiate the opinion: He hasn't the least thing in the world to do; he is a mere idler.

Such was the existence I led by way of seconding my aesthetic work. Incidentally it involved a breach with all coteries. And I formed the polemical resolution to regard every eulogy as an attack, and every attack as a thing unworthy of notice. Such was my public mode of existence. I rarely visited anyone, and at home the rule was strictly observed to receive no one except the poor who came to seek help. For I had no time to receive visitors at home, and any one who entered my home as a visitor might easily get a presentiment of a situation about which he should have no presentiment. Thus I existed. If Copenhagen ever has been of one opinion about anybody, I venture to say that it was of one opinion about me, that I was an idler, a

---

* It was for the same reason that at the moment when the whole of *Either/Or* was ready to be transcribed into a fair copy, I printed a little article in *Fædrelandet*, 'Open Confession' [1842], over my own signature, in which I gratuitously disclaimed that I was the author of a good many interesting articles which had appeared anonymously in various newspapers, acknowledging and admitting my idleness, and making one petition, that henceforth no one would ever regard me as the author of anything beneath which my name was not signed.

dawdler, a *flâneur*, a frivolous bird, intelligent, perhaps brilliant, witty, etc. – but as for 'seriousness', I lacked it utterly. I represented a worldly irony, *joie de vivre*, the subtlest form of pleasure-seeking – without a trace of 'seriousness and positivity'; on the other hand, I was prodigiously witty and interesting.

When I look back upon that time, I am almost tempted to make some sort of apology to the people of importance and repute in the community. For true enough, I knew perfectly well what I was doing, yet from their standpoint they were right in finding fault with me, because by thus impairing my own prestige I contributed to the movement which was impairing power and renown in general – notwithstanding that I have always been conservative in this respect, and have found joy in paying to the eminent and distinguished the deference, awe, and admiration which are due to them. Yet my conservative disposition did not involve a desire to have this sort of distinction for myself. And just because the eminent and distinguished members of the community have shown me in so many ways not only sympathy but partiality, have sought in so many ways to draw me to their side (which certainly was honest and well-meant on their part) – just for this reason I feel impelled to make them an apology, though naturally I cannot regret what I have done, since I served my idea. People of distinction have always proved more consistent in their treatment of me than the simpler classes, who even from their own standpoint did not behave rightly, since they too (according to the foregoing account) attacked me . . . because I was not superior enough to hold myself aloof – which is very queer and ridiculous of the simpler classes.

This is the first period: by my personal mode of existence I endeavoured to support the pseudonyms, the aesthetic work as a whole. Melancholy, incurably melancholy as I was, suffering prodigious griefs in my inmost soul, having broken in desperation from the world and all that is of the world, strictly brought up from my very childhood in the apprehension that the truth must suffer and be mocked and derided, spending a definite time every day in prayer and devout meditation, and being myself personally a penitent – in short, being what I was, I found (I do not deny it) a certain satisfaction in this life, in this inverse deception, a satisfaction in observing that the deception succeeded so extraordinarily, that the public and I were on the most confidential terms, that I was quite in fashion as a preacher of a gospel of worldliness, that though I was not in possession of the sort of distinction which can only be earned by an entirely different mode of life, yet in secret (and hence the more heartily loved) I was the darling of the public, regarded by every one as prodigiously interesting and witty, though no doubt everyone thought himself better, more serious, more honourable and more positive than me. This satisfaction, which was my secret and which sometimes put me into an ecstasy, might have been a dangerous temptation. Not that the world and such things could tempt me with their flattery and adulation. No, on that side I was safe. If I was to have been capsized, it would have to have been by this thought raised to a higher power, an obsession almost of ecstasy at the thought of how the deception was succeeding. This was an indescribable alleviation to a sense of resentment which smouldered in me from my childhood; because, long before I had seen it with my own eyes, I had been taught that falsehood, pettiness, and injustice ruled the world. – I often had to think of these words in *Either/Or*. 'If ye but knew what it is ye laugh at'[13] – if ye but knew with whom ye have to do, who this *flâneur* is!

B: *The personal mode of existence in relation to the religious works*

In the month of December 1845 the manuscript of the *Concluding Postscript* was completely finished, and, as was my custom, I had delivered the whole of it at once to Luno [the printer][14] – which the suspicious do not have to believe on my word, since Luno's account-book is there to prove it. This work constituted the turning-point in my whole activity as an author, inasmuch as it presents the 'Problem' – how to become a Christian. With this began the transition to the final stage, the series of purely religious writings.

I perceived at once that my personal mode of existence must be remodelled to correspond with this change, or that I must try to give my contemporaries a different impression of my personal mode of existence. So I myself had already become aware of what must be done, when there occurred in the most opportune way a little incident in which I perceived a hint from Providence to help me to act decisively in that direction.

However, I cannot proceed further with this subject until I have recalled to the reader's memory the situation in Copenhagen at that juncture – by a description which perhaps now will stand out in sharper relief by contrast with the present warlike situation.[15] At that time there developed little by little the rather remarkable phenomenon that the entire population of Copenhagen became ironical and witty – and just so much the more ironical in proportion as the people were more ignorant and uneducated. It was irony here and irony there, from one end to the other. If the case were not so serious, and if I could venture to contemplate it in a purely aesthetic manner, I do not deny that it is the most ludicrous thing I have ever beheld, and I really believe that one might travel far and still be lucky to encounter anything so fundamentally comical. The entire population of a city, with all the unemployed on the streets and alleys well in the lead, down to school-urchins and apprentices; all the legions of those classes which in our day are the only really privileged classes, those, namely, who amount to nothing, they become what they become . . . *en masse*; the entire population of a city, guilds, corporations, business men, persons of rank, they become (very much like a bourgeois sauntering out to the Deer Park), they become . . . *en famille*; these thousands and thousands become . . . just about the one thing I would venture to assert it is impossible for them to become (especially *en masse* and *en famille*) – they become *ironical*, with the help of a news-sheet, which in turn (ironically enough) leads the fashion with the help of editorial black-guards, and the fashion it sets is . . . irony.[16] It is impossible, I believe, to think of anything more ludicrous. For irony presupposes a specific intellectual culture, such as is very rare in any generation – and this *cohue* and rabble were adepts in irony. Irony is absolutely unsocial; an irony which is in the majority is *eo ipso* not irony. Nothing is more certain than this, for it is implied in the very concept. Irony tends essentially towards one person as its limit, as is so justly stated in the Aristotelian saying that the ironical man does all 'for his own sake' (*heauton heneka*)[17] – and here was an immense public, arm in arm, *in bona caritate* [in friendship], become as ironical as the devil.

But the case was too serious. The irony was of course sheer vulgarity. For even if the real instigator[18] possessed a talent by no means insignificant, it could not but become vulgarity in passing over to these thousands and thousands; and unfortunately vulgarity is always popular. So there was a demor-alization which only too dreadfully recalls the punishment with which the Prophet of old in the name of the Lord threatened the Jews as the worst of all punishments: 'Children shall rule over you.'[19] It was a demoralization which, considering the proportions of the little land, actually threatened it with complete moral disintegration. To form a conception of the danger one must see at close range how even good-natured and worthy people, as soon as they become a 'crowd', turn into quite different beings. One must see at close range the want of character exhibited by otherwise upright people, who say: It is a shame, it is shocking for any one to do or to utter anything of the sort – and then they themselves contribute their share to envelop the city in a snow-flurry of chatter and town-gossip. One must witness the hard-ness of heart which otherwise kindly people display in their capacity as 'the public', thinking that their intervention or non-intervention is a trifling thing – a trifling thing indeed which by the contributions of the many becomes a monster. One must see how laughter is feared above all other forms of attack, how even a man who had boldly encountered moral peril for a cause that did not concern him, would hardly hesitate to betray father and mother if the danger were laughter. For an attack of this sort isolates a man as no other does, and at no point does it offer him the support of pathos, while frivolity and curiosity and sensuality grin, and the nervous cowardice which itself shuns such an attack incessantly cries, 'It is nothing', and the contemptible cowardice which buys itself off from attack by bribery or by currying favour with the person concerned, it too says 'It is nothing', and even sympathy says 'It is nothing.' It is terrible when in a little land chattering and grinning become a menace on becoming 'public opinion'. Denmark was on the point of being absorbed in Copenhagen, and Copenhagen was just in the act of becoming a mere market town. It is only too easy to bring this about, especially with the help of the press; and when this is accomplished it will require perhaps a generation to live it down.

But enough of this. It was important for me to alter my personal mode of existence to correspond with the fact that I was making the transition to the statement of religious problems. I must have an existence-form corresponding with this sort of authorship. It was, as I have said, the month of December [1845], and it was desirable that everything should be in readiness by the time the *Concluding Postscript* came out. So the step was taken within this month of December. With the knowledge I possessed of the situation I readily perceived that it was enough to address two words to that organ of irony [the *Corsair*], which in a sense (i.e. if I had not been the man I am) had rather adroitly venerated and immortalized me – that two words would be enough to reverse dialectically my whole existence-relationship, by getting the entire interminable public of ironical adepts to take aim at me, so that I should become the target of the irony of all men. Alas for me, the Magister of Irony!

The command was issued, and in order that it might not be exploited as a newly invented and highly piquant form of irony, a pretty strong dose of the ethical was added by my requisition that I be made an object of the gross abuse of the loathsome organ of loathsome irony. That hydra of innumerable ironical heads naturally thought that I was crazy. The individuals who saw deeper into the affair beheld, not without a shudder, the leap which I made, or (because they thought only of what in a worldly sense is understood by worthiness and did not bethink them of what in a godly sense is understood by it) they found it beneath my dignity to take notice of such a thing, whereas I should have counted it beneath my dignity to have lived as a contemporary of such a demoralization without having acted decisively, content with the cheap virtue of behaving like 'the others', that is to say, shirking as far as possible all action, while journalistic vileness on a scale so disproportionately great was doubtless bringing people to their graves, mortifying and embittering, perhaps not always the direct objects of the attack, yet at all events their wives and children, their relatives and closest friends, penetrating defil-

ingly into every place, even into the privacy of school-life, even into the
sanctuary of the Church, spitting out lies, gossip, insolence, and urchin-pranks
– all in the service of pernicious passion and paltry greed for money . . . and
for all this a blackguard was 'responsible'! That in the service of my idea the
course I took was the right one I understood perfectly, and I did not vacil-
late. The consequences thereof, of which certainly no one at the time was
envious, I now lay historic claim to as my lawful property, the value of which
in perspective my eye easily discerns.

I had now reckoned out that dialectically the situation would be appropriate for recovering the use of indirect communication. While I was occupied solely with religious productions I could count upon the negative
support of these daily douches of vulgarity, which would be cooling enough
in its effect to ensure that the religious communication would not be too
direct, or too directly create for me adherents. The reader could not relate
himself directly to me; for now, instead of the incognito of the aesthetic,
I had erected the danger of laughter and grins, by which most people are
scared away. Even he who was not scared by this would be upset by the
next obstacle, by the thought that I had voluntarily exposed myself to all
this, giving proof of some sort of lunacy. Ah, yes! so did the contemporaries
doubtless judge of the Roman knight who made the immortal leap to save
his country![20] Ah, yes! and again, ah, yes! for it was dialectically the precise
expression for Christian self-denial – and I, poor wretch, the Magister
of Irony, became the pitiable target for the laughter of a 'highly esteemed
public'.

The costume was correct. Every religious author is *eo ipso* polemical; for
the world is not so good that the religious man can assume that he has triumphed or is in the party of the majority. A victorious religious author who
is *in the world* is *eo ipso* not a religious author. The essentially religious author
is always polemical, and hence he suffers under or suffers from the opposition which corresponds to whatever in his age must be regarded as the specific evil. If it be kings and emperors, popes and bishops . . . and powers that
constitute the evil, the religious author must be recognizable by the fact that
he is the object of their attack. If it is the crowd – and prating and the public
– and the beastly grin which is the evil, he must be recognizable by the fact
that he is the object of that sort of attack and persecution. And the essentially religious author has but one fulcrum for his lever, namely, a miraculous
syllogism. When anyone asks him on what he bases the claim that he is
right and that it is the truth he utters, his answer is: I prove it by the fact
that I am persecuted; this is the truth, and I can prove it by the fact that I
am derided. That is, he does not substantiate the truth or the righteousness

of his cause by appealing to the honour, reputation, etc., which he enjoys, but he does quite the contrary; for the essentially religious man is always polemical. Every religious writer, or speaker, or teacher, who absents himself from danger and is not present where it is, and where the evil has its stronghold, is a deceiver, and that will eventually become apparent. For every one who comes to the gates of death and its doors open for him has to lay aside from him all the pomp and grandeur and wealth and worldly reputation, and stars of knightly orders and other tokens of honour – whether they were distributed by kings and emperors or by the crowd and the public – has to lay them all aside as things which are entirely inappropriate and superfluous. Only one exception is made, and that is with reference to the man who in his lifetime has been a religious writer or teacher or speaker on his own responsibility and at his own risk. If he is found in possession of any such things, he is not allowed to lay them aside. No, they are packed up in a bundle and returned to him, and he is compelled to keep them and carry them, as a thief may be compelled to carry his stolen goods. And with that bundle he must enter the place where he is to be judged. Having been a religious teacher, he will be judged by the true religious teachers, who all of them so long as they lived were mocked, persecuted, derided, scorned, and spat upon. Ah! how frightful it is for the natural, sensual man to stand here on earth and be derided, mocked, and spat upon! More frightful still to stand in eternity with this bundle under his arm, or attired in . . . his finery!

The costume was correct. In a grinning age, such as that was of which I speak (and, in my opinion at least, the 'war' has in this respect been a fortunate thing for Denmark),[21] the religious author must, for God's sake, see well to it that he be derided above all others. If it is from the crowd that the evil proceeds, the contemporary religious author must, for God's sake, see well to it that he become the object of its persecution, and that in this respect he be found in the front line. And the estimate I formed of the crowd, which at one time even the more perspicacious may perhaps have considered a little exaggerated, now, in 1848, now, by the help of the gesticulations of existence (which are more effective than the weak voice of an individual and are like the raging of the elements), *now* the objection might rather be that I did not put it strongly enough. And that category, 'the individual', which was regarded as an oddity, the invention of an odd person – which in fact it is, for was not he who in a sense was the inventor of it, namely, Socrates, called in his day 'the oddest' (*atopotatos*)?[22] – the credit for having decisively brought that category to notice in its time I would not exchange for a kingdom. If the crowd is the evil, if chaos is what threatens us, there is salvation only in one thing, in becoming a single individual, in the redeeming thought of 'that individual'.

One triumph I have experienced, and one only, but that satisfies me absolutely, so that as a thinker I demand nothing more in this world. The revolutionary world-historical events of the past few months brought forward unripe visionaries as bewildered spokesmen of bewildering thoughts, and on the other hand reduced to silence all who had hitherto in divers ways presumed to guide opinion – had brought it either to silence or to the embarrassment of having to manufacture for itself in the greatest haste an entirely new dress. Every system was shattered – shattered as completely in the course of a few months as if between the present and the immediate past a whole generation had intervened. During this catastrophe I sat and read the proofs of a book (*Christian Discourses*) which, consequently, was written before it. Not one single word was added or subtracted; it expressed the view which I, 'the odd thinker', had already for several years been propounding. Anyone who reads it will get the impression that the book was written after the catastrophe. Such a world-historical catastrophe, which ranks so high that not even the dissolution of the ancient world was so imposing, constitutes for every one who *then* was an author the absolute *testamen rigorosum* [rigorous examination]. I experienced the triumph of not needing to modify or alter one tittle of what I had written, the triumph, indeed, of seeing that what I had written before the event will be, if any one now reads it, far, far more intelligible than when it was written.

And now only one thing more. When some day my lover comes, he will easily perceive that at the time when I was regarded as ironical the irony was by no means to be found where 'the highly cultivated public' thought. It was to be found – and this goes without saying, for my lover cannot possibly be so foolish as to assume that a public can understand itself ironically, which is just as impossible as to be an individual *en masse* – he will perceive that the irony lay precisely in the fact that within this aesthetic author, under this worldly appearance, was concealed the religious author, who just at that time was perhaps consuming quite as much religiousness for his own edification as commonly suffices for the provision of an entire household. Moreover, my lover will perceive that irony appeared again in relation to the next period, and is to be discovered precisely in the fact which 'the highly cultivated public' regarded as lunacy. In an ironical generation (that great aggregation of fools) there remains nothing else for the essentially ironical man to do but to invert the relationship and himself become the target for the irony of all men. My lover will perceive how it all fitted to a nicety, how my existence-relationship was transformed in precise correspondence with the requirement of my productivity. If I had not had an eye for this or courage enough for it, if I had altered the productivity but not the existence-relationship, the situation would have been undialectical and confused.

Chapter Three: The share divine Governance had
in my authorship

What I have written up to this point has in a sense been neither agreeable nor pleasant to write. There is something painful in being obliged to talk so much about oneself. Would to God I might have ventured to hold my peace even longer than I have, yea, even to die in silence about a subject which, like my labour and my literary work, has silently occupied me day and night. But now, thank God, now I breathe freely, now I truly feel an urge to speak, now I have come to the theme which I find inconceivably pleasant to think about and talk about. This God-relationship of mine is the 'happy love' in a life which has been in many ways troubled and unhappy. And although the story of this love affair (if I dare to call it such) has the essential marks of a true love story, in the fact that only one can completely understand it, and there is no absolute joy except in relating it to one only, namely, the beloved, who in this instance is the person by whom one is loved,★ yet there is a joy also in talking about it to others.

★ Perhaps now the reader may be ready to recognize how it is that what thus has been the misfortune, humanly speaking, of the whole productivity, what has more and more caused it to stand apart as a superfluity, instead of actually coming to grips with the situation, is the fact that it is too religious, or that the author's existence is too religious, that the author *qua* author has been absolutely weak, and therefore has been absolutely in need of God. If the author had been less weak, that is to say, in a human sense stronger (that is, less religious), he would as a matter of course have laid claim to the authorship as his own, he would presumably have acquired a number of confidants and friends, he would have made known to others beforehand what he proposed, would have taken counsel with them and asked their assistance; and they in turn, acting as godfathers, would have enlisted others, so that the authorship would have been active and effective in the instant – instead of being a superfluity . . . such as God himself is in sooth, more than everything else and everybody else. – Perhaps now the reader may be ready to recognize why I have laboured with so much effort and sacrifice, day in and day out, to prevent falsehood from emerging, a falsehood, it is true, which (as it always does) would have brought me money, honour, reputation, applause, etc., the falsehood that what I had to deliver was 'what the age demands', that it is presented to the indulgent judgement of 'a highly respected public', and furthermore that it owes its success to the support and acclamation of this same highly respected public. In exact opposition to this, in the fear and love of God, I had to watch sleeplessly to ensure that the truth be expressed: that it was God's aid alone I relied on, that I owed nothing either to the public or to the age (except the wrong it has done to me, to truth, and to the rousing epigram at a time when everything was general assemblies and societies and committees, their appointment, continuation, and dissolution, whereas all the while nothing was done), that at this time there was bestowed upon a weakly and solitary man the talent to work on a scale so great that anyone might suppose it was more than the labour of a committee. In short, it was my religious duty to give expression, both in my personal existence and in my author-existence, to the fact – which I every day ascertained and convinced myself of anew – that a God exists. – Perhaps now the reader may

As for the fact that I have needed God's aid, and how constantly I have needed it, day after day, year after year – to recall this to my mind and to report it exactly, I do not need the aid of memory or recollection, or of journals or diaries, nor do I need to check the one by the other, so vividly, so feelingly do I live it over again in this very instant. What could not this pen produce if it were not a question of hardihood, of enthusiasm, of fervour to the verge of madness! And now that I am to talk about my God-relationship, about what every day is repeated in my prayer of thanksgiving for the indescribable things He has done for me, so infinitely much more than ever I could have expected, about the experience which has taught me to be amazed, amazed at God, at His love and at what a man's impotence is capable of with his aid, about what has taught me to long for eternity and not to fear that I might find it boring, since it is exactly the situation I need so as to have nothing else to do but give thanks. Now that I am to talk about this there awakens in my soul a poetic impatience. More resolutely than that king who cried, 'My kingdom for a horse',[23] and blessedly resolute as he was not, I would give all, and along with that my life, to be able to find what thought has more blessedness in finding than a lover in finding the beloved – to find the 'expression', and then to die with this expression on my lips. And lo, it presents itself – thoughts as enchanting as fruits in the garden of a fairy-tale, so rich and warm and heartfelt; expressions so soothing to the urge of gratitude within me, so cooling to my hot longing – it seems to me as if, had I a winged pen, yes, ten of them, I still could not follow fast enough to keep pace with the wealth which presents itself. But no sooner have I taken pen in hand, at that very instant I am incapable of moving it, as we say of one that he cannot move hand or foot. In that situation not a line concerning this relationship gets put down on paper. It seems to me as if I heard a voice saying to me: Silly fellow, what does he imagine? Does he not know that obedience is dearer to God than the fat of rams?[24] Then I become perfectly quiet, then there is time enough to write each letter with my pen almost painfully. And if that poetic passion awakens in me again for an instant, it seems as though I heard a voice speaking to me as a teacher speaks to a

(cont'd from p. 320) be ready to recognize why it was that I found myself compelled to counteract in a finite sense my own effort, for the sake of ensuring that the responsibility should be all my own. I must at every instant be quite alone, absolutely alone, yes, I must even reject assistance, lest my responsibility be too light. Given but one friend and one fellow worker, responsibility becomes a fraction – not to speak of getting a whole generation to come to one's aid. But in the service of truth the point for me was that if I were to go astray, if I were to become presumptuous, if what I said were untrue, Governance might have an absolutely sure hold on me, and that in the possibility of this examination which at every instant hung over me I might be kept alert, attentive, and obedient.

boy when he says: Now hold the pen right, and form each letter with equal precision. And then I can do it, then I dare not do otherwise, then I write every word, every line, almost without knowing what the next word or the next line is to be. And afterwards when I read it over it satisfies me in a quite different way. For though it may be that one or other glowing expression escapes me, yet the production is quite a different one: it is the outcome, not of the poet's or the thinker's passion, but of godly fear, and for me it is a divine worship.

But what now at this instant I am living over again, or just now have been, is something I have experienced time and again during my whole activity as an author. It is said of the 'poet' that he invokes the muse to supply him with thoughts. This indeed has never been my case, my individuality prohibits me from even understanding it; but on the contrary I have needed God every day to shield me from too great a wealth of thoughts. Give a person such a productive talent, and along with that such feeble health, and verily he will learn to pray. I have been able at any instant to perform this prodigy, and I can do it still: I could sit down and continue to write for a day and a night, and again for a day and a night; for there was wealth sufficient for it. If I had done it, I should have been broken. Oh, even the least dietetic indiscretion, and I am in mortal danger. When I learn obedience, as I have described above, when I do the work as if it were a sternly prescribed task, hold the pen as I ought, write each letter with pains, then I can do it. And thus, many and many a time, I have had more joy in the relation of obedience to God than in thoughts that I produced. This, it can readily be perceived, is the expression of the fact that I can lay no claim to an immediate relationship with God, that I cannot and dare not say that it is He who immediately inserts the thoughts in me, but that my relationship to God is a reflection-relationship, is inwardness in reflection, as in general the distinguishing trait of my individuality is reflection, so that even in prayer my *forte* is thanksgiving.

Thus it is that in the course of my whole activity as an author I have constantly needed God's aid so as to do the work simply as a prescribed task to which definite hours every day were allotted, outside of which it was not permissible to work. And if once that rule was transgressed, I had to pay for it dearly. Nothing is less like my procedure than the stormy entrance of genius upon the scene, and then its tumultuous *finale*. Substantially I have lived like a scrivener at his desk. From the very beginning I have been as it were under arrest and every instant have sensed the fact that it was not I that played the part of master, but that another was Master. I have sensed that fact with fear and trembling when He let me feel His omnipotence and my nothingness;

have sensed it with indescribable bliss when I turned to Him and did my work in unconditional obedience. The dialectical factor in this is that whatever extraordinary gift may have been entrusted to me, it was entrusted as a precautionary measure with such elasticity that, if I were not to obey, it would strike me dead. It is as if a father were to say to his child: You are allowed to take the whole thing, it is yours; but if you will not be obedient and use it as I wish – very well, I shall not punish you by taking it from you; no, take it as yours . . . it will smash you. Without God I am too strong for myself, and perhaps in the most agonizing of all ways am broken. Since I became an author I have never for a single day had the experience I hear others complain of, namely, a lack of thoughts or their failure to present themselves. If that were to happen to me, it would rather be an occasion for joy, that finally I had obtained a day that was really free. But many a time I have had the experience of being overwhelmed with riches, and every instant I bethought me with horror of the frightful torture of starving in the midst of abundance – if I do not instantly learn obedience, allow God to help me, and produce in the same fashion, as quietly and placidly as one performs a prescribed task.

But in still another sense I have needed God's aid, time and again, day after day, year after year, in the whole course of my activity as a writer. For He has been my one confidant, and only in reliance upon His complicit knowledge have I dared to venture what I have ventured, and to endure what I have endured, and found bliss in the experience of being literally alone in the whole vast world, alone because wherever I was, whether in the presence of all, or in the presence of a familiar friend, I was always clad in the costume of my deceit, so that I was then as much alone as in the darkness of the night; alone, not in the forests of America with their terrors and their perils, but alone in the company of the most terrible *possibilities*, which transform even the most frightful *actuality* into a refreshment and relief; alone, almost with human speech against me; alone with torments which have taught me more than one new annotation to the text about the thorn in the flesh,[25] alone with decisions in which one had need of the support of friends, the whole human race if possible; alone in dialectical tensions which (without God) would drive any man with my imagination to madness; alone in anguish unto death; alone in the face of the meaninglessness of existence, without being able, even if I would, to make myself intelligible to a single soul – but what am I saying, 'to a single soul'? – nay, there were times when it could not be said in the common phrase, '*that* alone was lacking', times when I could not make myself intelligible to myself.[26] When now I reflect that years were passed in this manner, I shudder. When but for a single instant I see amiss, I sink in deep waters. But when I see aright and find repose in the assurance of God's complicit knowledge, blessedness returns again.

And now for details. It would be in vain for me to attempt to relate how I have sensed God's aid. As in the inexplicable occurrence which often was repeated, that when I did something without knowing why or even thinking to ask why, when as a single individual I followed the prompting of my natural inclination, that then this which for me had a purely personal significance verging on the accidental, that this then proved to have an entirely different and a purely ideal significance when it was viewed later in relation to the authorship as a whole; that, strangely enough, much I had done purely personally was exactly what I should have done *qua* author. It has been inexplicable to me that trivial and, as it seemed, accidental circumstances in my life (which, it must be said, were made to loom large by my imagination) brought me into a definite situation where I did not understand myself and became melancholy – and lo, there developed from this a mood, and precisely the mood I had use for in relation to the work I was then occupied with, and precisely at the right place. For the productivity has never suffered the least check; what was needed for use was always at hand, just at the instant it was needed. The whole productivity has had in a certain sense an uninterruptedly even course, as if I had had nothing else to do but to copy daily a definite portion of a printed book.

However, in this accounting I must make a more precise reckoning of the share Governance had in the authorship. For if I were to affirm out and out that from the very first instant I could survey the whole dialectical structure of the entire authorship, or that at every instant, stage by stage, I had by anticipation so far exhausted the possibilities that later reflection had nothing further to teach me – not even this other thing, that though what I had done was surely right, yet only afterwards was I in a position to understand thoroughly that this was so – if I were to do this, it would be a denial of God and dishonesty towards Him. No, I must say truly that I cannot understand the whole, just because to the merest insignificant detail I understand the whole; but what I cannot understand is that now I can understand it and yet cannot by any means say that at the instant of commencing it I understood it so precisely – though it is I that have carried it out and made every step with reflection. In the parlance of pure idiocy one could easily explain this by saying – as someone has said of me, without having any conception of my literary work as a totality – that I had a genius for reflection. But just because I acknowledge the justice of ascribing reflection to me, I am verily too reflective not to perceive that this juxtaposition of reflection and genius explains nothing. For just so far forth as one has genius, he has not reflection, and vice versa, inasmuch as reflection is precisely the negation of immediacy.

Were I now to express with the utmost categorical precision the share Governance had in my whole activity as a writer, I know no more suggestive or decisive expression than this: it is Governance that has educated me, and the education is reflected in the process of the productivity. In view of this it must be admitted that what I set forth above about the whole aesthetic production being a deceit is not quite true, for this expression assumes a little too much in the way of consciousness. At the same time, however, it is not altogether false, for I have been conscious of being under instruction, and that from the very first. The process is this: a poetic and philosophic nature is put aside in order to become a Christian. But the unusual feature is that the two movements begin simultaneously, and hence this is a conscious process – one is able to perceive how it comes about, and the second movement does not supervene after a series of years which separate it from the first. So the aesthetic production is certainly a deceit, yet in another sense it is a necessary elimination. The religious is decisively present from the very first instant and has a decisive predominance, but for a while it waits patiently to give the poet leave to talk himself out, yet all the time on the watch with the eyes of Argus[27] to make sure the poet does not fool it and make of himself the whole.*

It is from this point of view, I take it, that the significance my authorship has for this age is to be seen to most advantage. If with one word I were to express my judgement of this age, I would say that it lacks religious education. Becoming and being a Christian has become a triviality. The aesthetic has plainly got the upper hand. By 'going farther' than being a Christian (which every one is as a matter of course) one has got back into a refined aesthetic and intellectual paganism, with the admixture of a dash of Christianity. The task which has to be proposed to the majority of people in Christendom is: Away from the 'poet'! Or away from having a relation to, or from having one's life in, that which the poet declaims. Away from speculation! From the fantastic conceit (which is at the same time an impossibility) of having one's life in speculating (instead of existing) – and to become a Chris-

---

* This thought, that it is the 'poet' that must be got rid of, already finds its expression in *Either/Or*, although when it is understood in view of the authorship as a totality this question of getting away from or back from the 'poet' has naturally a deeper meaning than the second part of *Either/Or* could explain. That this is the case with *Either/Or* was already noted in the *Concluding Postscript*. [See the opening section of 'A Glance at a Contemporary Effort in Danish Literature' in *Concluding Unscientific Postscript*; cf. KW XII.1, pp. 252–3.] Indeed the transition made in *Either/Or* is substantially that from a poet-existence to an ethical existence.

tian! The first movement (away from the poetical) constitutes the total significance of the aesthetic production within the totality of the authorship. The second movement (away from speculation) is that of the *Concluding Postscript*, which, while it draws or edits the whole aesthetic production to its own advantage by way of illuminating its problem, which is the problem of 'becoming a Christian', makes the same movement in another sphere: Away from speculation! From the System, etc. – to become a Christian. The movement is *Back*! And although it is all done without 'authority', there is, nevertheless, something in the accent which recalls a policeman when he faces a riot and says, Back! Hence also more than one of the pseudonyms applies this expression to himself, saying that he is a policeman, a member of the detective force.

And now as for me, the author, what, according to my opinion, is my relation to the age? Am I perhaps the 'Apostle'? Abominable! I have never given an occasion for such a judgement. I am a poor insignificant person. Am I then the teacher, the educator? No, not that at all; I am he who himself has been educated, or whose authorship expresses what it is to be educated to the point of becoming a Christian. In the fact that education is pressed upon me, and in the measure that it is pressed, I press in turn upon this age; but I am not a teacher, only a fellow student.

To illuminate farther the share of Governance in the authorship, it is necessary to explain, so far as I have an explanation at my disposal, how it was I became an author.

About my *vita ante acta* [earlier life] (i.e. from childhood until I became an author) I cannot expatiate here at any length, however remarkable, as it seems to me, the way I was predisposed from my earliest childhood, and step by step through the whole development, to become exactly the sort of author I became. For the sake of what follows I must allude, however, to a few traits of my earlier life, which I do with the diffidence a person surely must always feel when he has to speak quite personally about himself.

From a child I was under the sway of a prodigious melancholy, the depth of which finds its only adequate measure in the equally prodigious dexterity I possessed of hiding it under an apparent gaiety and *joie de vivre*. So far back as I can remember, my one joy was that nobody could discover how unhappy I felt. This proportion (the equally great magnitude of melancholy and of the art of dissimulation) signifies that I was relegated to myself and to a relationship with God. As a child I was sternly and seriously brought up in Christianity. Humanly speaking, it was a crazy upbringing. Already in my earliest childhood I broke down under the grave impression which the melancholy old man who laid it upon me himself sank under. A child – what a crazy thing! – travestied as an old man! Frightful! What wonder then that there were times when Christianity appeared to me the most inhuman cruelty – although never, even when I was farthest from it, did I cease to revere it, with a firm determination that (especially if I did not myself make the choice of becoming a Christian) I would never initiate anyone into the difficulties which I knew and which, so far as I have read and heard, no one else has alluded to. But I have never definitely broken with Christianity nor renounced it. To attack it has never been my thought. No, from the time when there could be any question of the employment of my powers, I was firmly determined to employ them all to defend Christianity, or in any case to present it in its true form. For very early indeed, by the help of my upbringing, I was in a position to ascertain for myself how seldom Christianity is presented in its true form, how those who defend it most commonly betray it, and how seldom its opponents really hit the mark – although, in my opinion at least, they often squarely hit established Christendom, which might rather be called the caricature of true Christianity, or a monstrous amount of misunderstanding, illusion, etc., mixed with a sparing little dose of true Christianity. So I loved Christianity in a way: to me it was venerable – it had, to be sure, humanly speaking, rendered me exceedingly unhappy. This corresponds to my relationship with my father, the person whom I loved most deeply. And what is the meaning of this? The point precisely is that he made me unhappy – but out of love. His error did not consist in lack of love, but in mistaking a child for an old man. To love him who makes one happy is, to a reflective mind, an inadequate definition of what love is; to love him who made one unhappy out of malice, is virtue; but to love him who out of love, though by a misunderstanding, yet out of love, made one unhappy – that is the formula never yet enunciated, so far as I know, but nevertheless the normal formula in reflection for what it is to love.

So I went forth into life, favoured in every way, so far as intellectual gifts go, and outward circumstances. Everything was done and continued to be done to develop my mind as richly as possible. Self-confident, yet with a decided sympathy or predilection for suffering, or for whatever in any way is suffering or oppressed. In a certain sense I may say that I went out into life with a proud and almost foolhardy bearing. I have never at any instant in my life been deserted by the faith that one can do what one will – only one thing excepted (all else unconditionally, but one thing not), the throwing off of the melancholy in whose power I was. What I am saying will seem to others a vain conceit, but so it was with me in truth, as truly as what I tell next, which to others again will seem a conceit. I say that it never remotely occurred to me that in my generation there lived or was to be born a man who had the upper hand of me – and in my inmost self I was the most wretched of all men. It never remotely occurred to me that, even if I were to attempt the most foolhardy enterprise, I should not be victorious – only one thing excepted (all else unconditionally, but one thing not), the throwing off of the melancholy and its attendant suffering from which I was never entirely free even for a day. This, however, must be understood in connection with the fact that I was very early initiated into the thought that to conquer means to conquer in an infinite sense, which in a finite sense means to suffer. So this corresponded with my melancholy's inward apprehension that, in a finite sense, I was utterly good for nothing. What reconciled me with my fate and with my sufferings was that I, the so unhappy, so much tortured prisoner, had obtained this unlimited freedom of being able to deceive, so that I was allowed to be absolutely alone with my pain. It goes without saying that this was quite enough to render all my other abilities anything but merry for me. When this is given (i.e. such a pain and such a close reserve), it depends upon the personal characteristics of the individual whether this lonesome inward torment demonically finds its expression and satisfaction in hating men and cursing God, or in the very reverse. The latter was my situation. As far back as I can remember I was in agreement with myself about one thing, that for me there was no comfort or help to be looked for in others. Sated with the many other things bestowed upon me, filled as a man with longing after death, as a spirit desirous of the longest possible life, my thought was, as the expression of a melancholy love for men, to be helpful to them, to find comfort for them, above all clearness of thinking, and that especially about Christianity. The thought goes very far back in my recollection that in every generation there are two or three who are sacrificed for the rest, are led by frightful sufferings to discover what redounds to the good of others. So it was that in my melancholy I understood myself as singled out for such a fate.

So I fared forth into life – initiated into all possible enjoyments, yet never really enjoying, but rather (to indulge the one pleasure I had in connection with the pain of melancholy) labouring to produce the impression that I enjoyed. I fared forth into acquaintance with all sorts of men, yet it never occurred to me that I had a confidant in any of them, and certainly it never occurred to any one of them that he was my confidant. That is to say, I was constrained to be and was an observer. By such a life, as an observer and as spirit, I was extraordinarily enriched by experiences, got to see quite near at hand that aggregation of pleasures, passions, moods, feelings, etc., got practice in seeing a man through and through and also in imitating him. My imagination and my dialectic constantly had material enough to operate with, and time enough, free from all bustle, to be idle. For long periods I have been employed with nothing else but the performance of dialectical exercises with a dash of imagination, trying out my mind as one tunes [*stemmer*] an instrument – but I was not really living. I was tossed about in life, tempted by many and the most various things, unfortunately also by errors, and, alas, also by the path of perdition. So I was in my twenty-fifth year, to myself an enigmatically developed and extraordinary possibility, the significance and character of which I did not understand, in spite of the most eminent reflection which if possible understood everything. I understood one thing, that my life would be most properly employed in doing penance; but in the proper sense of the word I had not lived, except in the character of spirit. A man I had never been, and child or youth even less.

Then my father died. The powerful religious impressions of my childhood acquired a renewed power over me, now transformed by ideality. Also I had now become so much older that I fitted better to my upbringing, which has just this misfortune, that it would not turn out completely to my advantage until I was forty years old. For my misfortune (almost I might say from my birth, completed in my upbringing) was . . . that I was not to be a human being. But when one is a child – and the other children play or jest or whatever else they do; ah, and when one is a youth – and the other young people make love and dance or whatever else they do – and then, in spite of the fact that one is a child or a youth, then to be a spirit! Frightful torture! Even more frightful than if one by the help of imagination knows how to perform the trick of appearing to be the youngest of all. But this misfortune is already diminished when one is forty years old, and in eternity it does not exist.

I have never had any immediacy, and therefore, in the ordinary human sense of the word, I have never lived. I began at once with reflection; it is not as though in later years I had amassed a little reflection, but I am reflection from first to last. In the two ages of immediacy (childhood and youth) I, with the dexterity which reflection always possesses, helped myself out, as I was compelled to do, by some sort of counterfeit, and not being quite clear myself about the talents bestowed upon me, I suffered the pain of not being like the others – which naturally at that period I would have given everything to be able to be, if only for a short time. A spirit can very well put up with not being like the others – indeed that is precisely the negative determination of spirit. But childhood and youth stand in a close relation to determinations such as 'species' or 'human race'; and just for this reason it is the greatest torment of that period not to be like the others, or, as in my case, so strangely topsy-turvy as to begin at that point where a few in every generation end, whereas the majority, who live merely in the separate factors of the soul–body synthesis, never reach it – that is to say, the determination 'spirit'. But for this same reason I have my life now before me, in a sense very different from the ordinary meaning of that phrase. Nothing is more completely unknown and foreign to me than that wistful longing for child-hood and youth. I thank my God that all this is through with, and I feel happier with every day I grow older – yet only blessed in the thought of eternity, for temporality never is and never will be the element of spirit, but in a sense must mean suffering for it.

An observer will perceive how everything was set in motion, and how dialectically: I had a thorn in the flesh, intellectual gifts (especially imagina-tion and dialectic) and culture in superabundance, an enormous development as an observer, a Christian upbringing that was certainly very unusual, a dialectical relationship to Christianity which was peculiarly my own, and in addition to this I had from childhood a training in obedience, absolute obe-dience, and I was armed with an almost foolhardy faith that I was able to do anything, only one thing excepted, to be a free bird, though but for one whole day, or to slip out of the fetters of melancholy in which another power held me bound. Finally, in my own eyes I was a penitent. The impression this now makes upon me is as if there were a power which from the first instant had been observant of this and said, as a fisherman says of a fish: play it awhile, it is too soon to pull it in. And strangely enough there is some-thing that reaches far back in my recollection, impossible as it is for me to say when I began this practice or why such a thing ever occurred to me: I prayed to God regularly, i.e. every day, that He would give me the zeal and patience to perform the work He would assign me.

Thus I became an author.

Before my real activity as an author began there was an occurrence, or rather a fact,[28] since presumably an occurrence would not have been sufficient, for I had to be the active agent in the affair. I cannot elucidate this fact more particularly, telling in what it consisted, how terribly dialectical it was in its combination (although in another sense it was quite simple), or where the collision really lay. I can only beg the reader not to think of revelations or anything of that sort, for with me everything is dialectical. On the other hand, I shall describe the consequence of this fact in so far as it serves to illuminate the authorship. It was a double-fact. However much I had lived and experienced in another sense, I had, in a human sense, leapt over the stages of childhood and youth; and this lack, I suppose, must (in the opinion of Governance) be somehow made up for: instead of having been young, I became a poet, which is a second youth. I became a poet, but with my pre-disposition for religion, or rather, I may say, with my decided religiousness, this fact was for me at the same time a religious awakening, so that I came to understand myself in the most decisive sense in the religious, or in reli-giousness, to which, however, I had already related myself as to a possibility.

The fact made me a poet. Had I not been the man I was, and the occurrence, on the other hand, what it was, and if I had not acted as I did, it would have amounted to nothing more: I should have become a poet, and then perhaps after the lapse of many years should have come into relation with the religious. But just because I was so religiously developed as I was, the fact took far deeper hold of me and, in a sense, nullified what I had become, namely, the poet. It nullified it, or at least I was led simultaneously to begin in the same moment at two points, yet in such a way that being a poet was essentially irrelevant to me – something I had become by means of another person. On the other hand the religious awakening, though it was certainly not a thing I had achieved by means of myself, was nevertheless in accordance with myself, that is to say, in a deeper sense I did not recognize myself in becoming a poet, but rather in the religious awakening.

Here the reader can easily perceive the explanation of the duplicity of the authorship as a whole, but he must note that the author was at the same time conscious of this. What was to be done? Well, obviously the poetical still had to be given exhaustive expression – anything else was impossible for me. But the whole aesthetic production was put under arrest by the religious. The religious consented to the continued expression of the poetical but incessantly spurred it on, as though it were saying: Are you not through with that yet?*

---

* One will now perhaps be aware of what I myself promptly understood as the misfortune, humanly speaking, of the whole authorship. It was too grandiose, there was no appropriate place for it in any instant of reality, partly because of the very great haste with which it was produced, and partly because it comprehended such a decisive development as that from the aesthetic to the religious, the Christian. In relation to *Either/Or* as the first work, this misfortune was obscured; no yardstick had yet been presented, nor had the duplicity been posited. People regarded *Either/Or* as the fruit of many years' labour. That illusion helped, and there were many other factors which helped *Either/Or*. For example, by the help of the illusion the public could perceive the pains that were taken in a stylistic sense; and yet *Either/Or* was written in the shortest time, and perhaps the least pains were taken about style. But this is natural. The public may have thought that the first part of *Either/Or* was written several years before the second part but in fact the opposite was the case: the second part was written first. So it was with *Either/Or*. But when subsequently the illusion was made impossible and the yardstick was supplied, no one could fail to see that it was hasty work and not worth the trouble of following. This was natural enough – the literary output upon which I had spent five years would ordinarily have required fifteen. Perhaps one will also understand now, and be in agreement with me, that I did not want any reviews because I could not expect any essential review. In such a little land how could I count upon any contemporary who had the presuppositions and likewise the time to survey such a consciously crafty production? And direct communication I dared not use because I understood silence as my religious duty. Or is it possible that for a single instant it could really have occurred to any man when he got hold of *Either/Or* that the author was a religious man, or that he himself, if he were to follow my activity as an author, would in the course of three or four years of such a journey find himself in the midst of the most decisive Christian productivity?

While the poetical works were being produced the author was living under decisively religious terms.*

In a certain sense it was not at all my intention to become a religious author. My intention was to finish with the poetical as speedily as possible – and then go out to a country parish. By this compass I steered. I felt myself foreign to the whole poetical production, but I could do no other. It was not my intention, as I have said, to become a religious *author*. I had reflected that the most vigorous expression of the fact that I had been a religious man and that the pseudonyms were something foreign to me was the abrupt transition – to leave the city immediately and find a living as a country parson.

However, the urge of productivity in me was so great that I could not do otherwise. I let the *Two Edifying Discourses* come out, and I came to an understanding with Governance. There was allowed me again a period for poetical production, but always under the arrest of the religious, which was on the watch, as if it said: Are you not through with that yet? And I found a way to satisfy the religious by becoming a religious author.

Governance now had me securely bound. Like a suspicious character perhaps, I have been put on a very spare diet. I have been accustomed so to live that the maximum time I expect to have left is a year – sometimes, and not seldom, when a special tension is required, I live with the prospect of a week, yes, even of a day. And Governance had put checks upon me in every sense. It was impossible for me to run away from the aesthetic production, understood in such a way as to imply that I had lived my life in the aesthetic. For even if the religious had not been in the background, that thorn in the flesh would have prevented any such thing. And in relation to the religious authorship, Governance had a check on me in the fact that I did not arrogate anything to myself because I understood myself to be in too great a debt.

And now I come to an expression about myself, the author, which I am accustomed to use of myself when I talk to myself, an expression which is related to the inverse procedure of the whole productivity (that I did not begin by saying whither I designed to go), and related to me also in my capacity as observer, along with my consciousness of being one who himself is in need of upbringing. The expression I use is, that in relation to the intellectual and religious fields, and with a view to the concept of existence, and hence to the concept of Christendom, I am like a spy in a higher service,

---

* Here one will perceive the significance of the pseudonyms and why I had to be pseudonymous in relation to all aesthetic productions, because I led my own life in entirely different categories and understood from the beginning that this productivity was of an interim nature, a deceit, a necessary clearing out.

the service of the Idea. I have nothing new to proclaim; I am without authority, being myself hidden in a deceit; I do not go to work straightforwardly but with indirect cunning; I am not a holy man. In short, I am a spy who in his spying – in making inspection of questionable conduct and illusions and suspicious characters – is all the while himself under the closest inspection. Observe that this is the sort of people the police make use of. They will hardly select for their purpose the sort of people whose life was always highly honest; all that they take into account is that they are experienced, cunning, intriguing, shrewd people who can nose anything out, always follow a clue and bring things to light. Hence the police are far from disinclined to have under their thumb a person who – by reason of his *vita ante acta* [previous life] – they can compel to put up with everything, to obey, and to make no fuss about his personal dignity. So, too, it is with Governance, only that there is this infinite difference between it and the civil police, that Governance, being merciful love, employs such a person just for love's sake, saves him and educates him while he is employing his shrewdness, which is thus sanctified and consecrated. But such a person, who himself stands in need of education, understands that he is duty-bound to the most unconditional obedience. It is certain that of every man God can require all, that man must put up with everything, but it is also certain that the consciousness of earlier errors helps considerably to encourage promptness and nimbleness in this respect.★

★ If any one were to make what I would call the sharp-witted observation, 'Then if that is the case, if the notion that you are a spy is true, your whole activity as an author is a sort of misanthropic treachery, a crime against humanity'; then I should answer, 'Oh yes, the crime is that I have loved God in a *Christian* Way.' I have not endeavoured with the slightest fraction of the talents granted me to express the thought (which perhaps is what is meant by loving humanity) that the world is good, that it loves the truth, or desires the good, that what the age demands is truth, that the human race is the truth or even is God, and that the (Goetheo-Hegelian) task is therefore to content the age. On the contrary, I have endeavoured to express the thought that the world, if not evil, is mediocre, that 'what the age demands' is foolishness and frippery, that in the eyes of the world the truth is a ludicrous exaggeration or an eccentric superfluity; and that the good must suffer. I have endeavoured to express the thought that to employ the category 'human race' to indicate what it is to be human, and especially as an indication of the highest attainment, is a misunderstanding and mere paganism, because the human race, mankind, differs from animal races not merely by its general superiority as a race, but by the *human* characteristic that every single individual within the race (not merely distinguished individuals but every individual) is more than the race. This follows from the relation of the individual to God, and essentially this is Christianity, whose category, 'the individual', is so much derided by this highly-lauded Christian age. For to relate oneself to God is a far higher thing than to be related to the human race and through the race to God. This is what I have endeavoured to express. I have not declaimed or thundered, and I have not lectured, but I have made it plain that this is the case also in our age, that our age

But in any case this surely is evident, that with respect to reflection and shrewdness Christendom has run wild and exceeded all limits. Immediate pathos is of no avail – even if in immediate pathos one were to sacrifice one's life. The age has at its disposal too much reflection and shrewdness not to be able to reduce this significance to zero. Even for a martyr to accomplish anything in these times he must possess reflection, in order to so intrigue the age that it cleaves to him even when it puts him to death – that thus the awakening may follow.

So it is that I understand myself in my activity as an author. It makes the illusion of Christendom evident and opens the eyes to what it is to become a Christian. I do not know whether there could be religiousness of such a high grade that it would regard the aesthetic production as something that must simply be repented of, and refuse to accept that it required exhaustive expression, or was a holy deceit. I have never understood it thus, and surely such a thought will not occur to any one before I utter it. But since with me everything is reflection, it is a matter of course that this thought has not escaped my notice. I can imagine this objection made from the point of view of a scrupulous and pusillanimous notion of the duty of telling the truth, a notion which consistently leads to being always mute for fear of saying something false; and since silence may be a falsehood, it consistently leads to the dilemma: Do it or don't do it; be silent or speak out; both are equally futile.

(cont'd from p. 333) and generation is pitifully confused about the good and the true. I have endeavoured to make this manifest by all the cunning and craftiness I had at my command. In opposition to the theory and practice of living which humanly and with human self-complacency loves what it is to be human and turns traitor to God – in opposition to this I have committed the crime of loving God and have endeavoured by every means (but indirectly, qua spy) to make this treason manifest. Supposing that I had been free to use my talents as I pleased (and that it was not the case that another power was able to compel me every moment when I was not ready to yield to fair means), I might from the first moment have converted by whole productivity into the channel of the interests of the age, it would have been in my power (if such betrayal were not punished by reducing me to naught) to become what the age demands, and so would have been one more (Goetheo-Hegelian) testimony to the proposition that that world is good, that the human race is the truth and that this generation is the court of last resort, that the public is the discoverer of the truth and its judge, etc. For by this treason I would have attained extraordinary success in this world, etc. Instead of this I became (under compulsion) a spy. In this there is nothing meritorious: I certainly do not build my hope of salvation upon it. Yet it delights me childishly that I have served in this way, whereas in relation to God I offer this whole activity of mine with more diffidence than a child when it gives as a present to the parents an object which the parents had presented to the child. Oh, but the parents surely are not so cruel that, instead of looking kindly upon the child and entering into its notion that this is a present, they take the gift away from the child and say: This is our property. So it is also with God: He is not so cruel when one brings Him a gift . . . a gift which is His own.

But timorousness to the verge of lunacy is hardly to be regarded as a higher form of religiousness. Teleological suspension in relation to the communication of truth (i.e. suppressing something for the time being in order that the truth may become truer) is a plain duty to the truth and is comprised in the responsibility a man has before God for a proper use of the reflection bestowed upon him.

Well acquainted as I was with the suffering of inwardness in relation to the task of becoming a Christian, and strictly brought up as I was in this apprehension, the other side of the matter almost escaped me. Here Governance came to my aid, and helped me in such wise that the consequence of what I did turned out truly to my advantage and to the advantage of my cause. If one may compare intellectual talents with a stringed instrument, I may say that not only was I not put out of tune, but I acquired an extra string to my instrument. This was the fruit of my more complete education in what it means to become a Christian. For at the decisive instant when I was radically altering my existence-relationship on account of the *Concluding Postscript*, I had opportunity to observe what one will never believe until he has experienced it, namely, this Christian truth that love is hated. Verily nothing has ever been farther from me than pretension to social superiority. Being myself of humble origin, I have loved the common people, or what is spoken of as the simple classes. Indeed I did, as I well know, for in that I found a melancholy joy – and yet it was precisely they who were incited against me and made to believe that I gave myself airs of superiority. If I had really belonged to the superior classes, this would never have happened to me. Observe that here we have precisely the Christian proportions, and on a scale so great that it enabled me to illuminate Christianity from this side. The complaint which might have been brought against my mode of life (if the merely human were to be the judge, and not Christianity) can only be expressed thus: that I have not shown enough regard for myself, have not been sufficiently aloof; that humanly speaking I have in a light-minded way (Christianly understood, a God-fearing way) made sport of worldly honour and prestige, that by possibly impairing my own worldly prestige I have at the same time contributed to impairing worldly prestige in general. As I have said, I should regard it as perfectly natural if in consideration of this the people who are in the enjoyment of superior place and reputation had shown themselves a bit hostile, and hence I am the more grateful for the fact that exactly the opposite is and has been the case. But the fact that, because I have lived as I have, I am exposed to the hatred of the common people – that is to say, because I have not been 'superior' enough, that I have therefore been attacked, not by the superior classes but by the common people – that is lunacy . . . and the Christian proportion.

Thus it is that the whole literary activity turns upon the problem of becoming a Christian in Christendom; and this is the expression of the share Governance had in the authorship, that it is the author himself who has been educated, yet with consciousness of this from the very first.

Epilogue

'But what have you done now?' I hear somebody say. 'Do you not perceive what you have lost in the eyes of the world by making this explanation and public acknowledgement?' To be sure, I perceive it very clearly. I have lost thereby what in a Christian sense it is a loss to possess, namely, every worldly form of the interesting. I lose the interesting distinction of proclaiming the seductive craftiness of pleasure, the glad report of life's most subtle enjoyments, and the insolence of derision. I lose the interesting distinction of being an interesting possibility, suggestive of the query whether it might not after all be the case that he who represented the ethical with warmth and enthusiasm – whether he might not after all be exactly the opposite, *either* in one way *or* in another, since it is (so interestingly) impossible to say which he is. I lose the interesting distinction of being an enigma, seeing it is impossible to know whether this thoroughgoing defence of Christianity is not a covert attack most cunningly conceived. This interesting distinction I lose, and for it is substituted, at the farthest remove from the interesting, the *direct communication* that the problem was, and is, how to become a Christian. The interesting is what I have lost in the eyes of the crowd, in the world's eyes – if indeed I get off so easily as to lose only that, and the world does not become enraged at the fact that a man has presumed to be so crafty.

True enough, things are going backward with me, in a sense – though in a Christian sense it is forward. As an author I began with the tremendous advantage of being regarded privately as not much better than a scoundrel – but naturally all the more likeable on that account, especially as I was so interesting and witty. This was needed in order to get the 'crowd' of Christians a little bit on my side. Even if one were a saint, one could not begin with holiness without losing the game in advance. For in the age of reflection in which we live people are prompt to parry, and even the death of the saint is of no avail. No, in reflection everything must be done inversely. Thus it was that I began. At that time I stood at the pinnacle of favour with the human crowd, and (since we live in Christendom where all are Christians) with the Christian crowd also, the monstrous crowd of Christians, all the novel-readers of both sexes, the aesthetically refined, the beautiful souls, all of whom are at the same time Christians.

This was the beginning. As time went on and I got farther ahead, and the great Christian public became aware or had a suspicion (ah, this was going backward with a vengeance!) that I really was not so bad after all, the public fell away more and more, and I began to be included under the boring category of the good. And in the meanwhile, I proceeded with the edifying discourses, and perceived with joy that 'the single individual whom I with joy and gladness call *my* reader' became more than one, almost a multitude, yet certainly not anything like a public. And then when I performed a decisive act which had a little bit of Christian flavour about it, an act which at the same time I was conscious of performing as a true benefaction to little Denmark, and an act which will give me unconditional joy at my hour of death – that is to say, when I cast myself as a sacrifice before the insurrection of vulgarity – then I was regarded by the public as crazy and queer, condemned almost as a criminal. Naturally enough, for there was not the least trace of the scoundrel or the rascal in what I did. How perfectly this all fits together! I do not see how more could be required of a spy.

And now – now I am no longer interesting. That becoming a Christian should *really* be the fundamental thought in my whole activity as an author – how boring! And this business about 'The Diary of a Seducer',★ this tremendously witty production! Why, it seems now that even this belonged to the plan! If any one asks me out of a purely aesthetic interest what my judgement is about the aesthetic production, I will not make any attempt to conceal the fact that I know perfectly well what has been accomplished, but I will add that for me even the aesthetic value of the accomplishment consists in a deeper sense in the indication it furnishes of how infinitely important the decision to become a Christian is. It is a perfectly *direct* thing to become a Christian in immediacy; but the truth and inwardness of becoming a Christian in reflection is measured by the value of that which reflection discards. For one does not become a Christian through reflection; but to become a Christian in reflection means that something else must be discarded. One does not reflect oneself into

★ Psychologically it is quite remarkable, and worthy perhaps to be recorded, that a person to whose name I will concede a place here in order to take him with me – that Herr P. L. Møller quite rightly regarded 'The Diary of a Seducer' as the central point in the whole authorship. That reminds me so vividly of the motto to *Stages on Life's Way* – precisely the work which he, from the point of view of 'The Diary of a Seducer', fell upon or fell over – which motto I therefore reminded him of in a little lesson I gave him, but it may be appropriate to repeat it here since it is well adapted as an epigram to preserve a pious memory of Møller's aesthetic and critical services on behalf of my authorship: 'Such works are mirrors: when an ape peers into them, no Apostle can be seen looking out.' [Peter Ludvig Møller (1814–65) offended Kierkegaard in 1846 by publishing a critical article on the pseudonymous works.]

being a Christian; in order to become a Christian, one must reflect oneself out of something else. And this is especially the case in Christendom, where one must reflect oneself out of the semblance of being a Christian. The depth and significance of the movement of reflection depends on the nature of this 'something else'. The character of the reflection will be determined by the fact that there is a journey to be made in order to reach the point of becoming a Christian, and by how long the journey is. The character of the reflection is defined by the difficulty, which is proportional to the value and significance of the thing left behind.

Thus it is, as I believe, that I have rendered a service to the cause of Christianity while I myself have been educated by the process. He who was regarded with astonishment as about the shrewdest fellow (and this was attained with *Either/Or*), he to whom the place of 'the interesting man' was willingly conceded (and this was attained with *Either/Or*) – precisely he, as it turned out, was engaged in the service of Christianity, had consecrated★ himself to this from the very instant he began that pseudonymous activity; he, personally and as an author, was striving to bring out this simple thing about becoming a Christian. The movement is not from the simple to the interesting, but from the interesting to the simple, the thing of becoming a Christian, which is the place where the *Concluding Postscript* comes in, the 'turning-point' of the whole authorship, which states the 'Problem' and at the same time, by indirect attack and Socratic dialectic, inflicts upon the System a mortal wound . . . from behind, fighting the System and Speculation in order to show that 'the way' is not from the simple to the System and Speculation, but from the System and Speculation back again to the simple thing of becoming a Christian, fighting for this cause and vigorously slashing through to find the way back. So we have to do here not with a onetime aesthetic author who subsequently turns away from the world, but with one who decisively turned away from the world and the world's wisdom; he may rightly be said to have had from the earliest time quite exceptional pre-

---

★ The consecration, in so far as it dated from an earlier time, consisted in the resolution before God that, even if I were never to attain the goal of becoming a Christian, I would employ all my time and diligence to getting it made clear at least what Christianity is and where the confusions in Christendom lie – a labour for which I had prepared myself substantially from my earliest youth. Humanly speaking, this was surely a magnanimous resolution. But Christianity is a power far too great to be willing as a matter of course to make use of a man's magnanimous resolution (which in my case was for the most part an expression of my relationship to my father), wherefore Governance took the liberty of so arranging my subsequent life that there could be no misunderstanding (as indeed there was not from the beginning) as to whether it was I that stood in need of Christianity, or Christianity that stood in need of me.

dispositions for becoming a Christian, but they were all dialectical. Nor does he feel at this instant any impulse to go farther than becoming a Christian. With his conception of this task, and with the consciousness he has of how far he is from being perfect, he feels only an impulse to go farther in becoming a Christian.

If the benevolent reader has read this little book with attention, he now knows what sort of an author I am.* So it is I represent myself. Should it prove that the present age will not understand me – very well then, I belong to history, knowing assuredly that I shall find a place there and what place it will be. Humble as I am before God, I also know this – and at the same time I know it as my duty definitely not to suppress it in silence, but to proclaim it; for if pride and arrogancy in claiming something for oneself is an abomination to God, so too, and just as much so, is the cowardly fear of men which depreciates itself with mendacious modesty – I also know *who*, humanly speaking, I was (the past tense because it is in God's power, every day, and even to-day, to alter it), that (in respect to genius) extraordinary gifts had been bestowed upon me.

With this present little book, which itself belongs to a bygone time, I conclude my whole previous authorship, and so as the author (not an author, but the author) I advance to meet the future. What may betide me in the immediate future I know not; how it will be in the following age when I have passed into history, that I know. But whatever it be that I know in this respect, it would be of no comfort to me, were I not in faith and confidence, though in humility and also in penitence, advancing to meet that future which is nearest of all and at every instant equally near – eternity. Suppose that, if I should live longer, time deprives me of all, and suppose that the following age makes the fullest reparation – how can that really harm me, or how can it profit? The former does not harm me if I merely take care to be absent, and the latter will not profit me, since then I shall have become an 'absent one'.

Conclusion

I have nothing further to say, but in conclusion I will let another speak, my poet, who when he comes will assign me a place among those who have suffered for the sake of an idea, and he will say:

'The martyrdom this author suffered may be briefly described thus: He suffered from being a genius in a market town. He set a standard for talent,

---

* For that I myself possess a more exact and purely personal interpretation of my life is a matter of course.

industry, disinterestedness, devotedness, absolute definiteness of thought, etc., which was far too high for the average level of his contemporaries; prices went up, prices went down, and so wildly that it was almost as if the majority in the market town had lost its *dominium absolutum* [absolute sovereignty], but that there was a God. So for a while people entertained one another with voluble arguments about why on earth he had such extraordinary talents, and why he should have independent means and yet be so industrious. They argued for such a long time (while also taking offence at various peculiarities in his mode of living, which, however, were not really peculiar at all, but peculiarly calculated to serve the purpose of his life) that in the end it came to this: 'It is his pride, everything can be explained by his pride.' Thereupon they went farther, from argument to action. Since it is his pride, they said, every covert opposition, every insolence towards him or maltreatment of him is not only permissible but is a duty to God – it is his pride that should be punished. O priceless market town! How inestimable thou art when attired in thy comical dressing-gown[29] and in the way of becoming holy, when abandonment to every disgusting inclination of envy, rudeness, and vulgarity becomes an expression of the worship of God! But what about his pride? Was it really pride, or simply great talent? That would be like reproaching the golden sparrow, saying that it wears its golden finery out of pride. Or was it his diligence, etc.? If a child who had been very strictly brought up were to study in a class together with others, would it not be strange to say that his diligence, etc., was pride, even if the others could not keep up with him? But such a case seldom occurs, for the child would be moved up to a higher class. For one who is in many ways well prepared for eternity's class, there is unfortunately only one class, that of temporality, and he may have to remain there a long while.

'This was the martyrdom. But therefore I, his poet, perceive also the epigram, the satire – not any particular one he wrote, but the one which his whole life expressed – which lies in the fact that now that all the "real" people with whom he could not stand comparison (especially when legs are the criterion – not for beasts, but for human beings), are dead and gone, and their legs like his are mouldering in the ground, and he has arrived in eternity (where, in parenthesis be it said, legs do not decide anything, neither their thinness nor their thickness) where (in parenthesis be it said) he is for ever spared, praise God, from brutish company – now that all these "real" people are dead I can see that their participation was essential: a priceless market-town chorus clinging to what it understands – namely his trousers, which became "what the age requires" – and, more precious still, a chorus which ironizes . . . the ironist. I have only to think of this, and I burst out laughing. In eternity it consoles him that he suffered thus, and voluntarily exposed himself to this suffering, that he did not bolster his cause by any illusion, or hide behind any illusion, but with God-fearing shrewdness transmuted his sufferings into a treasure for eternity: – the recollection of sufferings endured, and of fidelity to himself and his first love, apart from whom he loved only those who have suffered in the world. Humble as he is, he will not advance to meet those glorious ones shamefacedly, as he would if his earthly life had expressed the conviction that their lives were inessential, false, or unripe, and if he had gained great honour and reputation by serving the truth, encountering spiritual affinity and understanding everywhere, whereas they on the contrary met with little but brutishness and misunderstanding.

'Yet it is true that he found also here on earth what he sought. He himself was "that individual", if no one else was, and he became that more and more. It was the cause of Christianity he served, his life from childhood on being marvellously fitted for such a service. Thus he carried to completion the work of reflection, entirely transposing into reflection what Christianity is and what it means to become a Christian. His purity of heart was to will only one thing. What his contemporaries complained of during his lifetime – that he would not compromise, would not give in – is precisely the eulogy pronounced upon him by posterity, that he did not compromise, did not give in. But he did not get carried away by his grand enterprise. As author he dialectically surveyed the whole, but Christianly he understood that it signified his own education in Christianity. The dialectical structure which he had brought to completion, of which the different parts are themselves whole works, was not something he could ascribe to anyone, least of all himself. Or if he were to ascribe it to anyone, it would be Governance, to which it had in fact already been ascribed, day after day and year after year, by the author, who historically died of a mortal sickness, but poetically died of a longing for eternity, where uninterruptedly he would have nothing else to do but thank God.'

Notes

1 Shakespeare, *II Henry IV*, 2, ii.
2 Hans Adolf Brorson (1694–1764), *Op al den Ting*.
3 Cf. Ecclesiastes 3, 7: 'A time to rend, and a time to sew; a time to keep silence, and a time to speak'.
4 Cf. Plato, *Apology of Socrates*, 30 d–e.
5 Cf. Matthew 16, 26: 'For what is a man profited, if he shall gain the whole world, and lose his own soul?'

6   Another reference to *The Crisis and a Crisis in the Life of an Actress.*

7   *Either/Or* part one; cf. KW III, pp. 301–445.

8   Johannes de Silentio is the pseudonym responsible for *Fear and Trembling.*

9   'Kts' was the pseudonym used by Jakob Peter Mynster, derived from the initial consonant of the second syllable of each of his names; see above, p. 285, n. 29.

10 Kierkegaard offers five theses on the aesthetic works, of which only the fifth is included here.

11 Cf. Romans 8, 16: 'The Spirit itself beareth witness with our spirit, that we are the children of God.'

12 Jens Finsteen Giødwad (1811–91), journalist and editor of the Journal *Fædrelandet.*

13 An approximate quotation from *Either/Or* Part Two; 'Equilibrium between the Aesthetic and the Ethical'; cf. KW IV, p. 205.

14 Christian Peter Bianco Luno (1790–1852), printer of *Postscript* and most of Kierkegaard's other works.

15 Kierkegaard alludes to the political crisis in Denmark in March 1848 precipitated by German attempts to annex Schleswig-Holstein.

16 A reference to the *Corsair*, a satirical journal which had subjected Kierkegaard to savage and relentless mockery throughout 1846.

17 Cf. Aristotle, *Rhetoric*, 1419b: 'Irony suits a gentleman better than buffoonery: the ironist makes jokes to amuse himself, the buffoon to amuse others.'

18 Kierkegaard refers to Meïr Aron Goldschmidt (1819–87), editor of the *Corsair.*

19 Cf. Isaiah 3, 4: 'And I will give children to be their princes, and babes shall rule over them.'

20 According to Livy (*History of Rome*, VII, 6), Marcus Curtius leapt with his horse into a chasm that opened up in the middle of the forum in Rome.

21 Another reference to the Schleswig-Holstein crisis; see above, n. 15.

22 Cf. Plato, *Phaedrus*, 230c: 'you, my excellent friend, strike me as the most eccentric of men'.

23 See Shakespeare, *Richard III*, 5, iv.

24 Cf. I Samuel 15, 22: 'And Samuel said, Hath the Lord as great delight in burnt offerings and sacrifices, as in obeying the voice of the Lord? Behold, to obey is better than sacrifice, and to hearken than the fat of rams.'

25 Cf. II Corinthians 12, 7: 'And lest I should be exalted above measure through the abundance of the revelations, there was given to me a thorn in the flesh, the messenger of Satan to buffet me, lest I should be exalted above measure.'

26 Cf. Luke 10, 42: 'But one thing is needful: and Mary hath chosen that good part, which shall not be taken away from her.'

27 In Greek mythology, Argus was a giant with a hundred eyes which took turns in watching over the beautiful Io.

28 Kierkegaard uses the Latin word *factum*, meaning an action or deed.

29 An allusion to Ludvig Holberg's play, *Den politiske Kandestøber.*

11

Johannes Climacus

Johannes Climacus was one of Kierkegaard's most prolific pseudonyms – the author, in particular, of *Philosophical Fragments* (1844) and *Concluding Unscientific Postscript* (1846). But he was also the subject of an incomplete short story called 'Johannes Climacus, or *De Omnibus Dubitandum Est*' ('Everything Should Be Doubted'), written when Kierkegaard was just beginning to embark on his career as an author, probably in 1842. Like the other great works of that time – *Repetition* and *Either/Or* – it proposes a philosophical argument against the Hegelian idea of a total system of knowledge, and it presents the argument in the form of a story.

By Kierkegaard's standards it is a very straightforward story: not an indirect first-person tale whose significance lies, at least in part, in the unreliability of its narrator, but a direct third-person narrative whose philosophical content is provided by the thoughts of its hero. Johannes Climacus is a young man living in a town rather like Copenhagen, of about the same generation as Kierkegaard himself; and he is passionately in love both with thinking and with the idea of living a life devoted to thought. People used to laugh at him when he was young, but he paid them no heed: he was utterly absorbed in a kind of fantasy life, sharing a strange intellectual existence with the only other person who mattered to him – his father. Johannes's father was also his teacher, and a man with a remarkable but recessive talent – a genius for extending the imagination of others by allowing them to think they are complete geniuses compared with him.

When the imaginative Johannes started attending the university, he was naturally eager to learn about philosophy in the high tradition, and hence about 'becoming a philosopher' (*at blive philosoph*) too.[1] He was enthralled by the injunction *de omnibus dubitandum est* – an echo, presumably, of the very first of Descartes's *Principles of Philosophy*, which states that 'The seeker after truth should, once in the course of his life, doubt everything, as far as it is possible.'[2] Indeed the principle came to sum up the whole of Johannes's existence – not because he found it easy to accept or even understand, but because, unlike all his teachers and his fellow students, he found it utterly challenging and perplexing. Everyone seemed to accept the proposition that 'modern philosophy [*den nyere Philosophie*, i.e. philosophy since the time of Descartes] begins with doubt', but Johannes was bewildered by it: what could 'modernity' mean, and if philosophy in other periods began somewhere else, why was it still called philosophy? So he started to wonder instead what could be meant by saying that philosophy as a whole begins with doubt: presumably, that admission to philosophy's universal certitudes was open only to those who have undergone a dark night of doubt. But this would put us in an impossible position, a double bind, since we would not be able to experience genuine doubt, and thus gain access to philosophy, if we knew in advance that our doubts would eventually be rewarded with certainty.

Johannes reflected that it must have been different for the very first philosopher, with no manuals of the history of philosophy to rely on and no teachers to guide him: he would have had to plunge into the depths of doubtfulness without any assurance that he would ever surface again. But if he survived the experience he would immediately be trapped in another dilemma, for if he turned what he had learned into a doctrine and communicated it to his pupils, then he would effectively prevent them from following him: their capacity to experience doubt would have been compromised by his assurances about the eventual return of certitude. Of course his pupils might try to get round the problem by forgetting their teacher, or indeed 'murdering' him; but even if they managed to cheat their way into an education in this way and thus to enjoy an authentic experience of doubt, the problem would catch up with them soon enough, since they could never pass on the hard-won fruits of their experience without having to be forgotten or murdered in their turn. Johannes is shocked: he always knew that 'a transformation must take place in anyone if they are to become a philosopher', but he had not realized that it might involve becoming a murderous Bluebeard.[3]

So Johannes turns to a third interpretation: that 'in order to philosophize one must have doubted', in which doubt is no longer treated as a constitutive part of philosophizing, but only as an optional preparation for it, rather like taking a walk or drinking a cup of coffee: but in that case, of course, doubt would lose its philosophical fascination.

This story of the discouragements which face Johannes in his quest for the meaning of philosophical doubt occupies the whole of part one of 'Johannes Climacus'. In part two he sets off to do some authentic doubting on his own account, though with a proper sense of the difficulty of the task. He begins to sense that the ancient Greek sceptics may have been wiser than the modern systematic philosophers, for they regarded doubt as a state of mind we should always aspire to rather than a phase which we pass through on our journey to something higher. But there the story breaks off, and we are left uncertain whether anyone can ever succeed in repeating the moment of doubt from which true philosophizing begins.

Kierkegaard never completed 'Johannes Climacus' and the story was first published as part of his Journals and Papers in 1869. It has not received much attention, though Hannah Arendt described it in 1958 as 'perhaps still the deepest interpretation of Descartes's doubt', adding that 'no one perhaps explored its true dimensions more honestly than Kierkegaard'.[4] And the incomplete story can serve as an introduction to Kierkegaard as well as to Descartes: a broad prospectus of his principal themes, and far less partial, obstreperous and domineering than *The Point of View for My Work as an Author*. It returns its readers to the questions that Kierkegaard made his own – about the relations between individual existence on the one hand and communication, teaching and tradition on the other, the origins of evil and of error and the nature of newness and repetition; and above all it brings us back to his first and abiding problem: the difficulty of 'becoming a philosopher'.

Notes

1   See for instance pp. 351, 354, 371 below.
2   'Veritatem inquirenti, semel in vita de omnibus, quantum fieri potest, esse dubitandum.' See René Descartes, *Principia Philosophiae* (1644), I, 1.
3   See below, pp. 370–1.
4   Hannah Arendt, *The Human Condition* (Chicago: Chicago University Press, 1958), p. 275, 275n.

Johannes Climacus, or
De Omnibus Dubitandum Est:
A Narrative

I speak of real doubt existing in the mind, not the kind of doubt we see when someone says he doubts, even though his spirit is not doubtful. The correction of the latter belongs not to Method, but to studies of stubbornness and its cure.[1]

Let no man despise thy youth.[2]

Please Note

Those who believe that philosophy has never been closer to solving its problems (or explaining all secrets) may well find it strange, vain, or even scandalous that I choose the narrative form rather than helping, in my humble way, to put the final coping stone on the System. On the other hand, those who are convinced that philosophy, in spite of all its definitions and distinctions, has never been more preposterous or confused – rather like the bizarre weather last winter when mussels and prawns and watercress were all for sale at the same time, so that you might think it was winter or spring or

The first English translation of *Johannes Climacus*, by T. H. Croxall, appeared in 1958, and a new version, by Howard V. Hong and Edna H. Hong, was published alongside *Philosophical Fragments* in *Kierkegaard's Writings* vol. VII, 1985. The present translation of the entire text as Kierkegaard left it (incomplete and sometimes a little inelegant or unclear) is by Jane Chamberlain and Jonathan Rée and appears here for the first time. Copyright © Jane Chamberlain and Jonathan Rée, 2001.

midsummer, depending which trader you listened to, while someone who listened to all of them at once would imagine that nature herself had become confused and the world would not last till Easter – they will certainly think it appropriate that I should be trying, by means of the narrative form, to counteract the vile untruthfulness of the modern [*nyere*] philosophy: a philosophy which differs from previous philosophy in realizing that, once we have made our claims and promises, it is ridiculous to go to the trouble of carrying them out. They will find it appropriate and will only regret, as I do, that the task is not being tackled by someone with rather more authority than me.

Introduction

Once upon a time in the city of H—— there lived a young student by the name of Johannes Climacus. He had no ambition to become prominent in the world – on the contrary, it was his joy to live in quiet seclusion. Those who knew him well tried to explain his self-sufficiency [*indesluttede væsen*] and his avoidance of closeness with others by imagining that he was either melancholy or in love. In a sense, the idea that he was in love was not far off the mark, though it would certainly be a mistake to suppose that he was dreaming about a girl. Such feelings were totally alien to his heart, and just as his external appearance was fine and ethereal – almost transparent – so his soul was far too intellectual or spiritual to be captivated by feminine beauty. He was in love – ardently in love – but with thought or, rather, with thinking. No young lover, stirred by the unintelligible transition through which love has been awakened in his breast, and by the stroke of lightning which kindles an answering love in the beloved, could be more deeply moved than he was by the intelligible transition through which one thought leads on to another. For him this transition was the happy moment when something he had intuited and anticipated in the silence of his soul really came to pass. When his pensive head was nodding like a ripe ear of corn, therefore, it was not because he was hearing the voice of his beloved, but because he was listening to the secret whispering of his thoughts. And if he gazed into the distance, it was not because he was contemplating her image but because he was observing the movement of an emerging thought. What pleased him most was to start with a single thought and then climb up step by step along the path of logical inference.

For Johannes logical inference was like a *scala paradisi* [a ladder reaching to heaven], and it seemed to him that his blessedness was even more glorious than that of the angels.[3] When he had climbed up to a higher thought it was his indescribable joy and passionate delight to plunge headlong back down the same chain of inferences till he reached the point from which he had started. He was not always as successful as he could have wished, and when he did not receive exactly the same number of bumps on his descent as there were links in the chain he became despondent, for that meant his movements had been imperfect. He would therefore start all over again. But if he succeeded his soul would thrill with delight; at night he would be unable to sleep for joy, and he would continue with the same movements for hours on end, so great was his pleasure in the up-and-down and down-and-up of thought. On such occasions he was at ease with himself; he almost floated. But at other times he grew anxious, and troubled with uncertainties. When the climbing was hard, it meant that the path of logical inference had not yet been cleared, and this would depress him, since he was frightened of losing the many inferences he had already made but which were not yet fully clear to him in their necessity. When we see someone carrying a precarious stack of fragile crockery, we are not surprised that he walks unsteadily, constantly struggling to keep his balance; but if we cannot see the crockery, we smile. Hence many people smiled at Johannes without suspecting that his soul was carrying a stack far taller than it would normally take to astonish us, and that he was anxious not to let a single logical inference fall, lest the whole lot should crash to the ground. He did not realize that people smiled at him on such occasions, any more than he noticed at other times when they turned cheerfully to watch him as he hurried through the streets as lightly as if he were dancing. He paid no attention to others, and never imagined that they might pay attention to him. He was and remained a stranger in the world.

But if young Johannes's behaviour seemed slightly odd to those who did not know him well, it made sense to anyone who understood something of his earlier life, for he was much the same now, at the age of twenty, as he had always been. His natural disposition was allowed free rein in childhood under the most favourable conditions. His home offered few diversions, and since he rarely went out he became accustomed from an early age to his own company and that of his thoughts. His father was very stern, and outwardly dry and prosaic, but under this plain cloak of severity there was a sparkling imagination which remained undimmed despite his great age. When Johannes asked permission to go out, he was usually refused, but by way of compensation his father would sometimes suggest that they hold hands and take a walk up and down the room. This might seem a poor substitute, and yet, like his blunt manner, it concealed something very different. Johannes would accept the offer, and was at complete liberty to choose where they should go. So they went through the city gate to a castle in the countryside, or out to the beach, or round and about the streets – wherever Johannes wished, for there was nothing his father could not do. While they walked up and down the room his father would describe everything they saw. They greeted passers-by, carriages clattered past and drowned his father's voice, the baker-woman's cakes were more tempting than ever. The descriptions of familiar scenes were so precise, so realistic, and so vivid, down to the most insignificant detail, and the descriptions of unfamiliar ones so elaborate and graphic, that after half an hour walking with his father Johannes felt as dazed and weary as if they had been gone for a whole day. Before long he developed magic powers like his father's, and then what had been an epic became a drama – their journeys became conversations rather than monologues. When they were following familiar paths, they kept an eye on each other to make sure they overlooked nothing. And if Johannes had never passed that way before, he would try to make things up on the basis of past experience, while his father applied his all-powerful imagination to creating whatever he wanted, turning every childish fancy into an ingredient of the unfolding drama. For Johannes it was as if the world came into existence through these conversations, as if his father was the Lord our God and he himself one of the elect, permitted to weave his own poor fancies into the drama however he pleased. His father never lost his composure and denied him nothing – every suggestion was incorporated, and always to Johannes's complete satisfaction.

In this way, life in his father's house encouraged the growth of Johannes's imagination – it taught him to relish ambrosia[4] – and so did the education he received at school. The immense authority of Latin grammar and the God-like majesty of its rules inspired a new enthusiasm in him, but it was Greek grammar that appealed to him above all – so much so that he forgot to read Homer out loud to himself, as he had once done in order to enjoy the poetic rhythms. His Greek teacher explained grammar on somewhat philosophical principles, and when he said, for example, that the accusative case implies a certain relationship in time and space, or that it is the relationship rather than the preposition that governs case, Johannes felt his world expand. Prepositions disappeared, and extension in time and space became like a vast empty canvas waiting to be filled with his intuitions. His imagination was busy once again, but not in the same way as before. What used to entertain him on his walks was a densely packed space in which he would wrap himself up as tightly as possible, for his imagination was so efficient that it needed very little to get it started. There were a few blades of grass outside the drawing room window, for instance, and when the young Johannes found some little creatures scurrying around amongst them, the setting had become an enormous forest, with the same dense darkness as the grass. Now, however, he was confronted with vast emptiness instead of density: when he looked again, there was nothing but endless expanse.

The power of his imagination grew steadily – both aesthetically and intellectually – but another aspect of his soul was growing alongside it: a feeling for the sudden and the surprising. This came about not through the ordinary magical means which children always find fascinating, but through something far higher. Johannes's father combined an irresistible dialectic with his powerful imagination, and when he engaged in discussions, Johannes was all ears – especially as they were conducted with a certain formality which was almost playful. His father would always allow his opponent to state his case, and take care to inquire whether he had anything to add before beginning his reply. Johannes, having followed the exposition with close attention, had in his own way acquired a vested interest in the outcome. Then came the pause, followed by his father's rejoinder . . . and in no time everything was altered. How it came about remained a mystery to Johannes, but the drama never failed to delight his soul. The opponent spoke again, and Johannes was still more attentive, determined that nothing should escape him. He would sum up, and Johannes could almost hear his own heart beating as he impatiently awaited the outcome. And sure enough . . . in no time everything was turned upside-down: the explicable became inexplicable, certainties grew doubtful, and the opposite position was now self-evidently correct. A shark has to turn on its back to catch its prey, since its mouth is on its belly side. Its back is dark, its belly silvery white, and the sudden change of colour must be a magnificent sight – perhaps flashing so brightly as to hurt the eyes, but wonderful to behold none the less. Johannes witnessed a similar switch listening to his father in debate. He might forget what had actually passed between his father and his opponent, but he could never forget the thrill in his soul. Nor did he lack similar experiences at school. He saw how a single word could change an entire sentence, and how a subjunctive in the middle of an indicative sentence could put everything in a different light. As he grew older, and more intimate with his father, he became more and more alert to this inexplicable quality. It was as if his father secretly understood what Johannes was going to say, and could therefore confound him completely with a single word. When his father was not simply opposing him, but expounding some idea of his own, Johannes observed how he went about it, and how he approached his goal in successive stages. He came to suspect that the reason his father could turn everything upside down with a single word must be that he, Johannes, had overlooked some link in the chain of thoughts.

Johannes took the same pleasure in quiet contemplation and the permutations of dialectic that other children get from the magic of poetry and the surprise of fairy tales. They were the delight of his childhood, the sport of his boyhood, and the yearning of his youth. Thus his life unfolded with exceptional steadiness, without any marked discontinuities between distinct periods of time. Johannes did not have to set aside his toys as he grew up, since from his earliest days he had learned to play with what would eventually be the most serious preoccupation of his life – and it never lost its attraction for him. A little girl plays with her doll for so long that it is gradually transformed into her lover, her husband, for love is a woman's whole life; and Johannes's life had a similar continuity, for his whole life was thinking.

Johannes entered the University, took the second examination, and reached the age of twenty, but still he did not change: he was and remained a stranger in the world. He did not avoid company, however; on the contrary, he sought out all those who were of like mind. Yet he did not express any opinions, or give any indication of what was going on inside him – his love ran too deep for that. He thought he would blush if he tried to talk about it, and he was afraid of knowing too little or finding out too much. On the other hand, he was always attentive when others spoke. Just as a young girl deeply in love will not talk about her love, yet listens with almost painful concentration when other girls talk about theirs (silently checking whether she is as happy or perhaps happier, and seizing on any hint to guide her), so Johannes observed everything in silence. And when he got home he would mull over what the philosophizers had said, since it was of course their company he had sought.

It never occurred to him to want to be a philosopher, or dedicate himself exclusively to Speculation; he was still far too restless for that. Of course thinking remained his only passion – he was no butterfly, flitting from one thing to another – but he did not yet have the self-discipline to achieve deep coherence. He was equally tempted by the significant and the insignificant as points of departure for his inquiries, and results were not important to him. All he was interested in was the movement of thought. From time to time he might notice that he kept arriving at the same result from very different starting points, but this did not engage his attention in any deeper sense. His delight lay in simply forging ahead. Wherever he suspected a labyrinth, he had to find a way through, and once he had started, nothing could distract him. If he found it difficult or grew tired, he would adopt a very simple remedy: he would shut himself away, carefully arrange everything in his room, and ceremoniously utter the following words: it *can* be done! From his father he had learned that one can always do what one wills, and the doctrine was fully confirmed by his father's way of life. Johannes took great pride in this lesson, and could not bear the thought of things that could never be done no matter how intensely one willed them. But Johannes's pride did not arise from weakness of will, since when he pronounced these energetic words he really was ready for anything, and he set himself a still higher goal – to forge through the labyrinthine complexities of the difficulty by sheer will-power. It was another inspiring adventure for him, and in this way his life never lacked adventure. His adventuring required neither forests nor long journeys, but only what he already possessed – a small room with a view.

Although his soul had always been inclined towards ideality, his faith and trust in actuality never faltered. The ideality which nourished him worked itself out so naturally, and he was so close to it, that ideality became actuality for him, and he counted on finding it in the actuality that surrounded him. In this respect he was helped by his father's melancholy. It took a long time for Johannes to understand how extraordinary, humanly speaking, his father was; he found him more astonishing than anyone else, but he met so few people in his father's house that he had no standard of comparison. Now and then when an old and trusted friend was visiting them, and engaging his father in confidential conversation, Johannes would hear his father saying, 'It's no use: I cannot do anything, and I only wish I could find a place for myself in an institution.' He was entirely serious, and there was no trace of irony in his words. Indeed, there was a dark seriousness in them which made Johannes anxious. And they were not spoken casually, for Johannes's father was capable of demonstrating that the most insignificant person in the world was a genius compared to himself. Counter-arguments were of no avail, since the irresistible force of his dialectic could transfix his listeners as if there were nothing else in the world, making them forget facts which were staring them in the face. Johannes's whole outlook on life was so bound up with his father (indeed he saw very little of anyone else) that he became entangled in a contradiction. For a long time he failed to realize that his father contradicted himself – not least in the virtuosity with which he could defeat all challengers and reduce them to silence. Hence Johannes's confidence in actuality was undiminished: he had not absorbed ideality from the kind of books which persuade those they nurture that the glory they describe is too good for this world, and he had been educated by a teacher who, instead of making his knowledge appear valuable, knew how to make it seem as worthless and insignificant as could be.

Part One, in which Johannes Climacus Begins to Philosophize with the Help of Traditional Ideas

Introduction

Although he had been at the University for several years, Johannes had not read very much, especially for a student. He had made a thorough study of the classics at grammar school, and now and then he enjoyed going through them again, though they had no connection with the deep stirrings within him. Occasionally he would come across some modern book or other, but he never had any clear idea what significance it was supposed to have. Historical studies did not interest him much: the predominant tendency of his mind had destroyed his sense of empirical actuality, and just as he was uninterested in anything that people said or did unless it had some relation to thinking, so he was indifferent to accounts of the deeds and thoughts of those who had lived in earlier times. If he came across a modern philosophical work he would not put it aside unread, but after reading it he would grow dissatisfied and listless. His whole cast of mind made him uncomfortable about reading. Sometimes a title would tempt him, and then he would take up a book in happy anticipation. But then . . . it would turn out to deal with lots of extraneous questions and to have very little to say about its purported topic. If he worked at it and eventually unearthed something like what the title had promised, then the reasoning would usually prove to be so fractured that the issue was left undecided. It often irritated him to see so much attention paid to things that seemed merely incidental. The author would interrupt his exposition in order to correct some recondite opinion put forward by an author Johannes had never heard of, and Johannes would not be able to understand the digression without reading that author's work, which in turn would probably presuppose others, and so on. He also sometimes thought that the reason the opinion of a particular author had been included was very peculiar: he lived in the same town as the writer, for example, or wrote for the same journal. He did not always find strict dialectical movement, and sorely missed the wondrous spectacle of the dialectic with all its mysterious surprises. After several such attempts he gave up reading and abandoned himself to his own thoughts again, even though they might lead nowhere. Meanwhile he refrained from over-hasty judgements about particular books or books in general. On hearing others judge very differently, he concluded that it was his own fault and that his education had been imperfect, though it had at least taught him to recognize as much.

He also realized, from listening to what others had to say, that he was not acquainted with the writings of the great thinkers of modern philosophy. He often heard their names mentioned with an enthusiasm bordering on reverence, and this gave him indescribable joy, though he would not dare read their works, as they were said to be so difficult that they required years of study. It was not cowardice or indolence that deterred him, but a painful sense, which had been with him since early childhood, that he was different from other people. He was far from happy about this difference; indeed he regarded it as a burden he would probably have to bear all his life. He was like a child who could not help remembering the pain that attended his birth, though his mother had forgotten it entirely in her joy over her new baby.

As for his reading, Johannes now encountered a curious contradiction. He was not satisfied by the books he had read, but he dared not blame the writings themselves; and he did not have the confidence to approach the great books directly. He therefore read less and less, and followed his inclination to ponder his thoughts in silence. He became increasingly shy and withdrawn, fearing that thinkers of distinction might smile at him if they heard that he was hoping to become a thinker, just as fine ladies smile at the presumption of a poor girl who longs for the bliss of love. He remained silent, but listened with ever closer attention.

Attending to other people's conversations, he noticed one theme that cropped up again and again, and he seized upon it and made it the object of his thinking. So it was that fate came to his aid and provided him with exactly what he needed. The purer his task – the more virginal, so to speak – the more he prized it; and the less help he had with his thinking, the better everything went and the happier he became. Nevertheless he considered it an imperfection that he could think his thoughts best when he came across them like freshly fallen snow, innocent of any trace of others, for he had a great regard for those who, unlike him, could grapple with the manifold thoughts of manifold thinkers. His pain was soon forgotten, however, in the joy of thinking.

The conversations he heard drew his attention to one proposition in particular, which came up over and over again, and was invariably praised and revered as it passed from mouth to mouth: *De omnibus dubitandum est* – 'Everything should be doubted.' He heard it repeated many times, and it came to be decisive for him. Sometimes a name can epitomize the whole story of a life; and so it was with this proposition for Johannes. It became a task for his thinking. He did not know how long it would take before he had thought it through to the end, but he knew he would not let go of it before that moment came, even if it should cost him his life.

What inspired him even more was the relationship generally posited between this proposition and the process of becoming a philosopher. He did not know if he would ever manage to become a philosopher, but he would certainly try; and with quiet solemnity it was decreed that he should begin. He strengthened his resolve by reminding himself of the courageous Dion, who had said – as he set out to sea with a small band of men to begin his war against Dionysius – 'I will be satisfied to have taken part; if I should die the moment I set foot on land, without achieving anything, I will still regard my death as fortunate and glorious.'[5]

Johannes now set about trying to understand how the proposition that everything should be doubted related to philosophy. The task would be a bracing overture; the more clarity he could achieve, the more enthusiastically he would be able to proceed to philosophy as such. So he retreated into himself with his philosophical thesis, while looking around for every clue he could find. If he noticed his thoughts diverging from other people's, he tried to memorize theirs and went home to begin again from the beginning. The speed with which they reached their conclusions startled him, but he saw this as yet another sign of their superiority.

So he set to work, and began by laying out the three main theses he had heard concerning the relationship of doubt to philosophy. The theses were as follows:

(1) philosophy begins with doubt;
(2) in order to philosophize one must have doubted; and
(3) modern [*nyere*] philosophy begins with doubt.

Chapter One: Modern philosophy begins with doubt

What immediately struck him about the three theses was that they seemed to be of very different kinds. For whilst the first two were strictly philo-sophical, on account of their universality (they made general statements about philosophy or philosophizers in all times and places), the third appeared to be a historical report, and it would have to undergo a transformation before it could claim to be philosophical in the strict sense of the word. It might of course be historically interesting to know that modern philosophy begins with doubt, in the same way as it might be interesting to know whether it began in Germany or France, and with whom. On the other hand, if the thesis underwent a philosophical transformation, it could probably be sub-sumed under one of the others. So, hoping to ascertain whether this might be possible, Johannes decided to explore the thesis in more detail.

§1 How should the third thesis be understood literally?
First he tried to work out what could be meant by attaching the adjective 'modern' – which is of course a historical predicate – to the word 'philoso-phy'. It seemed to imply that the thesis was restricted to a particular histori-cal form of philosophy. Since he had neither the scholarship nor the experience to investigate the question for himself, he decided to assume that the thesis was true, and then noted the implication – unless the thesis was very badly formulated – that there must have been a more ancient form of philosophy which began differently. Then he started to wonder whether this

meant that a future form of philosophy might begin in yet another way, so that philosophy could begin in several different ways without ceasing to be philosophy. To be as brief as possible, he wondered whether a future philosophy could begin in exactly the same way as the more ancient philosophy and still be philosophy, or whether modern philosophy's having begun with doubt could have a decisive influence on the future. And in that case, might it also have retroactive power, raising doubt as to whether the more ancient philosophy could still be considered philosophy if it began with something other than doubt? In other words, if the beginning of modern philosophy excludes the possibility of a different beginning forever, then it must be a beginning in more than a historical sense — it must be an essential beginning. In that case modern philosophy would be the only true philosophy, and the more ancient version would be called philosophy only as a courtesy. And if the third thesis (that modern philosophy begins with doubt) is interpreted in this way, then it will have undergone a transformation and become identical with the first — that philosophy begins with doubt.

Johannes had no idea if this was philosophy's opinion, and he listened in vain for enlightening hints in other people's conversations. If it was, then it struck him as strange that people should express themselves so loosely, mixing eternal categories with historical ones in such a way that when they said something which seemed historical they really meant something eternal. Why did they not stick to the first thesis — that philosophy begins with doubt — since then nothing would be left in doubt, as anything that did not begin with doubt would not be philosophy, whatever else it might be? This would of course have the strange implication that the eternal beginning had a beginning in time, so that there would need to have been a time when it had not yet begun — whereas Johannes imagined that the eternal beginning must always have existed. As he understood it, philosophy had always had difficulty with the claim that Christianity came into the world through a beginning that was both historical and eternal; so it would be very problematic for philosophy to claim the same thing about itself.

Johannes now considered the words of the third thesis from a different angle. It speaks not of an individual philosopher who, as history relates, began by doubting; rather it speaks of modern *philosophy* as a whole. And it does not employ the past tense, nor even the historical present (as when we say 'Descartes begins with doubt', referring to an event in the past through a present-tense historical narrative). The thesis that modern philosophy begins with doubt uses the eternal present, as if what it claimed were more than merely historical, and as if modern philosophy were more than individual philosophers.

And there was another reason for thinking that what the thesis claims is not merely historical. We must of course assume that modern philosophy is still in the process of coming into existence, since otherwise we would be confronted with a more modern philosophy in relation to which it would no longer be modern. But is it not conceivable that modern philosophy, as it rose to dominance, could have become conscious that it began incorrectly, and that its beginning was not really a beginning after all? On what authority would this beginning be treated as the beginning of modern philosophy as a whole? Surely this could not be justified unless the beginning itself were the essential beginning for modern philosophy – which could only be settled, historically speaking, after modern philosophy had finally come to an end. If the thesis is to be affirmed before that time, then it has to be interpreted eternally – with the implication that this beginning is the essential beginning for every conceivable philosophy. But in that case, the thesis that modern philosophy begins with doubt has again been transformed and made identical with the first thesis, that philosophy begins with doubt.

Why then has philosophy made use of two different formulations, which either mean the same as each other, so that one of them must be incorrect, or else mean different things, so that one of them must be obscure?

This apparent ambiguity might have made Johannes hesitate about going further, but he nevertheless decided to examine what the implications of the thesis would be if it were taken in a historical sense. As such it was of course distinct from the first thesis, and his only option was to assume either that it was completely superfluous and confusing, or that it was a historical thesis somewhat strangely expressed.

§2   How did it come to pass that modern philosophy began with doubt?
Johannes now inquired how it had come to pass that modern philosophy began with doubt – assuming that it had – and whether it happened by accident or necessity, in other words, whether its beginning was accidental or necessary.

(a) WAS IT BY ACCIDENT THAT MODERN PHILOSOPHY BEGAN WITH DOUBT?
Johannes wondered whether it could have been the kind of accident which would always remain an accident – like the accident by which purple dye was discovered.[6] In that case the thesis that 'modern philosophy begins with doubt' would refer to a historical accident with no implications for philosophy before or since, or for philosophy in general; after all, we cannot conclude from what happened to that particular dog that every dog is going to discover purple dye. The thesis would then amount to no more than a historical report, but then it contradicts the first thesis – that philosophy begins

with doubt – since if the two are compared it would appear that the essential came about by accident.

Next he wondered whether the accident by which modern philosophy began with doubt might be of such a kind as to conceal within itself a necessity by which the accident would be explained a moment after it happened – like the accident by which Newton discovered the law of gravitation: it was of course an accident, but the moment it happened it revealed the law which showed that the accident was itself a necessity. In that case it would be only in an imperfect historical sense that it could seem accidental that modern philosophy began with doubt, since the moment it happened, modern philosophy would have discovered that this beginning was necessary. Regarded as a historical fact, however, modern philosophy could not yet have established this necessity, since it still has not reached its conclusion. The only way the necessity could be demonstrated, then, would be in an eternal sense, in so far as modern philosophy was identical with philosophy in general. The revelation about the beginning of philosophy would thus be decisive for the future as a whole, as well as retroactively valid for the entire past. Thus the thesis would have undergone a transformation and become identical with the first thesis again.

(b) WAS IT BY NECESSITY THAT MODERN PHILOSOPHY BEGAN WITH DOUBT?

Johannes now turned to the question of what came before modern philosophy: was it philosophy or something else, and how did it make it necessary that modern philosophy began with doubt? Given the wording of the thesis, it seemed to him that it must have been philosophy. But what would this philosophy have had to be like to make it necessary that modern philosophy begin with doubt? Were these two philosophies – modern philosophy, and the philosophy which preceded it and made it necessary that it begin with doubt – the only ones which deserved to be called philosophy? And supposing there had been earlier philosophies which began in some other way . . . would they have to relinquish their claim to the title of philosophy?

Johannes then wondered whether the philosophy that preceded modern philosophy had itself begun by accident or necessity. So as not to be led too far afield, he concentrated on the following proposition: if modern philosophy necessarily begins with doubt, then its beginning is determined in continuity with some earlier philosophy. Hence if we want to say something historical about the beginning of modern philosophy, we must describe the beginning of the previous philosophy, since the beginning of modern philosophy would be a consequence of that earlier beginning. (And this assumption would of course have a disruptive effect on the first thesis – that philosophy begins with doubt.) Here Johannes noted a problem which he would need to confront later − that such a connection would be difficult to think, since the beginning with which modern philosophy began was supposed to be a break from the past. So it would have to be a special kind of connection − a connection through which an effect is produced by its opposite. A connection of this kind is usually called a leap.

Meanwhile Johannes did his best to cling to the thought that it was by necessity that modern philosophy began with doubt. He therefore drew the conclusion that the beginning of modern philosophy must be an essential beginning for philosophy as such, since we could never be justified in asserting anything (except in a purely historical and accidental sense) about the essential nature of a process before it has concluded. After all, it might later become apparent that the beginning was simply a misunderstanding, and so not really a beginning at all, and certainly not a beginning for philosophy. No beginning philosopher could ever be justified in saying 'modern philosophy begins with me', and endorsements by his successors would not help either − unless of course the assertion concerned the essential nature of philosophy as such. Interpreted in this way, the third thesis (that modern philosophy begins with doubt) was once again transformed into the first (that philosophy begins with doubt).

§3 Intimations

It pained him; but despite all his efforts, Johannes had not advanced a single step. He found it hard to accept that the third thesis was identical with the first, since such tautologies were disconcerting and could not inspire confidence. They were disconcerting because they encouraged people to think there were several thoughts where in fact there was only one. If the two theses were treated as if they meant the same thing, then there was a disconcerting tautology. He could not keep them distinct except by modifying the thesis and reducing it to a historical triviality, such as 'Descartes began with doubt and many others followed his example.' Philosophically speaking, it would be impossible to take exception to such a statement, and any difficulties it presented would be of a purely historical kind − had anyone actually claimed to have followed his example in this way, for instance, or had they really done what they claimed?

Johannes had hoped that the difficulty would be cleared up for him if he listened to what others had to say − but in vain. They used the first and third theses as if they were completely interchangeable; sometimes the one, sometimes the other, and sometimes both at once. One philosophizer would state one of the theses, another would respond with the other, and they would assume they were both talking about the same thing. They never explained the thesis, though an explanation was precisely what Johannes needed, and his own private thinking had made him all the more receptive to guidance from others. But no explanation was forthcoming; on the contrary, they repeated the thesis at such a rate that the relentless uniformity almost made him dizzy. It was giving him the utmost difficulty, yet they seemed to find it easy and could chat about it carelessly. Johannes would always return home with a troubled mind.

He went over the thesis again and again, trying to forget his previous thoughts and get back to the beginning; but he always ended up at the same point. He could not let it go, however; it was as though he was drawn to the thesis by a mysterious power – as though someone were whispering in his ear: 'Behind this misunderstanding something lies hidden.' He now tried to bring together the elements he had put asunder when he thought that the thesis must be either purely philosophical or purely historical. It is certainly a mystery, he thought, that modern philosophy can be both historical and eternal at the same time and, moreover, that it can be aware of the fact. The unity must be like that of the two natures of Christ. Modern philosophy becomes conscious of its eternal significance with every step it takes, or, rather, it must be conscious of it before it takes its first step: otherwise the step might be such that philosophy could never acquire eternal significance – unless by chance the historical development of philosophy was absolutely identical with the movement of the Idea itself. But then such a development would not really be historical, and modern philosophy would not need to undergo any transformation, any retrospective transfiguration, any purification of forgetfulness, in order to be taken up into the System. It would all fit straight into the System down to the most insignificant detail, just as a historical human being who was so poetic that all his words and gestures were pure poetry would not have to undergo any transformation in order to step onto the stage – he could go on as he is, straight from the street without the slightest embarrassment.

But Johannes could not yet work out how to bring the two elements together. His soul was troubled, full of premonitory anxiety, and he sensed that being a philosopher must be something extraordinary – that being a philosopher nowadays must be indescribably difficult. If this was the condition of modern philosophy, then it must be the same for individual philosophers. Individual philosophers *would have to become conscious of themselves, and in this self-consciousness they would have to become conscious of their significance as a moment in modern philosophy as well. And modern philosophy would in turn have to become conscious of itself as a moment in the philosophy that came before, which in turn would have to become conscious of itself as a moment in the historical unfolding of the perennial philosophy.* The consciousness of individual philosophers would therefore have to encompass the most dizzying contrasts: on the one hand their own personality and their own little contribution to philosophy, and on the other the philosophy of the whole world as the unfolding of the perennial philosophy.

It was a long time before Johannes could grasp this monstrous thought correctly and distinctly. He was like a man pushing a heavy load up a mountain, so overwhelmed on occasion that his foot would slip and the load start rolling back again. Eventually, however, he became confident that he could make the movement with ease, and decided to let the thought work with all its weight – for he drew a distinction between the difficulty of the thinking and the weight of the thought. As a historical thought, it was easily grasped. He had mustered new strength, felt sure of himself, so he put his back into the idea, so to speak . . . and then it overwhelmed him and he *fainted*. When he regained consciousness he hardly dared turn his attention to it again; he realized that it was a thought that could drive people mad, at least if their nerves were no stronger than his. He had ever more admiration for those who could grasp such thoughts as if they were all just child's play.

He became discouraged, but even as he was sinking into dejection he grasped the monstrous thought almost in spite of himself. He was too upset to think clearly, but it occurred to him that the monstrous thought, though it had at first struck him as extremely positive, might really be a form of scepticism, since it implied that an individual had no knowledge except of himself as a moment [*moment*] and of his significance as a moment. If this was really a possibility – and he was still not sure he could really grasp it – then it was not clear to him how a moment could become conscious of itself purely as a moment. Such a consciousness would require a consciousness that was more than a consciousness of itself as a moment, since otherwise it would have to reside in someone else – in which case it would become purely relative, and very far removed from absolute knowledge. But how could individual moments become conscious of their eternal validity as moments in a whole? They could not, unless individuals were omniscient; but in that case the world would already have come to an end.

He could perhaps see how a single individual might become conscious of the eternal; and presumably the earlier philosophy – if there was such a thing – had been of the same opinion. But to become conscious of the eternal in the process of concrete history as a whole, and to do so by a standard which did not apply merely to the past – this he believed must be reserved for the deity. Nor could he grasp how, at a particular moment of time, anyone could be so transfigured as to become past to themselves, while still remaining present to themselves. He believed that this was possible only in eternity, and that the eternal exists in time only in a purely abstract sense.

The individual philosophers of an earlier age would presumably have drawn on their predecessors too. They would have realized that they could adopt some things and correct others, but the thought of an eternal necessity by which philosophers always emerged from their predecessors in an eternal continuity would never have crossed their minds. Even though we might get some sense of such an inner necessity by thinking about the past (though the more distant it was, the greater the chances of being deceived), it seemed to him impossible with regard to the present. The present was not given leave to become present out of eagerness that it should become past – and the sooner the better – since then it would become neither. This was made clear to Johannes through the observation of personal lives. When we look back over our lives they may appear to be permeated by necessity, especially in the earlier years. But if we refused to set out on a new phase without first understanding its eternal validity as a moment in our lives, then we would prevent it from acquiring its significance, since by insisting that the present should manifest itself as past and present in the same moment, we would have transcended it before it ever happened.

Johannes considered prophecy a very questionable undertaking. And yet, if we can sense a certain necessity in the past, we can also imagine discovering it in the future. But philosophy seems to have set its heart on something far harder – it wants to bathe everything in the thought of eternity and necessity, and to do so in the present moment, which means slaying the present with the thought of eternity while still preserving its fresh life. It means wanting to see what happens both as having already happened and as happening still; it means wanting to know the future both as present and as future.

This is how far Johannes had progressed in his consideration of the thesis. Of course the process took a long time – far longer than it has taken to recount it here; it cost him time and hard work. Yet he still had scant reward for his pains, for if he were to venture an opinion on the substance of the first thesis it would have to be that it was simply impossible – which he did not have the courage to believe.

Chapter Two: Philosophy begins with doubt

Johannes now began to compare the first thesis – that philosophy begins with doubt – with thesis two, which states that in order to philosophize one must first have doubted. He could easily see that they did not say the same thing, for while the first states that doubt is the beginning of philosophy, the second treats it as preceding the beginning. He had turned his attention to the three theses in the hope that they might among other things shed light on the relation between philosophy and the statement *de omnibus dubitandum est*, and hence improve his prospects of gaining admission to philosophy. Thesis one therefore gladdened him, as it seemed to offer the quickest route. It did not speak of doubt as something that precedes philosophy; rather, it stated that when in doubt we are already at the beginning of philosophy.

§1   Is the first thesis identical with thesis three?

Johannes found it strange that doubt should be integral to philosophy. It seemed to him that this thesis developed in the opposite way to thesis three (that modern philosophy begins with doubt). Thesis three seemed to be historical, but turned out on closer examination to be philosophical, even if he found it impossible to understand it as such. The first thesis, on the other hand, appeared at first glance to be philosophical, since it describes philosophy in general, but on closer inspection it seemed to be historical. It asserts that philosophy begins with a negative principle, but one directed not only against principles lying outside philosophy, but also against a principle which belongs within it. This implies an antecedent, however, since it would obviously be absurd to polemicize against nothing. But if the antecedent was not itself a principle, then the polemic would be unworthy of philosophy – indeed the thesis would be positive rather than negative, for the polemic would be intended merely to exclude what was alien to it, and would not really be a polemic so much as a declaration of some higher principle. But the thesis cannot abrogate its polemic against something of the same nature as itself, since a negative principle can never be ignorant of what it excludes, though an immediate positive principle can be. The thesis itself therefore implies an antecedent philosophical principle.

If philosophy had begun with a positive principle, we would certainly have no right to draw any historical conclusions from it. Johannes knew that the ancient Greeks maintained that philosophy begins with wonder; but this kind of principle cannot give rise to historical consequences. If a later thinker were to promulgate the same doctrine, we could not assume that he thought we should begin with wonder at the wonderment of Plato and Aristotle. For wonder is an immediate category, involving no reflection on itself – unlike doubt, which is a reflection-category. Later philosophers who say 'Philosophy begins with wonder' put themselves in direct continuity with the ancient Greeks. The Greeks wondered, and later philosophers wonder too, even if they wonder at different things. When later philosophers utter or repeat the words 'Philosophy begins with doubt', however, then the continuity is broken, for doubt is precisely a polemic against what went before. The more important the person who repeats the thesis of doubt, the greater the break; but the more important the person repeating the thesis of wonderment, the more the continuity is confirmed and strengthened. Of course the thesis of doubt is also confirmed by repetition, but its confirmation serves precisely to emphasize the break.

The more he thought about the thesis, the more historical it seemed and the closer to thesis three; thus, by a reverse process, he ended up at the same position as before. But that was not all, for he discovered a new difficulty as well. Johannes could understand how particular individuals might take it into their heads to doubt, but he could not see why they should think of mentioning it to other people – especially when they offered it as advice (it would have been different if they meant it as a warning). The recipients of such advice, provided they were not extremely slow-witted, would surely respond by saying: 'Thank you very much, but forgive me if I also doubt the correctness of that statement.' The first group might be pleased by such gratitude, announcing to a third group that they were now in agreement about doubting everything; but the declaration would be a mockery, since the supposed agreement would be no more than a thoroughly abstract expression of disagreement – unless of course they were so impolite as to regard each other as of no account. But this would be another contradiction, since it would be pointless to advance the thesis unless one believed oneself to count for something, and not only oneself but one's audience too – otherwise it would not be worth initiating them into it. Nor could the first group get angry at the second, since they could not want them to be less perfect than themselves, let alone inconsistent – just as Anaxarchus in antiquity, when he fell into a deep ditch, could not get angry as Pyrrho walked past without offering to help: on the contrary Anaxarchus praised Pyrrho for demonstrating that he agreed that philosophers ought to be calm and dispassionate.[7]

Although Johannes could certainly appreciate this point, he was too timid to be so consistent with regard to highly prized truths. It might be inconsistent for a genius to demand such consistency, but it was consistent for a lowly student to do so. He was fully aware of the imperfection of his way of appropriating the truth, but that was not enough to make him abandon the thesis. So he tried to think it over yet again to try to find out how he could enter into relation to it. He was not yet ready to consider the thesis itself, for he first had to establish whether he could relate to it successfully. Hence he did not ask such questions as: is doubt, as the beginning, a part of philosophy or is it the whole? And if it is only a part of philosophy, then what of the other part? Could it perhaps consist in certainty? And are these two parts put asunder for all eternity? How can we speak of a whole if the parts exclude each other? Epicurus's sophistical remark about how we should not fear death – when I am, death is not, and when death is, I am not –

seemed applicable here:[8] could anything unite the two parts into a single whole? But Johannes did not spend time on such questions; his only concern was the relation between the thesis and particular individuals.

§2   How do particular individuals relate to the first thesis?
When Johannes found himself unable to ask questions, he felt as if thought was twining itself alarmingly around him; but if he could ask questions he was happy – thought unfolded itself for him in dialogue and he could escape. One day, when his soul was pregnantly pondering this question, he overheard one of the philosophizers saying: 'The thesis does not belong to any particular philosophy – it is part of the perennial philosophy, which is embraced by all who wish to dedicate themselves to philosophy.' Johannes trembled with delight at the thrill of enthusiasm that ran through the audience as these words were spoken. He hurried back home happier than Robinson Crusoe when he found Friday, repeating the words to himself to make sure his memory would not fail him.

The perennial philosophy, he said to himself, the perennial philosophy – but what did perennial mean? It sounded glorious, and no epithet could be too glorious for philosophy; yet surely a glorious epithet ought to be clear and perspicuous too. *The perennial philosophy.* Was it a philosophy indifferent to time? In that case it would have to be the most abstract philosophy – a philosophy which in its abstraction had neither beginning nor end. But that could not be right, since the thesis spoke of a beginning. Or was it a philosophy that contained history within itself – the blessed transfiguration of philosophy's inner riches, comparable perhaps to the transfiguration in eternity which all of us expect when our life comes to an end? If so, then strictly speaking it could be approached only by way of anticipation. Johannes was already beginning to feel discouraged; those powerfully inspiring words were proving so treacherous! He still put his trust in the last part of the statement: 'the perennial philosophy is embraced by all who want to dedicate themselves to philosophy', but no one gave any hints as to how to set about it. What was the good of saying that there is a perennial philosophy which everyone should embrace, if no one could find out how to approach it, or if no one even knew, or at any rate if no one in the audience knew any better than he did? And yet it pained him; the words seemed to him so beautiful that he could not help dwelling on them, just as we might gaze wistfully at wild geese flying across the sky. If we want to belong to that world then we must join them, and yet no one has ever been seen flying with a flock of wild geese.

The words of the philosophizer had not helped Johannes on his way; in fact, after closer consideration, they seemed to lead to precisely the place where he had been about to begin before he heard them, for that was precisely what he wanted to investigate – how particular individuals ought to relate to the thesis, and how they could thereby come to embrace philosophy. He realised how unedifying this coincidence was, since it could well mean that he, as a beginner, had to begin where others had already ended. Hence his apparent similarity to them. The conclusion of a mathematical proof resembles the beginning in just the same way. The proof begins, for example, with the statement that: 'The square on the hypotenuse of a right-angled triangle is equal to the sum of the squares on the other two sides', and it ends with exactly the same statement, except that it is now followed by: QED – *quod erat demonstrandum* [as was to be proved]. It pained him to find the philosophizers conducting themselves in this way. They should be ashamed of never explaining anything, since there might well be people listening who really needed an explanation.

Johannes was about to abandon himself once more to the drift of his own thoughts, and the question was already hovering on his lips, when he was brought up short by one of the philosophizers making what was apparently an extremely important remark. The thesis that 'philosophy begins with doubt' was a regular subject for discussion, but now he heard it said that the beginning of philosophy is threefold: it has its *absolute* beginning in the concept that is also the end of the System, the concept of Absolute Spirit; but its *objective* beginning lies in the concept of absolutely indeterminate being, the simplest determination that exists; and its *subjective* beginning is the labour by which consciousness raises itself to the level of thinking and to positing the abstract.

Johannes found fresh encouragement in this remark. It seemed solid and trustworthy, and even if it lacked the power of intoxicating inspiration, it still seemed clear and level-headed. But he found it strange: it was supposed to shed light on the thesis about philosophy's beginning with doubt by explaining that philosophy has a threefold beginning and by naming each part separately – and yet none of the three referred to philosophy beginning with doubt. This might mean that philosophy has four beginnings, with doubt as the fourth, but then he was in the awkward position of having to assume that the explanation explained everything except what needed to be explained. It was clear that if any of the three beginnings was the one that interested him, it could only be the third, since reflection on philosophy's absolute and objective beginnings would have to be left to those who had already become philosophers. The subjective beginning, on the other hand, was certainly the one through which an individual who was not yet a philosopher could begin to become one. So this had to be the one that interested him, though of course he was not concerned with the relation of the thesis to philosophy, but only with his own relationship to the thesis and hence his possible relation to philosophy.

'The *subjective* beginning', it was said, 'is the labour by which consciousness raises itself to the level of thinking and to positing the abstract.' Johannes considered this statement very beautiful and extremely uplifting, but still his consciousness was not uplifted by it. If this was the beginning that interested him, it was not clear why it now took a positive form instead of the usual negative one. He was well aware that we could arrive at the same point either by raising ourselves up or by doubt, but the connection would obviously be completely different in each case. If some people raise themselves above the world of the senses in order to philosophize, while others doubt the world of the senses from the same motive, they may end up in the same place, but their movements will have been different – and the movements were of course precisely Johannes's concern. Moreover, since raising oneself up is a positive principle, it does not – unlike the principle of doubt – imply any historical conclusions about the philosophy that preceded it. So how can the two formulations – doubting or raising oneself up – be regarded as interchangeable? It would obviously be absurd, since they are not identical. But why use two different formulations? Why use the easier expression to explain the more difficult one, when it really refers to something very different and not what it is supposed to explain? The statement he heard repeated over and over again was: philosophy begins with doubt; the other statement (about the subjective beginning) was far less common. Was the latter in fact the real thesis, then, and the former merely a misunderstanding? Even if that were possible – which of course it was not – the thesis would presumably still require some explanation, and saying that 'the beginning is the act by which one begins' is not much help. It was therefore necessary to get clearer about the nature of this act and also how individuals can become capable of performing it.

Johannes therefore resolved to begin where he had originally meant to begin, following the inclination of the question as he felt it in his soul.

(a) HOW DOES AN INDIVIDUAL WHO AFFIRMS THE FIRST THESIS RELATE TO IT?
Bearing all this in mind, Johannes now wondered whether the thesis (that philosophy begins with doubt) had existed in the temporal sense at all times, so that everyone had always been aware of it even if no one had ever stated it explicitly. Was it valid in the same way as 'All men are mortal'? Did it state something which, though perhaps unknown, had always been the case? Did it involve something immediately inherent in human nature? Was it perhaps similar to wonder, for even if no one had ever explained the meaning of wonder, still everyone would have experienced it? Alternatively, had the thesis

always existed in the eternal sense, and yet been discovered in time? Was it valid in the same way as mathematical propositions, which, when discovered, are discovered in their eternity? Would it continue to exist in the eternal sense at all times, just as philosophical theses do? Was the personality of the discoverer a matter of indifference, as it is with mathematical and metaphysical theses, or was it important to know the personality through which it was asserted? We certainly need to know something about the personality behind a religious thesis, and to some extent an ethical thesis too. Anyone can utter a religious or ethical thesis, after all, but it will not be really religious or ethical in everyone's mouth – unless we assume that it makes no difference whether it was Christ or someone else who said he was the Son of God, or whether 'Know thyself' was said by someone who really knew himself. The thesis remains the same, yet it becomes different – in the one case it is a thesis, in the other mere chatter, whereas with a mathematical thesis it makes no difference whatsoever whether it is asserted by Archimedes or by tradition, as long as it is asserted correctly. In the one case personality means everything, in the other nothing, just as in civic life anyone has the formal right to act as a guarantor, and yet it makes all the difference who the guarantor is.

So what is required in the personality of those who assert the thesis? Must they be talented, and would talent be sufficient to authorize them in asserting the thesis? The assertion of a mathematical proposition requires mathematical talent; a talent demonstrated by anyone who can make such an assertion. Even if we could imagine it being stated by someone with no talent (which would be utterly absurd, since talent would be manifested in the presentation), the thesis would still retain its truth, its mathematical truth – that is, its essential truth – just as in civic life a bond payable to the bearer is equally valid whether it is held by a rich man or a pauper, a thief or its rightful owner. It is quite different with religious and ethical propositions. If we taught a 2-year-old a mathematical thesis, it would essentially be just as true in the child's mouth as in the mouth of Pythagoras. But if we taught the child to say: 'I believe in the existence of God' or 'Know thyself', no one would pay any heed. Apparently talent itself is not a sufficient authority in this case. Religious and ethical truths surely require something different, or a different kind of authority, or rather what we might call genuine authority, since there is certainly a distinction between talent and authority. Even if someone had sufficient talent to assert such a thesis and understand all its implications, he might still not believe or practise it himself, and in that case the thesis would be historical or metaphysical rather than religious or ethical.

It was clear to Johannes that the thesis that interested him had to belong with the subjective beginning, since there could not be four beginnings to philosophy – and even if there were, the conclusion would remain the same. This was confirmed by the fact that it would be ridiculous to talk about objective doubt, since objective doubt is not doubt but deliberation. Like any philosophical thesis, therefore, it could not lay claim to mathematical necessity, but neither did it have the necessity of theses in absolute and objective philosophy. The thesis therefore had to be such that it could only be asserted by those who understand it and have the necessary talent and authority.

(b) HOW DOES THE INDIVIDUAL TO WHOM THE FIRST THESIS IS PROPOSED RELATE TO THE INDIVIDUAL WHO PROPOUNDS IT?

At this point Johannes realized that some of the questions he faced were simply the obverse of previous questions, so that he could deal with them quite swiftly. He wondered whether, like the thesis that all men are mortal, the thesis that philosophy begins with doubt continues to validate itself once it has been proposed, whether we like it or not. Was its validity so necessary that by denying it we would expose ourselves to a reverse inference, just as those who deny a mathematical thesis must be prepared for the inference that they have no head for mathematics? Was the thesis like a mathematical one in that it made no difference how many people proposed it?

The question he particularly focused on was this: can the thesis only be propounded, or can it actually be grasped? In the case of mathematics, a thesis can really only be propounded, since we have not genuinely grasped it until we can state it for ourselves – otherwise it does not exist for us at all. For Johannes this was explained by the abstract nature of mathematics. But surely the thesis about doubt, given its negativity, must be of the same kind? Surely negativity lacks the continuity which is necessary for communication? Would it not be a deception to give negativity the appearance of continuity? Surely negativity is to the sphere of thought what evil is to the sphere of freedom – a break in continuity?

So can the thesis be propounded but never actually grasped? Or do we grasp it in such a way that the moment we propound it, it no longer matters how or by whom it was communicated to us, since we have not grasped it until we can propound it for ourselves? Can one individual receive it through another? Can it be received at all, and should it be believed? When we accept a thesis on trust, for example, we cannot grasp or apply it at once, but we accept it because we trust the one who propounds it. Perhaps the thesis is such as to depend on the authority of those who propound it, and the submission and trust of those who accept it? Are those who believe it supposed to apply it to themselves, or can they just believe that others have done so? Or perhaps one philosopher doubted for us all, as Christ suffered for us all, so that if we believe *this* we need not doubt for ourselves. But in that case, the thesis is poorly formulated, since philosophy would not begin with doubt for the individual, but with a belief that some philosopher had doubted for us. Was the thesis to be appropriated so trustingly that the individual would simply do as it says? Did its propounder doubt everything so thoroughly that individuals need only repeat his doubt and, by believing in him, make the movements of doubt exactly as he described them? Does every individual add a new moment [*moment*] of doubt for the benefit of the next? And as regards those things which had already been called into doubt, should we assume that earlier individuals doubted them sufficiently rigorously, or should we undertake to doubt them all over again?

The more Johannes thought about it, the more he grew certain that it was impossible to enter into philosophy in this way, since the thesis of doubt simply destroyed the continuity. He had once read a story in an old saga about a knight who accepted a troll's gift of a special sword. Besides its other rare qualities, this sword thirsted for blood as soon as it was drawn. When the troll handed it to him, the knight was so impatient to see it that he instantly drew it out of its scabbard, and . . . the troll had to bite the dust! It seemed to Johannes that it must be the same with the thesis: as soon as one person stated it to another, it became in the latter's hand a sword which would slay the first, however much it might pain him to repay his benefactor in this way.

Of course the first person to discover that we must begin with doubt was spared this predicament. Presumably he set out on a bold adventure, not knowing whether it would lead to victory or ruin. But the individual who learns doubt from someone else is not so lucky, and the teacher, if he is not quick enough, will become the victim of his own teaching.

Johannes could not bear the thought of such bloodthirsty ingratitude, and as he plucked up his courage, he began to foresee another problem: that once he had murdered his teacher – albeit unwillingly, as he could say with a clear conscience – he would become a teacher in his turn. He would not have gained anything from his predecessors; on the contrary, he would either have to become the absolute sovereign of philosophy (through being the last to assert the thesis and having no successors, so that he would become the sovereign philosopher by being the only one left), or else he would meet the same end as his great predecessors. *Aller Anfang ist schwer* [every beginning is difficult] – he had always thought the Germans were right about that, but this particular beginning seemed to him to be worse than difficult: to call it a beginning and categorize it as 'difficult' seemed to him like classifying a fox which is being skinned under the category of 'transition'.

These reflections were far from encouraging, but Johannes could not help laughing to himself from time to time; laughter, after all, is often strangely close to tears. Johannes – who would never hurt a fly and was so innocent of blood that he might be taken for a girl rather than a man – could see what a ridiculous figure he would cut if he were transformed into a blood-thirsty Bluebeard who chopped down immortal philosophers for his food instead of corn; he thought the whole thing could only come about through sorcery. He knew perfectly well that some sort of transformation must take place when someone becomes a philosopher . . . but such a transformation?

He therefore resolved to let the sword slumber in its scabbard for a while, and to carry on being himself rather than becoming a philosopher on such terms.

Whatever else might be implied in the thesis and its relation to philosophy, Johannes saw that this kind of beginning had the effect of excluding the individual from philosophy: either philosophy endures despite the fact that the beginning shuts individuals out, or the beginning annihilates philosophy, which excludes us no less effectively. The beautiful prospect which the thesis had opened up for Johannes had vanished. The only way out was to assume that this beginning preceded the beginning of philosophy. And in that case, thesis one was identical to thesis two.

Chapter Three: In order to philosophize one must have doubted

The reader will recall that what originally intrigued Johannes was the statement *de omnibus dubitandum est*. He had wanted to prepare himself for the main investigation by exploring the statement's relation to philosophy. But this long ordeal had not yielded much joy, since it reduced him to the very meagre assertion that the statement lay outside philosophy and was at best a preparation for it. Even so, his efforts would not have been wasted, since such preparations should surely have made him a little worthier of beginning philosophy at some later time.

In one sense there was nothing to stop him proceeding directly to the statement, since it would presumably teach him what he needed to do to put it into practice. Yet he thought it worth beginning by investigating what it could mean that philosophy demanded such preparation. And thesis two ('in order to philosophize one must have doubted') gave him his opportunity.

It seemed to him entirely proper that philosophy should demand such preparation. Indeed the thought appealed to him greatly; his disposition, which was as humble as it was bold, gave it complete approval. Even if he had succeeded in understanding thesis one and slipping inside philosophy with its help, he would still have worried lest he had got in too easily; easy victories were a paradox to his adventurous soul, which was always attracted by adversity. He knew that this kind of preparation had once been customary in the world. He knew that Pythagoras required his disciples to be silent,[9] and that Egyptian and Indian philosophers imposed a similar period of probation; and he knew that novices went through a lengthy apprenticeship before being received into the Church. Indeed, the more important the matter into which you were being initiated, the more rigorous the test should be, and this was illustrated for Johannes by the example of ascetic monks or the vast Jesuit order. Johannes could hardly be surprised that philosophy in our age should also require an ordeal. He also knew that it was not proper for a disciple to criticize his master; whatever the master thinks fit to command should be performed trustingly and wholeheartedly, however offensive or humiliating it might be. Johannes could understand why Pythagoras demanded silence, as disciples ought to keep quiet; he could also understand why Diogenes required a would-be follower to walk behind him carrying a pot;[10] and why novices had to stand outdoors, kneeling when others stood, standing when others sat, and always undertaking the roughest work. This seemed perfectly correct to Johannes, and he would have complied unhesitatingly if it had been required of him. His reason for hesitating before the preparation now prescribed for him was different: it did not seem sufficiently lowly.

Doubters tend to raise themselves above their teachers, and that is why there is nothing that teachers deplore in their disciples as much as doubt. And yet Johannes knew that it was doubt that was required of him; it was by doubting that he was supposed to prepare to become a philosopher. Once again he was in difficulties. It may be a benevolent ruse, he thought. Perhaps the disciple was taught to depend upon his master rather as, without warning, a child is allowed or even encouraged to get hurt by fire, because experience is supposed to be the best teacher. He was not entirely satisfied with this explanation, but then he began to notice that there is a certain nobility and dignity in the way philosophy conducts itself. A disciple's life will be easier if his master positively tells him what to do, since the teacher then carries the responsibility; on the other hand it also makes the disciple less perfect, because his life is given over to another. By imposing negative requirements on a disciple, however, the teacher emancipates him and makes him just as great as himself. Indeed the relation of teacher and disciple is nullified, as Johannes could easily see. 'I cannot even be sure that doubt really is a preparation', he said to himself. 'I have been left to myself and now I have to do everything on my own responsibility. I might have preferred to wait a little longer before coming of age, and be ordered around so that I could enjoy the pleasure of obedience; but even if I have the anxious feeling of growing up too soon, like a girl who marries too young – still, this is how it has to be. The statement *de omnibus dubitandum est* is now engraved on my consciousness, and I have no choice but to think it through with all my strength and put it passionately into practice. I will stake everything on it, and whatever happens I will not let go of it, whether it leads to everything or nothing, whether it makes me wise or mad. My misty dreams of disciplehood are over. I have grown old without having leave to be young, and now I must sail the open seas. My fantasies about the statement and its relation to philosophy are at an end. I know nothing about its relation to anything else at all, and I, simply follow in its wake – like a man rowing a boat, I turn my back on my destination.'

Part Two, in which Johannes Tries to Think *Propriis Auspiciis* [on his Own Account]* *De Omnibus Dubitandum Est*

Introduction

Just as a fish dives down to the bottom of the sea when it has snatched its prey from the surface, so Johannes now plunged down with the statement into the depths of his soul. For a while he surrendered to the various moods induced by the mere possession of something whose true significance has not yet been grasped. He allowed himself to be swayed by numerous thoughts about the difficulty of his task and its captivating charms, about his failures and moments of triumph, and about the romantic existence that could be his. In short, he enjoyed the sweet joy and suffering of a first love, for as Hippel says '*es geht mit den Wissenschaften wie mit der Liebe; die verstohlne ist die angenehmste* [in science as in love, furtiveness gives greatest pleasure]'.[11]

He slowly began to collect himself and, sensing a growing desire and energy for tackling the task in a more definite form, he tried to recall

---

* Out of solicitude for young Johannes, and so that he should not appear to be occupying himself with sheer nonsense – though it is easy to see that he has no genius for paragraphs and that he has not been trained in the philosophical compendia of the past ten years – I shall take this opportunity to recall that the issues he raises have been dealt with in philosophy before.

whether anything the philosophizers had said offered any clues to guide him. A journey round the world requires more preparation, after all, than an afternoon stroll. Not knowing how hard it will be, the soul takes refuge in solemn but elevating devotions, as courage and enthusiasm compete with anxiety in constructing audacious adventures. But even as we yield to ourselves in this way, it is natural to pay close attention to the testimonies of those who have already made the attempt. Johannes realized that sailors have far better information in their maps than he could expect to glean from the conversations of the philosophizers, but he also knew that the mind is not so subject to multiplicity as the sea, its movements being far more uniform.

A strange feeling came over him as he racked his memory, for he realized that the philosophizers had said hardly a word about all the trials and adventures by which we will be tested when we set out to doubt everything. And this was really quite surprising; indeed one might have expected it to be their favourite topic – rather as sailors love to reminisce about the extraordinary ordeals they have endured, especially when conversing with companions who have sailed the same seas. Johannes would have understood them if they sometimes claimed to have undergone such trials when in reality they had not, but he hoped he could tell the men of experience from the windbags by the inwardness with which they spoke. So he found it incredible that they all remained silent. Were the things they had seen so frightful that they dreaded to speak of them? Yet their companions must have witnessed such things too. . . .

It was not entirely true that Johannes had heard nothing of these matters from the philosophizers, but when he refreshed his memory about the little he had heard, he admitted that it amounted to nothing, and that it was not surprising if the odd phrases he remembered had discouraged him at the time. On one occasion when they were discussing the significance of doubt as a preliminary to philosophy, Johannes heard someone say that 'instead of wasting time on doubt, we should simply get started on philosophy'. The company welcomed this suggestion with the same joy with which Catholics would seize on an indulgence. Johannes, however, was so ashamed for the speaker that he wished himself miles away so that no one could see what was written on his face. 'Even the most ordinary person', he said to himself, 'tries to practise what he preaches.' Of course for want of skill or self-understanding he may not always succeed; but surely this could not apply to a philosopher? And for a philosopher openly to say that it is not worth trying to do what at other times he assures us he has achieved, and deliberately to give up what he normally stresses as a necessary condition – that, surely, was to hold both oneself and philosophy in contempt.

On another occasion, Johannes had heard one of the philosophizers (and one whose statements usually inspired confidence) express himself as follows: 'Universal doubt is no easy matter, for it is not doubt about one thing or another, or about this or that: rather, it is a speculative doubt about everything – and this is not so easy.' Johannes remembered how attentive he had been at the beginning of the lecture, and how depressed when it was over, since he realized that it had really said nothing at all. It would have been better if the speaker had stopped after his opening words, since despite appearances what followed amounted to absolutely nothing. Indeed it was surprising that the lecture had not lasted even longer, since those who talk in this way always have an infinite amount to say.

So Johannes bade the philosophizers a final farewell. Occasionally he might still hear a stray remark of theirs, but he was determined to pay no more heed, since long and painful experience had taught him how treacherous their words could be. He therefore returned to the method he had always followed in the past: he would try to make everything as simple as possible.

Chapter One: What is it to doubt?

§1   How must existence be constituted in order for doubt to be possible?
When Johannes began to consider the question, he knew very well that he was not looking for an empirical answer, since life would present him with a multiplicity, displaying a bewildering variety between its extremes. And if doubt could be awakened by many very different things, the opposite was also the case: if we try to awaken doubt in others, we may end up by evoking faith, just as faith, conversely, can evoke doubt. Johannes could easily see that this paradoxical dialectic – which, as he had noted before, had no analogy in any sphere of knowledge, since knowledge is always directly and immanently related to an object and a knower, rather than inversely and transcendently to some third term – meant that empirical observation would serve no purpose. He would not be able to answer his question unless he approached it in a different way. He had to try and discover *doubt's ideal possibility in consciousness*. This ideal possibility would of course remain the same, however various the phenomena associated with it, since it would explain the action of the phenomena rather than being explained by them. The occasions of doubt in the individual can be as various as may be, but if the ideal possibility is not already present, doubt can never arise. Moreover, since the various phenomena occasioning doubt can be diametrically opposed, the possibility itself must be all-embracing, and essential for human consciousness.

Johannes then tried to explore consciousness as it is in itself – as that which underlies each individual consciousness without itself having any individuality. He wondered how consciousness would be constituted if doubt were not part of it, as is the case with children. But how is the consciousness of children determined? Surely it is quite indeterminate, or in other words, immediate, for *immediacy* is precisely *indeterminacy*. In immediacy there is no relation, and as soon as relation is given, immediacy is nullified. *Immediately, therefore, everything is true;*★ but in the next moment this truth is untruth, since *in immediacy everything is untrue*. If consciousness can remain in immediacy, then the question of truth is nullified.

How does the question of truth arise? Through untruth, because the moment I ask about truth, I have already asked about untruth. In the question of truth, consciousness is brought into relation to something else, and it is untruth which makes this relation possible.

Which comes first, immediacy or mediacy? A deceptive question, which made Johannes think of the answer Thales is said to have given to the question whether night or day came first: 'Night is one day earlier', he said.[13] Can consciousness not remain in immediacy, then? Another foolish question, for if it could there would be no consciousness at all. How then is immediacy nullified? By mediation, which nullifies immediacy by *pre*supposing it. What, then, is immediacy? It is reality. What is mediacy? It is language. And how does the one nullify the other? By giving expression to it, for what is expressed is always *presupposed*. Immediacy is reality; language is ideality; and consciousness is contradiction. Contradiction is there the moment we express reality, for what we say is ideality. Hence the possibility of doubt is implicit in consciousness, and the essence of consciousness is a contradiction that is produced by, and itself produces, doubleness.

Such doubleness necessarily calls for two different expressions: it is reality and ideality, and consciousness is the relation between them. I can bring reality into relation with ideality, or can bring ideality into relation with reality. In reality itself there is no possibility of doubt; but contradiction arises when I express reality in language, since I do not in fact express reality, but rather produce something else. In so far as what is said is supposed to express reality, I have brought it into relation with ideality; and in so far as what is said is produced by me, I have brought ideality into relation with reality. And as long as this exchange continues without mutual contact, consciousness exists only according to its possibility. In ideality, every-

---

★ Cf. the thesis of the Greek Sophists, that everything is true, and Plato's efforts to refute them by showing, in particular, that the negative exists; or Schleiermacher's doctrine of feeling – that everything is true; or Heraclitus's thesis that everything is and everything is not, which Aristotle glossed as 'Everything is true.'[12]

thing is as perfectly true as it is in reality. Just as I can say that immediately everything is true, therefore, so I can also say that immediately everything is actual, for *possibility* arises only in the moment when ideality is brought into relation with reality. In immediacy, the most false and the most true are equally true, and the most possible and the most impossible equally actual. As long as the exchange takes place without collision, consciousness does not really exist; and hence the tremendous falsity does not produce any supersessions, any transitions to a higher level. Consciousness is neither reality nor ideality, but it requires both of them in order to exist, and this contradiction constitutes consciousness both in its coming into existence and in its essence.

Before proceeding any further, Johannes wondered whether what he was calling consciousness here was what is usually called reflection.* In that respect he fixed his definitions as follows: reflection is the *possibility of the relation*, and consciousness is *the relation whose first form is contradiction*. He also noted that this meant that the categories of reflection are always *dichotomous*. (Thus ideality and reality, soul and body, knowledge and truth, will and goodness, love and beauty, God and world, and so on, are all categories of reflection; and in reflection they touch each other in such a way that a relation becomes possible.) The categories of consciousness, on the other hand, are *trichotomous*, as language itself demonstrates, since if I say '*I am conscious of this sensory impression*', I give expression to a triplicity. Consciousness is spirit [*aand*], and it is worth noting that when unity is sundered in the world of spirit, it always becomes three rather than two. Hence consciousness presupposes reflection − otherwise doubt would be inexplicable. Language might seem to dispute this, of course, since − at least as far as Johannes knew − the word 'doubt' is etymologically related in most languages to the word 'two'. In his opinion, however, this was merely an indication of what doubt presupposes, especially as it was clear to him that when, as spirit, I become two, I am *eo ipso* three. If there were nothing but dichotomies, then doubt would not exist, for the possibility of doubt depends precisely on the third which sets the first two into relation to each other. If we say that reflection produces doubt, therefore, then we are expressing ourselves backwards; we should rather say that doubt *pre*supposes reflection, though not in a temporal sense.

* Johannes's concern is not without significance. The terminology of modern philosophy is often confusing; it speaks of *sinnliches Bewußtsein* [sensory consciousness], *wahrnehmendes Bewußtsein* [perceptual consciousness], *Verstand* [Understanding], and so on, even though it would be far better to use the terms 'sense-perception' and 'experience', since the term 'consciousness' implies something further. It would be very interesting to see how Hegel would formulate the transition from consciousness to self-consciousness and from self-consciousness to reason − though of course it is easy enough if the transition is no more than a chapter-heading.

Doubt arises from a relation between two terms, which must already exist even though doubt, as a higher expression, comes before them.

Reflection is the possibility of relation, and this can also be expressed as follows: reflection is *disinterested*. Consciousness, however, is itself relation, and hence it is interest – a doubleness to which the word 'interest' (*interesse* [being between]) gives perfect expression, and with pregnant ambiguity. Disinterested knowledge (mathematics, aesthetics, metaphysics) is therefore only the presupposition of doubt, and doubt is overcome not when interest is nullified, but when it is neutralized; and all such knowledge is mere regression. Those who imagine that they can overcome doubt through so-called objective thinking are therefore mistaken: doubt is higher than objective thinking, since it not only presupposes it but also involves something more – a third term, namely interest or consciousness.

Thus Johannes considered the attitude of the ancient Greek sceptics far more consistent than that of the modern vanquishers of doubt. The Greeks knew very well that doubt is founded on interest, and they concluded very logically that doubt would be nullified if interest were transformed into apathy. This procedure was entirely consistent, but it is an inconsistency – evidently due to ignorance as to the nature of doubt – which gave modern philosophy the desire to control doubt systematically. Even if the System were absolutely complete, or if actuality exceeded all expectations, doubt would still not be vanquished. Doubt is based on interest, and all systematic knowledge is disinterested. Hence it is clear that doubt is the beginning of the highest form of existence, because it can take everything else as its presupposition. The ancient Greek sceptics understood exceptionally well that it is unreasonable to talk about doubt once interest has been nullified, and probably they would also have understood that the idea of objective doubt is just another play on words. Ideality and reality may struggle with each other for all eternity, but without consciousness or interest – without a consciousness that has an interest in the struggle – there will be no such thing as doubt. And even if they were totally reconciled, doubt could still continue unabated.

Consciousness, then, is relation – a relation whose form is contradiction. But how does consciousness discover the contradiction? If the falsity mentioned earlier could continue – in other words, if ideality and reality communicated with each other in all innocence – then consciousness would never emerge, since consciousness arises precisely through their collision, and presupposes it. In immediacy there is no collision, but mediately there is. And collision occurs as soon as the question of *repetition* arises, for repetition is conceivable only in relation to what has already existed.

In reality as such there is no repetition. But this is not because everything is different from everything else. If all the things in the world were absolutely identical, there would still be no repetition in reality, because repetition occurs only in the moment. If the world had no beauty, and contained nothing but identically shaped boulders, all exactly the same size, there would still be no repetition. We would see nothing but boulders at every moment for all eternity, but the question whether we were looking at the same one as before would never arise. Nor can there be repetition in ideality alone, for the Idea is and remains the same, and hence can never be repeated. Repetition arises only when ideality comes into contact with reality. When we see something in the moment, for example, ideality intervenes and explains it as a repetition. This is the contradiction, for that which exists in one mode also exists in another. We can see that the external exists, but in the same instant we relate it to something else which also exists – something which is the same and which will also explain that the other is the same. Here we have a redoubling; and hence a question of repetition.

Thus ideality and reality collide, but in what medium? In time? That is of course impossible. In eternity? That of course is impossible too. In what then? In consciousness – for here there is contradiction. The question is not disinterested, as if we were wondering whether existence as a whole is only an image of the Idea, or, if not, whether in a weak sense the world of the senses is itself a repetition. But the present question concerns repetition in consciousness, and hence recollection as well. For recollection involves the same contradiction. It is not ideality; it is ideality which has passed away. And it is not reality; it is reality which has passed away; and this too is a double contradiction, for according to its concept ideality cannot have passed away, and the same holds true of reality.

[At this point the manuscript breaks off.]

Notes

1   'Loquor de vera dubitatione in mente, & non de ea, quam passim videmus contingere, ubi scilicet verbis, quamvis animus non dubitet, dicit quis se dubitare. Non est enim methodi hoc emendare, sed potius pertinet ad inquisitionem pertinaciae et eius emendationem.' See Benedictus de Spinoza (1632–77), *Tractatus de Intellectus Emendatione* (*Treatise on the Correction of the Understanding*, 1677), §77.
2   I Timothy 4, 12.
3   Cf. Genesis 28, 12: 'And he [Jacob] dreamed, and behold a ladder set up on the earth, and the top of it reached to heaven: and behold the angels of God ascending and descending on it.'
4   In Greek myth, ambrosia is the food of the immortals.
5   Dion, a disciple of Plato, was banished from his native Syracuse by Dionysus the younger, but took his revenge in 356 BCE.

6 Kierkegaard refers to the legend according to which the dye known as Tyrian purple, which is extracted from a species of mollusc, was discovered by a dog rooting amongst sea-snails.

7 The story of Pyrrho of Elis and Anaxarchus of Abdera ('the happy man' who fell into a bog) is related in Diogenes Laertius, *Lives of the Philosophers*, IX, 63–4.

8 In the letter to Menoeceus, Epicurus wrote that death 'is nothing to us, seeing that, when we are, death is not come, and when death is come, we are not'. See Diogenes Laertius, *Lives of the Philosophers*, X, 125.

9 'For five whole years they had to keep silent, listening to his lectures without seeing him'; see Diogenes Laertius, *Lives of the Philosophers*, VIII, 10.

10 Diogenes of Sinope; cf. Diogenes Laertius, *Lives of the Philosophers*, VI, 36, where the philosopher asks one follower to carry a fish, another a cheese.

11 Kierkegaard quotes from the first volume of the autobiography of Theodor Gottlieb von Hippel (1741–96), *Lebensläufe nach aufsteigender Linie* (1778).

12 Kierkegaard's note makes elliptical reference to the following sources: (a) Plato's *Sophist* (e.g. 241d, where the Stranger says it may be necessary to commit parricide against Parmenides by maintaining that 'things that are not' must nevertheless have being, since otherwise it would be impossible to distinguish falsehoods from truths); (b) *Der Christliche Glaube* (1821–2, second edition 1830–1) by Schleiermacher, which argued that religion is essentially a determination of feeling; (c) some rejoinders to Schleiermacher by J. E. Erdmann in Bruno Bauer's *Zeitschrift für spekulative Theologie* (1838); (d) Aristotle's *Metaphysics* (IV, 7, 1011b–1012b); and (e) a note in the first volume (1798) of W. G. Tennemann's *Geschichte der Philosophie*.

13 'To the question which is older, day or night, he replied "Night is older by one day".' See Diogenes Laertius, *Lives of the Philosophers*, I, 36.

Kierkegaard's Works and their Authors: A Chronology

1813
Søren Kierkegaard born in Copenhagen, 5 May

1838
From the Papers of One Still Living, published 'against his will' by S. Kierkegaard
(7 September)

1841
The Concept of Irony, by S. Kierkegaard (16 September)

1843
Either/Or, edited by Victor Eremita (20 February)
Two Edifying Discourses, by S. Kierkegaard (16 May)
Fear and Trembling, by Johannes de Silentio (16 October)
Repetition, by Constantin Constantius (16 October)
Three Edifying Discourses, by S. Kierkegaard (16 October)
Four Edifying Discourses, by S. Kierkegaard (6 December)

1844
Two Edifying Discourses, by S. Kierkegaard (5 March)
Three Edifying Discourses, by S. Kierkegaard (8 June)

Philosophical Fragments, by Johannes Climacus, edited by S. Kierkegaard
  (13 June)
The Concept of Anxiety, by Vigilius Haufniensis (17 June)
Prefaces, by Nicolaus Notabene (17 June)
Four Edifying Discourses, by S. Kierkegaard (31 August)

1845

Three Discourses on Imagined Occasions, by S. Kierkegaard (29 April)
Stages on Life's Way, by Hilarius Bookbinder (30 April)

1846

Concluding Unscientific Postscript, by Johannes Climacus, edited by S. Kierkegaard
  (28 February)
Two Ages: A Literary Review, by S. Kierkegaard (30 March)

1847

Edifying Discourses in Various Spirits, by S. Kierkegaard (13 March)
Works of Love, by S. Kierkegaard (29 September)

1848

Christian Discourses, by S. Kierkegaard (26 April)
The Crisis and a Crisis in the Life of an Actress, signed 'Inter et Inter' (24–7
  July)

1849

The Lilies of the Field and the Birds of the Air, by S. Kierkegaard (14 May)
Two Minor Ethico-Religious Treatises, by H. H. (19 May)
The Sickness Unto Death, by Anti-Climacus, edited by S. Kierkegaard (30 July)
Three Discourses at Communion on Fridays, by S. Kierkegaard (14 November)

1850

Practice in Christianity, by Anti-Climacus, edited by S. Kierkegaard (25
  September)
An Edifying Discourse, by S. Kierkegaard (20 December)

1851

On my Work as an Author, by S. Kierkegaard (7 August)
Two Discourses at Communion on Fridays, by S. Kierkegaard (7 August)
For Self-Examination, by S. Kierkegaard (10 September)

1855

This Must be Said, So Let It be Said, by S. Kierkegaard (24 May)
Christ's Judgement on Official Christianity, by S. Kierkegaard (16 June)
The Unchangeableness of God, by S. Kierkegaard (3 September)
Died 11 November

1859

The Point of View for my Work as an Author, by S. Kierkegaard

1869

'*De omnibus dubitandum est* (Johannes Climacus)', by S. Kierkegaard

1872

A. P. Adler and his 'Revelation' (The Book on Adler), by S. Kierkegaard

1876

Judge for Yourself, by S. Kierkegaard

Bibliography

Kierkegaard's works

In Danish

Samlede Værker, edited by A. B. Drachmann, J. L. Heiberg and H. O. Langes (14 vols, Copenhagen: Gyldendal, 1901–6); second edition (15 vols, Copenhagen: Gyldendal, 1920–36); third edition, with additional editorial material provided by Peter Rohde (20 vols, Copenhagen: Gyldendal, 1962–4)

Efterladte Papirer, edited by H. P. Barfod and Hermann Gottsched (9 vols, Copenhagen: Reitzel, 1869–81)

Søren Kierkegaards Papirer, edited by P. A. Heiberg, V. Kuhr and E. Torsting (11 vols, Copenhagen: Gyldendal, 1909–48); second edition, with supplementary volumes, edited by Niels Thulstrup (13 vols, Copenhagen: Gyldendal, 1968–70)

In English translation: Journals and Papers

The Journals of Søren Kierkegaard, translated by Alexander Dru (London: Oxford University Press, 1938)

Søren Kierkegaard's Journals and Papers, translated by Howard V. Hong and Edna H. Hong, assisted by Gregor Malantschuk (7 vols, Bloomington: Indiana University Press, 1967–78)

Vol. 1, A–E (1967)

Vol. 2 F–K (1970)

Vol. 3, L–R (1976)

Vol. 4, S–Z (1976)

Vol. 5, Autobiographical. Part 1, 1829–1848 (1978)

Vol. 6, Autobiographical. Part 2, 1848–1855 (1978)

Vol. 7, Index and composite collation; index prepared by Nathaniel J. Hong and Charles M. Barker (1978)

Papers and Journals: A Selection, translated by Alastair Hannay (London: Penguin, 1996)

In English translation: the Princeton *Kierkegaard's Writings*

Vol. I: *Early Polemical Writings*, translated by Julia Watkin (Princeton: Princeton University Press, 1990); includes *From the Papers of One Still Living, Articles from Student Days* and *The Battle Between the Old and the New Soap-Cellars*

Vol. II: *The Concept of Irony, Schelling Lecture Notes*, translated by Howard V. Hong and Edna H. Hong (Princeton: Princeton University Press, 1989)

Vol. III: *Either/Or*, vol. 1, translated by Howard V. Hong and Edna H. Hong (Princeton: Princeton University Press, 1987)

Vol. IV: *Either/Or*, vol. 2, translated by Howard V. Hong and Edna H. Hong (Princeton: Princeton University Press, 1987)

Vol. V: *Eighteen Upbuilding Discourses*, translated by Howard V. Hong and Edna H. Hong (Princeton: Princeton University Press, 1990)

Vol. VI: *Fear and Trembling, Repetition*, translated by Howard V. Hong and Edna H. Hong (Princeton: Princeton University Press, 1983)

Vol. VII: *Philosophical Fragments, Johannes Climacus*, translated by Howard V. Hong and Edna H. Hong (Princeton: Princeton University Press, 1985)

Vol. VIII: *The Concept of Anxiety*, translated by Reidar Thomte and Albert B. Anderson (Princeton: Princeton University Press, 1980)

Vol. IX: *Prefaces/Writing Sampler*, edited and translated by Todd W. Nichol (Princeton: Princeton University Press, 1997)

Vol. X: *Three Discourses on Imagined Occasions*, translated by Howard V. Hong and Edna H. Hong (Princeton: Princeton University Press, 1993)

Vol. XI: *Stages on Life's Way*, translated by Howard V. Hong and Edna H. Hong (Princeton: Princeton University Press, 1988)

Vol. XII: *Concluding Unscientific Postscript*, translated by Howard V. Hong and Edna H. Hong (2 vols, Princeton: Princeton University Press, 1992)

Vol. XIII: *The Corsair Affair and Articles Related to the Writings*, translated by Howard V. Hong and Edna H. Hong (Princeton: Princeton University Press, 1982)

Vol. XIV: *Two Ages, A Literary Review*, translated by Howard V. Hong and Edna H. Hong (Princeton: Princeton University Press, 1978)

Vol. XV: *Upbuilding Discourses in Various Spirits*, translated by Howard V. Hong and Edna H. Hong (Princeton: Princeton University Press, 1993)

Vol. XVI: *Works of Love*, translated by Howard V. Hong and Edna H. Hong (Princeton: Princeton University Press, 1995)

Vol. XVII: *Christian Discourses, The Crisis and a Crisis in the Life of an Actress*, edited and translated by Howard V. Hong and Edna H. Hong (Princeton: Princeton University Press, 1997)

Vol. XVIII: *Without Authority: The Lily of the Field and the Bird of the Air, Two Minor*

Ethical-Religious Essays, Three Discourses at the Communion on Fridays, An Upbuilding Discourse, Two Discourses at the Communion on Fridays, edited and translated by Howard V. Hong and Edna H. Hong (Princeton: Princeton University Press, 1997)

Vol. XIX: *The Sickness Unto Death*, translated by Howard V. Hong and Edna H. Hong (Princeton: Princeton University Press, 1980)

Vol. XX: *Practice in Christianity*, translated by Howard V. Hong and Edna H. Hong (Princeton: Princeton University Press, 1991)

Vol. XXI: *For Self-Examination; Judge for Yourself!*, translated by Howard V. Hong and Edna H. Hong (Princeton: Princeton University Press, 1990)

Vol. XXII: *The Point of View: On My Work as an Author, The Point of View for My Work as an Author, Armed Neutrality*, translated by Howard V. Hong and Edna H. Hong (Princeton: Princeton University Press, 1998)

Vol. XXIII: *The Moment and Late Writings: Articles from Fædrelandet; This Must Be Said, So Let It Be Said; Christ's Judgement on Official Christianity, The Changelessness of God; The Moment*, translated by Howard V. Hong and Edna H. Hong (Princeton: Princeton University Press, 1998)

Vol. XXIV: *The Book on Adler*, translated by Howard V. Hong and Edna H. Hong (Princeton: Princeton University Press, 1998)

Vol. XXV: *Kierkegaard: Letters and Documents*, translated by Henrik Rosenmeier (Princeton: Princeton University Press, 1978)

Vol. XXVI: *Cumulative Index to Kierkegaard's Writings*, compiled by Nathaniel J. Hong, Kathryn Hong and Regine Prensel-Guthrie (Princeton: Princeton University Press, 2000)

Other English translations: a historical selection

Philosophical Fragments; or, A Fragment of Philosophy, translated by David F. Swenson (1936); translation revised by Howard V. Hong (Princeton: Princeton University Press, 1962)

The Journals of Søren Kierkegaard, translated by Alexander Dru (London: Oxford University Press, 1938)

The Point of View for My Work as An Author: A Report to History, translated by Walter Lowrie (Oxford: Oxford University Press, 1939)

Christian Discourses, The Lilies of the Field and the Birds of the Air, Three Discourses at the Communion on Fridays, translated by Walter Lowrie (London: Oxford University Press, 1940)

Concluding Unscientific Postscript, translated by David F. Swenson and completed by Walter Lowrie (Princeton: Princeton University Press, 1941)

For Self-examination, and Judge for Yourselves!, and Three Discourses, translated by Walter Lowrie (London: Oxford University Press, 1941, and Princeton: Princeton University Press, 1944)

On Authority and Revelation, The Book on Adler, or a Cycle of Ethico-religious Essays, translated by Walter Lowrie (Princeton: Princeton University Press, 1941, and New York: Harper & Row, 1966)

Either-Or, translated by David F. Swenson and Lillian Marvin Swenson with Walter Lowrie (1944); translation revised by Howard A. Johnson (2 vols, Princeton: Princeton University Press, 1959)

The Concept of Dread, translated by Walter Lowrie (Princeton: Princeton University Press, 1944)

Fear and Trembling and The Sickness Unto Death, translated by Walter Lowrie (Princeton: Princeton University Press, 1954)

Works of Love, translated by Howard V. Hong and Edna H. Hong (New York: Harper & Row, 1962)

The Concept of Irony, with Constant Reference to Socrates, translated by Lee M. Capel (London: Collins, 1966)

Crisis in the Life of an Actress and Other Essays on Drama, translated by Stephen Crites (London: Collins, 1967)

Fear and Trembling, translated by Alastair Hannay (Harmondsworth: Penguin, 1985)

Prefaces, translated by William McDonald (Tallahassee: Florida State University Press, 1989)

The Sickness Unto Death, translated by Alastair Hannay (Harmondsworth: Penguin, 1989)

Either/Or: A Fragment of Life, abridged and translated by Alastair Hannay (London: Penguin, 1992)

Glossary

Danish–English glossary

aabenbar; aabenbare; aabenbarelse   obvious, evident; reveal, disclose; revelation

aand   spirit, mind, *also* breath; cf. German *Geist*

æsthetisk   aesthetic, aesthetical (used in accordance with the Greek *æsthesis*, sensation)

afgjørende; afgjørelse   decisive; decision

almene   universal, general

alvor   seriousness, earnestness

anfægtelse   spiritual trial, trial of temptation, temptation in a higher sense; see also *fristelse*

angest, angst   anxiety, dread

arvesynd   original sin, hereditary sin

bedrage   deceive, defraud, cheat

begreb   concept; cf. German *Begriff*

beslutning   resolution, decision, resolute decision

bestaae   subsist, endure, exist

bestemmelse   determination, category, quality, trait, characteristic, qualification, term, specification, form, definition; cf. German *Bestimmung*

bevægelse   movement, motion

bevist; bevisthed   conscious; consciousness

blive; blive til   become; come into existence, come into being

Christen, at blive Christen   Christian, becoming a Christian

Christendom   Christianity

Christenhed   Christendom

dæmonisk demonic
dobbelthed doubleness, duplexity, duality
dobbelt-reflexion double-reflection
duplicitet duplicity, duplexity

eenhed unity
elskov love, erotic love; cf. Greek *eros*; cf. *kærlighed*
enkelte individual, single individual, particular individual
erindre; erindring recollect; recollection (often contrasted with *gjentagelse*, repetition)
erkjenden knowledge
erotisk erotic
ethisk ethical
ethnisk ethnical, pagan
evighed eternity
existents existence
existents-forhold existence-relationship
existere exist

forbigangne past
fordobling, fordobelse reduplication, redoubling, duplication
forestilling representation, notion, conception, idea; cf. German *Vorstellung*
forfatter author
forfatter-virksomhed work as an author, literary activity
forfører; forførelse seducer; seduction
forhold relation, relationship
fornuft reason; cf. German *Vernunft*
forsøg attempt, essay
forsone; forsoning atone; atonement
forstand understanding; cf. German *Verstand*
fortvivlelse despair
forundring wonder
fraværelse absence
frihed freedom
friste; fristelse tempt; temptation

gjenstand object
gjentagelse repetition; cf. *erindre*
glemme forget
Gud God
Guden the deity
Guds-forhold God-relation, relationship to God

hæve elevate, cancel, nullify
historisk historical

idee   idea
ikke-væren   non-being, non-existence
inderlighed   inwardness
indesluttet   reserved, enclosed
indirekt meddelelse   indirect communication
interesse; interessant   interest; interesting
intet; intethed   nothing; nothingness
ironie   irony

jeg   I, ego

kærlighed   love; cf. Greek *agapé*; cf. *elskov*
kategori   category
kjedelig; kjedsomhed   boring; boredom

lide; lidelse   suffer; suffering
lidenskab   passion
ligefrem meddelelse   direct communication
livs-anskuelse   life-view

meddelelse   communication
mediation; mediere   mediation; mediate
modsætte; modsatte; modsætning; modsætningsforhold   oppose; opposite; opposition;
     relation of opposition
modsige; modsigelse   contradict; contradiction
modtagelighed   receptivity
moment   (a) instant, moment (of time); cf. German *der Moment*; (b) moment, aspect,
     element; cf. German *das Moment*; see also *øieblik*
moral   moral; cf. German *Moralität*
mulige; mulighed   possible; possibility
myndighed   authority

nærværende   present
negativ; negativitet   negative; negativity
negere; negation   negate; negation
nødvendig; nødvendighed   necessary; necessity

øieblik   moment, instant; literally, 'the glance of an eye'; cf. I Corinthians 15, 52 'we
     shall all be changed in a moment [Greek *atomos*, Latin *momenta*, German *plötzlich*,
     Danish *haft*], in the twinkling of an eye [*rhipe ophthalmou, in ictu oculi, in einem
     Augenblick, i et øieblik*]'; see also *moment*
onde   evil, bad
opbyggelige   edifying, upbuilding
opdragelse   education, upbringing

opfatte; opfattelse   conceive, grasp, apprehend; conception, apprehension
ophæve   supersede, annul, transcend; cf. German *Aufheben*
oprindelighed   originality, primitivity, originariness
overgang   transition

pathos   pathos, emotion, excitement
philosopherende   philosophizers
poetisk   poetic
prøvelse   ordeal, test, trial

realisere   realize, actualize
realitet   reality
redupplikation   reduplication
reflexion   reflection
religiøs   religious

sædelig; sædelighed   ethical; social morality; cf. German *Sittlichkeit*
sær   eccentric or peculiar
salighed   blessedness, bliss, happiness, salvation
samtidig; samtighed   simultaneous, contemporary; simultaneity
samvittighed   conscience
sandhed; det Sande   truth; the true
sandselighed   sensuality
sikkerhed   assurance, security
sjæl, sjel   soul, psyche
skjebne   fate
skjulthed   hiddenness, concealment
slette Uendelighed   bad infinity; cf. Hegel's *schlechte Unendlichkeit*
slutning   conclusion
speculation   speculation; i.e. Hegelian philosophy
spring   leap
stemning   mood, attunement
Styrelse   Providence, Governance
synspunkt   point of view

tid   time
tilblivelse; bliver til   coming into existence; come into existence
tilegnelse   appropriation
tilfældige   contingent, accidental, inessential
tilintetgjørelse   annihilation
tilkommende   future
tilstede   present
tilværelse; være til   existence; exist, becoming
timelighed   temporality

tro   faith, belief, trust
tungsindig   melancholy, depression
tvetydighed   ambiguity, equivocalness, double meaning
tvivl   doubt

uendelighed   infinity
umiddelbarhed   immediacy
uvidenhed   ignorance
uvished   uncertainty

være; væren   be; being, existence (sometimes contrasted with *væsen*)
være til   exist
væsen   essence; cf. *være*
verdens-anskuelse   world-view
viden   knowledge
videnskab; videnskabelig   science, scholarship; scientific, scholarly
virkelighed   actuality, reality
vished   certainty
vorde   become

English–Danish glossary

absence   *fraværelse*
accidental   *tilfældige*
actuality   *virkelighed*
actualize   *realisere*
aesthetic   *æsthetisk*
ambiguity   *tvetydighed*
annihilation   *tilintetgjørelse*
annul   *ophæve*
anxiety   *angest, angst*
apprehension   *opfattelse*
appropriation   *tilegnelse*
atone; atonement   *forsone; forsoning*
attunement   *stemning*
author   *forfatter*
authority   *myndighed*

be; being   *være; væren*
become   *blive, vorde*
becoming a Christian   *at blive Christen*
belief   *tro*
boredom; boring   *kjedsomhed, kjedelig*

cancel *hæve*
category *kategori, bestemmelse*
certainty *vished, sikkerhed*
Christendom *Christenhed*
Christianity *Christendom*
coming into existence; come into existence or into being *tilblivelse; blive til*
communication *meddelelse*
concealment *skjulthed*
concept *begreb*
conception *opfattelse, forestilling*
conclusion *slutning*
conscious *bevist*
contemporary *samtidig*
contingent *tilfældige*
contradict; contradiction *modsige; modsigelse*

deceit; deceive *bedrag; bedrage*
decisive *afgjørende*
the deity *Guden*
demonic *dæmonisk*
despair *fortvivlelse*
direct communication *ligefrem meddelelse*
double meaning *tvetydighed*
doubleness *dobbelthed*
double-reflection *dobbelt-reflexion*
doubt *tvivl*
dread *angest, angst*
duality *dobbelthed*
duplexity *dobbelthed, duplicitet*
duplicity *duplicitet*

earnestness, seriousness *alvor*
edifying, upbuilding *opbyggelige*
education, upbringing *opdragelse*
elevate *hæve*
equivocalness *tvetydighed*
erotic *erotisk*
essence *væsen*
eternity *evighed*
ethical *ethisk, moral, sædelig*
ethnical *ethnisk*
evil *onde*
exist; existence *existere, være til; tilværelse, existents*

faith   *tro*
fate   *skjebne*
freedom   *frihed*
future   *tilkommende*

general   *almene*
God   *Gud*
Governance   *Styrelse*

hereditary sin   *arvesynd*
hiddenness   *skjulthed*
historical   *historisk*

I   *jeg*
idea   *idee, forestilling*
immediacy   *umiddelbarhed*
indirect communication   *indirekt meddelelse*
individual, single individual   *enkelte*
infinity   *uendelighed*
instant   *moment, Øieblik*
interest; interesting   *interesse; interessant*
inwardness   *inderlighed*
irony   *ironie*

knowledge   *erkjenden, viden*

leap   *spring*
life-view   *livs-anskuelse*
love   *elskov, kærlighed*

mediate; mediation   *mediere; mediation*
melancholy   *tungsindig*
mind   *aand*
moment   *moment, Øieblik*
mood   *stemning*
motion   *bevægelse*
movement   *bevægelse*

necessary; necessity   *nødvendig; nødvendighed*
negate; negation   *negere; negation*
negative; negativity   *negativ; negativitet*
non-being   *ikke-væren*
nothing; nothingness   *intet; intethed*
nullify   *hæve*

object *gjenstand*
oppose; opposite; opposition *modsætte; modsatte; modsætning*
original sin *arvesynd*

passion *lidenskab*
past *forbigangne*
pathos *pathos*
philosophizers *philosopherende*
poetic *poetisk*
point of view *synspunkt*
possible; possibility *mulige; mulighed*
present *nærværende, tilstede*
Providence *Styrelse*
psyche *sjæl, sjel*

reality *realitet, virkelighed*
realize *realisere*
reason *fornuft*
recollect; recollection *erindre; erindring*
reduplication *fordobling, fordobelse, redupplikation*
reflection *reflexion*
relation, relationship *forhold*
religious *religiøs*
repetition *gjentagelse*
representation *forestilling*
resolution *beslutning*
reveal, disclose *aaberbare*
revelation *aabenbarelse*

scholarship; scholarly *videnskab; videnskabelig*
science; scientific *videnskab; videnskabelig*
seducer; seduction *forfører; forførelse*
sensuality *sandselighed*
seriousness *alvor*
simultaneous; simultaneity *samtidig; samtidighed*
soul *sjæl, sjel*
speculation *speculation*
spirit *aand*
subsist *bestaae*
suffer; suffering *lide; lidelse*
supersede *ophæve*

temporality *timelighed*
time *tid*

transcend   *ophæve*
transition   *overgang*
truth; the true   *sandhed; det Sande*

uncertainty   *uvished*
understanding   *forstand*
unity   *eenhed*
universal   *almene*

wonder   *forundring*
work as an author   *forfatter-virksomhed*

Index

CPSIA information can be obtained
at www.ICGtesting.com
Printed in the USA
JSHW031516080722
27837JS00002B/5